Acid Hype

THE HISTORY OF COMMUNICATION

Robert W. McChesney and John C. Nerone, editors

A list of books in the series appears at the end of this book.

Acid Hype

American News Media and the Psychedelic Experience

STEPHEN SIFF

UNIVERSITY OF ILLINOIS PRESS
Urbana, Chicago, and Springfield

Library of Congress Cataloging-in-Publication Data
Siff, Stephen, 1972–
Acid hype: American news media and the psychedelic experience
/ Stephen Siff.
pages   cm. — (History of communication)
Includes bibliographical references and index.
ISBN 978-0-252-03919-5 (hardback)
ISBN 978-0-252-08076-0 (paper)
ISBN 978-0-252-09723-2 (e-book)
1. Drugs and mass media. 2. Hallucinogenic drugs—United
States—History—20th century. 3. Hallucinogenic drugs—Social
aspects—United States—History—20th century. 4. LSD (Drug)—
United States—History—20th century. 5. LSD (Drug)—Social
aspects—United States—History—20th century.
I. Title.
P96.D78S54   2015
302.23—dc23   2014042889

Volume supported by
Figure Foundation.
nigh stir through
the night before creation.

To Sarah, Harvey, and Miriam

Contents

Acknowledgments   xi

Introduction: Midcentury Media's Trip with LSD   1

1. Early Restrictions on Drug Speech, 1900–1956   17

2. Introducing LSD, 1953–1956   42

3. Creating a Psychedelic Past, 1954–1960   68

4. Research at the Intersection of Media
   and Medicine, 1957–1962   89

5. Luce, Leary, and LSD, 1963–1965   115

6. Moral Panic and Media Hype, 1966–1968   145

Postscript: Psychedelic Media   181

Notes   191

Index   227

Acknowledgments

This project would not have been possible without the guidance and support of colleagues and mentors. The project that ultimately grew into this book was launched by a conversation with Ohio University professor Joseph Bernt, who was then graduate director of the university's E. W. Scripps School of Journalism, and nurtured by the advice of fellow Ohio professor Patrick Washburn. At Miami University of Ohio, now my academic home, I have received invaluable advice from professors Richard Campbell, James Tobin, and Joseph Sampson. I would also like to thank the anonymous reviewers for University of Illinois Press for suggestions that improved this book immeasurably. Nanette Schwartz, Sacha Bellman, and John Wing provided vital assistance at various stages of this project, as did Miami University undergraduate research assistants Holly Jeric and Joseph Bushur. I am also grateful for the financial support for research related to this project from the Miami University Committee on Faculty Research and E. W. Scripps School of Journalism.

I would like to thank the staff at the following libraries and individuals for their help in locating materials: the Library of Congress Manuscript and Prints and Photographs divisions; the Botany Libraries at the Harvard University Herbaria, and particularly Lisa DeCesare; Arianne Hartsell-Gundy and Laura Crosby and the staff of Miami University's King Library; Bob Deis at MensPulpMags.com; and the Olive Kettering Library of Antioch College.

I would like to thank my parents, John and Lynda Siff, for their love and support. Finally, I would like to thank Sarah Brady Siff, who has stood with me from the beginning of this project, offering suggestions, reading drafts, and displaying remarkable patience and understanding.

Acid Hype

Introduction

Midcentury Media's Trip with LSD

This study examines media coverage of the powerful hallucinogenic drug lysergic acid diethylamide, also known as acid or LSD, during the roughly decade-and-a-half period between the first news reports on the drug in the mid-1950s and its tumble from the news agenda after 1968, by which time it had become thoroughly associated with hippie counterculture and prohibited under federal law. During this period, LSD was subject to an extraordinary amount of media attention, despite the fact that its most widespread use was still to come. Beginning in the mid-1950s, mainstream, commercial mass media embraced the challenge of explaining and illustrating for their audiences the realms of experience said to be accessed through this strange new drug. In the years that followed, magazine, newspaper, and broadcast journalists pioneered new ways for conveying a seemingly novel and significant drug effect. News coverage of LSD in the 1950s and 1960s introduced America to an alluring experience credited to drugs, but which most Americans would encounter reliably only through media.

Midcentury fascination with LSD and the mystical, mind-expanding, "psychedelic" experience it was said to create was fanned by coverage in *Time* and *Life*, magazines owned by Henry Robinson Luce and identified with the publisher's socially and politically conservative point of view.[1] At these iconic magazines, the corporate culture was far more *Mad Men* than *Woodstock*. The publishing house Time Inc. accepted and even celebrated alcohol consumption as part of its corporate culture. During the 1950s and 1960s, at *Life* magazine's high-rise offices in Manhattan's Rockefeller Center, bottles of scotch and bourbon appeared on layout tables as each week's issue approached completion. A feast day in Nepal or a shift in the exchange rate of the British pound sufficed as excuses for impromptu parties, often signaled by a martini-emblazoned flag hung over the doorway to the foreign news department. Christmas gatherings and staff outings were professionally catered and buoyed by seas of liquor. The annual Hunt Ball, inaugurated in the early 1960s and named for the managing editor George Hunt, ranked among the most lavish. The entire staff of *Life*, including correspondents flown in from around the world, gathered in a New York hotel ballroom for the formal, boozy affair. Luce, who founded *Time* in 1923 and remained editorial chairman of all his publications, including *Life* and *Fortune*, until his death in 1967, presided from the head table. He delivered speeches "variously exhilarating, rambling, elegant, boring, hilarious, pompous, brilliant and incomprehensible," the longtime *Life* writer and editor Loudon Wainwright recalled.[2]

At one such ball, probably in 1964, Luce held forth to the assembled editors, writers, and photographers about LSD, which he and his wife, the playwright and Republican operative Clare Boothe Luce, had first tried several years earlier. As the former *Life* publisher and *Time* chairman Andrew Heiskell recollected more than two decades later: "Without any preamble that I can remember, [Luce] said that he and Clare were taking LSD! And two hundred and fifty people fainted. And then he went right on. I don't think he had any notion of what he had said. I don't know whether he thought all of us took LSD and therefore he would be one of the boys—maybe that. You know, he was very specific about it. He said, 'Yes, yes, we take LSD. We do it under doctor's supervision.'"[3]

Luce was a lifelong Republican, a patriot for free enterprise and middle American values, who drank alcohol moderately, chain smoked, and had no sympathy for the antiwar movement or the emerging hippie subculture. Through much of the 1950s and 1960s, Luce, the magazines he controlled, and the news-media industry of which he was a leading light were also entranced by psychedelic drugs.

Critics have applied the term "hype" when news media focuses attention on a particular issue far out of proportion to its place in the real world. During an episode of media hype, news coverage feeds on itself, as different news outlets follow and expand on one another's stories, reacting among themselves and to real-world developments. Influence seems to flow from larger news organizations to smaller ones, as editors at smaller or more marginal media operations look toward the decisions made by major outlets for ideas and confirmation of their own judgment.[4] The process "is more like a square dance than a forced march," Lucig H. Danielian and Stephen D. Reese observed after charting cocaine coverage across prominent newspapers, news magazines, and nightly television news during a forty-week period in 1986. "The patterns and partners continually change as both external events and the media 'dancers' themselves call the steps."[5]

The history of the label "psychedelic" reveals a kinship between media experience and the experience of these drugs. Coined in 1957 specifically to suggest the mind-expanding and transporting capacity of LSD and similar substances, it was soon applied to light shows, rock music, art, or film meant to provide audience members the same effect. In 1969, the prominent media scholar Marshall McLuhan theorized in *Playboy* (1969 circulation 5.1 million), "The upsurge in drug taking is intimately related to the impact of the electric media. Look at the metaphor for getting high: turning on. One turns on his consciousness through drugs just as he opens up all his senses to a total depth involvement by turning on the TV dial. Drug taking is stimulated by today's pervasive environment of instant information, with its feedback mechanism of the inner trip. The inner trip is not the sole prerogative of the LSD traveler; it's the universal experience of TV watchers."[6]

This book presents a history of the media hype over LSD and related psychedelic drugs: a grand arrival, heralded in particular by *Time* and *Life,* to a 1950s cultural landscape that had been deliberately scrubbed of alluring descriptions of drug use; the picturesque drug trips related in mainstream magazines and newspapers; sensational television specials and radio discussions; the contradictory, at times hysterical, reactions in mass media as the drugs accrued both casualties and countercultural cachet; and, finally, the loss of interest in psychedelic drugs by mainstream media outlets at the end of the 1960s, despite continued increase in the use of these substances and the insurgent popularity of films and popular music inspired by their effect. As a history, the goal is not to build a general theory but to shed light on a particular case through close examination of the media content and circumstances surrounding it. Still, theory informs this study in two ways: by suggesting explanations of cause and effect, and by offering a history of how similar phenomena have been considered by previous scholars. While media historians have discussed coverage of LSD and psychedelic drugs only in passing, theorists have examined the media's role in influencing public opinion and encouraging new behaviors. Insights from this scholarship speak to the coverage's significance and its seemingly contradictory effects.

The American news media's hype over LSD stands out for breaking the pattern of magazine, newspaper, and televised antidrug crusades that historians have observed in nearly every decade of the twentieth century. From muckraking investigations of the patent-drug industry at the beginning of the century, to newspaper crusades against Prohibition-era opiate and cocaine use, to televised assaults on crack cocaine and designer drugs at century's end, American mass media frequently has been observed exploiting what David F. Musto and Pamela Korsmeyer have described as the public's "reflexive fear of drugs . . . always there and ready to be inflamed."[7] Detailed scholarship has examined how media attention to recreational drugs at various times echoed the rhetoric of alcohol prohibition and anti-subversion,[8] demonized crack cocaine users,[9] and heightened society's anxiety about newer synthetic drugs including PCP, ecstasy, and methamphetamine.[10] A media history of LSD expands this scholarship by showing that beyond exhorting the public to "Just Say No," mainstream, commercial mass media have also challenged members of the audience to consider saying "yes."

Literature Review

Generations of American social scientists have been preoccupied with understanding how mass media influence the adoption of new attitudes and behaviors, including the use of new and innovative drugs.[11] Researchers in the 1940s and 1950s, led by Paul F. Lazarsfeld, an Austrian émigré trained as a mathematician, pioneered new polling techniques and sophisticated methods of analysis to try to measure the effect of the expanding mass media, defined initially as newspapers, magazines, and radio, on socially consequential behavior. The work was centered at the Columbia University Bureau of Applied Social Research, created by Lazarsfeld in 1944, staffed from the rich talent pool of displaced European scientists, and supported nearly entirely by research conducted on behalf of government, foundations, and industry.[12]

Counterintuitively, the first studies in this tradition found that mass media had only a limited effect on audience views and behavior. To collect data for the groundbreaking *The People's Choice: How the Voter Makes Up His Mind in a Presidential Campaign* (1944), Lazarsfeld supervised multiple interviews—monthly, in some cases—with a panel of 2,400 registered voters in Erie County, Ohio, to track changes to their political opinions in the seven months leading up to the 1940 presidential election. Researchers found that the preelection "floodtide of political propaganda" in radio and print media rarely caused voters to change their minds. "The people who did most of the reading about and listening to the campaign were the most impervious to any ideas which might prompt them to change their vote," the researchers found. "Insofar as campaign propaganda was intended to change votes, it was most likely to reach the people least susceptible to such changes."[13] Those most likely to change their views were individuals who held their views weakly to begin with, and were least immersed in the flood of broadcast and printed election propaganda. Researchers theorized that ideas spread from mass media to a more active and media-engaged audience of "opinion leaders," who then diffused them to the less engaged segments of the population through social contact, in a process described as a two-step flow.[14] Landmark Bureau studies focusing on the new antibiotic tetracycline appeared to confirm the limited role of media in fostering a drug's spread. Although tetracycline was surely a mundane drug by comparison with LSD, it was introduced to physicians during the same time period and through a similar process. Prior to 1962, most of the LSD consumed in the United States also flowed from medical channels.[15] The bureau's tetracycline study, *Medical Innovation: A Diffusion Study* (1966), is cited by leading scholars of diffusion as "one of the most influential diffusion studies in showing that the diffusion of an innovation is essentially a social process that occurs through interpersonal networks."[16] By correlating time-stamped prescribing records with information about physicians' social relationships gleaned from interviews with physicians in four midwestern cities, researchers seemed able to plot how the decision to prescribe the new drug spread epidemiologically, like a disease, through personal contact between physicians in professional and social settings.[17]

The analogy of the new drug spreading like disease, with only minor influence from media, had a profound influence on communication scholarship, despite immediate doubts about its empirical validity. Many scholars preferred to think that physicians acted on the basis of published scientific opinion, or at least on drug-company outreach and marketing, which in the case of tetracycline was extensive. Other studies and national surveys conducted around the same time found that physicians were more influenced by medical journals and drug-company marketing than by peers.[18] Even the authors of *Medical Innovation* found that doctors most frequently cited drug-company representatives when asked the "most important source of information in your decision to adopt" a drug, although the scholars concluded that the question was worded poorly for determining the source that actually prompted a final decision.[19] In 2001, a reanalysis of the *Medical Innovation* data set published in the *American Journal of Sociology* found that evidence for the social-contagion effect between physicians highlighted in the original study evaporated when variables measuring drug-company marketing were added to the mix.[20]

Contemporary research confirms that the media plays a role in diffusing innovation, and new drugs in particular. Diffusion theorists describe media's influence as taking place early in the individual's decision-making process. As a result, the influence was easily overlooked in studies that focused only on the final moment in which individuals tried an innovation for the first time.[21] Media coverage alerts audiences that an innovation exists and informs them what it is supposed to do. Even news coverage that seems harshly negative in tone can spread information about a new drug or new way of using drugs and "ensure the new drug gains a popularity it might never have acquired if it had simply been ignored," noted Philip Jenkins in a study of media drug panics. "Instead, the substance is described in the most exaggerated terms, stressing its extremely powerful, pleasurable and enduring effects in a way that in other contexts would be seen as unabashed advertising."[22] In regard to highly regulated or illegal drugs, it is worth noting too that the appearance of epidemiological, person-to-person transmission may be predetermined by the fact that it is the only way the drugs could be obtained.

Beyond offering information about the existence and benefits of a new drug, coverage of a subject in the news media has the effect of increasing that subject's salience to members of the audience: that is, the more something is discussed in the news, the more easily it comes to mind. "The mass media force attention to certain issues," the communication scholars Kurt Lang and Gladys Engle Lang observed. "They are constantly presenting objects suggesting what individuals in the mass should think about, know about, have feelings about." Hundreds of studies have confirmed that the news media's selection and emphasis of particular issues or topics, the news media's agenda, influences the public's agenda, typically operationalized by a list of concerns cited by respondents in public-opinion polls.[23] The effect is most pronounced when the media directs attention to issues about which most members of the public have no direct experience (such as the national debt or balance of trade) and much weaker for issues that are experienced personally. In a study of U.S. media coverage of drugs between 1972 and 1986, Pamela Shoemaker, Wayne Wanta, and Dawn Leggett found that the level of media attention to drugs alone appeared to be responsible for half of the variation in public concern measured through public-opinion polls. "The more the mass media emphasize drugs, the more the public is concerned with drugs as a problem," the authors concluded.[24] However, agenda setting is formally agnostic about how audience members will respond to the issues they are alerted to by media, beyond suggesting that the issues will come more easily to mind. This ambivalence was stated succinctly in 1963 by Bernard Cohen, who said that the press "may not be successful much of the time in telling people what to think, but it is stunningly successful in telling its readers what to think about."[25]

Scholars noted that media that increases the salience of illegal drugs may draw attention to forbidden fruit, potentially leading some audience members to curiosity or desire for something that would otherwise be out-of-mind.[26] The effect may occur regardless of the tone of the coverage; even antidrug advertising can "boomerang" when it reminds people about something they are not supposed to do. "Campaigners are constantly wrestling with the question of whether the forbidden fruit appeal might sell the fruit," the communications scholar Charles Atkin wrote. And even media content as seemingly unambiguous as antidrug advertising may influence different audience members differently, provoking antidrug reactions in some while sparking curiosity in that fraction of the audience psychologically prone to risk-taking. Antidrug advertising can also inadvertently encourage drug use through what Atkin called "inadvertent social norming," by providing the impression that drug use is more common and accepted than it actually is.[27]

The tendency for news organizations to look toward one another when formulating their individual news agendas explains how particular issues seem to explode to prominence and linger with seemingly little regard to the actual prevalence of the problem, as well as why particular themes, sources, and explanations seem to be repeated across the media landscape. The media hype over cocaine in the mid-1980s, Danielian and Reese concluded, was more the result of news organizations following one another's stories, a process described as intermedia agenda setting, than any real-world event. News media publicized cocaine use during this period not because use was increasing (in fact, it had been leveling off since the late 1970s) but because they were following a trail blazed by other media outlets, foremost the *New York Times*.[28] Studies conducted decades apart have found that the volume of mass-media attention to major political issues, including drug abuse and crime, has had little relationship to the actual prevalence of the problem in society or the risk posed to individuals.[29]

Many factors influenced how LSD and psychedelic drugs appeared on the media agenda. The development of the LSD story was shaped by the journalists and sources who told it, and the processes by which journalists turned items from the realms of science, culture, and crime into news. During the hype over LSD and psychedelic drugs, several of the most prominent sources doubled as occasional journalists, and the most effective approached news coverage functionally as a way to publicize pro-drug views. At particular news outlets, the agenda was affected by editorial outlook and the desire to appeal to a particular presumed audience. In the case of *Time* and *Life,* discussion of LSD was also influenced by an owner who had the wherewithal and authority to see his preferences realized.

Government activity also influences the news agenda, in direct and indirect ways. In the United States, the First Amendment discourages direct government interference with the content of printed publications. Nevertheless, regulatory structures discouraging certain types of content—including content about drugs—within some broadcast and entertainment media, and efforts of government officials to influence media makers by intimidation and moral suasion, affected the way drugs were discussed (see chapter 1). Subtler was the general inclination of news media to align with government policy positions, a tendency observed in many contexts.[30] News attention to crime, by definition, reflects legislative decisions about legal and illegal behavior. Routine journalistic practices, such as coverage of government activities, pronouncements, and reports and attention to police stations and courtrooms as sources of news, reveal other pathways of government influence on the kinds of stories that become news.

Moral beliefs also influence the news agenda. News creators draw on traditional cultural themes that resonate with audiences and typically accept fundamental views of contemporary society, such as, for example, belief in the Protestant work ethic or free enterprise.[31] Distaste toward certain types of drug use is also deeply imbedded in the American psyche; so too is the pursuit of instant gratification through material goods, including drugs.[32] The sociologist Jock Young argued that the moral deviance of certain kinds of drug use caused the media in the 1960s to discuss these drugs as a moral rather than a public-health issue. Young proposed that mass-media attention to any particular drug reflected—and defended—a social consensus about "what activities are praiseworthy and what are condemnable" and was unrelated to the actual health threat. He, like many others, pointed out that tobacco and alcohol caused far more casualties than any illicit drug. "It is when drug use is seen as unrelated to productivity, when it gives rise to experiences which question the taken-for-granted 'reality,' that forces of condemnation are brought into play," Young argued.[33] Sociologists who examined coverage of drugs in the late 1960s concluded that journalists were attuned to and selected stories that satisfied moral expectations: that an evil drug must have evil effects, or that undeserved pleasure must result in extraordinary suffering. Erich Goode and Nachman Ben-Yehuda argued that false and unlikely stories about LSD circulating through the media in the late 1960s seemed credible to journalists and the public because they corresponded to incipient notions about what the newly deviant drugs were supposed to do.[34] Young perceived the coverage more cynically, as an opportunistic bid to appeal to readers by stoking moral outrage. "The mass media has discovered that people read avidly news which titillates their sensibilities and confirms their prejudices," he wrote. "Moral indignation, if first galvanized by the newspapers and then resolved in a *just* fashion, is a fine basis for newspaper readership."[35]

Media coverage may influence social beliefs, as well as be influenced by them. In addition to increasing the overall salience of an issue, news attention raises the salience of particular attributes with which an issue is described. The effect, described as second-level agenda setting, is thought to work on a basic cognitive level: the attributes associated with an object in media coverage are more accessible and come more quickly to mind than those that were not. In effect, the public not only learns what topics are important from news coverage, it learns what is important about them.[36] Through this mechanism, news media participate in the construction of meaning around topics, including drugs. The attributes applied to drugs can influence not only attitudes but also how the drug is experienced. In regard to marijuana, Rogers concluded, "Enjoyment is introduced by the favorable definition of the situation that one acquires from others."[37] Looking toward the more metaphysical claims made about LSD, the sociologist Todd Gitlin explained: "Drugs are physical substances, and intoxication is a physiological and psychological state. But the meaning of a given drug to the people who use it, even the experience of the drug itself, differs considerably from one society, one sector, one group, even one moment in time to another. That meaning is not preordained in nature; it is constructed—and not by wholly free human beings, but rather by people with specific opportunities, desires and limits, operating in and among specific institutions."[38] Some have suggested that it was the far-out attributes associated with LSD, rather than anything about the substance itself, that triggered the drug's condemnation. "Most commentators at the time argued that the use of LSD posed a threat to the hegemony of the middle class work ethic, morality and world view," Goode and Ben-Yehuda wrote, referring to the late 1960s. "The very notion of otherworldliness that psychedelic propagandists were peddling, which very few users subscribed to, was what seemed so fearful."[39]

How audiences use media content has been addressed by decades of research in uses and gratifications, another theory with roots in the studies of audiences conducted by the Columbia Bureau of Applied Social Research. With surveys and self-reports, early scholarship in this tradition sought to understand the social and psychological reasons for people's media use by asking them. "This approach to mass communications is essentially functional," pioneers of uses and gratifications explained in 1973. "It argues that people bend media to their needs more regularly than the media overpower them."[40] Audience members are envisioned as active consumers who purposefully use media to gratify social or psychological needs, needs that otherwise might be gratified through non-media means. In this sense, media compete with social and other activities that also gratify these needs. Research has not established a clear-cut list of gratifications, with each major study seemingly introducing its own classification scheme.[41] A list of gratifications offered by Denis McQuail included: getting information and advice; reducing personal insecurity; learning about society and the world; finding support for one's own values; gaining insight into one's own life; experiencing empathy with problems of others; having a basis for social contact; feeling connected with others; escaping from problems and worries; filling time; experiencing emotional release; and acquiring a daily routine. Of special relevance to the news coverage of psychedelic drugs is "gaining entry into an imaginary world."[42] Lawrence A. Wenner argued that audience members also use news to participate in imagined relationships with people depicted. They may feel as though they were on a team with the reporter, actually confronting a source, or right there cheering with a spokesman. "We feel both involved and knowledgeable," Karen S. Johnson-Cartee summarized.[43]

While describing an innovative drug, news coverage of LSD through the 1950s and 1960s frequently, and often quite explicitly, promised an innovative use of media: taking readers or viewers on the mind-blowing experience of a psychedelic drug trip. To accomplish this, journalists pushed against formal constraints, introducing trick photographic effects, artistic renditions, literary flights of fancy, and extended narration of internal drug effects. The accounts kept pace with the evolving interpretation of the significance of LSD experience, from simulacrum of madness in the mid-1950s, to personal psychological insight at the end of that decade, to mystical connectedness in the mid-1960s. The coverage gratified audience members' curiosity, provided information about and a sense of participation in a marginal cultural movement, and, most weirdly, offered through media the psychedelic experience said to be offered by the drug itself.

Historiographic Context

From the first deliberate human experience with LSD, a 1943 trip by Albert Hofmann that is celebrated as Bicycle Day by psychedelic devotees, the activities and experiences of the founding generation of LSD users has been extraordinarily well documented, almost certainly to a greater extent than any other drug in common recreational use. The discrete origin of the drug, which until 1962 flowed entirely or almost entirely from the stores of its manufacturer, the chemical company Sandoz, the publications of early academic researchers, and the celebrity of many adopters in arts and media have enabled the initial diffusion of LSD to be mapped to a remarkable degree. Careful accounts by journalists have traced the person-to-person spread of LSD among notable figures in

Boston, New York, and California, as one cultural icon seemingly turned on the next. Even the drug's clandestine use by the military and Central Intelligence Agency has been brought into the light following the declassification of documents and congressional investigations. Many of these accounts also consider the intellectual history of the drug. A fascinating aspect of LSD was the extent to which it appeared to encourage users to contemplate the significance of the experience they just endured.[44] The same factors that permitted detailed accounting of the drug's early diffusion have allowed researchers to observe how public intellectuals constructed meanings around the disorienting and irrational psychedelic experience. Recent scholarly and popular books have examined the activities and motivations of the outspoken LSD pitchman Timothy Leary and other figures within his orbit, many of whom published their own stories.[45]

A history of mass communication about LSD contributes to this scholarship by illuminating how and why these new and challenging ideas about drug use were disseminated to the public at large. From the mid-1950s to about 1970, magazine and newspaper articles, television documentaries, and radio programming about LSD reached the great majority of Americans who had no connection to the obscure experimental drug and no natural inclination to seek information about it on their own. Unlike the books in which intellectuals like Leary, Aldous Huxley, Alan Watts, and others formulated their theories about LSD and psychedelic experiences for self-selecting audiences of perhaps tens of thousands of readers, mass media spoke to millions, whether they knew they were interested in the subject or not.

In a nation with thousands of daily newspapers and hundreds of broadcasters and national magazines, generalizing about the whole of the news media is a formidable challenge. The discussion of newspaper coverage here emphasizes the places where extraordinary coverage of LSD was located, rather than those where it was not, while providing context through examination of four geographically diverse metropolitan newspapers, including several in areas that were early centers of LSD use: the *New York Times, Boston Globe, Los Angeles Times,* and *Chicago Tribune.* Television and radio programming about LSD was located by searching program guides and newspaper television grids. Abundant magazine articles about LSD and related subjects were located through the *Readers' Guide to Periodical Literature,* bibliographies, and other secondary sources. Magazine circulation figures are drawn from the *N.W. Ayer and Son's Directory of Newspapers and Periodicals,* which was published most (but not all) years during the period covered by this study.

When journalists introduced LSD to the public in the 1950s and 1960s, they heralded it as an innovation in the most robust sense. Minute doses of LSD seemed to transport patients to a dramatically altered reality for eight to twelve hours while preserving their ability to communicate with the researchers who launched their trips. It was not only a new drug, but suggested a new use for drugs in exploring the unconscious mind. Research with LSD coincided roughly with the discovery of the first effective antipsychotic drugs and the realization that mental illness is influenced by brain chemistry. To many psychiatrists, it appeared as though LSD would be the tool to illuminate the chemical underpinnings of human consciousness. More than one thousand medical-journal articles published before 1961 examined the therapeutic use of LSD and explored the experience it seemed to create. Some LSD volunteers analogized their experience to insanity, bolstering the hope that the drug could lead to a better understanding of that condition. Others reported cinematic visions, with imagery borrowed from literature, religion, or personal history, and sensations of spiritual fulfillment and insight.[46]

Beginning in the mid-1950s, when depictions of drug effects were still blocked from entertainment television and major studio films, and continuing through the late 1960s, the news media—newspapers, broadcast television, and particularly popular magazines—lavished attention on the strange new drug.[47] The first U.S. clinical trial with LSD generated articles in 1954 and 1955 not only in the *American Journal of Psychiatry* but also *Scientific American* (1955 circulation 129,000) and the picture magazine *Look* (1954 circulation 3.4 million), which invited readers to "Step into the World of the Insane" with a six-page spread of staged and manipulated photos intended to show what taking LSD is like.[48] Researchers who worked with the drug were alarmed by the enthusiastic media attention. Albert Hofmann, the chemist who first synthesized LSD in 1938 from a chemical found in the grain fungus ergot, charged that sensational magazine and newspaper articles in the 1950s "made effective lay propaganda for LSD" that "introduced and expedited" its spread from medicine and psychiatry to the drug scene.[49] In 1964, the *Journal of the American Medical Association* similarly blamed "a series of articles in national popular magazines" for focusing major attention on "these drugs, their effects, and the personal eccentricities and misadventures of the people advocating their use."[50] A sociological study of black-market LSD users, also published in 1964, observed that in 1962 and 1963 nearly every important national magazine had printed a major article about LSD. "With the clanging acclaims and denunciations, the national noise level has become a din," the authors observed.[51] In 1967, a psychologist began an essay on the motivations of LSD users by noting, "It would be easy enough to rest upon the observation that the chemical substance most instrumental in the spread of the psychedelic movement is printer's ink."[52] In 1968, another

LSD researcher claimed, "In the past twenty years no other medication, except possibly thalidomide and 'the pill,' has aroused such widespread public and professional interest."[53] Scholars have subsequently suggested that the swell of magazine articles about LSD was the primary reason why the drug is widely considered to have been a 1960s phenomenon, even though in the following decades the actual use of the drug was often above 1960s levels.[54]

Breathless initial coverage of LSD was followed by an onslaught of highly negative publicity in the late 1960s, as the drug was increasingly prohibited through state-by-state legislation. One turning point was in 1967, when the journal *Science* published a study claiming that the drug caused birth defects. Its results were hyped in dozens of inflammatory magazine articles, some equating the damage from LSD to that of a nuclear bomb and predicting a generation of deformed children. The exaggeration and falsification in magazine reporting about LSD has become a textbook example of moral panic, a theory in the field of sociology that sees a role for media in whipping up irrational public concern over something that appears to threaten the social order.[55] Several observers floated the theory that the negative media coverage made users so nervous about taking the drug that it caused an increase in bad LSD trips.[56] No actual cases of birth defects from LSD were confirmed, and *Science* retracted the study in 1971. In the interim, a mass-media consensus against LSD had hardened, and the glories of the drug experience ceased to make news. While the actual number of LSD users continued to rise into the 1970s, journalistic interest in describing their trips withered.[57]

While it lasted, this was mind-expanding stuff. Through coverage of LSD and similar drugs, the mass media introduced a broad swath of America to the existence of a psychedelic experience that was mostly unknown and certainly unconsidered. Between the public introduction of the drug in 1954 and the period of its prohibition in the late 1960s, coverage in magazines, newspapers, television, and radio reports focused the public's attention on the amorphous inner experience of LSD. From its initial interpretation as madness, the dissociative drug experience was heaped with cultural and mystical attributes that were often quite desirable.

The desire for the kind of mystical, transformative experience described in the early 1960s media led down many paths—maybe to marijuana, which was sometimes hailed as a psychedelic drug and sometimes credited with similar mind-expanding qualities, despite its comparatively meek effect.[58] Or to meditation, Buddhism, neo-paganism, or New Age spirituality, all of which have been cited as beneficiaries of the 1960s psychedelic drug culture.[59] A shift in emphasis toward personally accessible mystical and spiritual experiences budged even mainline Christian churches. By the end of the decade, "the talk of God, even those at theological odds with the radical side of the Sixties, was laced with the new jargon of highs, trips, and liberation," wrote the religion scholar Robert S. Ellwood.[60]

Most, however, accessed psychedelic experience only through media. From magazines' literary flights of fancy and distorted photos to broadcasters' surrealistic visual effects and trippy music, the subject of LSD gave license to media creators to experiment with novel effects intended to immediately engage and transport the audience and to work on a level beyond rational comprehension. By reporting the LSD experience, the media also familiarized the public with this more abstract, immersive, and immediate way to use media. Experimental re-creations of LSD trips faded from the news media after 1968, but the gratification of this immediate connection to engrossing, psychedelic effects was increasingly offered in popular music and movies. Psychedelic experience became a media sensation, in both senses of the word.

The book proceeds as follows:

Chapter 1 explains the media's contribution to America's naiveté about illegal drugs—heroin, cocaine, marijuana—and drug effects before psychedelic drugs were introduced. Until the 1960s, pressure from U.S. government agencies and industry self-regulation discouraged information about drug use in television and film. Government officials and prohibition ideologues played determinative roles in setting a news-media agenda that was hostile toward drug use and drug users and omitted acknowledgment of drugs' potentially enticing effects. Themes about drug use that were initially raised in antinarcotics crusades following World War I were revived in the 1950s by public officials in highly publicized hearings reported by newspapers and covered live in broadcast media. Social beliefs about the harm of drug use and the influence of prominent experts and public officials made informative descriptions of drug use and drug effects out of bounds for mass media.

Chapter 2 explains the dramatic appearance of LSD on the news agenda in reports on scientific studies using drugs to simulate madness and the concurrent discussion of mystical, mind-expanding drug use sparked by the publication of Aldous Huxley's *Doors of Perception*. In addressing these topics, journalists introduced American audiences to new drugs and to the use of drugs to create mental states considered to have significant scholarly and academic importance. Scholarly interest gave journalists license to describe drug states that previously had been considered inappropriate for public view. Reports in mainstream media outlets were followed quickly by even more sensational coverage in more marginal publications.

The third chapter explains how the new salience of hallucinogenic drugs inspired a media interest in Indian drug rituals. Indian practices that were previously described as backward and superstitious were seemingly rehabilitated in 1950s news coverage to align with contemporary theories about the drugs. Of particular interest was the "discovery" of hallucinogenic mushrooms by an amateur scientist writing for *Life* magazine in 1957 and the frenzy that discovery sparked in the media, in part due to the author's coordinated publicity campaign. As well as creating a market for magic mushrooms, the coverage disseminated a seemingly authentic backstory for contemporary psychedelic drug use.

Chapter 4 examines cross-fertilization between researchers and media figures in the late 1950s, as LSD spread from controlled trials to the black market. News reporters gravitated toward research documenting astonishing results with LSD, even as those studies were becoming further removed from the scientific consensus about the drug. The movie star Cary Grant seconded descriptions of LSD as a wonder drug, endorsing the drug in interviews that appeared widely in newspapers and magazines.

Chapter 5 describes the celebrity coverage of Timothy Leary in the early 1960s and interest in LSD at *Time* and *Life,* where the publisher Henry Luce was becoming increasingly outspoken about his interest in the drug. Reporters often treated Leary, a Harvard psychologist removed from his job as a result of drug experimentation, with skepticism while still permitting him to explain the LSD phenomenon and relying on his scholarship and wit. Journalists were often surprisingly accepting of Leary's conclusions about the drug experience, even while condemning his encouragement of drug use. Among the many magazines focusing attention on LSD, *Time* and *Life* were particularly protective of the technology and hopeful it could be productively used by regular people.

Chapter 6 examines how media coverage of LSD changed as recreational use of the drug was increasingly identified as an aspect of the blossoming hippie movement. Horror stories about LSD side effects and tales of nightmarish trips, including several that were demonstrably false, circulated through media. Still, the apparent cultural currency of psychedelic experience encouraged magazines in particular to continue to describe and depict drug experiences for their readers. A number of publications, including *Time* and *Life,* defended the importance of LSD and psychedelic experiences even while condemning its reckless use. The significance of LSD experiences was weighed against its harm to users in a number of television specials, radio documentaries, and printed reports.

The concluding postscript discusses the dramatic decline in interest in LSD by the news media after about 1968, when the federal government finally prohibited possession of the drug. In the face of growing government activism against drugs, elaborate reenactments of LSD trips faded from the news agenda. But the psychedelic world introduced by the news media was increasingly enacted by television and film producers emboldened by the decline of the television and motion-picture production codes. As the 1960s faded into history, entertainment programming frequently offered itself as a substitute for the psychedelic drug experience that journalists had taught Americans to seek.

CHAPTER 1

Early Restrictions on
Drug Speech, 1900–1956

In 1968, when the public interest in and media attention to psychedelic drugs seemed to be reaching a crescendo, the LSD researcher and addiction expert Sidney Cohen reflected that the lavish descriptions of psychedelic drug trips and breathless testimonials proliferating in contemporary media were not genuinely new. Cohen noted that in 1822, the Englishman Thomas De Quincey, enthralled by a preparation of opium, wrote in *Confessions of an English Opium-Eater,* "[H]appiness might now be bought for a penny, and carried in the waistcoat-pocket; portable ecstasies might be had corked up in a pint-bottle; and peace of mind could be sent down by the mail." In the classic poem "Kubla Khan," Samuel Taylor Coleridge described fantastic visions brought on by opium. Other Victorian writers, including Edgar Allan Poe and Elizabeth Barrett Browning, "spoke of the extract of Oriental poppy capsule in terms singularly similar to the eulogies of today's LSD advocates," Cohen observed.[1]

Even the sensations of mystical insight and cosmic understanding attributed to LSD were earlier associated with other drugs, particularly nitrous oxide—laughing gas—which had a long history of recreational use. William James, a founding father of American psychology, wrote about achieving mystical experiences through laughing gas in a number of places, including an 1874 review in the *Atlantic Monthly* (1880 circulation 12,000).[2] In his 1902 masterwork *The Varieties of Religious Experience,* James concluded that laughing gas offered insights of genuine "metaphysical significance" that were appropriate for serious philosophical consideration, although one was under no obligation to accept the drug-inspired insights of anyone else.[3] A contemporary of James scoffed, "Truly the new beatitude is a hard saying: 'Blessed are the intoxicated, for to them the kingdom of spirits is revealed.'"[4]

An even closer analog to LSD was mescaline, the psychoactive component of the hallucinogenic peyote cactus, long used by American Indians in religious observances and first isolated from peyote buttons in 1896 by the German chemist Arthur Heffter.[5] The British psychologist and intellectual Havelock Ellis introduced mescaline to others, including the poet W. B. Yeats, and wrote about his experiences with the drug in the British periodical *Contemporary Review* in 1898 and *Popular Science Monthly* (1901 circulation 10,000) in 1902. Ellis described how a potion derived from three cactus buttons produced brilliant, kaleidoscopic visions and a fresh appreciation for the beauty of simple objects. He added that an acquaintance reported obtaining "objective knowledge" of his own personality by way of mescaline use. "Mescal intoxication may be described as chiefly a saturnalia of the specific senses, and, above all, an orgy of vision. It reveals an optical fairyland, where all the senses now and again join the play, but the mind itself remains a self-possessed spectator," Ellis summarized in the *Contemporary Review* article. "It may at least be claimed that for a healthy person to be once or twice admitted to the rites of mescal is not only an unforgettable delight but an educational influence of no mean value."[6]

By 1950, these drug experiences described vividly in turn-of-the-century magazines had disappeared from public memory. The leading drug-control historian David F. Musto in 1973 identified a persistent cycle in the history of American drug use, in which successive generations forgot the harm caused by a drug and repeated the excess of the past. At midcentury, Americans' knowledge was at a low point. With the decline in drug use since the century's start, fewer Americans had firsthand experience taking recreational drugs and hence were less familiar with both risks and rewards.[7]

Extra-media and ideological influences on the mass media worked to compound Americans' naiveté. Beginning shortly after the turn of the century, censors attacked cinematic depictions of drugs for fear that any representation might serve as an enticement. Industry codes governing film, and later television, forbade any portrayal of drugs. Although the obscenity laws, industry codes, and government activism intended to keep practical or potentially alluring information away from the public did not focus directly on news media, journalists were influenced by the social ideology that labeled the material inappropriate. Sympathetic portraits of drug addicts persisted for a few years after the passage of the Harrison Narcotic Act in 1914, which criminalized possession of opium-based drugs and cocaine. However, by the mid-1920s journalists had largely adopted the apocalyptic language of antinarcotic crusaders.[8] As the news media turned its attention to narcotics, it was frequently to sensationalize their dangers to play on readers' worst fears.

History of Censorship of Drug Information

The genesis of laws used to censor information about drugs was the post–Civil War crusade against obscenity led by U.S. Postal Inspector Anthony Comstock, the founder of the New York Society for the Suppression of Vice. The 1873 federal Comstock Law forbade publishing or mailing information, instructions, "or any drug or medicine, or any article whatever, for the prevention of conception or for causing unlawful abortion," as well as "obscene, lewd or lascivious" materials.[9] Forty years later, Comstock boasted that he had "convicted persons enough to fill a passenger train of sixty-one coaches, sixty coaches containing sixty passengers each and the sixty-first almost full. I have destroyed 160 tons of obscene literature."[10]

Progressive crusaders and government officials who enforced censorship at the local level did not fear simply that people who viewed obscene material would mimic the behavior portrayed. Rather, they believed that the act of viewing itself was harmful, leading to juvenile delinquency and social decline. Comstock-era attacks on obscenity drew on an understanding articulated in the 1868 British court ruling in *Regina v. Hicklin*.[11] Under that decision, obscenity was defined as that which could be harmful to women, children, or the mentally deficient. "The tendency of the matter charged as obscenity is to deprave and corrupt those whose minds are open to such immoral influences and into whose hands a publication of this sort may fall," the ruling read.[12] Using this definition, courts found ample grounds to ban printed information about birth control and abortion, as well as racy books. Among the hundreds prosecuted under the Comstock Law was Edward Bliss Foote, inventor of the rubber diaphragm, and Margaret Sanger, founder of the modern birth-control movement, who fled indictment in 1915 for sending birth-control information through the mail.[13]

Enforcers of Comstockery turned their sights on recreational drug use in the moving pictures, a new medium whose very intimacy challenged Victorian norms of propriety. "Picture galleries of hell," William Randolph Hearst's *New York Journal* called moving-picture arcades in 1899, charging that they showed schoolchildren obscene, indecent, and immoral pictures "too vulgar to be described," but almost certainly including short films of women dancing or in tights.[14] Opium smoking was included in motion pictures of this vintage by W. K. Laurie Dickson, George Méliès, the Lumière brothers, and others.[15]

Depictions of urban low life, nightlife, and crime offended the official watch-dogs of early films, which in New York included police, agents of Comstock's Society for the Suppression of Vice, and the mayor's office, which licensed the-aters. A popular genre along these lines was the "slumming" comedy, which typically followed tourists on a night on the town, including a visit to a Chinese opium den. In 1909, after protests caused New York Mayor George McClel-land to temporarily shutter all 550 of the city's theaters, a censorship board was created in New York at the request of the city's film exhibitors. Named the National Board of Censorship, the board quickly gained support and financing from a trade group representing the ten largest film manufacturers. By 1914, the National Board of Censorship claimed to be reviewing 95 percent of U.S. films, and its weekly bulletin was mailed to city officials and civic groups around the country. Almost 20 percent of the films it reviewed were rejected for depicting sexuality, prostitution, drug use, or violent crime.[16]

Other municipalities and states soon established censorship boards with more strident standards, often targeting images of drug use. Instructive de-tails of the "use of opium and other habit-forming drugs" were prohibited in Maryland. Ohio prohibited "scenes which show the use of narcotics and other unnatural practices dangerous to social morality as attractive." In Massachusetts the law read, "[P]ictures and parts of pictures dealing with the drug habit: e.g., the use of opium, morphine, cocaine, etc. will be disapproved."[17] In 1915, the U.S. Supreme Court established that films were not protected under the First Amendment but were rather "business pure and simple," and hence subject to state regulation just as any other business. By 1923, Pennsylvania, Ohio, Kansas, Maryland, New York, Virginia, and Massachusetts had formed state censorship boards, as had dozens of local jurisdictions.[18]

Disapproval by state and local censorship boards did not prevent the produc-tion of a few hundred silent films about illegal drugs, addiction, and the drug trade, nearly all of which are now lost. Most followed the trajectory of an up-per- or middle-class character who becomes hooked on drugs and subsequently loses his job, family, and self-respect. While many of these films depicted a sympathetic drug user's descent into addiction and degeneracy, the antidrug message was often undercut by glamorous stops along the way.[19] Notable drug films included D. W. Griffith's *For His Son* (1914), the story of a father who grows rich off a cocaine-laced soft drink called Dopokoke, but whose son becomes hopelessly addicted to the Coca-Cola-inspired product. In the notoriously bi-zarre 1916 *The Mystery of the Leaping Fish,* drugs are used to justify the madcap behavior of detective Coke Ennyday, played by Douglas Fairbanks Sr. The char-acter lives up to his name by injecting himself with hypodermic needles worn in a sash around his chest, inhaling clouds of cocaine, and eating opium by the fistful. The detective's office clock divides the day between "dope," "drinks," "sleep," and "eats."

Films like these, along with a series of scandals in the early 1920s, seemed to expose Hollywood as a hotbed of sin. There were rumors of cocaine use following the death of the actress Olive Thomas, wife of Jack Pickford, in Paris in 1920. The following year, the comedian Roscoe "Fatty" Arbuckle was accused of raping starlet Virginia Rappe during a party at a San Francisco hotel, leading to her death. Arbuckle was eventually acquitted of rape and manslaughter, but the episode soured attitudes toward Hollywood. While the second of Arbuckle's three jury trials was still under way, Paramount Studios director William Desmond Taylor was murdered in Los Angeles. Newspaper reports on the latter murder and subsequent investigation alleged that Taylor was killed by drug dealers associated with his friend and rumored lover, the silent-screen bad girl Mabel Normand, who had a long-standing affinity for cocaine. Public disgust with Hollywood contributed to declining box-office sales and the introduction of nearly one hundred new censorship bills in thirty-seven states.[20]

To forestall greater regulation, studio executives tapped Will H. Hays, the U.S. postmaster general and former campaign manager for President Warren G. Harding, to head up a new trade association, the Motion Picture Producers and Distributors of America, responsible for creating a set of standards for the movies its members would distribute. Shortly after accepting the post, Hays requested that distributors cancel all bookings and showings of Arbuckle's films. In 1921, the association instituted the "morality clause," subjecting actors to dismissal for behavior that was offensive to public decency, and studio executives circulated a blacklist of more than one hundred drug users and addicts who were warned to sober up or lose their jobs. A statement the same year condemned "stories that make gambling and drunkenness attractive or scenes that show the use of narcotics and other unnatural practices dangerous to social morality." Depictions of drug use were forbidden regardless of in-plot consequences. In 1927, the Association of Motion Picture Producers and the Motion Picture Producers and Distributors of America issued a resolution discouraging the use of the word "drugs," even in connection with smuggling. It read, "naturally, the methods of distributing illegal drugs, and of peddling dope may never be shown since this is an art of the 'traffic' in drugs." Guidelines issued from the Hays office, however, did little to head off the production of troublesome films; the number of cuts demanded by local censors reached a new high in 1929.[21]

To quiet critics and preclude the possibility of federal censorship, the Hays office adopted a detailed Motion Picture Production Code in 1930. Its attitude toward drug use was blunt: "Illegal drug traffic must never be presented. Because of its evil consequences, the drug traffic should never be presented in any form.

The existence of the trade should not be brought to the attention of audiences." Four years later, the Production Code Administration was empowered to enforce the code by pre-screening movies. The major Hollywood studios, which owned most urban first-run theaters, vowed not to distribute or show unapproved films, and many independent theater owners followed suit. For nearly two decades, not a single major Hollywood film dealing with drug use was distributed to the public.[22]

Newspaper Antidrug Crusades

Print media had more latitude in depiction of drug use, but it also responded to the governmental and cultural disapproval of narcotics. Although middle-class and medical narcotics addicts had been subjects of sympathy before narcotics prohibition, the devious, criminal drug addict became a staple of reporting on narcotics after their prohibition. Newspaper and magazine articles about drugs reflected the sensitivities of motion-picture censorship by avoiding descriptions or instructive information about drug use, while often adopting the most heated rhetoric of antidrug campaigners and government officials. The historian Susan L. Speaker observed that the drug problem was described as an "evil," a "menace," an "infection," or in similar terms in two-thirds of the fifty-four articles she examined for a history of 1920s and 1930s drug-reform rhetoric. Nearly three-quarters of the articles offered numbers exaggerating the scope of the drug problem.[23]

Overheated antidrug rhetoric perhaps reached its zenith in the roughly two dozen Hearst newspapers, which frequently ran the same articles and editorials and by the 1920s accounted for approximately 10 percent of daily and 20 percent of Sunday newspapers sold across the country.[24] During the 1920s, Hearst newspapers built on the interest in Hollywood drug scandals with a series of crusades against illicit drugs that redirected some of the anxieties and rhetoric that undergirded alcohol prohibition. Arbuckle's first trial was under way in San Francisco when the *San Francisco Examiner* launched its 1921 salvo with the headline, "Drug Evil Invades Cities, Towns as Ruthless Ring Coolly Recruits Victims," by the celebrity reporter Annie Laurie:

There are more than one million drug addicts in the United States today.
Ten years ago, there were less than half a million.
Twenty years ago, the "dope" habit was contained to the underworld—today it is reaching, creeping closer to the very doorsteps of the plain, everyday home—

and it has already trailed its slimy length into the very heart of what we call society.[25]

For the next several weeks, editorials, editorial cartoons, and feature stories pressed the case: "The Twentieth Century pestilence that stalks at noonday commands your attention," one editorial proclaimed. "The diligent dealer in deadly drugs is at your door!"[26] Contributions from Laurie (a.k.a. Winifred Black) included first-person accounts of visits to "Paradise Alley," "Evil Town," and San Francisco's "Street of the Living Dead," where addicts congregated. "So how many today—how many tomorrow? How far does it reach . . . and into what unsuspected homes does it throw its dreadful shadow this very hour?" Laurie asked.[27] Another editorial offered the shocking—and exaggerated—figure of two million drug addicts from coast to coast, about one in every fifty-five Americans.[28]

The death of the silent film star Wally Reid from morphine addiction in 1923 coincided with a revival of Hearst's antidrug crusade. In an article on the front page of the *San Francisco Examiner,* Laurie asked: "Is there a dope problem in the United States of America? And does that problem deeply and vitally concern you and your home and your children, and every young and easily influenced boy and girl in this country, from Maine to California and from Seattle to Galveston?" The answer, she concluded, was clearly yes. "The narcotic traffic has almost trebled in volume in America in the past two years," Laurie reported. "We use in the United States forty times more narcotic drugs per capita than any other white nation."[29] Editorial cartoons supporting the 1923 crusade showed the "dope evil" as the cloaked figure Death.[30] Even more dramatic was the promotion, published in newspapers from coast to coast, for a related article in the February 1923 edition of *Hearst's International Magazine* (1923 circulation 443,000) that showed dope as a monstrous hyena, with the body of a woman in its jaws (figure 1).

A literary magazine featuring short stories by prominent writers, *Hearst's International Magazine* was advertised under the tagline "A Liberal Education," but it incorporated the publisher's sensationalistic sensibilities. "When it starts after the secrets of the dope ring, or the Ku Klux Clan, or any other menace to the wholesomeness and integrity of family and national life, the International has a way of getting the WHOLE STORY," it boasted.[31] "The Inside Story of Dope in This Country," by Sidney Howard, who two years later would win the Pulitzer Prize for drama, promised "to deal with vice at its most depraved and least romantic, where processes are more menacing and physiological results more tragic than any melodrama."[32] Howard depicted a drug problem of national reach, dwelling on the suffering and debased circumstances of

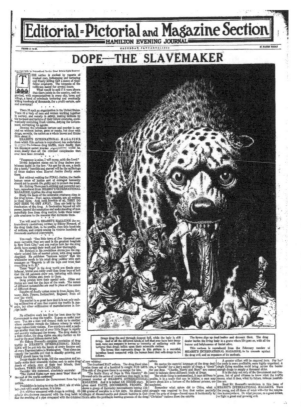

Figure 1. The text for this 1923 full-page advertisement for the dramatist Sidney Howard's story on dope in *Hearst's International Magazine* equates drug trafficking with murder and slavery. Advertisements for the series, clipped here from the January 27, 1923, *Hamilton (Ohio) Evening Journal,* appeared in other newspapers, including the *Indianapolis Star* and the *San Francisco Examiner.*

morphine addicts trapped by their habits. While sparing no hyperbole in the description of the harmful effects of dope, and opiate addition in particular, he called for more effective and human treatment of addicts than was offered through the criminal justice system. At the start of the series and in newspaper articles promoting it, Hearst promised to place the magazine in the hands of every member of Congress. "The rulers of the country shall know the ravages and the headway of this vice," read a note introducing the series. "They will be compelled to act."[33]

The portrait of dope as a threat to a wholesome family and national life reflected the rhetoric of an increasingly vocal antinarcotics movement, led by the temperance alumnus Richmond P. Hobson, for a time the Anti-Saloon League's best-paid public speaker. In speeches and interviews, Hobson warned that foreign powers pushed narcotics to make money and "to weaken a financial, commercial, or industrial rival or an imagined enemy in war."[34] The invocation of shadowy foreign forces weakening America from within resonated with post–World War I fears about foreign entanglements and influence. In 1924, for example, Hobson warned the readers of the *New York Times*: "The United States is assailed by opium from Asia as a base, by cocaine with South America as a base and by heroin and synthetic drugs with Europe as a base. This deadly drug warfare that is striking from three sides at our citizens and homes is more destructive and biologically more dangerous to our future than would be united warfare against us from these three continents."[35] As had been the case with alcohol, drug use was credited with potentially ruinous effects on not only the individual but also society, and often the "race." Drug use was not an unfortunate or degrading habit, as it had been described in the past, but a creeping infection that threatened to undermine white society. Hobson's rhetoric borrowed from the anti-alcohol script, including scientific-sounding descriptions of brain damage allegedly caused by drugs. Drug use, he claimed, led to a transformation in character.[36] In a 1928 radio address, Hobson explained, "The question of securing the drug supply becomes absolutely dominant. To get this supply the addict will not only advocate public policies against the public welfare, but will lie, steal, rob and if necessary, commit murder." Among the drug's effects was an uncontrollable "mania" to bring others into addiction.[37]

Hearst revived his crusade against drugs to commemorate Hobson's National Narcotics Education Week in 1927 and 1928, each time with multi-part stories by Laurie filled with dire warnings and tear-jerking anecdotes. While confirming the criminal tendencies of drug users, some of the sob sister's portraits of addicts oozed sympathy. "Dope Habit Traps College Girls, Evil Robs Woman of Mate, Home," was the headline over a 1928 interview with four female addicts in a New York prison. After discussing their plight, Annie Laurie concluded with the observation that all these women were someone's daughter:

Your girls and mine—how safe are they from this creeping horror of drug addiction? What are we doing, you and I, to protect them?

Do you suppose that any one of the mothers of these poor, broken creatures ever saw, even in her wildest dreams, the black shadow of a prison?

Heroin, cocaine, morphine, marihuana, opium—what does it matter which it is? One horror is worse than the other.

How can we be sure that our young people are in no danger from these deadly perils? [38]

By the 1928 crusade, Laurie had widened her focus to include another villain, the drug of "murder and torture, and hideous cruelty," marijuana.

The man under the influence of hasheesh [*sic*] catches up his knife and runs through the streets hacking and killing everyone he meets. No, he has no special grievance against mankind. When he is himself, he is probably a good humored, harmless, well-meaning creature. But hasheesh is the murder drug, and it is the hasheesh that makes him pick up his knife and start out to kill. Marihuana is American hasheesh.

It is made from a little weed that grows in Texas and in Arizona and Southern California. You can grow enough marihuana in a window box to drive the whole population of the United States stark, staring, raving mad.[39]

William Randolph Hearst was involved with the decision to push the drug issue onto his publications' agendas, as he was with all major editorial decisions. In 1923, Hearst lofted the banner for his papers' crusade against dope with a signed, page-one editorial.[40] "He keeps this subject alive whenever the occasion arises, forces it under the noses of his readers and continues to demand that the Government kill this dreadful traffic. And finally, when it is killed, he will have done more than any man in the United States to accomplish its death," Laurie wrote in the foreword to her 1928 book *Dope: The Story of the Living Dead.*[41] Nothing in Hearst's biography reveals a particular antipathy toward drugs.[42] Certainly with regard to alcohol, however, Hearst was troubled by others' lack of restraint. Although he gave up drinking while a student at Harvard in the 1880s, Hearst continued to supply guests at his palatial home on the central California coast with alcohol throughout Prohibition, but in carefully metered quantities. One cocktail before dinner was acceptable, but drunkenness was forbidden and could result in an involuntary early departure. Personal liquor bottles were subject to confiscation. These idiosyncrasies may have been motivated by Hearst's desire to keep liquor away from his companion, the movie star Marion Davies, whose alcoholism caused him no end of concern. In any case, narcotics were a natural fit within Hearst's larger portfolio of causes. Hearst unleashed his writers on causes that he believed had populist appeal and would cast his papers in the role of protagonists in a fight. During the heyday of yellow journalism, Hearst directed sustained attacks on the railroads and trusts, monopolies that controlled prices of milk, coal, and power. The drug problem was attractive for a Hearst editorial crusade: it afforded the opportunity to raise the alarm about a heretofore-invisible threat, to indulge in apocalyptic rhetoric, to demand action from lawmakers, and to take credit when it occurred. Surely, it also helped that drug users were sufficiently marginalized that they could hardly object to even the most unflattering portrayals. The commercial success that Hearst's newspapers enjoyed with a formula that included these splashy, sensational stories and broad, fear-based appeals goes a long way toward explaining their regular place on the papers' agenda.[43]

Other newspapers did not share Hearst's enthusiasm for this cause. The *Chicago Daily Tribune* editorialized against attempts to reduce narcotics use through criminal statutes in 1935, arguing that they were ineffective and resulted in drug addicts turning to crime.[44] The paper, which offered relatively scant coverage to Hobson, objected in 1928 that his narcotic-education week was part of a drive for antidrug legislation, rather than a purely educational effort.[45] The *Boston Globe* published a half-dozen articles about addresses by Hobson between 1920 and his death in 1937, while the *New York Times* published scores of articles reporting on Hobson's statements in his official and semiofficial capacities, along with other news about government narcotic control efforts and local narcotics crime. Neither paper exhibited Hearst's fascination with lurid tales of drug-induced downfall. In Los Angeles, home base during the 1920s of Hobson's International Narcotics Education Association, the *Los Angeles Times* covered numerous local antinarcotics marches and organizing activities, but likewise without Hearst's sensationalism. Nevertheless, the paper supported tough antidrug laws and had no sympathy for drug use. "The disgusting, filthy drug habit is an exotic, an alien, the most un-American poison that ever took root in the life of our nation," the *Los Angeles Times* editorialized in 1923. "God help the republic in the dangerous years ahead if this curse is not speedily stamped out!"[46] On the eve of narcotics week in 1928, a *Los Angeles Times* reporter wrote a column, "The Narcotic Bogey," suggesting that the scale of narcotics addiction was exaggerated by the campaigners, and that the annual effort had little effect beyond raising further money for "education" and tantalizing schoolchildren by "hav[ing] their interest whetted in a mysterious verboten which they are quite likely to wish to experiment with themselves—as bright children often do in such cases."[47]

Agenda-setting theory predicts that the press coverage should increase public concern with narcotics as a political problem. The theory is agnostic about the direction in which news coverage would shift beliefs, predicting only that the issue will seem more salient. Still, merely considering the issue as a problem that should be addressed through politics would seem to lead to support for greater—not less—government intervention. That the increase in the prominence of narcotics could also lead some to an increase in curiosity certainly seems possible. Given the lack of detail about the pleasures offered by drugs in these articles, it would be a curiosity that readers would have to go elsewhere to satisfy.

Harry J. Anslinger and the Media Agenda

The federal government adopted a higher profile in the fight against domestic drug trafficking in the late 1930s, led by Harry J. Anslinger, commissioner of the new Federal Bureau of Narcotics (FBN). Anslinger, a former official in the

Bureau of Prohibition, was tapped to head the narcotics bureau within the U.S. Department of Treasury in 1930. He quickly established himself as, in his words, the "world's greatest living expert on the international narcotic traffic,"[48] and he strategically used his position to influence the media agenda. On the one hand, he spoke forcefully on the drug issue, provided a file of cherry-picked antidrug anecdotes to news organizations, penned magazine articles, and even participated in commercial films starring his agency. On the other hand, he brought pressure to squelch research and reports that threatened to introduce contrary views and used the resources of his small agency to keep depictions of drug use off of television and the big screen.

In pressing a campaign for uniform state laws against narcotics and marijuana in the 1930s, Anslinger drew on the rhetoric of earlier antinarcotics crusaders, modified with a generous sprinkling of horrific anecdotes and a hard-boiled sensibility. The marijuana addicts he described were so violently and criminally deranged that they deserved only punishment and jail. In interviews and articles for the popular press, Anslinger offered a litany of drug-induced horrors, from racial mixing to rape and murder. A 1937 article, "Marijuana, Assassin of Youth" in *American* magazine (1937 circulation 2.1 million) credited to the commissioner, opened with a Chicago girl's suicidal plunge from a building and mentioned an unnamed addict who was hanged for assaulting a ten-year-old girl; another sexual assault on a child; three different cop killers; burglars and thieves; and a dazed marijuana addict who murdered his entire family with an ax. ("'I had a terrible dream,' he said. 'People tried to hack off my arms!'")[49] Anslinger included the story of the ax murderer when testifying to Congress about the effects of marijuana, without mentioning that local authorities had found the killer criminally insane and concluded that the episode was not marijuana-induced. Under the influence of marijuana, the slightest opposition may provoke "a state of menacing fury or homicidal attack. During this frenzied period, addicts have perpetuated some of the most bizarre and fantastic offenses and sex crimes known to police annals," he testified at a 1937 congressional hearing.[50]

The file of horror stories that Anslinger opened for journalists and at congressional hearings had a mythological character. While he placed some in particular states or cities, the incidents were stripped of names or other identifying details. He left out details about criminals' backgrounds or motivations, such as the psychiatric diagnosis of his ax murderer, in favor of the naive assumption that if crime was committed under the influence of a drug, the drug was the primary cause of the violent act. The tales were also embroidered with racial stereotypes, sexual innuendos, and prurient details absent from the original reports.[51] In a

1943 article for *Scientific American* (1943 circulation 47,000), "Marijuana More Dangerous than Heroin or Cocaine," the commissioner described marijuana as the most horrifying substance imaginable, transforming the individual, destroying intellect, and giving rise to "evil instincts." Its effect was nothing short of madness.[52]

While offering journalists and lawmakers tales of depraved drug addicts and swashbuckling narcotics agents, Anslinger worked ceaselessly behind the scenes to squelch dissenting views. The Federal Bureau of Narcotics "had an iron clamp" on addiction research and "had essentially driven out physicians for thirty years or more," according to Dr. Vincent Dole, a pioneer in methadone maintenance treatment for heroin addiction.[53] The bureau also used its influence against research into alternative drug-control policies. A former FBN detective and staff lawyer recalled: "[Anslinger] tried to suppress anyone's reports or information that would be contrary to his policy. If push came to shove and he couldn't effectively suppress it in its early stages, he would try to suppress the man, the preparer of the report, as some weirdo. Some person of poor judgment who should be discredited."[54]

A frequent foe of the bureau was the Indiana University sociologist Alfred Lindesmith. In 1940, he published an article in the *Journal of Criminal Law and Criminology* arguing that the "mythology" of the violent, criminal "dope fiend" did not comport with scholarly studies and was based on "superstition, half-truths and misinformation that bolsters up an indefensible repressive law."[55] Years later, Lindesmith recounted being visited by a bureau agent who threatened to have him fired. Deploying a tactic that would become familiar, Anslinger also recruited a San Francisco judge to pen an indignant rebuttal for the same journal that ran more than twice as long as Lindesmith's original piece.[56] Before a 1944 report by New York Mayor Fiorello LaGuardia and the New York Academy of Medicine concluding that marijuana is only a mild intoxicant was even released, Anslinger coordinated a rebuttal in the *American Journal of Psychiatry*. Fourteen years later, he reacted similarly to an American Bar Association–American Medical Association joint study "gently suggesting that severity of punishment might not be the only or even the best way to deter addiction," in the words of the panel chairman. The narcotics bureau distributed a comprehensive attack on the study while Treasury agents convinced a foundation to withdraw funding for the original study's publication. Through Lindesmith's efforts, Indiana University Press published the ABA-AMA report a few years later.[57]

The bureau's reach extended to the entertainment industry. In 1948, Anslinger prevailed on the State Department, the Public Health Service, and the Canadian government to block any U.S. screening of the Canadian documentary

The Drug Addict, which included realistic footage of drug traffickers and addicts of all races and raised doubts about the possibility of completely stopping the flow of illegal drugs. Anslinger claimed that the film, produced by National Film Board of Canada and winner of the Academy of Canadian Film and Television award for best documentary, "would do incalculable damage in the way of spreading drug addiction." After Lindesmith agitated for the release of the film, Anslinger asked FBI director J. Edgar Hoover for information about Lindesmith's membership in any "Communist-Front organizations." More than a decade later, a narcotics-bureau agent filed a report identifying Lindesmith as a member of a youth organization sponsored by the Communist party.[58]

Anslinger maintained agents in Hollywood to monitor the activities of celebrities. In 1948, bureau agents were involved in the high-profile arrest of Robert Mitchum for smoking marijuana with a movie hopeful, Lila Leeds. Movie audiences reacted sympathetically to Mitchum's arrest, which seemed to burnish his rebel persona, and his career quickly rebounded. Leeds was less fortunate. Upon release from jail in 1949, she accepted an offer from an exploitation filmmaker to make a low-budget movie capitalizing on the publicity around the Mitchum arrest. *The Wild Weed,* also exhibited as *She Shoulda Said No,* told the story of an orphaned chorus girl whose experimentation with marijuana causes a brother to commit suicide and leads to her own arrest for drug peddling. Shooting for the film was completed in six days. Anslinger was outraged by the movie, which a subordinate reported displayed "lewd and lascivious conduct of men and women under the influence of marijuana."[59] The film was distributed without Production Code Administration approval. The narcotics bureau's supervisor in Philadelphia complained to the Pennsylvania Board of Censors that the movie was "insidious propaganda that would teach juveniles the method of using narcotics."[60]

When the Production Code Administration considered removing its prohibition against drugs in 1948, Anslinger met with MGM studio chief Louis B. Mayer and threatened to go public with a list of stars who were addicts. An agenda for the meeting on file with Anslinger's papers included his handwritten notations, "The case of Peter Lorre" and "Case of Errol Flynn."[61] The prohibition against drugs was not dropped. The first film depicting drug use or drug trafficking to receive Production Code Administration approval was *To the Ends of the Earth* (1948), an adventure about an international narcotic investigation that featured Anslinger as himself.[62] The storyline about heroic narcotics agents successfully defending the nation from drugs was the sort Anslinger approved.[63] The bureau also participated in the making of *Johnny Stoolpigeon* (1949), reviewing scripts and enjoying prerelease screenings. Another movie that received Production

Code Administration approval despite depicting drug smuggling was *Slattery's Hurricane* (1949), perhaps because it was made with navy cooperation.[64] With cooperation from law enforcement and Anslinger's FBN, popular magazines offered sensational accounts of the drug trade that went beyond what was permitted on screen, while still presenting the problem from the approved police perspective. Anslinger continued to supply magazines with sensationalized horror stories from his bureau's files and to participate with newspaper photographers on undercover shoots.[65] A 1943 *Life* (1943 circulation 3.8 million) feature reporting on fears of a postwar spike in drug use, for example, included photographs and dramatic accounts of street drug sales, as well as pictures of busts and interrogations by narcotics-bureau agents.[66] Whether or not Anslinger's FBN initiated the story, it influenced its content to the extent that it was largely indistinguishable from the bureau's perspective.

The triumph of the police perspective was particularly vivid in the new medium of television. Drug addicts and traffickers routinely filled the roster of villains on crime dramas such as *Dragnet* in the 1950s, but the shows would not portray their crimes. Among prohibitions on sexual content, lotteries, and swearing, the 1951 National Association of Radio and Television Broadcasters code stated: "Drunkenness and narcotic addiction are never presented as desirable or prevalent"; and, "The administration of illegal drugs will not be displayed."[67] This prohibition was also enforced by informal means. Anslinger told a reporter for *Variety* (1955 circulation n.a.) that when he knew that a "dangerous" program was planned, he telephoned the radio or television station manager and had it pulled.[68]

The restriction of drug information on television and major studio films had the related effects of decreasing public knowledge about drugs and adding to the topic's sensational appeal for media makers not subject to the same restrictions. Several exploitation films of the late 1930s drew directly from Anslinger's antidrug campaign, including *Marijuana, Assassin of Youth* (1937), which not only borrowed its title from Anslinger's *American* magazine article but also appropriated the article's opening image for a promotional trailer. The embrace of self-regulation by major studios established the niche for extremely low-budget films that offered spectacle that the majors would not show. These so-called exploitation films, often exhibited by traveling promoters or in theaters in run-down parts of town, tantalized audiences with graphic depictions of drug use, as well as childbirth, diseased sexual organs, half-dressed Africans, and nudity that couldn't be seen elsewhere. (Hardcore pornography was illegal and was not an element in these films.) The drug exploitation films typically posed as educational, with introductions that stressed the importance of knowledge in combating the drug threat while relentlessly sensationalizing the topic and providing remarkably little information about the drugs' actual effects. *Marijuana, Assassin of Youth* and a second exploitation film, *The Burning Question* (1936), both recounted Anslinger's story about the marijuana addict who killed his family with an ax. The films' outlandish portrayal of marijuana as a murderous vice surely seemed ridiculous to those few audience members actually familiar with the drug. This was demonstrated fifty years later, when *The Burning Question* was rescued from obscurity by the National Organization for the Reform of Marijuana Laws and eventually distributed for exhibition as a comedy on the midnight-movie circuit under one of its alternate titles, *Reefer Madness.*[69]

Book publishers also exploited the sensational nature of drug use, along with sex, homosexuality, and violence, to sell cheap, pulp paperback books distinguished by lurid cover art. The marketing and distribution of these pocket-sized books was more like the periodical business than traditional bookselling. The paperbacks were printed in huge quantities (a 100,000- to 250,000-copy initial press run was typical) and sold on racks at corner stores, supermarkets, train stations, newsstands—in short, at just about any type of retail outlet except traditional bookstores. In 1953, *Fortune* estimated that mass-market publishers distributed 250 million paperbacks in 1952, outselling traditional trade books by 50 percent. Intended to shock, the paperbacks dealing with drug use were often erotic and unconcerned with the reality of drugs or drug users.[70]

The books' potentially alluring and instructional descriptions of drug use worried the U.S. House of Representatives Select Committee on Current Pornographic Materials, which held hearings on the paperback book industry in 1952. The committee's general counsel, H. Ralph Burton, led questioning. "In examining an enormous number of books, our staff has found that they now deal with narcotics, and deal with them in such a way as to almost provide an inducement, to those to read them, to become addicts. They describe the pleasures of narcotics, how to use them, how to use the needle. They expand upon homosexuality, and one book advises or supports polygamy, and any number of books deal with lesbianism and nymphomania. I have the names of them here." Burton was particularly worried about *Marijuana Girl,* published in 1951, for describing the "wonderful feeling" of marijuana smoking and the ritual of sniffing and shooting up drugs. "Even the eventual effects of drug addiction are made to appear not so very unattractive by artful manipulation of the imagination," he complained.[71]

Publication of these novels was protected by a series of court decisions that chiseled away at the government's authority to directly suppress books. In 1933, an influential federal court decision to allow James Joyce's *Ulysses* to be imported from France redefined obscenity in terms of its imagined effect on an "average reader," rather than on women or children or others deemed especially impressionable. While talk about sex, politics, and drugs often went hand in hand, two disparate traditions of analysis developed for political and sexual speech. Antigovernment or political speech fell under the legal tradition stemming from sedition, while obscenity became increasingly narrowly defined in terms of sex.[72] As the Supreme Court incrementally refined the circumstances under which either of these free-speech exceptions could be applied, speech about drugs fell between the cracks. Neither sexual nor seditious, by default drug speech became more difficult to prosecute.

But while prosecution based on drug content alone was unlikely, harassment by the Federal Bureau of Narcotics or a local law-enforcement agency loomed. Perhaps the most faithful portrayal of drug addiction published during this period was William S. Burroughs's 1951 semi-autobiographical novel *Junky*, which abandoned the pretensions of drama to describe a desultory life of addiction and petty crime. In the introduction to a 1977 edition, Allen Ginsberg, a friend of Burroughs, wrote that the book's editor complained, "The damn thing almost gave me a nervous breakdown—buildup of fear and terror, to work with that material." Ginsberg explained:

> There was at the time—not unknown to the present with its leftover vibrations of police state paranoia, cultivated by narcotic bureaus—a very heavy implicit thought-form, or assumption: that if you talked about "tea" (much less junk) on the bus or the subway, you might be arrested—even if you were only discussing a change in the law. It was just about illegal to talk about dope. . . . The fear and terror that [editor Carl] Solomon refers to was so real that it had been internalized in the publishing industry, and so, before the book could be printed, all sorts of disclaimers had to be interleaved with the text—lest the publisher be implicated criminally with the author, lest the public be misled by arbitrary opinions of the author which were at variance with "recognized medical authority"—at the time a forcible captive of the narcotics bureau.[73]

The first significant novel about drug addiction was Nelson Algren's 1949 *The Man with the Golden Arm,* which won the National Book Award for fiction. The novel detailed the struggles of a World War II veteran who returns to his old Chicago neighborhood with an addiction to morphine stemming from a shrapnel wound he had received in the war. In the works of both Burroughs, who was an unrepentant drug user, and Algren, who was not, drug use and addiction stood for an inward-turning rejection of society and its expectations, an alternative to bourgeois life. Subsequent "beat" writers dealing with drug themes did not try to rehabilitate the outsider status of the drug user, but rather embraced it as an authentic critique of society.[74] Although not strictly obscene, intimate descriptions of drug use—like intimate descriptions of sex—were not considered proper for public consumption. Writing about sex and writing about drugs were similar acts of rebellion against social constraint. Indeed, the works of three beat writers credited with sparking the 1960s interest in drugs, Burroughs, Jack Kerouac, and Ginsberg, were all prosecuted between 1957 and 1962 based not on drugs, but on crude language and sexual content.[75]

In adapting Algren's book for the screen, director Otto Preminger challenged the Motion Picture Production Code Administration by including scenes of drug use by the star, Frank Sinatra. Anslinger condemned the film in a front-page story in the weekly entertainment trade magazine *Variety* (1955 circulation n.a.) before production was even complete. In 1956, it became the first major studio film distributed without Production Code Administration approval since the group's creation. *The Man with the Golden Arm* was a commercial and critical success, winning three Oscar nominations.[76] Following this debacle, the Code was amended to permit showing drugs as long as it was in a negative light:

> Drug addiction or the illicit traffic in addiction-producing drugs shall not be shown if the portrayal:
>
> > Tends in any manner to encourage, stimulate or justify the use of such drugs; or
> >
> > Stresses, visually or by dialogue, their temporarily attractive effects; or
> >
> > Suggests that the drug habit may be quickly or easy broken; or
> >
> > Emphasizes the profits of the drug traffic; or
> >
> > Involves children who are shown knowingly to use or traffic in drugs.[77]

The 1950s Narcotics Scare

The junky lifestyles described in cheap 1950s paperbacks appeared to reflect a growing reality. Recalling what was believed to have happened following World War I, the FBN worried that returning veterans, including some who had been treated with morphine during the war, might again, in the historian David F. Musto's words, "be habituated through the devious methods of the enemy."[78] As shipping lines closed by World War II reopened and international trade resumed, so too did smuggling. The war also restricted FBN efforts to attack international drug trafficking, which had not been particularly effective in any case. The agency's fears appeared to be confirmed by reports of increasing drug use in black and Puerto Rican ghettos of northern cities at the end of the 1940s. Even more alarming were the reported increases in drug use among two groups that seemed particularly vital to the nation's future security: schoolchildren and members of the armed forces. In an appearance on the former first lady Eleanor Roosevelt's televised talk show in 1951, Anslinger said that the efforts of his bureau, which fielded only about 180 agents, was "like using a blotter to try to blot up the ocean."[79] Anslinger testified to Congress that a tough enforcement of existing drug laws was necessary to protect society from a weakness that aided our enemies.

In 1951, Congress passed the Boggs Act, the first federal law to treat marijuana alongside cocaine and opiates, such as heroin, as a narcotic. The federal law instituted a two-year minimum sentence for first drug convictions and eliminated the possibility of suspended sentence or probation for subsequent offenses. While the Boggs Act was still pending before Congress, Anslinger began lobbying state legislatures to pass similar "little Boggs Acts," increasing state penalties for drug use. Twenty-eight states and the territory of Alaska passed little Boggs bills by 1956.[80]

The Boggs Act was passed in an emotional atmosphere that Musto compared to that of the first Red Scare. "There is a noticeable parallel between the association of internal subversion in the postwar periods of both 1919–20 and 1951–55," Musto wrote. "Both led to extremely punitive sanctions against addicts and those who catered to addicts. Toleration of addiction was attacked as a dangerous weakness of soft-hearted or ill-informed persons; at least some of them must harbor evil intentions. Public sympathy was up against a social fear of addiction that had almost no connection with physiology or pharmacology."[81]

The 1951 scare over drug abuse nestled perfectly with other cold war fears: the pervasive influence of organized crime, subversion, weakness in the face of enemies abroad and at home. The frightening associations between narcotics and shadowy foreign powers that had spiced the Hearst antidrug crusades in the 1930s were now embedded in the sober claims of government officials. In testimony to lawmakers, Anslinger linked communist China's export of heroin to drug pushers in the United States to its efforts to get hard cash for war materials and to undermine Western society.[82] Postwar global politics fanned the paranoia. When, at a United Nations meeting in 1952, Anslinger accused China of smuggling opium to U.S.-occupied Japan to pay for war materials, the *New York Times* covered the charge and the Soviet representative's response that U.S. troops in Japan and Korea arrived at their stations already addicted to drugs.[83]

Normally unobtrusive to most Americans, the traffic in narcotics was thrust onto the public agenda in 1951 and 1952 by the highly publicized investigation of the U.S. Senate's Special Committee on Organized Crime in Interstate Commerce, popularly known as the Kefauver Committee after the committee's chair, first-term Tennessee Senator Estes Kefauver. The committee was formed in

1949, after the American Municipal Association petitioned the federal government to examine the growing influence of organized crime. Over the course of a fifteen-month investigation, the committee convened hearings in fourteen cities and interviewed hundreds of witnesses, including drug addicts and notorious gangsters like Bugsy Siegel and Frank Costello. In New York, Kefauver hearings addressing narcotics were broadcast on stations affiliated with all three major broadcast networks.[84] "Illegal drug use has reached epidemic proportions, according to information secured by this committee from different parts of the country. One of the most alarming aspects is the reported increase in addiction among the younger generation, some of school age," Kefauver stated before the committee a few weeks after the New York commission heard testimony.[85]

Broadcast on both radio and television, the hearings captured the nation's attention, reaching an estimated thirty million television viewers during hearings in New York. "From Manhattan as far west as the coaxial cable ran, the U.S. adjusted itself to Kefauver's schedule. Dishes stood in sinks, babies went unfed, business sagged and department stores emptied while the hearings were on," *Time* magazine (1952 circulation 1.7 million) claimed in an article the following year.[86] Some movie theaters showed the hearings. According to the U.S. Senate historian, the televised hearings were the most-viewed congressional investigation to date. "I do not think any of you can possibly realize how much good it has done to have these hearings televised," one viewer wrote the committee. "It has made millions of us aware of conditions that we would never have fully realized even if we had read the newspaper accounts."[87]

In New York, believed to have the greatest narcotics problem in the country, state and local officials also pushed the narcotics problem onto the news agenda. The Kefauver Committee hearings were succeeded by an investigation and hearings by State Attorney General Nathaniel Goldstein intended to "arouse an apathetic public" with the "shocking details" of juvenile narcotics use in the city, according to his spokesman. Like the Kefauver hearings, they were planned as a media event. "It is anticipated that phases of the hearings will be as dramatic as those held by the Senate Crime Investigating Committee," the *New York Times* reported.[88] They were premised on the concern that juvenile drug use was rising dangerously. Governor Thomas E. Dewey, a former prosecutor who rose to prominence fighting organized crime, signed the bill authorizing the fifty-thousand-dollar investigation on the same day that he signed measures increasing criminal penalties for possession and sale of heroin, cocaine, and morphine. In signing the bill, Dewey called on Goldstein "to determine the reason for the present inadequacy of our law-enforcement efforts."[89] Three days of hearings, including recorded testimony from teenaged addicts, were covered intensely by newspapers and broadcast live on radio.

The most widely reported item from the hearings, the acknowledgment by the New York schools superintendent that as many as one in two hundred New York schoolchildren used narcotics, demonstrated the pervasive influence of government officials and policy on news on this subject. The estimate was splashed on the front page of the following day's *Times* and made headlines from coast to coast. "A startling statistic last week made a front-page sensation out of a subject usually discussed only in the improbable columns of Sunday supplements: narcotics addiction," *Time* (1951 circulation 1.6 million) reported.[90] Prior to the hearings, school officials had reported 154 known cases of narcotics addiction among students. But on the witness stand, confronted with figures from law enforcement that suggested dramatic increases in youthful drug use and, according to the *New York Times*, "taunted" by the state attorney general for suggesting that the number of cases could really be so low, school superintendent William Jansen conceded a much larger estimate suggested by police. The low number was the result of school administrators' decision to leave it to individual school principals whether or not to include students caught with marijuana, he said.[91] The inclusion of marijuana, condemned as a gateway drug by federal narcotics officials but generally less concerning to medical authorities, increased the scale of the "narcotics" problem tenfold. In the hearings and subsequent news coverage, the teens were referred to as "addicts." Higher numbers served the political interests of the state officials who organized hearings and their desire for publicity. Journalists participated in the addict inflation by focusing attention on the most shocking estimates. A *Washington Post* headline, "6,000 Children in New York Called Dope Addicts," referred to a figure offered by a police lieutenant on the last day of testimony that bested even Goldstein's "at least 1,500," mentioned lower in the article.[92]

The *New York Times* published about nine hundred articles dealing with narcotics in 1951 alone, as state, federal, and United Nations committees held hearings, the Boggs Act moved through Congress, and the New York legislature considered bills intended by sponsors to prepare for "total war," with tougher sentences and a new state bureau of narcotics control.[93] In its news columns, the *Times* published numerous stories offering official assessments of the drug problem, tracking the progress of legislation and international negotiations. Statewide, narcotics arrests doubled in 1951 as a result of the heightened official interest,[94] while the salience of the issue made arrests and trials more likely to make the news. Articles in the *New York Times* described drug busts and trials from as far away as Buffalo, Washington, D.C., and Wichita Falls, Texas.[95] As well as the live coverage of hearings, broadcasters attended to concern over the drug problem with special reports and forums relying on government sources. The month after the New York hearings, NBC radio broadcast a series of three weekly programs on "The Truth about Narcotics," including interviews with addicts, narcotic experts, and the Kefauver Committee's chief counsel.[96] Other programs broadcast in 1951 included a half-hour television program on "International Narcotics Traffic" on CBS and a forum on "Teen-age Narcotic Victims" on the New York independent television station WPIX, as well as a discussion with Anslinger and New York school officials on Eleanor Roosevelt's live, Sunday-afternoon talk show on NBC.[97]

By the 1950s, the attitudes about drug use that were expressed in the 1920s antidrug crusades had become ingrained, and as such did not require extended explanation. Since the Hearst campaigns a generation earlier, many government officials had come to embrace the most extreme fears about narcotics use and, in the 1950s, used their positions to push the issue onto the media agenda. Officials, including Anslinger, warned about drugs as an immediate threat to youth and national security during what was by all accounts a fearful time. Newspapers in Boston, Chicago, and Los Angeles reported on the hearings in New York, as well as on local drug busts and programs to combat the dope menace. At a California state assembly committee meeting in 1951, Los Angeles Police Chief William H. Parker offered his opinion that communists in Europe and Asia were directing, in part, the flow of narcotics into the United States. "We have reason to believe that much of the traffic is Communist-inspired, following the pattern used in certain Asiatic countries to bring about a moral deterioration of their people," Parker was reported as saying in the *Los Angeles Times*.[98] Nine years later, the paper won the Pulitzer Prize for public service for a 1959 series by Gene Sherman that elevated concern about narcotics as a local problem and refocused attention on a drug threat not from overseas communists but from south of the Mexican border.[99]

The gratification offered by news coverage during this narcotics scare was closely related to the audience's presumed desire for surveillance: information about what was described as an imminent threat to society at large. The news reflected the societal rejection of narcotics use. Although news coverage was not subject to the regulations imposed on broadcast entertainment, newspaper and broadcast journalists held themselves to similar standards, steering clear of descriptions that could be construed as alluring or of practical, instructional value. Most readers had negative opinions about narcotics anyway, and would have little tolerance for news articles that seemed to promote narcotics use or revel in its appeal. While it is possible that the increased salience of the issue nudged some people toward narcotics use, the main effect was to increase public concern about narcotics as a political issue and subsequently build support for increasingly punitive antinarcotics legislation.

While newspapers generally favored official sources and a flat, objective style, magazines occasionally offered the voyeuristic pleasure of melodrama by dramatizing the horror of lost children and their heartbroken mothers. An 8,200-word fictional account in *Look* (1953 circulation 3.3 million), "A Monkey on My Back," described the author's interactions with teenagers who died or were jailed for violent crimes after becoming involved first with marijuana, then heroin.[100] A few months later, the magazine published an article, "Your Child May Be Hooked," including photographs of desolate teen addicts, aimed at educating parents about an epidemic that cut across economic levels. A psychiatrist explained:

"The war, the draft and the general uncertainties of the times have made this a period of extreme anxieties and frustrations for our youth," he said. "It's natural that they should seek an escape, some release from their fear and insecurity.

"But why are they turning to dope for an escape? We never had a serious dope menace before. Sometimes we suspect that this thing is coming dangerously close to a national fad—almost like the panty-raids craze.

"What's happening to American home life? Don't parents take the time to tell their children the facts of life anymore?"[101]

Other magazines addressed concerns about drugs with long accounts glamorizing the careers of law officers, a perspective encouraged by Anslinger and accommodated by police participation. In the *Saturday Evening Post* (1954 circulation 4.6 million), a two-part memoir of FBN agent Gon Sam Mue downplayed fears about an adolescent epidemic—"Our children prefer peppermint sticks to marijuana sticks in a ratio of 10,000 to 1," the agent wrote—before bringing readers along on an adventure in San Francisco's Chinese underworld.[102] Customs agents were "death on dope runners" in a 1952 *Saturday Evening Post* (1952 circulation 4 million) feature, working the Mexican border to nab "some of the dirtiest criminals on earth."[103] *Collier's* (1954 circulation 3.2 million) profiled Detective Kitty Barry, "ace detective of the narcotics squad and the most decorated lady cop in New York."[104] A 1953 first-person account in the *Saturday Evening Post* (1953 circulation 4.2 million) described a crusading U.S. Attorney's investigation into dope sold out of the Federal Bureau of Narcotics storeroom in Washington, D.C. Although the bureau frustrated the investigation, the author concluded that it was "mending its ways."[105] In each of these accounts, the drug issue was rendered as a heroic struggle between valiant law-enforcement agents and depraved drug addicts.

While magazines occasionally luxuriated in the seedier aspects of drug use, they avoided describing the experience, presumably pleasurable, that drugs could provide. Exposing the sordid life of an addict to raise sympathy for mothers or prosecutors was fine, but sharing the exultant experience of a drug high—which was, after all, a crime—would have crossed a line. An account by Lila Leeds, the pot-smoking companion of Robert Mitchum, in *Collier's* (1952 circulation 3.2 million) four years after her arrest approached this line, but merely tantalized:

> Now for the test. I loosened the tourniquet a bit. Instantly, the milky solution in the eyedropper turned red with blood pulsing back through the needle into the tube. I'd hit! The needle was in the vein solid.
>
> Nothing remained now but the joy-pop—the squeeze of the syringe that shoots reddish heroin out of the eye dropper into the vein. I waited, tasting the moment—scraping my dry tongue against the roof of my mouth—anticipating the sharp bitter flow of heroin induced saliva . . . and the dreamy calm that vanishes aches and fever.
>
> I squeezed the syringe—hard. Nothing happened. My right hand seemed paralyzed. I bent over and tried to sink my teeth into the syringe—anything to shoot the heroin. I bit savagely.
>
> Then suddenly I was awake.[106]

It was only a reformed addict's dream. Even in a shamelessly exploitive setting, the drug experience itself was off limits.

Notably absent from the news coverage were the testimonials about positive drug experiences and alternate academic viewpoints that would make the coverage of LSD so remarkable. During the decades of narcotics prohibition, media coverage of the narcotics problem was strongly influenced by the ideology of prohibition, words and actions from the federal antidrug bureaucracy, and a cultural belief that depictions of drug use caused harm. The belief that potentially alluring depictions of drugs had a pernicious effect was so prevalent that few seemed to believe drug speech was worth defending, or even worth serious consideration. Like the drugs themselves, descriptive media content about drugs was perceived as a source of immorality, threatening to lure youth down the path of delinquency. Speech about drugs fell into a grey area between sex and sedition, where government regulation was well established. As with sex, drug use was too intimate, shameful, and corrupting for public display. And while describing illegal drug use fell short of calling for the overthrow of the government (the legal definition of sedition), it telegraphed a disregard for its laws and would have seemed uncomfortably sympathetic toward what was perceived as an imminent, foreign threat to national health and independence.[107] Its exclusion from the mass media was rarely questioned.

As a result, during the half-century after Havelock Ellis recommended mescaline as an educational experience, the American public forgot the powerful, other-reality of subjective drug effects. When media descriptions of drug experiences reappeared in the 1950s, even as venerable a drug as mescaline seemed shocking, sensational, and new. Conceived by men in white lab coats and academic tweed, the new "psychedelic" drugs arrived as marvels of science rather than artifacts of crime. After years of assiduously avoiding any discussion of subjective drug effects, journalists jumped at the opportunity these new drugs provided to take readers to unknown lands. It was as though they discovered the gate to a forgotten world and could not wait to push on through.

CHAPTER 2

Introducing LSD, 1953–1956

After decades of willful disregard, the news media turned its attention to the otherworldly, internal effects of drugs as a result of external developments that cast these experiences in an unexpected new light. First was the extravagant scientific interest in LSD, a new drug that seemed to illuminate the divide between sanity and madness. The second was the unlikely advocacy of Aldous Huxley, an author widely considered among the leading literary intellectuals of his time,[1] and his publication of several books describing the effects of hallucinogenic drugs on himself and promoting their wider, nonmedical use as a spiritual tonic. In both cases, the interest in the drug by ostensibly soberminded individuals cracked the door to sensational descriptions of drug trips that previously had no place in mass media.

As with much of the LSD story, the first, accidental human experience with the drug was extraordinarily well documented. On Friday, April 16, 1943, a research chemist named Albert Hofmann in the Basel, Switzerland, laboratories of pharmaceutical company Sandoz was re-creating the twenty-fifth in a series of molecules he had earlier derived from lysergic acid found in the grain fungus ergot. Through a mishap that remains mysterious (Hofmann insisted that he maintained "meticulously neat" work habits), he absorbed a small amount of LSD through his lungs or fingertips. In a note to his boss, he explained what happened next:

I was forced to interrupt my work in the laboratory in the middle of the afternoon and proceed home, being affected by a remarkable restlessness, combined with a slight dizziness. At home I lay down and sank into a not unpleasant intoxicated-like condition, characterized by an extremely stimulated imagination. In a dreamlike state, with eyes closed (I found the daylight to be unpleasantly glaring), I perceived an uninterrupted stream of fantastic pictures, extraordinary shapes with intense, kaleidoscopic play of colors. After some two hours this condition faded away.[2]

Hofmann had joined Sandoz in 1929 after earning a doctorate with distinction from the University of Zurich. For his first six years on the job he examined the active compounds in the Mediterranean squill, a spiny plant whose bulb seemed to have the same effect on the heart as digitalis. In 1935, with "creative joy" and "eager anticipation," he embarked on a second program of research, methodically synthesizing the alkaloids in ergot.[3]

Midwives had used grain infected with ergot to quicken childbirth for centuries. But the herbal, listed in medical texts as early as 1582, also had a dark side. Seventeenth-century scientists linked the consumption of bread made with infected grain with localized epidemics of "St. Anthony's fire," a horrific disease with symptoms that included rotting limbs, madness, and death.[4] By creating a synthetic version of the active components, Hofmann hoped to make a drug that could be more accurately and reliably dispensed than the natural product. Sandoz already sold one synthetic drug, trademarked "Gynergen," modeled after a component of ergot and used in obstetrics and for the treatment of migraines. Hofmann had synthesized the substance he accidentally absorbed on April 16, 1943, once before, in 1938, but it was set aside after animal testing revealed only unexplained restlessness and a moderate effect on uterine activity. Hofmann credited what he said was an unusual decision to produce the drug a second time five years later to "a peculiar presentiment—the feeling that this substance could possess properties other than those established in the first investigations."[5]

The Monday following his first, inadvertent trip, Hofmann conducted a deliberate self-experiment with LSD-25, consuming a minute amount of the substance dissolved in water. After experiencing "dizziness, visual distortions, symptoms of paralysis, desire to laugh," he and his assistant left the laboratory by bicycle for Hofmann's home. On the ride, commemorated by devotees of LSD as "Bicycle Day," the chemist experienced intense visual hallucinations and strange contortions of self-perception. Back at home, he felt himself possessed by a demon, removed from his body, taken to another world, perhaps mad, perhaps dying.

My surroundings had now transformed themselves in more terrifying ways. Everything in the room spun around, and the familiar objects and pieces of furniture assumed grotesque, threatening forms. They were in continuous motion, animated, as if driven by an inner restlessness. . . . Even worse than these demonic transformations of the outer world were the alterations that I perceived in myself, my inner being. Every exertion of my will, every attempt to put an end to the disintegration of my ego, seemed to be wasted effort. . . . I was seized by a dreadful fear of going insane. I was taken to another world, another place, another time. My body seemed to be without sensation, lifeless, strange. Was I dying? Was this the transition? At times I believed myself to be outside my body, and then perceived clearly, as an outside observer, the complete tragedy of my situation. I had not even taken leave of my family. . . . Would they ever understand that I had not experimented thoughtlessly, irresponsibly, but rather with the utmost caution, and that such a result was in no way foreseeable?

Hofmann's fear subsided, and he slowly began enjoying the play of shapes and colors. He fell asleep exhausted, waking the following morning with a clear head and the sensation of well-being and renewed life. "The world was as if newly created," he wrote.[6]

Hofmann turned LSD-25 over to the Sandoz pharmacological department for animal testing. Under the influence of LSD, cats stood in fear of mice or ignored them. Fish swam in strange positions. Under low dosage, spiders spun unusually exacting webs, which became more rudimentary when the dosage was increased. Giving LSD to a single chimpanzee in a caged community created a reaction that now seems prophetic. Hofmann recalled: "Even though no changes appear in this single animal, the whole cage gets in an uproar because the LSD chimpanzee no longer observes the laws of its finely coordinated hierarchic tribal order."[7]

Initial research was oriented toward finding a use (and, ideally, a market) for the discovery. The first published study of LSD, by Dr. Werner Stoll, a University of Zurich psychiatrist and the son of Sandoz president Arthur Stoll, appeared in the *Swiss Archives of Neurology* in 1947. Stoll concluded that the drug could be used to induce abnormal mental states in normal subjects, he himself having experienced depression and ecstasy while under the influence of the drug. He also saw psychodynamics in its visions. Beginning in 1948, Sandoz shipped LSD to researchers under the trade name Delysid, as both sugarcoated tablets and a liquid solution in small glass vials.[8] The product insert suggested two uses:

Analytical: To elicit release of repressed material and provide mental relaxation, particularly in anxiety states and obsessional neurosis.

Experimental: By taking Delysid himself, the psychiatrist is able to gain an insight into the world of ideas and sensations of mental patients. Delysid also can be used to induce model psychoses of short duration in more normal subjects, thus facilitating studies on the pathogenesis of mental illness.[9]

The suggested applications for LSD appealed to psychologists with vastly differing theoretical orientations. On the one hand, its analytical use could facilitate psychoanalysis, the talk-based treatment for mental problems that originated in the work of Sigmund Freud, who postulated that abnormal behavior was rooted in repressed memories and desires buried in the patient's subconscious. Where else could the substance of these visions come from, if not some forgotten corner of the patient's mind? In the psychoanalytic tradition, treatment was closely linked with diagnosis: by making patients aware of their repressed memories, psychoanalysts helped dispel the symptoms these memories caused. In terms of Freud's mental geography, the drug seemed to break down barriers around the ego to allow repressed memories to pass more easily into consciousness.[10]

Experimental researchers, on the other hand, were drawn to LSD because it seemed to create mental illness without relying on repressed memories or unobservable mental states. As well as giving doctors greater personal insight into their patients, a pill that reliably triggered an episode of insanity meant that insanity could be used as the manipulation in controlled experiments; for example, to test new antipsychotic drugs against a known, replicable level of illness. And perhaps most importantly, if the drug caused mental illness, biochemical researchers might be able to trace its actions to find a metabolic cause.[11]

Since the late 1930s, psychiatrists had suggested that they could learn about mental insanity by studying the effects of mescaline, which researchers observed brought on hallucinations, mood swings, and confusion. With mescaline, "an opportunity is gained by psychiatrists of personally experiencing mental changes similar to those of schizophrenics," a researcher noted in a 1936 article in *Journal of Mental Science.*[12] (Although marijuana was also discussed in terms of madness in the 1930s, the interpretation was more popular with law-enforcement officials than medical authorities.) However, the line of inquiry did not take off until the 1950s, energized by LSD's discovery and advances in psychiatry and related fields. "With new insights in pharmacology, physiology, psychology, and sociology, we now have appropriate instruments to properly study and understand the effects of such psychologically potent drugs," researchers concluded in 1956.[13]

Midcentury was a fertile period for scientific research on the human mind. In the 1940s, researchers found spots in the brains of animals where a jolt of electricity could stimulate pleasure, overriding the creature's usual urges. Other technological breakthroughs demonstrated that physical manipulation of the brain, as in a lobotomy, could bring about psychological change.[14] Scientists also seemed to make new inroads to understanding the brain's chemical mechanisms, with two Nobel Prizes awarded for psychopharmacological research in the 1950s. The decade also witnessed the first generation of antipsychotic drugs, including chlorpromazine, which appeared to resolve cases of mental-asylum inmates who had been hospitalized for years.[15] The number of psychologists and psychiatrists working in the United States more than doubled between 1940 and the mid-1950s, and federal funding for psychiatric health care and research increased even faster.[16]

Psychiatrists discovered that LSD was a sort of doppelganger of chlorpromazine, the powerful sedative and antipsychotic sold under the trade names Largactil and Thorazine. Given beforehand, chlorpromazine blocked the effects of LSD. Administered after, it ended the LSD trip. "Psychiatry, it seemed, had overnight become scientific. Madness could be induced and resolved within hours. If this was the case, it could surely be studied systematically and would quickly yield up its secrets," wrote the historian of psychopharmacology David Healy.[17] If LSD indeed caused subjects to experience mental illness, researchers hoped it might be used to isolate a metabolic cause.[18] Scientists also felt a need for a drug that could produce a model psychosis against which new and better antipsychotic agents could be tested.[19]

LSD had tantalizing physical differences from earlier drugs that seemed to cause people to go crazy. For one thing, it had a pure scientific pedigree, delivered in glass vials directly from the laboratory in which it was created. And it was effective in amazingly small amounts. The standard dose was 0.025 milligrams, equivalent to 0.0000009 ounces of the pure chemical. At the same time, the drug seemed safe. While scientists demonstrated that injections of LSD between three hundred and one hundred thousand times the effective dose could cause respiratory arrest in mice, rabbits, and an unfortunate elephant, there have been no recorded cases of toxic overdose by humans.[20] The fact that it was so effective in microscopic doses suggested to researchers that LSD acted on a specific site in the brain, upending a previous view that consciousness-altering drugs worked by flooding the brain with a poison that overwhelmed normal function.[21]

The first shipment of LSD-25 to American researchers was received by a team headed by Max Rinkel at Boston Psychopathic Hospital, a clinic associated with Harvard University, in 1949. At the 1950 meeting of the American Psychiatric

Association, Rinkel announced results showing that LSD induced temporary psychotic episodes in normal subjects, setting forth hope that it would soon be possible to study mental disorders objectively in laboratory settings.[22] By 1951, scholarly journals published more than one hundred articles on LSD experiments, many including the authors' own experiences taking the drug. By 1961, the number of published studies had reached one thousand. That number doubled again by 1965, by which time the drug had been the subject of several dozen books and six international conferences and administered by researchers to between thirty thousand and forty thousand psychiatric patients and thousands more normal volunteers.[23] A 1972 book published by the Consumers Union summarized: "Few drugs known to man have been so thoroughly studied so promptly."[24]

The peculiar qualities of LSD conspired against researchers facing the fundamental challenge of objectively measuring the impact of a drug whose main effect was innately subjective, unobservable, and ambiguous. The problem of measuring mind-drug effects was illustrated by the story behind a biochemical theory of madness that was current around the time that LSD was introduced. After noting similarities between a molecular diagram of mescaline, printed in a thirty-year-old French text, and that of the hormone adrenaline, the British psychiatrists Humphry Osmond and John Smythies speculated that schizophrenia, a "disease marked by disordered thinking, hallucinations, social withdrawal and, in severe cases, a deterioration in the capacity to lead a rewarding life," resulted when the body's adrenal system created a mescaline-like substance in the body. To test their theory, they gave the adrenaline-related drug adrenochrome to volunteers and observed psychosis-like effects.[25] But at Boston Psychopathic, researchers observed no mental effect from adrenochrome at all.[26] To this day, there is no consensus on whether adrenochrome is psychoactive, despite continued experimentation.[27] Even LSD seemed to produce extraordinary responses in some researchers who took the drug, while others reported only unpleasant or inconsequential effects.[28]

There was a persistent problem of measurement. Something happened to subjects given the drug, but how to describe and quantify something taking place principally in the subjects' minds? Among the tools at researchers' disposal were external observations, interviews, and standardized psychological tests; physiological tests like blood pressure and urinalysis; and self-experimentation. All had shortcomings. Standardized intelligence and personality tests offered researchers the possibility of generating more objective, quantitative data. However, the answers found by standardized questionnaires were bound by the questions asked. The most commonly used questionnaire for LSD research, developed by a New York laboratory, presented all of its questions in negative terms, asking whether subjects felt unsteady, anxious, peculiar, weak.[29] But just as with schizophrenics, subjects on LSD could become hostile when doctors insisted that they participate in Rorschach or Draw-a-Person tests. The school psychologist–turned–LSD guru Arthur Kleps explained one aspect of this problem at a congressional hearing: "If I were to give you an IQ test and during the administration one of the walls of the room opened up, giving you a vision of the blazing glories of the central galactic suns, and at the same time your childhood began to unreel before your inner eye like a three-dimension color movie, you would not do well on the intelligence test."[30]

As a result of these difficulties, some studies relied entirely on narrative observations of drugged subjects by researchers. These observations have been shown to be surprisingly frail. A critique of data produced by fifteen years' worth of studies examining the effects of LSD on autistic children was largely worthless because of the way observations were conducted:

> Observations were naturalistic with little apparent appreciation for the value of controlling the conditions under which observations were made. The observers themselves were not blind to the fact that the children had received the medication, and the reliability of their narrative descriptions was never assessed. The resulting data are for the most part purely qualitative and presented in a narrative form that is highly subjective, potentially biased by observer expectations, and of unknown reliability and validity. . . . Whatever promise LSD might have was never going to be validated through these types of studies. Despite a good number of independent studies, it remains impossible to determine whether or not LSD had any therapeutic value for the children with autism who participated in these studies.[31]

Most of the autism studies examined did not randomly assign subjects to a control group, or use control groups at all. In most cases, researchers selected the severely disabled children for LSD trials on the sole basis that no other treatment had worked. The children were given the drug either once or twice or repeatedly for months, or, in some instances, years. Researchers following this methodology reached an initial consensus that children were happier and more responsive while on LSD. However, the consensus was eventually reversed as patients in later studies were observed as unresponsive and withdrawn.[32] In addition to autistic patients, researchers tested the therapeutic potential of LSD in clinical trials on juvenile delinquents, drug and alcohol addicts, schizophrenics, neurotics, and institutionalized mental patients.[33] Lee and Shlain argued that the approach employed by researchers in controlled trials "was inherently flawed not only because it sought to quantify creative experience but also because it ignored the input of the observer, which always influenced the result of an LSD experiment."[34]

Normal subjects on LSD were exceptionally emotionally reactive and suggestible. In experiments, volunteers responded to coldness from investigators with hostility, to warmth with affection. At Boston Psychopathic, the most common motivation of volunteers, largely drawn from hospital staff, was "to have a temporary psychotic experience in order to approach an understanding of a mental patient." Researchers suggested that this was one reason that hospital staff members displayed more response from the drug than did other volunteers.[35] While some of the experiments were double blind, with neither volunteers nor observers told who was given LSD and who was given plain water, distinguishing the effect of the powerful hallucinogenic drug from a placebo was generally not the problem; the problem was reducing the influence of expectations on what observers saw and volunteers experienced. In short, reactions to LSD experiments were influenced by both volunteers' frame of mind and their surroundings, "set and setting," in the formulation that later would be popularized by Timothy Leary.[36]

In the absence of good tools for measuring the subjective effects of LSD, researchers frequently turned to self-experimentation. LSD was recommended by Sandoz for consumption by psychologists in order to enhance their understanding of their patients. Indeed, many experts on LSD therapy advocated that it could only be responsibly conducted by therapists who had experienced the drug firsthand. Self-experimentation had a distinguished history in medical research. Freud himself conducted a course of self-experimentation with cocaine, early in his career, using spring-powered devices to graph reaction times and muscle strength under the influence of the drug. Freud appreciated the "cheerful and efficient mood" cultivated by cocaine and published an article recommending it against fatigue. Although data developed from Freud's self-experimentation improved understanding of cocaine dosages and the time-course of its effect, he was later criticized for ignoring its potential for abuse.[37] More than other volunteers, researchers were often assumed to have a sophisticated understanding of the risks and benefits involved in trying a new drug or procedure.[38] "It would be simply unethical to think that someone else should go first," LSD discoverer Hofmann told an interviewer.

One can only speculate the extent to which the sensation of profundity characteristic of LSD experiences influenced the researchers who experimented on themselves to pursue the research further. While the nature of the drug experience may be unclear, an aspect of the drug is to impress users with the feeling that what they underwent was of the deepest significance. As LSD fell out of favor, investigators' self-experiments seemed less like a qualification than a liability. "At one time, it was impossible to find an investigator willing to work with LSD who was not himself an 'addict,'" a 1964 editorial in the *Journal of the American Medical Association* charged.[39]

Ironically, these characteristics of LSD that encouraged and confounded researchers also made it particularly well suited for journalistic treatment. If the disoriented world opened through LSD is best explained from the perspective of one who has been there, who better to send than a trained journalist?

Reporting Sensations of LSD Madness

A smattering of newspaper articles in the mid-1950s reported on conference presentations and articles in scientific journals that discussed hopes for research with LSD, although without going deeply into the drug experience. "Maybe people go insane because their bodies start making a queer new chemical," began an Associated Press article, distributed to newspapers across the nation in 1954, which described research with adrenochrome and LSD.[40] A British study that found that LSD caused adults to relive childhood events was described in a 1954 Reuters wire-service story in a similar, matter-of-fact tone. "An 'Alice in Wonderland' drug which makes adults feel they have shrunk back to child-size has been tested on patients at the British Mental Hospital, it was revealed today," the article began.[41] The hope that research with drugs including LSD would transform treatment of mental illness was the subject of four of Dr. Walter C. Alvarez's nationally syndicated medical columns, which appeared in papers including the *Los Angeles Times* and *Boston Globe*.[42] "Is the human brain just a fantastically complex chemical and electrical machine?" asked the lead sentence in a 1956 Associated Press article that explored questions raised by the new mind drugs, including LSD.[43] Another Associated Press article in 1957 explained how, for three dollars a day, prisoners at a penitentiary in Atlanta volunteered to go "temporarily crazy to help humanity," by participating in LSD trials.[44] Other straightforward descriptions of research projects with LSD appeared in science columns in the *New York Times* and *Washington Post*.[45] In style and tone, the articles were not much different from the coverage of other scientific subjects in the daily news columns. In routine newspaper reports, journalists did not deviate far from their source material in journal articles and scientific presentations, explaining the research without digging any more deeply into its implications or the drug experience itself.

The mind-bending effects of LSD were explored more thoroughly by journalists who worked in the longer magazine formats. While daily newspaper coverage trumpeted scholarly presentations and publications, extended descriptions of LSD trips were a better fit for print magazines that occupied a niche for longer, more in-depth stories that went beyond timely hard-news coverage.[46] In the 1950s, and particularly before the dominance of broadcast television, magazines were important sources of information about science for the general public, educating while they also entertained.[47] LSD lingered on the news agenda of magazines thanks to the journalists' professional assessments of the story possibilities. Other groundbreaking drugs of this era, including the antipsychotic drug Thorazine and minor tranquilizers such as Miltown, the prototypical "Mother's Little Helper,"[48] went into greater use more quickly and had greater impact on public health but did not offer comparable possibilities for storytelling and art. Both received a fraction of the attention garnered by LSD.[49] Delivering readers to the world of the insane, as several magazine articles promised to do, was a project that allowed writers to flex their literary muscles, photographers to experiment with trick effects, and designers to violate the usual constraints of their medium.

LSD did not fit within the framework of concerns that circumscribed coverage of illegal drugs, but showing drug effects was still particularly sensational fare. "Next shocker due on TV—A film showing an insane man in a sensual trance," began a wire-service article about a 1955 episode of the syndicated half-hour television program *Confidential File,* carried on fifty stations nationwide, in which the reporter and newspaper columnist Paul Coates interviewed a man judged temporarily insane on LSD. "Such programs have had TV critics and viewers charging that 'Confidential File' purposely picks sensational subjects," the news article on the program reported.[50] Although LSD was not an illegal drug, graphically showing its effects nevertheless pushed the limits of propriety, which for some no doubt added to its appeal.

A few magazines discussed the potential of laboratory madness to advance scientific research without diving too deeply into the drug experience. In 1955, the *Saturday Evening Post* (1955 circulation 4.6 million) dramatized "New Help for the Living Dead" by telling the story of a middle-class man who was institutionalized after developing schizophrenia. Research using LSD provided the hope that a cure or biochemical treatment for the disease might soon be found.[51] "Experimental Insanity" in *Today's Health* (1956 circulation 362,000) similarly concluded that "now it is at least possible to hope that learning what makes the personality of man tick normally or abnormally lies just around the corner and that the war on mental disease may produce a major victory in a few years." The four-page article paraphrased heavily from the study the Boston Psychopathic team published in the *American Journal of Psychiatry* two months before.[52] The *American Weekly* (1954 circulation 9.1 million), a Sunday newspaper supplement published by Hearst, also embraced the viewpoint of scientists while dramatizing the British study that found LSD resurrected long-forgotten memories. "Alice-in-Wonderland Drug," illustrated with a drawing of a little girl in Victorian dress, began:

"This medicine," the doctor said, holding out a spoonful to the young woman, "is going to make you live over again a day in the past. You are going to be a little girl again."

"Will I like it?" she asked.

"I don't know," the doctor said. "But it may be good for you. Now, swallow."

The young woman afterward described how she relived an experience, long forgotten, of being separated from her mother in a large store and being nearly abducted by a stranger. According to her doctors, she remained at the age of eight or nine for nearly two weeks. "'It seemed real,' she said. 'All that I know is: I was a child again.'"[53]

One of the first magazine articles re-creating for readers the experience of volunteers in laboratory madness trials described experiments not with LSD, but mescaline. In 1953, under the headline "Mescal Madness," *Newsweek* (1953 circulation 866,000) explained,

"In mescaline, we have an agent which can reproduce in the normal subject under experimental conditions all those phenomena which are found in the subject of so-called psychogenic psychosis," declares Dr. G. Taylor Stockings, Birmingham, England, psychiatrist, in the *Journal of Mental Science*. "The drug is therefore of the greatest importance as a method of approach to the understanding of mental disorder."

Cocaine, morphine, and marijuana could also induce "experimental psychoses," the magazine explained, but these drugs were habit-forming and left subjects unable to describe what they had experienced. Mescaline was better because it allowed subjects to visit bizarre realms and describe them with "un-blurred consciousness." Oddly, despite this explanation, the article did not include any of the subjects' descriptions, instead offering a paragraph of generalities and noting that Havelock Ellis "saw 'dazzling lights and beautiful gems.'" In place of detailed description, nine photographs from a German photographer "portrayed more vividly than with words what mescaline madness can mean." In the staged photographs, a young woman marvels at swirling forms and dazzling crystals and recoils from wallpaper figures come to life. The experience was visually alluring, packaged as educational, and represented by a woman with model good looks (see figure 2). Cutlines read, "Enchanted eyes probe the corridor's fateful secret: dazzling crystals grow, interweave, melt away, and reappear," and, "Time stands still as golden cobwebs burst into flights of song."[54]

The photographs offered an odd blend of the subject's and the scientists' perspectives, depicting hallucinations from the woman's point of view while

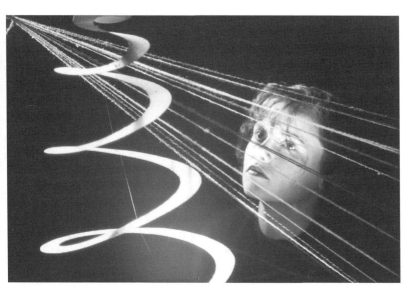

Figure 2. The 1953 *Newsweek* feature "Mescal Madness" included a two-page spread with a half-dozen photographs by the German photographer Leif Geiges that attempted to capture the mescaline experience. *Newsweek*'s caption on this photo was "Mescal maze: Bright spirals turn to music, sounds to colored designs." "Mescal Madness," *Newsweek,* February 23, 1953, 94. Haus der Geschichte Baden-Wuerttemberg, Sammlung Leif Geiges.

her face remained in the frame. While explaining the subject's experience, it was fundamentally the account of an observer who watched the patient while also trying to record that patient's experience. It offered a compromise between describing the experience from an outside observer's perspective and delivering subjective experience itself.

"Step into the World of the Insane," a 1954 feature in *Look* (1954 circulation 3.4 million) the following year, walked a similar tightrope between objective and subjective description of drug experience, this time with LSD. After declaring, "Today, scientists have the key to insanity," the article described the first American administration of LSD, to Dr. Robert Hyde at Boston Psychopathic Hospital, although the name of the physician and the hospital were not used. An anecdote dramatized the challenge of pulling the drug-trial volunteers' wildly subjective experiences into science's objective realm:

The attendant [who had been given LSD at 8:15 a.m.] stared vacantly for a few moments, and when he spoke again his voice had lost its cheerful tone: "What is this, Madame Tussaud's waxworks? The way you sit there staring at me—you don't look human." The doctors looked at each other knowingly; the one with the pad wrote: "8:47. Emotional flatness. Distorted vision." . . .

The young man looked at him with the utmost annoyance and said, "Don't scowl at me like that. And don't come so close. Your head looks enormous a . . . a leering gargoyle. And you don't need to shout. I can hear you. I'm not deaf!" The doctor had not moved an inch, nor had he changed his expression or the quiet tone of his voice. His colleague noted: "Suspiciousness. Feelings of persecution. Perceptual distortion."[55]

As in *Newsweek,* the volunteers' descriptions of their own experiences had been limited to a few words. But *Look* also offered pictures, spread over six pages, staged to "simulate the sensations that a volunteer would experience on such a mad journey," according to the cutline under the first. In one photograph, the distorted faces of doctors loom menacingly from three corners of the frame (see figure 3); in others, a confused woman enacts the experience by clapping a hand to her head, peering from behind a cracked door, recoiling against a wall, and crouching in a corner. "Haunted by fears of persecution, she listens for steps that follow her in the night," read the caption under a picture of the woman walking down a dark street. Like the text, the photography strove to convey the

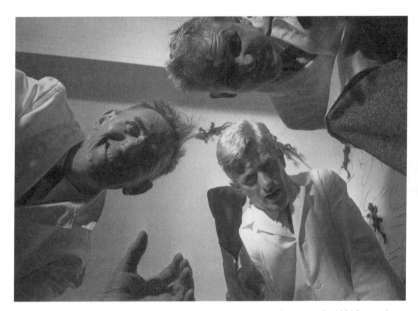

Figure 3. This photograph by Jim Hansen ran full-page alongside the first page of a 1954 feature in *Look* headlined "Step into the World of the Insane." Other photographs include distorted images of a distressed experimental subject clutching her head and waving her arms. Robert M. Goldenson, "Step into the World of the Insane," *Look,* September 21, 1954, 30–35. Jim Hansen, photographer, *Look* magazine photograph collection. Image courtesy of *Look* Magazine Photograph Collection, Library of Congress, Prints and Photographs Division [LC-L9–54-3238-X, #21A].

volunteer's subjective experience, although in many of the photos the volunteer who was experiencing the strange sensations also appeared within the frame.[56] A 1955 *Scientific American* (1955 circulation 129,000) article describing the same experiments credited to "Six Staff Members of Boston Psychopathic Hospital" dwelt on the external, objective measurements scientists collected to explain the experience they were creating in subjects. Charts showed volunteers' pupil dilation and heart rates over time. Volunteers were subjected to a battery of psychological tests: Rorschach, Wechsler-Bellevue Block Designs, Draw-a-Person, Drawings of Feelings, and Thematic Apperception Cards, *Scientific American* explained. Tests were given to volunteers once before the drug was administered, then a second time while they were on the drug. Administered to a lobotomized mental patient, LSD temporarily reversed the good done by the surgery. The article bypassed narrative descriptions of particular drug trips in favor of a generalized account of the effect of "a standard dose of LSD" on "normal subjects," who typically had difficulty explaining the experience for themselves. "He becomes more or less inarticulate, apparently because he cannot put into words the unfamiliar ideas and strange sensations he is experiencing," the magazine explained. Nevertheless, the particular, subjective reaction to the drug was the "most important" fruit of their research: "The staffs of mental hospitals have struggled year by year to get a deeper understanding of what their patients are actually thinking and feeling. Only in this way can they come into communication with the patient and help him. Now that they can experience themselves something approaching the feelings of their patients, they will be able to communicate better. Moreover, mental illness will no longer be so strange or mysterious; there will be fewer barriers between the sick and the well."[57]

The direct view of this experience was presented not through narrative but rather through sketches and three drawings said to "illustrate stages of the reaction to LSD." Captions explained that the heavily symbolic drawings expressed a subject's feeling of euphoria, followed by bleak depression.

A particularly detailed narrative description of a trip appeared in 1953 in the Canadian magazine *MacLean's* (1953 circulation 424,000). In "My Twelve Hours as a Madman," the journalist Sidney Katz described participating in a study at Saskatchewan Mental Hospital conducted by a team of psychiatrists including Osmond and Smythies, the pair who had linked mescaline to adrenochrome a few years earlier. The doctors left London for the mental institution on the Canadian plains in search of a more supportive environment for their research. When the first shipment of mescaline arrived, Osmond volunteered to be the first to try the drug, choosing for the experiment the familiar surroundings of his home. The mescaline made him frightened, paranoid, and suspicious, and on a walk in his neighborhood, familiar sights seemed menacing. After experiencing similar effects with LSD, he made that drug the focus of research, because it generated strong responses and was easier to obtain. Osmond and his colleague Abram Hoffer's self-experiments expanded to include their wives, who helped compile the follow-up reports, and to graduate students and colleagues.[58]

Katz was among the first volunteers who did not come from Osmond's extended circle of friends and colleagues. The experiment took place in a hospital lounge, where the attending doctors treated him collegially. His published account of the experience began with an overview:

> On the morning of Thursday, June 18, 1953, I swallowed a drug which, for twelve unforgettable hours, turned me into a madman. For twelve hours I inhabited a nightmare world in which I experienced the torments of hell and the ecstasies of heaven.
>
> I will never be able to describe fully what happened to me during my excursion into madness. There are no words in the English language designed to convey the sensations I felt or the visions, illusions, hallucinations, colors, patterns and dimensions which my disordered mind revealed.
>
> I saw the faces of familiar friends turn into fleshless skulls and the heads of menacing witches, pigs and weasels. The gaily patterned carpet at my feet was transformed into a fabulous heaving mass of living matter, part vegetable, part animal. An ordinary sketch of a woman's head and shoulders suddenly sprang to life. She moved her head from side to side, eyeing me critically, changing back and forth from woman into man. Her hair and her neckpiece became the nest of a thousand famished serpents who leaped out to devour me. The texture of my skin changed several times. After handling a painted card I could feel my body suffocating for want of air because my skin had turned to enamel. As I patted a black dog, my arm grew heavy and sprouted a thick coat of glossy black fur.[59]

Over fifteen pages, Katz described this experience minute by minute, aided by a tape recording, photographs, and observers' notes. The overall effect was both alluring and terrifying. Drab photographs of men in a hospital setting ran alongside sketches of the grossly distorted faces, floating furniture, and Oriental visions imagined by the hallucinating journalist.

At the most basic level, the gratification offered by these illustrated trips into madness was, as with the newspaper articles about LSD research, informational. The coverage was forthright in its intention to alert its audience to this strange new drug and the use scientists found for it to explore weird and worthwhile mental states. In many cases, the coverage went further, trying to convey to readers what these states were like: not only what they looked like from the outside, but how they felt from within. True to the medium, magazines also strove to entertain their readers and to evoke emotional responses, often wonderment and horror.

Apart from any inherent appeal, the descriptions titillated because they revealed realms of experience that seemed not quite proper for public display. Simply by illustrating these drug experiences, journalists validated the reality of drugged states as an object of interest and study. The magazines showed audiences what was possible with drugs by offering a taste. While frightening and often unpleasant, the drug experience portrayed was undeniably fascinating—indeed, it was the journalist's obligation to his or her audience to make it so. To audiences that had been systematically denied sensory information about drug effects in regard to illegal substances, the possibility of these immersive and intellectually interesting experiences was as novel as the drugs themselves.

News articles describing episodes of laboratory insanity brought the topic to the attention of a number of magazines that were generally uninterested in sober science. The influence of intermedia agenda setting flowed from more respected publications eventually to pulp men's adventure magazines, emboldened by the mainstream attention to offer even more sensational treatments. In 1956, the bi-monthly *Man's Magazine* (1957 circulation 198,000), which more typically featured articles on sex and combat, ran "I Went Insane for Science," which emphasized the danger to the LSD taker's permanent sanity. The volunteer, a doctor, noted at the start of the experiment that a straitjacket and three strong attendants were on hand in case he flew out of control. "The tape recorder will expose all the deep-down, intimate things that make me what I am—all the frustrated desires, evil wishes and subconscious tortures I normally keep under control," he promised. Under the influence of LSD he ranted but did not fly out of control, the accompanying photographs of a mental patient being restrained to the contrary (see figure 4). "The doctors were right in diagnosing my constant allusions to Trixie (my fiancée) as a mild anxiety neurosis, with sexual overtones," he explained. The editors of *Man's Magazine* evidently believed that the article had enduring interest; it was reprinted in whole in 1961 by the same magazine (1961 circulation 216,000).[60]

Another pulp men's adventure magazine, *Argosy* (1959 circulation 1.4 million), published a similar first-person account in 1959. Again, the volunteer in the account was a psychiatrist:

I was now absolutely certain. The experiment was badly out of control. . . .
Some three and a half hours ago, I was a normal, sane man.
Now, as that incredible morning groped its way forward, I was moving—had, in fact, moved—across the Great Divide into the terror that is total insanity.

The paranoia, disorientation, and hallucinations convinced him that, as a doctor, he was glad to have glimpsed "the echoing terror that is insanity," but "as a man" he would never again take LSD.[61]

"I WENT INSANE

I think about the schizophrenic's nightmare life — his violent moments, the hours he spends in a death-like trance. And I am frightened — for I am about to leap into his snake-pit world by taking a drug that turns men into mental patients.

I AM SITTING on a tiny white stool in the seclusion room of a state mental hospital. Ninth floor, Section "G" is the polite clinical name. To the doctors here, privately, it is known as The Jungle. This is the place where they hide the worst of them.

Two colleagues stand over me, for I, too, am a doctor... a healthy young interne who some day hopes to be a first-rate psychiatrist.

I am about to voluntarily lose my mind.

The doctor standing on my right, one of the great new pioneers in the field of psychiatry-and-drugs, holds a glass in his hand. It is filled to the brim with six ounces of a clear, tasteless liquid.

"A few minutes after you drink this," he says quietly, "you will start to withdraw from the outside world. It is a venture into madness, you understand. For six hours, perhaps longer, you will undergo a full-fledged psychotic experience. You are likely to say anything and do anything — and yet you must come back to face what you have said and done.

continued on page 40

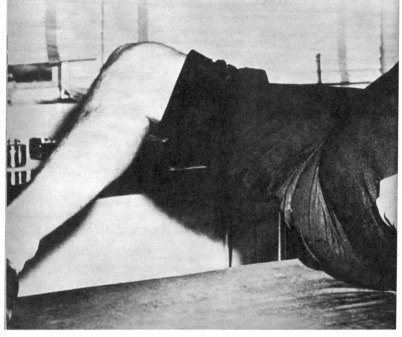

Figure 4. *Man's Magazine* published "I Went Insane for Science" twice, once in August 1956 and again in December 1961, with some of the same photographs. This image of a patient being restrained, which does not directly correspond to the experiences of the psychiatric intern described in the story, is from the 1961 version. See Robert H____, as told to William Michelfelder, "I Went Insane for Science," *Man's Magazine,* December 1961, 38–39.

FOR SCIENCE"

by DR. ROBERT H —— as told to WILLIAM MICHELFELDER

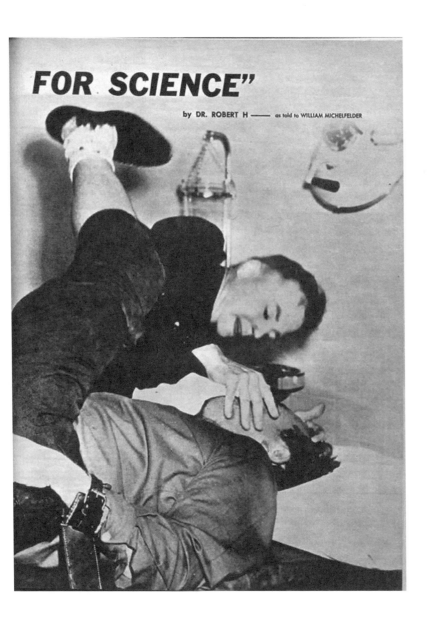

Perhaps inevitably, interpreting the LSD experience as insanity raised fears of loss of control and self. What may have been the drug's first film appearance was in the low-budget 1959 Vincent Price feature *The Tingler,* a movie better remembered for the gimmick of using buzzers installed in theater seats to goose unsuspecting patrons.[62] LSD figured in the plot as a drug that caused irrational, uncontrollable fear. "Well, what does that stuff do to you?" a female character asks her fiancé, a doctor. "Well, for one thing nightmares . . . you are wide awake, but you are having nightmares." The effect of LSD is dramatized in the mostly black-and-white movie in a scene in which blood-red water flows from bathroom taps and a hand rises from an apparently blood-filled bathtub.

As researchers became more familiar with LSD and similar drugs, they grew conscious of the differences between lab madness and the real thing. For one, LSD and mescaline rarely caused the sensation of hearing voices, common with genuine schizophrenics, and schizophrenics rarely experienced the visual distortions common with hallucinogenic drugs. Unlike schizophrenics, subjects under the influence of drugs generally did not believe the immediate, material reality of their visions. And the discovery that subjects rapidly acquired a short-term tolerance for LSD, requiring escalating dosages to achieve the same effect on consecutive days, cast doubt on the possibility that the drug effect was caused by the same biochemical mechanism as schizophrenia. Scientists remained at a loss to locate significant biochemical commonalities between the drug effect and genuine madness. Moreover, the interpretation of LSD as insanity relied on an imprecise definition of insanity, as well as an imprecise understanding of the drug. "The scientific literature and, even more, the popular press frequently state that recreational drug use produces a psychosis," the sociologist Howard Becker observed in 1967. "The nature of 'psychosis' is seldom defined, as though it were intuitively clear." Insanity, he argued, could simply be a facile explanation for unfamiliar mental states.[63]

Concurrent with the initial reports on LSD drug trials, discussion of hallucinogenic drug experiences was pushed onto the news agenda from another direction. In 1954, Aldous Huxley published the first of two short books detailing remarkable and illuminating experiences with LSD and mescaline, drugs he labeled "psychedelics." Huxley was a literary and intellectual celebrity of the first order, enjoying a kind of status that seems a holdover from a previous, more literature-oriented age. *The Doors of Perception* was not a bestseller,[64] but the oddity of its topic and claims, as well as the spectacle of such a prominent author embracing them, prompted a raft of reviews and rebuttals. While science journalists introduced the public to these drugs and drug experiences, literary and cultural critics for major publications began a debate about those experiences' deeper significance.

News Coverage of Huxley's Psychedelic Experience

The chain of events that culminated in Huxley's psychedelic experiences began at Saskatchewan Mental Hospital, where researchers working with LSD observed that self-experiments seemed to include moments of personal insight, experienced with remarkable clarity. "From the first we considered not the chemical, but the experience as a key factor in therapy—in fact, we used a sort of psychotherapy made possible by the nature of the experience," Hoffer recalled.[65] Over the course of an all-night conversation at an Ottawa medical conference in the fall of 1953, Osmond and Hoffer hashed out similarities between LSD intoxication and an alcoholic's episode of delirium tremens, or the shakes, a syndrome triggered by alcohol withdrawal that could include hallucinations and was often fatal. The researchers noted that many alcoholics gave up drinking after experiencing delirium tremens and reasoned that the same effect could be achieved by inducing simulated delirium tremens with LSD.

In trials conducted by several Canadian researchers, chronic alcoholics were encouraged to participate in the spiritually oriented Alcoholics Anonymous program, encouraged to talk about their drinking, and warned to expect an LSD experience that could resemble a religious conversion. The patients were given a single dose of the drug in a private room or doctor's office and encouraged to speak their minds. Upon discharge from the hospital, they were encouraged to continue participating with Alcoholics Anonymous. While the researchers claimed a 50 percent success rate with the treatment, others argued that it was necessary to control for therapy and meetings to isolate the effect of the drug. To overcome these methodological shortfalls, a group of Toronto researchers gave LSD to alcoholics who were isolated from observers, and in some cases blindfolded and restrained. Unsurprisingly, the same results were not achieved.[66]

Osmond's expertise was biochemistry, but he held a humanistic belief in a nonmaterial psyche influenced by religion and art. "All progress in psychological medicine is held up through lack of any clear understanding of the nature of the psyche and its relation to the brain," he and Smythies wrote in a 1953 essay in the *Hibbert Journal,* a British quarterly that published scholarly commentary on religion and philosophy. "The situation is complicated by the fact that its present state rests upon two orthodoxies. The field now covered by psychological medicine belonged in the past to religion on the one hand or Bedlam on the other."[67]

The essay caught the attention of the fifty-eight-year-old intellectual Aldous Huxley, whose place among the literary constellations was established by his 1932 dystopian novel *Brave New World,* which by the 1950s was basic to high-school curricula.[68] Huxley was the scion of a British family whose members included a grandfather, Thomas, renowned for his early defense of Charles Darwin's theories; a brother, Julian, who was a noted biologist and the first director-general of UNESCO; and a half-brother, Andrew, who won a Nobel Prize for research into the anatomical function of the central nervous system. Famously kindly and personable, in the 1950s Huxley lived in the Hollywood Hills, adapting screenplays for movie studios, writing essays for *Esquire,* and socializing in a rarefied circle of expatriate intellectuals, including the mystic and writer Gerald Heard, who emigrated with Huxley from England, the English novelist Christopher Isherwood, Igor Stravinsky, Greta Garbo, Charlie Chaplin, and Harpo Marx. In a characteristic gesture, Huxley sent a note congratulating Osmond and Smythies on their research and extending an invitation to visit if in Los Angeles.[69]

When Osmond agreed to stay with Huxley when in town for the American Psychological Association conference later that year, the writer asked him to bring along some mescaline, "for I am eager to make the experiment and would feel particularly happy to do so under the supervision of an experienced investigator like yourself." At 11:00 A.M. on the second-to-last day of Osmond's stay, the psychiatrist offered Huxley a glass of water in which four-tenths of a gram of mescaline crystals had been dissolved.[70]

"I did not relish the possibility, however remote, of being the man who drove Aldous Huxley mad," Osmond recalled.[71] But he also hoped that the writer's intellectual sensitivity and expressiveness would illuminate aspects of the drug experience that other subjects were at a loss to describe. One problem with LSD research, Osmond explained at a 1956 conference, was "a dearth of subjects skilled in self-observation."[72]

Huxley's engagement with questions surrounding drugs, science, and mysticism extended back to the 1930s and soma, the fictional drug that anesthetizes residents of *Brave New World* by raising "a quite impenetrable wall between the actual universe and their minds."[73] Before even trying the drug, Huxley had high hopes that mescaline would have the opposite effect, by allowing the direct experience of religious and artistic truth that had become lost in an overly materialistic world. In a letter to Osmond confirming travel arrangements, he explained:

> Under the current dispensation the vast majority of individuals lose, in the course of education, all the openness to inspiration, all the capacity to be aware of other things than those enumerated in the Sears-Roebuck catalogue; is it too much to hope that a system of education may someday be devised which shall give results, in terms of human development, commensurate with the time, money, energy and action expended? In such a system of education it may be mescaline or some other chemical substance may play a part by making it possible for

young people to "taste and see" what they learned at second hand, or directly but at a lower level of intensity, in the writings of the religious, or the works of poets, painters and musicians.[74]

Huxley's first experience with the drug exceeded even these lofty expectations. Under the influence of mescaline, mundane objects entranced the severely myopic writer. Table legs writhed, and the spines of books on the shelves of his study glowed like gems. He felt as though granted the vision of an artist. "It is a knowledge of the intrinsic significance of every existent," he wrote in the thin 1954 book describing his experience, *The Doors of Perception.* "This is how one ought to see," he recalled repeating during the experience. "This is how one ought to see, how things really are."[75]

It was not a brush with madness, Huxley concluded, but an encounter with a greater, mystical reality, "what Catholic theologians call 'a gratuitous grace,' not necessary to salvation but potentially helpful and to be accepted, thankfully, if made available," he explained. Huxley continued: "To be shaken out of the ruts of ordinary perception, to be shown for a few timeless hours the outer and the inner world, not as they appear to an animal obsessed with survival or to a human being obsessed with words and notions, but as they are apprehended directly and unconditionally by Mind at Large—this is an experience of inestimable value to everyone and especially the intellectual."[76]

To Huxley, the fact that the experience was rooted in chemistry did not negate its validity. "In one way or another, all our experiences are chemically conditioned, and if we imagine that some of them are purely 'spiritual,' purely 'intellectual,' purely 'aesthetic,' it is merely because we have never troubled to investigate the internal chemical environment at the moment of their occurrence," he reasoned in a second volume, *Heaven and Hell,* published two years later. Mescaline, he argued, provided a superior "chemical vacation" to alcohol, tobacco, opium, or cocaine, with fewer apparent side effects. Although the books described experiences with mescaline, Huxley claimed that the transcendent, mystical experiences also were achieved with LSD.[77] In a 1956 letter to Osmond, Huxley proposed the name "phanerothyme," coined from Greek roots relating to "spirit" or "soul," to describe the class of drugs that enable mystical consciousness. He offered the word in a couplet:

To make this trivial world sublime,
Take half a Gramme of phanerothyme.

Osmond replied with a word constructed from Greek roots for "mind manifesting," intended to suggest that these drugs allowed more ideas to come to the mind's attention.

To fathom hell or soar angelic
Just take a pinch of psychedelic.

Osmond used "psychedelic" in a scholarly paper the following year. The word stuck. Within a decade it was applied not only to drugs and therapy but to the range of art, music, and film that attempted to convey its sensations.[78]

Because of Huxley's personal celebrity and renown as a public intellectual, the author's startling advocacy of drug-induced spirituality attracted attention and widespread discussion in the press. *The Reporter* (1954 circulation 80,000), a respected biweekly news magazine, pointed out: "Coming from a lesser writer than Huxley, such suggestions for the salvation of mankind could be dismissed as the woolgathering of a misguided crackpot. But coming as they do from one of the masters of English prose, a man of immense erudition and intellect who usually demonstrates a high moral seriousness, they deserve more careful scrutiny."[79] Perhaps Huxley's thirtieth book in print, *The Doors of Perception* was promoted as "vivid and arresting" in display ads in the *New York Times*, reviewed in dozens of newspapers large and small, and debated in magazines with intellectual aspirations. The book was controversial in several respects. While Huxley's drug experiment was not illegal, it was sensational, an effect magnified by the book's intimate, confessional tone. And Huxley's conclusions from his experience could be perceived as not only nonscientific but potentially blasphemous, equating the most exalted human qualities to a drugged state. *The Reporter* put it: "And so, as an alternative to creativity and faith in the ultimate goodness of God and man, in place of either Christianity or alcohol, as a cure for the ten times ten gloomy sentiments of 1954, Huxley offers us four grams of mescalin [*sic*] in a glass of water."[80]

Journalists' squeamishness toward this material played out in unusual ways. In *Time* (1954 circulation 1.7 million), the editors condensed a passage from *Doors* in a way that eliminated explicit biblical and religious references that presumably would have offended some readers. The magazine's first article on Huxley—also its first article to describe LSD research—began: "'I took my pill at eleven,' reported Novelist Aldous Huxley in *The Doors of Perception*. 'I was in a world where everything shone with Inner Light . . . The legs, for example, of that chair—how miraculous their tubularity . . . I spent several minutes—or was it several centuries?—not merely gazing at those bamboo legs but actually being them . . .'" (ellipses in original).

A look at what was left out is illuminating. In *The Doors of Perception*, the sentence containing "was in a world where everything shown with Inner Light," continues, "and was infinite in its significance." And to get to that point from when Huxley popped his mescaline pill, *Time* editors skipped several arguably more colorful passages, including, "I was seeing what Adam had seen on the morning of his creation—the miracle, moment by moment, of naked existence," and, "Words like 'grace' and 'transfiguration' came to my mind." While willing to reproduce Huxley's sensational descriptions of drug use, *Time* seemed to balk at associating the experience with Christian faith. Still, his claims were too good to ignore entirely. "No psychiatrist will go as far as Author Huxley (who prescribed mescaline for all mankind as a specific against unhappiness)," the magazine reported.[81]

The *Saturday Review* (1954 circulation 127,000) discussed *The Doors of Perception* without addressing Huxley's visions at all, just his enthusiasm for mescaline. Under the headline "Mescaline—An Answer to Cigarettes?" the magazine offered a full page of excerpts from *Doors* touting the superiority of the exotic drug to alcohol and tobacco. In a sidebar, an anthropologist who studied Indian peyote use in the Native American church explained that mescaline did not create an artificial paradise but merely provided an easy way for a mystically inclined person to have a mystical experience. "I do not think most middle-class Americans would be interested in these effects of peyote," he concluded. "Certainly, they would not find it a substitute for tobacco, alcohol, barbiturates, or Benzedrine."[82] Other reviewers were less sure. A review in the *Tuscon Daily Citizen* that described both Huxley's visions and his mystic interpretations left that question open: "What is the average reader to make of this fascinating account? Huxley's report is impressive and his suggestions should be treated with the respect they deserve. However, the reader will have to decide for himself whether he feels he wants to share this strange ecstasy."[83]

Reviewers were often uncertain what to make of the author's philosophical examination of personal intoxication. The *New York Times Book Review* summarized the nature of Huxley's visions, while wishing that the author had focused less on his "intellectual preoccupations" and described the drug experience account more "objectively and mechanically."[84] A *Los Angeles Times* interview with Huxley following the publication of the book lingered on these preoccupations, congratulating him for his "literary audacity" in producing such a challenging work. "Few authors have had the courage to perform such an experiment, undertaken not for notoriety but in a spirit of serious inquiry," the journalist wrote.[85] The *Washington Post* review did not discuss the meaning that Huxley drew from his experience at all, but labeled his "strange campaign to induce civilization to switch from alcohol and tobacco" to mescaline "a little wacky." "Evidently the Federal Government does not consider mescalin [*sic*] a narcotic, and no law prevents the Indians from whooping it up at their religious festivals. But I rather hope we do not now experience a rash of mescalin [*sic*] parties among intellectuals who used to be satisfied with a few martinis," the article concluded.[86]

Consideration of recreational use often surfaced. In a capsule review of *The Doors of Perception,* the book columnist for the *Chicago Tribune* quipped, "Wonder if I could get a few pounds of mescalin [sic] without a prescription."[87] The pocket-sized magazine *People Today* (1954 circulation 654,000) researched the question in 1954 and found that it was indeed possible to order a ten-dollar bottle of mescaline from a Manhattan chain drug store without a prescription. The magazine worried that Huxley's book "might well drive thousands of thrill-hungry Americans to try mescalin [sic], a drug derived from a cactus plant, despite the dangers."[88] In Beckley, West Virginia, the afternoon newspaper fretted in 1954 that "Huxley might set off a widespread demand for mescalin [sic] with his writings" that could lead to addiction.[89] The following year, a San Mateo, California, newspaper reported that a local man whose interest was sparked by Huxley's book was arrested for ordering peyote buttons police said were worth three thousand dollars from Texas, where they were legal to sell.[90]

Despite these concerns, drug experience was becoming a legitimate topic for intellectual inquiry. The *New York Times* responded to *Heaven and Hell,* Huxley's 1956 follow-up volume to *The Doors of Perception,* with a review from a Yale psychologist who argued that "man" does not need drugs to experience beauty.[91] In a 1956 article in the *New Republic* (1956 circulation 27,000), the philosopher Hans Meyerhoff praised Huxley's erudition in *Heaven and Hell* but argued that there was little evidence that all artistic and religious incarnations of beauty reflected the same Other World.[92] In *The Nation* (1956 circulation 33,000), Richard Eberhart was less critical, praising *Heaven and Hell* as "fascinating and tantalizingly short." "Whether the reader will rush out and buy some mescaline, I don't know, but he might well rush out and buy a transporting book," the poet concluded.[93]

The discussion of Huxley's experiences in book reviews and intellectual journals introduced readers to a use for drugs that had been largely unknown to the public at large. While squeamish about describing the full scope of the drug experience claimed by Huxley, journalists informed their audiences of the possibility of personally transformative drug experiences that had been nowhere in public view. The discussion of Huxley's drug experiences in the news media introduced the seemingly novel attributes of psychedelic drugs, including mystical satisfaction, to many times more people than would have otherwise encountered his ideas. One appeal of the more high-minded publications was a promise to orient readers toward the intellectual debates of the time by offering them a sense of being informed about issues of the day and participating in contemporary cultural life. The drug experience was elevated not only by association with Huxley but also by the interest shown by the mass media.

The skepticism expressed in many articles did not squelch interest in Huxley's innovation. Scholars in the diffusion of innovations have concluded that two-sided appeals, messages that address both advantages and disadvantages of innovations, can more effectively spread the eventual adoption of a new practice than one-sided appeals, particularly if audience members are likely to initially disagree or be exposed to subsequent counter-propaganda.[94] In much of this coverage, journalists entertained the possibility that psychedelic drugs could someday be used recreationally with a mix of bemusement and chagrin. Alerting the public to their existence and seemingly miraculous effects was a step along that path. As researchers became increasingly interested in exploring the drug experience apart from its similarity to schizophrenia, the research at times assumed a more relaxed approach. Creativity, self-awareness, and mysticism seemed topics better explored in sitting rooms than hospitals, and better described with tools from art, literature, and journalism than notes from an observing clinician.

A 1955 article in *Time* (1955 circulation 1.9 million) that began with a description of experimental madness ("I felt sane but I knew that I wasn't," a volunteer in a Cincinnati study recalled) ended with a description of the less formal direction research was taking:

> In Manhattan, Psychiatrist Harold A. Abramson of the Cold Spring Harbor Biological Laboratory has developed a technique of serving dinner to a group of subjects, topping off the meal with a liqueur glass containing 40 micrograms of LSD. Instead of upsetting the subjects, it often helps them to recall and relive—in each other's presence—experiences and emotions of childhood that previously had been too painful to face.
> [...]
> So far, Dr. Abramson is almost alone among U.S. psychiatrists in using LSD for treatment, and like other doctors, he raises a warning finger: it is a dangerous drug, to be used only under strictest medical supervision.[95]

In a roundtable at a conference years later, Abramson commented, "It was all I could do to prevent all of Brookhaven, people in the school system, friends, and so on, to come to dinner with us on Friday evenings to take LSD." The hallucinogenic drugs were legal, after all, and scientists and doctors supervised the experiments—even when they consisted of offering LSD in a liqueur glass following dinner.[96]

CHAPTER 3

Creating a Psychedelic Past, 1954–1960

The new salience of psychedelic drug use in the mid-1950s triggered a flurry of magazine articles and broadcast accounts describing the apparently similar uses of drugs in Indian rituals and the effects of the drugs on intrepid journalists. Invariably referring to Huxley's *Doors of Perception,* these accounts capitalized on the contemporary interest in psychedelic drugs with first-person accounts of peyote and magic-mushroom trips in remote Indian villages that appeared to supply historical context to the practices while demonstrating the drugs' use. While news articles about LSD research and Huxley's remarkable experiences were prompted by the activities of individuals external to the news media, the descriptions of American Voodoo (so called by *Look*)[1] were more clearly the product of journalistic enterprise. Of these articles, the most famous by far was a 1957 article in *Life* (1957 circulation 5.7 million) by R. Gordon Wasson, a vice president of J. P. Morgan, public-relations man, and former journalist, describing his "discovery" of magic mushrooms—a phrase coined for his article[2]—in the hinterlands of Mexico. The discovery created a ripple through the media, spawned copycat accounts, and created commerce in the drug virtually overnight.

Wild stories about adventures with hallucinogenic drugs among Indians conceivably could have been written anytime in the previous forty years, but they were elevated to the media agenda in the 1950s as a result of several factors unrelated to the ostensible subject matter. Chief among these was the interest in mystical, psychedelic drug experience stirred by Huxley and the discussion of his views in the press. Indian drug use provided a forum to explore the mystical use of hallucinogenic drugs in a context that did not directly challenge social prohibitions against depictions of recreational drug experience. The weakening of these prohibitions, again enabled by Huxley and LSD, also played an assisting role, as did the sensationalism inherent in addressing a subject that was long taboo. But perhaps most remarkable was the campaign orchestrated by Wasson to publicize his role in discovering magic mushrooms and his personal theory about their place in history. Wasson's direct efforts led to numerous newspaper articles and stories in magazines of all types, and his tale was referenced in subsequent news articles on the topic. Wasson's role in promoting interest in the magic-mushroom story was bolstered by the corporate efforts of *Life*, which promoted the story on television with a scripted promotion on CBS's *Person to Person* and maintained an interest in the subject through the following decade.[3] Notably absent during this period was any particular government interest in the subject or coordinated campaign for prohibition.

While not about LSD, these articles directly explained the innovative psychedelic experience closely associated with that drug. Unlike Huxley's famous mescaline experiment, which took place in the familiar settings of his home and the book aisle at his neighborhood drug store, news-media voyages to American Voodoo sensationalized the seemingly weird, indigenous origins of the drugs themselves. Huxley's beliefs about the psychedelic experience were broadly grounded in English literature and letters, not Indian religion. Nevertheless, these accounts offered images of Indians taking drugs in all-night ceremonies as a historical, somehow authentic, backstory to the psychedelic drug phenomenon. The contemporary fascination with psychedelic drugs effected a transformation in journalistic attitudes toward Indian ritual drug use. Previously considered primitive and often distasteful, the native practice was rehabilitated in some of these articles to prefigure advances in the uses of pharmaceuticals believed to be just beyond the horizon.

The media attention to Indian drug use following the publication of *The Doors of Perception* was all the more interesting because many details of the practice had been known for centuries. The earliest conquistadors and missionaries to Mexico described Indian consumption of peyote, mushrooms, morning-glory seeds, and other intoxicating plants at festivals and religious ceremonies. In 1620, the Catholic church declared that the Indians' use of drugs for divination was "an act of superstition condemned as opposed to the purity and integrity of our Holy Catholic Faith." Between 1614 and 1779, church officials prosecuted at least ninety Inquisition cases against Indians accused of peyotism. Despite this effort, veneration of peyote spread to tribes well beyond the peyote cactus's natural range. In the late nineteenth century, Indians who had been forcibly relocated to the Oklahoma Territory formalized the practice of a religion that combined veneration of peyote and ceremonial use of the drug with belief in the Christian god. Peyote religion attracted the attention of the first generation of field anthropologists associated with the Smithsonian Institution and the U.S. Bureau of American Ethnology, who documented the practice with a sympathetic eye. But the Bureau of Indian Affairs, which held something of an overseer's role, viewed these scholars as exploiting the Indians as fodder for books and photographs while doing nothing to help them become more civilized.[4]

The first of many federal bills to prohibit Indian peyote use was defeated in the Senate in 1918 after extensive hearings pitting Indian witnesses and white academics against the Bureau of Indian Affairs, which counted among its allies the Anti-Saloon League, the Woman's Christian Temperance Union, and "all the Mission Boards of the Protestant Church and the Catholic Indian Bureau."[5] The campaign echoed rhetoric from the ongoing fights against alcohol and narcotics, even exaggerating the prohibitionists' concern about drug-induced degeneracy and damage to a "race." "It is an evil and nothing but an evil," proclaimed Harvey W. Wiley in a 1922 anti-peyote tract published by the Bureau of Indian Affairs. Wiley was a chemist remembered as the father of the 1906 Pure Food and Drugs Act, laboratory director of *Good Housekeeping* magazine, and head of the Good Housekeeping Institute, responsible for the famous Seal of Approval advertising guarantee. "So far as building up a peyote church is concerned, if that is established, we will have an alcohol church and a cocaine church and a tobacco church, and any other person who wants to use a drug and escape legal penalties for doing so can call it a religious rite," he wrote. According to his report for the bureau, digested and published over three columns in the *New York Times*:

"The peyote habit is bound to be one of the greatest hindrances to the industrial progress of the Indian. . . . Not only does it ruin the physical but it also ruins the intellectual development. Peyote destroys the power of concentration, logical thinking, strength of will and balanced judgment. It is fruitful of false notions in the minds of its users and gives them a wrong conception of life. Superintendents, teachers and matrons of the Government schools, agency physicians and mission workers are all practically unanimous in their verdict concerning the mental depression, stupidity and destroyed aspirations peculiar to its victims.

"Perhaps the most injurious of all the effects of peyote is found in connection with its extensive use in religious ceremonies. . . . This is a false worship carried under the guise of Christian teachings. It is utterly destructive of the morals, health and fellowship in the Christian Church and in the nation. How long will the Christian citizenship of this country, now giving its money to emancipate and Christianize the Indian, permit this menace to continue?"[6]

Measures to prohibit peyote were introduced annually to Congress and enacted in eleven states by 1933, although state laws do not normally apply on Indian reservations.[7] The Bureau of Indian Affairs officially ended its battle against peyote after the election of Franklin D. Roosevelt and his appointment of the liberal activist Harold Ickes as secretary of the interior in 1933. "No interference with Indian religious life or ceremonial expression will be tolerated," according to a policy statement published in 1934. The new policy did not instantly change state and local reservation officials' attitudes, and many peyote importers and roadmen were arrested and imprisoned in the following decades. In some cases, tribal officials themselves urged the repression of peyotism, which continued to grow while remaining, in most tribes, a minority religion.[8]

Even at the height of the political campaign against peyote, media attention to a problem contained in faraway reservations was sparse. Prior to the 1950s, most Americans had probably not heard much about the Native American church, although the idea of natives taking drugs in all-night religious rites maintained a place in the public imagination. With the passage of time, magazines remembered peyote religion as a curio of a crude culture gone by. A 1950 article in the magazine *Hobbies* (1950 circulation 40,000) on collecting Native American church artifacts explained: "The Indians found it difficult to imagine our God. They recognized His greatness, for they were easily defeated by this strange God's children. Soon, they found that their habit of eating peyote to dull pain or terror and give them a feeling of great strength, brought this foreign God to them in a way they understood."[9]

A long article in *Travel* (1950 circulation 21,000) on "The Cult of the Sacred Cactus" similarly explained that when Indians experienced the breathtaking hallucinations and rapturous ecstasy of peyote, "forgotten are the days of labor beneath the hot sun, the dust, the poverty. In their haven of fantasy they glimpse, however briefly, all the loveliness and joy of their utopian hunting grounds." The article by Vincent H. Gaddis, a freelance writer who specialized in strange tales, offered hope that scientists would confirm that substances in peyote allowed "supernormal abilities" such as ESP.[10]

Still, canards linking peyotism to crimes and moral decay lingered. In 1951, *Time* (1951 circulation 1.6 million) described Navajos, "already wretched in their poverty and disease," as "easy prey for peyote peddlers" in an article written from dispatches and news clippings to the magazine's punchy, opinionated style. Hopped up on peyote, men "are likely to grab the closest female, whatever age, kinfolk or not," *Time* reported, adding that a medical missionary had heard of two cases of infanticide and one of fatal child neglect due to the drug. "Until proof to the contrary is received the bureau [of Indian Affairs] is committed to the view that peyote is harmless. The men on the spot in the desert think they know better," *Time* concluded.[11]

The publication of Huxley's *Doors of Perception* in 1954 effected a shift in the magazine's attitude. In an article that year about the Native American church's annual convention, *Time* described a sedate ceremony, explaining that peyote helps Indians "experience their faith as immediate reality," while accepting the peyotists' declaration of Christian faith at face value. Huxley was mentioned in a footnote: "In his latest book, *The Doors of Perception*, Novelist Aldous Huxley prescribes mescaline, a derivative of peyote, for all mankind as an alternative to cocktails." It was an endorsement that elevated both the drug and those who took it, at least in the eyes of Time Inc.[12]

The interest generated by *The Doors of Perception* prompted other magazines to publish accounts in which the journalists turned their attention inward, promising to explain the drug experience as it was felt by a white adventurer. "Aldous Huxley's recent book *The Doors of Perception* makes it plain that he, like a good many people, is strongly taken with the romance, mysticism and folklore that have grown up around peyote, an untasty vegetable that I, too, have had an acquaintance with," began the anthropologist Alice Marriott in a long 1954 *New Yorker* (1954 circulation 377,000) article describing a peyote ceremony in South Dakota years before. At the ceremony, recommended to cure Marriott of attenuation in the summer heat, she became entranced by the colors of the fire in the center of a teepee, around which approximately thirty Indians were gathered. As the drug took hold, the door to the teepee came to represent an entrance to "beauty beyond the senses and beyond the earth." Marriott passed through the door, to gaze at cool stars and feel a cool breeze, and then returned to doze by the teepee fire. The following day, feeling strong and full of life, she returned to the house in which she stayed with Mary, an Indian friend and translator.

> "What was it like?" she asked as I began to undress. "You can describe it, can't you? No one else ever can—not even Wilma. Go on, tell me. What was it really like?"
>
> "Paradise," I answered, and fell across the bed, asleep. . . .
>
> The drought broke soon after, but the peyote had already strengthened me and helped me. The tremendous first exhilaration lasted for several days, and there

was no sudden drop following it. I tried once more to answer Mary's question, but I did not actually succeed. "It is like seeing the door to life swing open," I told her, rather helplessly, and she shook her head. "That's what they all say," she said, and we have left it at that ever since.[13]

A four-page spread in the weekly picture magazine *Look* (1957 circulation 4.2 million) also referred to Huxley, but diluted his descriptions of the mystical splendor of his mescaline trip to the observation that it "heightened his ability to concentrate while dulling his 'will to act.'" The text, by the staff writer Laura Bergquist, quoted an "Indian expert" who explained peyotism as an escape from a miserable reality. Bergquist described eating four peyote buttons at a Crow Indian ceremony, experiencing no visions but a subtle change in hearing. "Suddenly, the 'words' of the peyote songs, which are really unintelligible nonsense, spoke a language I could almost understand. And the drumming sounded as loud as any in the Congo," the piece concluded.[14]

Life Discovers the Magic Mushroom

The editors of *Life* wanted a more revealing account when they commissioned a Wall Street banker to write an article about his successful search for hallucinogenic mushrooms among the Indians of Mexico. "You will write an account of the expedition of approximately 5,000 words in which you will identify yourself and members of the expedition and include among other things a description of your own sensations and fantasies under the influence of the mushroom," specified *Life*'s contract with R. Gordon Wasson. He did not disappoint. "Seeking the Magic Mushroom" described a fascination with mushrooms that began with his wife Valentina thirty years earlier and culminated in a fantastic drug trip in a thatched-roof Indian home (see figure 5). Wasson described his experience (with his photographer, Allan Richardson) as "the first white men in recorded history to eat the divine mushroom" in lavish detail and wholly positive terms. "For the first time the word ecstasy took on real meaning," he wrote. "For the first time it did not mean someone else's state of mind."[15]

The story of Wasson's discovery echoed through the media. Six days after Gordon's article in *Life* (1957 circulation 5.7 million), at the time the nation's preeminent picture magazine, Valentina Wasson told the story from her perspective in the cover story for *This Week* (1957 circulation 11.7 million), a weekly magazine that was anchored to the *New York Herald Tribune* and inserted in the Sunday editions of more than three dozen newspapers nationwide, including major newspapers in New York, Baltimore, Philadelphia, Boston, Los Angeles, and Chicago (see figure 6). Published between 1935 and 1969, the magazine

Figure 5. This photograph of Wasson accepting a magic mushroom from Maria Sabina was one of ten images from the 1955 expedition published in *Life*. See R. Gordon Wasson, "Seeking the Magic Mushroom," *Life,* May 13, 1957, 110. Tina and R. Gordon Wasson Ethnomycological Archives, Harvard University, Cambridge, Mass.

contained a broad editorial mix, including fiction and articles on national affairs by notables including Herbert Hoover, Richard Nixon, and Nelson Rockefeller.[16] The story of the couple's adventure was also retold in a BBC radio newsreel, dozens of newspaper and magazine articles, and reviews for the couple's privately printed book.[17] Valentina died of cancer in 1958, but Gordon continued to stoke interest in their discovery by releasing a recording of an Indian mushroom ritual on the Smithsonian Folkways record label and giving public lectures, which were often covered in the local press.[18] In 1959, *Newsweek* (1959 circulation 1.2 million) and the *New York Times* reviewed the opening of Wasson's exhibit at New York's American Museum of Natural History, titled "The Quest for the Divine Mushroom: An Ancient Rite Rediscovered."[19] It generated additional local coverage as it traveled to museums in upstate New York and Michigan.[20]

The publicity had immediately tangible effects. A few months after publication of the seventeen-page "Seeking the Magic Mushroom" in *Life,* Wasson observed an influx of foreign tourists to the remote Mexican village Huautla de Jiménez, Oaxaca, where he had searched long to find someone willing to sell the sacred mushrooms. "The village was fully alive to the *Life* article," he wrote in a letter to a friend. "Mushrooms were offered to us by all and sundry as we went along the street. Huautla is having a hard time, because of a coffee crop failure, and mushrooms are a pleasant and profitable diversification."[21] By 1960,

Figure 6. Valentina Wasson's account of the discovery of magic mushrooms for *This Week* appeared about a week after her husband's account was published in *Life*. See Valentina P. Wasson, "I Ate the Sacred Mushrooms," *This Week,* May 19, 1957, 1, 8–10, 36. Tina and R. Gordon Wasson Ethnomycological Archives, Harvard University, Cambridge, Mass.

tourists in Mexico City could sign up for an overnight expedition to Huautla that included participation in a mushroom ritual.[22]

Combined with his talent for self-promotion, Wasson's social status helped to push his story onto the news agenda. His identification as a J. P. Morgan executive was a boon to his story, providing dramatic contrast between the author of the first-person account and the primitive surroundings and wild experiences he described. Additionally, solid social credentials insulated Wasson from criticism as a thrill seeker or even drug addict that could have more easily been heaped upon a less credentialed writer. As with Huxley, Wasson's personal background cast a halo on his claims.

Wasson was born in Great Falls, Montana, in 1898, but he spent his childhood in Newark, New Jersey, where his father was rector of an Episcopal church. A principled anti-Prohibitionist, Wasson's father was the author of a 1914 book, *Religion and Drink,* which drew on the Old and New Testaments to argue that there was an appropriate place for alcohol within the Christian faith.[23] Wasson's education included stints in France and Spain, followed by fourteen months as a private in the American Expeditionary Forces in France during World War I. After returning to the United States, he enrolled in the Columbia Graduate School of Journalism and was awarded the first Pulitzer Traveling Scholarship, which he used to study for a year at the London School of Economics. Upon return, Wasson spent a year teaching English at Columbia. In 1922, he joined the staff of the *New Haven Register* as editorial writer and state political correspondent. In 1925, he became the associate editor of the monthly *Current Opinion,* then moved to the *New York Herald Tribune,* where he wrote a daily by-lined financial-news column.[24] In 1926, Wasson married Valentina Pavlovna Guercken, who was born in Moscow in 1901 of a wealthy family that fled the country following the Communist Revolution. Valentina's father had been the director of Russian operations for Westinghouse Electric and Manufacturing Company. She was educated at Barnard College in New York and Bedford College in London and earned a medical degree from London University in 1927. She practiced pediatrics in New York and in 1939 wrote *The Chosen Baby,* a book explaining adoption to children.[25]

In *Life* and elsewhere, Wasson explained that he and his wife began thinking about mushrooms in 1927, while vacationing in the Catskills. During a walk in the woods, Valentina, who had recently qualified as a physician, delighted in collecting mushrooms that repulsed her new husband. From this experience, the couple speculated that their different reactions—her delight, his revulsion—were rooted in the difference in their backgrounds as a "Russian" and an "Anglo Saxon." "From that day on we sought an explanation for this strange cultural cleavage separating us in a minor area of our lives," Wasson explained in *Life.*[26] As a shared hobby, the couple collected etymologies of mushroom-related words and scoured volumes of history and art for clues to ancient attitudes about mushrooms. Wasson left journalism for banking in 1928, and was promoted to vice president of J. P. Morgan and Company in 1943, a position that afforded him the leisure to correspond with academics and scholars receptive to his Wall Street credentials. "As the years went on and our knowledge grew, we discovered a surprising pattern in our data: each Indo-European is by cultural inheritance either 'mycophobe' or 'mycophile,' that is, each people either rejects and is ignorant of the fungal world or knows it astonishingly well and loves it."[27]

The Wassons collected stories, myths, and folk beliefs about mushrooms from around the world to identify similarities suggesting a common past. The towering precedent for their comparative approach, using textual evidence about widely separated cultures to identify general patterns, was Sir James Frazer's *The Golden Bough: A Study in Magic and Religion,* first published in 1890. The abridged, 1922 version of Frazer's study had never gone out of print. Like Frazer, the Wassons amassed voluminous anecdotes from diverse sources to illustrate the presumably common features of primitive religion.[28] By the early 1940s, the couples' expanding collection of mushroom-related myths and references from around the world had drawn them to an even more startling hypothesis: attitudes toward mushrooms were rooted in the cultures' reaction to a forgotten, primitive, universal mushroom-worshiping religion. As Wasson asked in *Life*: "Was it not probable that, long ago, long before the beginnings of written history, our ancestors had worshipped a divine mushroom? This would explain the aura of the supernatural in which all fungi seemed to be bathed. We were the first to offer the conjecture of a divine mushroom in the remote cultural background of the European peoples, and the conjecture at once posed a further problem: what kind of mushroom was once worshiped, and why?"[29]

The couple was encouraged by Robert Graves, the English poet and translator whose 1948 book *The White Goddess: A Historical Grammar of Poetic Myth* took a similar approach in proposing a common goddess behind European, Celtic, and Middle Eastern myths. Valentina first contacted Graves in 1949 in regard to the substance used to poison the Roman emperor Claudius, the subject of Graves's highly regarded novel, *I, Claudius.* (They subsequently agreed the poison was a mushroom.) Over the next few years, Graves and Gordon Wasson corresponded as friends. The banker offered financial advice to the impoverished poet, while Graves let forth a stream of possible mushroom sightings across the span of Western history. "Isn't it strange how I seem to act like a lightning-conductor for these things on your behalf," Graves wrote.[30]

The fruit of the Wassons' scholarly hobby was to be *Mushrooms, Russia, and History,* a lavish book printed at their own expense, describing "the role of mushrooms in the life of the peoples of Europe" and their quest to uncover it. Years of poring over rare books and written consultation with expert sources led them to initially identify the divine mushroom as *amanita muscaria,* the red-capped, white speckled mushroom used as an intoxicant and in religious rituals by indigenous Siberians. They speculated that *amanita* could have spread east to become the unidentified soma of Indian legend, and even could have been the original source of good and evil (rather than the apple) in the Garden of Eden.[31]

Work on *Mushrooms, Russia, and History* was well under way in 1952 when Graves alerted Wasson to an article in a pharmaceutical journal referring to mushroom use by sixteenth-century Indians. At about the same time, Wasson received in the mail a drawing of a Mesoamerican mushroom statue held by a Swiss museum. The Wassons' attention turned to the New World. They located studies of mushroom statues in Central America, and reports from anthropologists suggesting that a mushroom cult might survive in the villages of Mexico. When a missionary in the remote village of Huautla de Jiménez in the state of Oaxaca confirmed by letter that local Indians indeed used mushrooms in healing rituals, Gordon and Valentina planned a field expedition—their first of this type—to Mexico the following summer. "Our objectives were simple: to obtain specimens of the sacred mushrooms, for purposes of identification and trial consumption by ourselves, to learn about the present state of the cult, and to attend the mushroom rite," they wrote. Wasson soon added a fifth objective to that list: to publicize their triumphant discovery.[32]

The Wassons' discovery of Mexican magic mushrooms was possible because a prominent scientist with the U.S. Department of Agriculture had lost them. In 1915, the economic botanist William E. Safford published an article claiming that historical accounts of intoxicating mushrooms were wrong after he failed to find the mushrooms himself during fieldwork in Mexico. Safford, who testified on behalf of American Indian peyotists during congressional hearings in 1918, concluded that what earlier investigators had actually seen were dried peyote buttons, which he claimed looked like mushrooms under some circumstances. Safford's stature in his field was such that his theory held sway for decades, despite the uninterrupted use of mushrooms by Mexican Indians and the doubts of other academics better placed in the field. By the 1950s, botanists and anthropologists in Mexico had assembled fresh evidence of "sacred mushrooms," including descriptions of Indian mushroom rites and the mushrooms themselves. When the Wassons embarked on their first expedition to Mexico in 1953, the primary milestone that remained was the collection of a specimen to formally identify the mushroom species and its place within the scientific taxonomy—the essence, by definition, of a botanical discovery.[33]

On August 8, 1953, Gordon and Valentina Wasson, along with their sixteen-year-old daughter Masha and a guide, set off from Mexico City in a chauffer-driven car. Two days later they reached Huautla de Jiménez by mule train, after an eleven-hour trip through the mountains, and paid fifty-five cents to rent an unoccupied house for the week. At last, on their final night in the village, a forty-five-year-old man they identified only as Aurelio agreed to hold a ceremony demonstrating for them the divinatory power of the mushroom. During a late-night ritual in Aurelio's home, he predicted that a relative of Gordon would fall seriously ill; that his eighteen-year-old son Peter was in New York, suffering an emotional crisis, rather than in Boston; and that the young man could face military service, perhaps in Germany. The Wassons left Mexico without a suitable specimen of the elusive mushroom, only to see the unlikely predictions come true: their son was in New York, he was enlisting in the army, and a cousin died. "We record, as in duty we are bound to do, but without further comment, these strange sequelae to our Huautla visit," they wrote in *Mushrooms, Russia, and History*, which was expanded with a second volume largely dedicated to Mesoamerica.[34]

The former magazine editor immediately grasped that his story was bigger than a privately printed book. The following year, he returned to Mexico by private plane with the New York society photographer Allan Richardson, who signed over all rights to his photos in exchange for payment and travel expenses. Trekking with guides through rural Mexico, they collected additional information and photographs, although nothing sensational enough to interest the *Saturday Evening Post* or *Vogue*, both of which rejected brief accounts of that trip.[35] The expedition in the summer of 1955 was more successful. Returning to Huautla de Jiménez, Wasson and Richardson were introduced to sixty-seven-year-old Maria Sabina, a shaman "of the first class,"[36] who provided Wasson with the magic-mushroom experience described in *Life* and modeled for Richardson's photos. (Sabina was referred to as Eva Mendez in Wasson's *Life* article in an unsuccessful bid to protect her privacy.) Wasson returned to New York with a collection of dried mushrooms that were still potent six weeks later. "The effects of these mushrooms are beyond belief," he wrote an old correspondent, Roger Heim, professor of mycology and director of the Muséum National d'Historie Naturelle in Paris, who agreed to accompany Wasson on a return expedition the following summer to identify the mushrooms and collect specimens.[37] Wasson also presented a slideshow and lecture about his discovery to a "couple of hundred" researchers at the Pennsylvania pharmaceutical firm Merck-Sharp and Dohme.[38]

On the 1956 trip Heim identified several previously unrecognized mushroom species, including one he named after his friend, *Psilocybe wassonii*. The name didn't stick. A rival group also in the field that year, led by the American mycologist

Rolf Singer and sponsored by a Chicago psychologist interested in mushrooms' therapeutic possibilities, beat Heim for naming rights by being first to publish their identification.[39] Wasson "jealously guarded his contributions," in the words of one associate, engaging in a lengthy dispute over primacy of the discovery that played out on the pages of *Mycologia* and *Ethnomycological Studies* into the 1980s. Mushroom specimens collected by Heim and cultivated back in his laboratory were provided to the chemist Albert Hofmann, who announced that he had isolated the psychedelic components psilocybin and psilocin in 1958.[40]

While Wasson's desire for scholarly recognition was initially frustrated (a mycologist named a different hallucinogenic mushroom for Wasson in 1979), his carefully managed story captured the public imagination. In February 1955, Wasson secured his long-coveted magazine contract from *Life*. While the contract called for the "definitive and final text" to be written in cooperation with *Life*'s editorial staff, Wasson retained veto power over any changes to the text, headlines, and photo captions.[41] "They respected my wishes on all important points," Wasson later told his friend Robert Graves.[42] Payment for the package was to be $8,500, including a $2,500 payment for photographs that Wasson forwarded to Richardson. "I personally think it will be quite a high point in *Life*'s continuing effort to bring new and fundamental information before the public," the assistant managing editor Philip H. Wootton Jr. wrote.[43]

On the eve of publication, *Life* promoted Wasson's story on CBS's news interview show *Person to Person*. Over photographs from the forthcoming story, an announcer read:

> Here in *Life* is one of the strangest adventure stories you'll ever read . . . the story of an age-old ceremony re-discovered in a little Mexican Village remote from civilization . . . here in this house, on a summer night in June 1955. It was the ceremony of the magic mushroom—an unbelievable ceremony, where certain types of mushrooms were eaten to conjure up fantastic visions, in the minds of all who took part in the ceremony.
>
> This is the lady, Eva Mendez [the pseudonym given Maria Sabina], who prepared the mushrooms, then conducted the ceremony. This boy is seen in *Life* as he was in the ecstasy brought on by the magic mushrooms.
>
> And at the ceremony too, was this American, R. Gordon Wasson, a vice president of J. P. Morgan and Co. and a longtime student of the strange ceremony. Wasson ate the mushrooms, even as the natives did, and tells of his weird and wondrous experience in an exclusive, first-person story in *Life*.[44]

As advertised, Wasson's story in *Life* was an adventure, opening with his entry to the "divine" ritual of the magic mushroom in a hut in a remote Mexican village. In the first section of the article, 1,300 words long, Wasson describes how he, a banker, and Richardson found their way to a basement room in an adobe hut in which Sabina conducted an all-night ritual before a simple altar with images of baby Jesus.[45] For the next 1,700 words, Wasson described his experience with hallucinogenic mushrooms in wholly positive terms. After vividly describing resplendent palaces and mythological beasts he saw under the influence of the drug, he wrote: "The visions were not blurred or uncertain. They were sharply focused, the lines and colors being so sharp that they seemed more real to me than anything I had seen with my own eyes. I felt that I was now seeing plain, whereas ordinary vision gives an imperfect view; I was seeing the archetypes, the Platonic ideals, that underlie the imperfect images of everyday life."[46] Wasson reported that he and his friends awoke the following morning "rested and heads clear, though deeply shaken by the experience we had gone through." The second half of the article went on to explain efforts to identify the Mexican mushrooms, his family's interest in mushrooms, and their unorthodox theory about an ancient mushroom religion.[47]

While Wasson described being transfixed by the indigenous ceremony, the meaning he drew from it was rooted more firmly in Huxley's *Doors of Perception* than Mixtec beliefs, about which he knew little. Like Huxley, with whom Wasson had corresponded since 1955, the banker felt that drugs allowed perception of the essence of things normally only seen by mystics and artists. (Both Huxley and Wasson considered the English poet William Blake in particular to exemplify this type of vision.) "At times there have been rare souls—the mystics and certain poets—who have had access without the aid of drugs to the visionary world for which mushrooms hold the key," Wasson wrote in *Life*, echoing *The Doors of Perception*. "But I can testify that the mushrooms make those visions accessible to a broader number." Although it took place in a far-off land, Wasson's interpretation of his drug experience tapped Western intellectual culture, not the indigenous folk traditions of divination and healing.[48]

Valentina's account of the expedition, published in *This Week* (1957 circulation 11.7 million) six days later, was more narrowly focused on personal experience with mushroom intoxication. The article began with Valentina lying in her sleeping bag on the floor of an adobe hut, waiting for the effects of the "supposedly sacred mushrooms" that her husband and Richardson obtained a few days earlier from Sabina to kick in. She wondered if the effects the men had felt at the ceremony could have been the result of a "primitive psychological ruse," or if the mushrooms contained a powerful, as yet unknown, hallucinogenic drug. "As a physician, I am usually content to leave this kind of experiment to more adventurous inquirers than myself," she wrote. "You have to be rained-in—in a place like that Indian Mixeteco [*sic*] village, to know how desperate you can get for diversion." She was not disappointed. Under the influence of mushrooms, she experienced visions "all in 3-D and in fantastic Technicolor" of a prehistoric cave, the French court of Louis XV, and a Spanish church. Like her husband, she awoke from the experience happy and alert, and set about writing notes from the "weird and wonderful experience."[49]

Wasson managed access to his story and Richardson's photographs for maximum impact. Prior to the choreographed debut of his and Valentina's stories in *Life* and *This Week*, Wasson denied permission to a British author to discuss it in a forthcoming book and told Richardson that he could not offer the photos to the photography magazine *Vision*.[50] After the articles appeared, Wasson participated in interviews, freely gave photo permissions, and even provided samples of mushrooms as news of his discovery rippled through the media. The couple reprised the story in 1958 for a six-page article in *Garden Journal* (circulation n.a.) but cooperated in publicity in less staid venues as well.[51] Behind a cover illustration of Italian soldiers gazing at a UFO, the October 1957 issue of *Fate* (1957 circulation 52,000) told the story of the Wassons' discovery from the perspective of an archeologist who accompanied them on several expeditions and witnessed the banker's rapture in the basement of Sabina's home. He quoted Wasson describing the mushroom experience at length, including Gordon's conclusions about its mystical importance: "'The creative faculty of man,' said Wasson, 'is probably unlocked by the mushrooms. It is as the Indians say, a truly divine experience. The memories of the race of mankind may be unlocked by the tiny mushrooms. And this inventory of wonders may be carried by each man within himself, waiting to be loosed by this key.'"[52] The archeologist wrote that he was excited to try mushrooms himself on another trip with the Wassons later that year. "What had started out as an adventure in archeology now had changed into an adventure of the mind," he wrote.[53] In 1958, *Time* (1958 circulation 2.2 million) published a brief article announcing that Hofmann had isolated the psychedelic components of magic mushrooms "thanks largely" to the adventures of the Wassons previously chronicled in *Life* and in the couple's privately printed book.[54] Gordon and Valentina's magazine articles also promoted their pet project, *Mushrooms, Russia, and History,* "a large, richly illustrated two-volume book," according to a sidebar in *Life*, "on sale now for $125."[55] This was a princely sum for a book, about one thousand dollars at 2012 rates. Wasson had only 512 copies of the book made by a prestigious Italian printer and used his proceeds from the *Life* article to pay for one hundred review copies to be shipped to scholars and institutions around the world.[56] Needless to say, potential readership of the remaining four hundred books was small.

The expense and limited availability of this luxurious book—combined with Wasson's success in attracting attention to its wildest story—actually raised its profile. A 1957 item in the *New Yorker* (1957 circulation 415,000) "Talk of the Town" column called the book "the latest novelty in the publishing world," while painting Wasson as a dilettante, detailing fantastic theories over lunch in his bank's private dining room.[57] "Probably one of the most expensive and certainly one of the most intriguing books of the year," said a 1957 BBC radio newsreel that briefly summarized its thesis about a widespread but forgotten mushroom religion.[58] *Mushrooms, Russia, and History* also received a positive notice in the *New York Times*: "Writing as amateurs in the various scientific disciplines, the Wassons are undaunted by settled conclusions of the pedants and eagerly welcome scholarly disputation," judged the reviewer, a former editor of *Art Digest*. "They handle their own erudition with engaging charm."[59] The *Saturday Review* (1957 circulation 165,000) and *The Atlantic* (1957 circulation 213,000) both printed long, glowing reviews by Graves, who wholeheartedly embraced his friend's conclusions about the global influence of the divine mushroom.[60]

The acquisition of such a rare and expensive book by the Toledo Public Library prompted a two-page article in the *Toledo Blade Sunday Pictorial* newspaper insert, including a sidebar "On the High Price of Books." The author explained, "though fortunately there are more good books now available on countless subjects at low cost than ever before in history, it is still a necessity to pay solid prices for items of solid worth."[61] The student newspaper at the University of Nebraska at Lincoln similarly covered the purchase of a copy by the university's Love Library.[62] A few years later, a *Milwaukee Journal* reporter observed that although only 512 copies of *Mushrooms, Russia, and History* were printed, "the book got almost that many reviews." Wasson told the reporter, "I couldn't believe my eyes. How did it get that play . . . I suppose we caught the popular fancy."[63]

Wasson did what he could to sustain interest in his tale. Along with interviews and Richardson's photographs, Wasson offered a supply of mushrooms for a 1959 article in *True, the Man's Magazine* (1959 circulation 2.4 million) titled "The Vegetable that Drives Men Mad." The first half of the six-page article described the writer William D. Cole's drug trip in his New York apartment, during which he marveled at visions of European castles and an Arabian camel train as a part of him "rose ecstatically to a new and supreme level of awareness." The journalist described the Wassons' expeditions and experiences at length, but said that his own motivations were less grand. "To me, intense curiosity alone was behind my desire to experience the weird dreams and highly colored hallucinations induced by the mushroom drug," he explained.[64]

With his magazine pitches, museum shows, and heavily promoted book, Wasson displayed a genius for self-promotion that surpassed his learning as an anthropologist. By self-publishing their book and writing for the popular press, the couple avoided a process of scholarly review that would likely have been unkind. By the time *Mushrooms, Russia, and History* was published, the practice of making inferences about past civilizations from later cultural practices was being rejected by the mainstream of anthropology, despite its hold on the popular imagination. By the 1940s, the Wassons' approach, using library research about civilizations widely separated in time and space to draw general conclusions, was being criticized by anthropologists for its susceptibility to selection bias and seemingly endless ability to confirm preexisting beliefs. The method allowed the Wassons to plumb a huge range of historical material for anecdotes to support their theory, without requiring detailed understanding of any particular one.[65]

Wasson's scholarly hobby was rewarded with speaking engagements and honors from universities and museum societies, but few scholars took his mushroom theories seriously. He published only a few articles in minor peer-reviewed journals, and foundations rejected his applications for grants. A fellowship at the Harvard Botanical Museum was self-funded. Until his death in 1986, Wasson continued investigating alleged magic-mushroom use in ancient civilizations, expounding on the theory that he traced back to his insight during the Catskills honeymoon so many years before. His books published in the 1960s, 1970s, and 1980s presented arguments that the Indian drug soma described in the Rig-Veda was a mushroom, as were drugs consumed as part of an ancient Greek festival, the Eleusinian mysteries. Although his books were published by commercial presses, they found their biggest following in the drug and New Age countercultures, much to the patrician banker's chagrin.[66]

Letters to the editor in *Life* following the publication of "Seeking the Magic Mushroom" offer a sense of how the fantastic stories about mushroom adventures were received by the general public. A Wichita reader declared, "Your article about mushroom worship is an outrage against faithful Christians," while a Fort Lauderdale woman wrote, "Seeking the Magic Mushroom is without doubt the most fascinating article I have ever read." A reader from San Francisco suggested that the ancient Chinese "probably" also indulged in hallucinogenic mushrooms, providing as evidence a photograph of a traditional mushroom-shaped ceremonial scepter. Another reader noted the similarities between Wasson's descriptions of mushroom hallucinations and the sensations described by Havelock Ellis after eating "mescal buttons" around the turn of the century. There was also this scrap of doggerel from Jenkintown, Pennsylvania: "Wasson's work is probably some fungi, if you're a lichen for it."[67] Most telling, however, was the letter instructing readers how they could have similar experiences on their own:

Sirs:

I've been having hallucinatory visions accompanied by space suspension and time destruction in my New York City apartment for the past three years. The essential difference between Mr. Wasson's vision and my own is that mine are produced by eating American-grown peyote cactus plants.

I first heard about peyote in Aldous Huxley's book, *The Doors of Perception*, in which he described this ancient "tranquilizer."

The chemicals in peyote are known. A drug called mescaline is made from it which is already in use effectively for psychotherapy and research.

I got my peyote from a company in Texas which makes C.O.D. shipments all over the country for $8 per hundred "buttons." It usually takes about 4 "buttons" for one person to have visions.

Jane Ross
New York, N.Y.[68]

The articles about American Voodoo gave at least a few readers an itch that in the 1950s took a moderate degree of industriousness to scratch. As well as peyote buttons, extracted mescaline sulfate could be purchased through the mail from chemical-supply companies at low cost and minimal legal risk. According to a longtime writer on psychedelic drugs, by the late 1950s peyote buttons were "fairly familiar" among beatniks and artists and on many college campuses. In New York, capsules of ground peyote could be purchased over the counter of a Greenwich Village café.[69] Never one to shy from recognition, in 1970 Wasson blamed himself in a *New York Times* essay for opening rural Mexico to drug tourism, "unleashing on lovely Huautla a torrent of commercial exploitation of the vilest kind."[70] His touch also poisoned Sabina, who was sought by many of the new visitors to Huautla and blamed by other residents for the village's transformation. Her home was burned, and she was briefly jailed. In the 1970s, a visiting anthropologist found her impoverished and living in rags, some years after a "symphonic tragedy" inspired by her life opened at Carnegie Hall.[71]

Beyond offering direct inspiration to a few people, the drug travelogues acculturated a much larger readership to recreational drug use driven by curiosity and the yen for adventure. In stark contrast with their Indian subjects, Wasson and most other practitioners of the genre did not believe that Indians' religion or rites were fundamental to the drug experiences they described. (Marriott, the anthropologist and chronicler of Indian life who wrote about peyote for the *New Yorker,* was an exception.) Descriptions of the drug experience were typically grounded in literary references, contemporary intellectual culture, and the amazing effects of Technicolor film, references that would have had little resonance to native worshipers. The accounts demonstrated how a religious rite could be stripped of original context and enjoyed with a secular, rational sensibility. In many cases, the physical and cultural remove of these Indian villages seem to allow journalists the freedom to provide the kinds of detailed, intimate descriptions of drug experiences that reputable publications had shied from in the past.

Although there was some attention from other media, the hype over magic mushrooms was centered in magazines. Apart from the efforts of its promoters, the story largely developed in the absence of any notable real-world events that might have attracted more attention from newspapers or other outlets focused on hard news. The fascination with magic mushrooms seemed an episode of hype in large part because coverage reflected and magnified earlier media accounts, more than events in the real world. The stories about indigenous hallucinogen use were on one level educational, providing readers with information about a drug and a cultural practice with which they may not have been familiar, while also offering entertainment, a few moments of escape from household tasks or the monotony of a doctor's waiting room. In the more elaborate accounts, the escapist gratification offered by a travelogue to a remote location merged with the voyeuristic, parasocial pleasure of sharing in the journalist's drug trip. When these trips were described, it was through descriptive language and literary flights of fancy enticing the reader to come along. Boring drug trips do not make good reading. Therefore, when they were described, frequently it was with attributes that made them seem inviting, involving, and transporting.

Not every outlet embraced this adventurous attitude toward drugs. The low-brow pulp magazines, in particular, described the rediscovered drugs with old tropes that played on audiences' fears. According to a 1958 article in *Uncensored* (1958 circulation 650,000), the real power of mushrooms was "sex stimulation." "When all the members of a tribe finish with a mushroom feast, the wingding that follows would make a Roman circus look like a prayer meeting of the W.C.T.U. [Woman's Christian Temperance Union]," *Uncensored* reported.[72] In a 1958 article in *Real for Men* (1958 circulation 283,000), they "lead to sex crimes and cause visions, insanity and suicide."[73] In 1960, *True Crime* (circulation n.a.) blamed Wasson by name for creating a sensation over poisonous mushrooms. As though to demonstrate Wasson's concept of mycophobia, *True Crime* explained, "the man who eats this poison, does so on purpose. He's a new and terrifying kind of addict, one that is becoming increasingly common—the poison eater!"[74]

But magazines with higher intellectual aspirations were curious about discoveries that would come through exploring the chemical mind. Peering at the psychedelic experience, they often found Wasson and Huxley peering back. "The men now exploring the frontiers of consciousness question whether the day will ever come when complete happiness and peace of mind—not to mention religious ecstasy—can actually be purchased in a pill," *Cosmopolitan* (1960 circulation 892,000) explained in "Drugs and the Mind's Hidden Powers" in 1960. "But they are convinced that the mental miracle drugs can be powerful aids in man's perpetual search for these spiritual goals." The article, like so many others, opened with a description of Wasson's Mexican trip.[75] In 1962, Graves talked about his own mushroom experience, undertaken in Wasson's New York apartment, in the travel magazine *Holiday* (1962 circulation 936,000). After describing "taking an ambrosial drug which conveys mortals to the Otherworld," while listening to a recording of Sabina, he explained its discovery in Mexico by Wasson and their theories about its place in history.[76] The following year, he wrote again about "The Sacred-Mushroom Trance" in *Story* (circulation n.a.), a magazine of short stories published in New York. Graves's contribution was promoted on the cover of an issue dedicated to "Unusual Stories off the Deep End," along with one of Richardson's photos of Sabina that had previously appeared in *Life*.[77]

As psychedelic experience persisted on magazines' agenda, through LSD, Huxley, and then stories of Indian rituals, it accumulated a range of contradictory attributes: pleasure on top of terror; mystical understanding on top of madness; hope for the future tied to a relic of a more primitive past. Amid these contradictions, the more elite voices and the more respected publications weighed on the side of experimentation and hope. Despite association with Indian rituals, psychedelic drugs were a highbrow fascination. The narrative power of the Wassons' and Huxley's visions was so great that even some who failed to achieve the promised self-transcendence remained convinced. Such was the case with the novelist and screenwriter Budd Schulberg, who described driving with friends to a remote corner of Mexico to participate in a mushroom ceremony in a 1961 article in *Esquire* (1961 circulation 859,000). "As departure day approached, this mysterious fungus and the effect it might have on us became topic A to Z. We read Huxley, Wasson and others who had navigated these voyages to the end of the mind," he explained. After long anticipation, Schulberg saw only geometric patterns while tripping on mushrooms, while others in his group experienced more baroque visions and flailed about on the floor, laughing manically. Despite his failure to achieve the state he had read about in Huxley and Wasson, Schulberg held to their vision of a drug state that was both part of a primal past and an inevitable future. He asked, "Is it conceivable that the only true American mystic, the self-contained American Indian, shunted aside by the Indianapolis Speedway of history, may still show us the way?"[78]

CHAPTER 4

Research at the Intersection
of Media and Medicine, 1957–1962

In 1953, while Sandoz was introducing the experimental drug LSD to researchers and psychiatrists, James Coleman, Elihu Katz, and Herbert Menzel launched the study of the diffusion of tetracycline that resulted in the landmark *Medical Innovation,* cementing the idea that innovations spread through interpersonal relationships. Allowing for a role for media in informing physicians of the existence of new drugs, the scholars emphasized the apparent importance of social relationships in spreading the determination to actually use them. They concluded that doctors who were more widely read and engaged with other physicians professionally and socially were quicker to adopt an innovation.[1] While they did not use the term, they described a process that resembled the two-step flow of communication introduced in *The People's Choice,* in which an initial role of media gave way to personal influence.[2]

In Los Angeles, home to Aldous Huxley and center of LSD therapy and research, the process of diffusion of that drug and the role of media were more deeply entangled. As studies of diffusion of innovation predicted, the adoption of LSD spread initially through interpersonal contact, in this case between researchers who had access to the drug and their patients and social acquaintances.[3] Among the earliest group of recreational users, and certainly the most socially prominent, was the network of psychiatrists and cultural luminaries that spun outward from Huxley.[4] Constructed in large part based on its members' contributions to arts and media, members were notable for their easy access to news-media channels and, frequently, the desire and ability to publicize their views. The resulting process less resembled a downward cascade from mass media to members of the public than a media echo chamber that increased in volume with time.

During the 1950s and early 1960s, access to LSD was restricted, but it was not illegal in today's sense. Categorized as an investigational drug, Sandoz Pharmaceuticals distributed LSD to physicians and researchers who completed paperwork attesting that they intended to use it for research and to publish their results. Until federal regulations over investigational drugs were tightened in 1963, Sandoz did not discriminate among the specialties of researchers to whom it provided the drug, or among their methods, which ranged from highly controlled trials to case studies with paying clients. Prior to 1966, simple possession of either investigational or regular prescription drugs was not a crime, even without a prescription.[5]

The dean of West Coast LSD researchers was Sidney Cohen, a professor at the University of California, Los Angeles, School of Medicine and internist at the Los Angeles Veterans Administration hospital. Handsome and prematurely gray, Cohen was born in New York in 1910 and educated in pharmacology at Columbia University and in medicine at the University of Bonn.[6] Cohen's reputation was undiminished by his interest in the increasingly controversial drug. From 1968 to 1970, he served as the first director of the National Institute of Mental Health's Division of Narcotic Addiction and Drug Abuse. He died in 1987.[7]

Cohen initially acquired LSD from Sandoz in 1955, with the intention of using the drug as a simulacrum of mental illness, but his focus shifted after trying it for the first time. Expecting to feel catatonic or paranoid, the doctor experienced "nirvana without ecstasy" in a drab hospital room. "I seem to have finally arrived at the contemplation of eternal truth," he wrote in his account of the trip. When he recovered from the drug, he was bothered by two things: first, that he could not recapture the essence of the LSD experience; and second, that he remembered reading a description of his vision somewhere before. He located it in the 1822 book by Thomas De Quincey, *Confessions of an English Opium-Eater.*[8] Prior reading of *The Doors of Perception* may also have influenced Cohen, according to his biographer, Steven J. Novak. Cohen had met Huxley the same year that he began his experimentation with LSD. Moved by his own experience, the psychiatrist launched a program of research to understand the drug. The first series of studies conducted by doctoral students under Cohen's supervision used psychological tests to measure the effect of LSD on eighty-one academics. Next, Cohen recruited psychoanalysts as subjects, hoping that experts in the unconscious would have special insight into the drug's effect on their own minds. He was again disappointed. Many psychoanalysts either did not respond or responded badly to the drug, and the psychological tests seemed to miss what Cohen experienced as LSD's indescribable essence.[9]

Like Humphry Osmond before him, Cohen believed that writers and intellectuals would be better equipped to describe the LSD experience that left normal subjects at a loss for words. By 1957, Cohen was collaborating with Huxley and his friend Gerald Heard (1889–1971), a thin, goateed popular philosopher and fiction writer who emigrated with Huxley from England twenty years before. Huxley and Heard both administered LSD obtained from Cohen to themselves and others, often at informal gatherings at Huxley's home in the Hollywood Hills, and Cohen collected volunteers' written reports. The volunteers from literary Los Angeles seemed not only better capable of describing the drug experience, they were also better able to integrate what they experienced into a coherent framework. "We learned from Gerald that, just as in some psychological experiments animals are inappropriate test subjects, so in certain experiments with the psychedelics *ordinary men are inadequate subjects,*" Cohen wrote in an unpublished tribute to Heard years later. "He was a skilled, articulate observer in entering into an indescribable, surging state, which could fragment some with its intensity and divert others with its entertaining visual displays."[10]

Despite these serious goals, the experiments themselves had an increasingly recreational feel. Oscar Janiger, an LSD researcher and psychiatrist who frequently shared an office with Cohen, recalled:

These people had first taken it experimentally, because that was the only way it was given at all. Then it was just a short step for people who had taken it to say, "Let's try it [again]" and make up some circumstance which would justify it. At the beginning, nobody would dare say, "Let's just take it." . . .

So in somebody's home there would be six to eight people, and they would take the drug. I was at one or two of those, and Huxley would be there, and Heard, and you would meet this strata of people. It was here that you met these people who were the investigators, plus those people who were some of their subjects—who had showed a special affinity or interest in the drug.[11]

Beyond advancing science, the Hollywood Hills philosophers viewed these experiments as a way to introduce psychedelic drugs to society. In an autobiography, Timothy Leary recalled a conversation in which Huxley maintained that successful integration of psychedelics into society depended on first gaining the approval of elites. "These are evolutionary matters," Leary recalled

Huxley saying in 1960, during a relaxed psilocybin trip while the author was in Cambridge for a temporary appointment at the Massachusetts Institute of Technology. "They cannot be rushed. Work privately. Initiate artists, writers, poets, jazz musicians, elegant courtesans, painters, rich bohemians. And they'll initiate the intelligent rich. That's how everything of culture and beauty and philosophic freedom has been passed on."[12]

One test subject recruited for expertise in philosophy and mysticism was Alan Watts, a San Francisco radio host and author of several popular books on Buddhism and mysticism. In 1958, Huxley helped put Watts in touch with Keith Ditman, head of an alcoholism research laboratory at UCLA and a frequent collaborator with Cohen. Watts explained:

> So many of their subjects had reported states of consciousness that read like accounts of mystical experience that they were interested in trying it out on "experts" in this field, even though a mystic is never really expert in the same way as a neurologist or a philologist, for his work is not a cataloguing of objects. But I qualified as an expert insofar as I had also a considerable intellectual knowledge of the psychology and philosophy of religion: a knowledge that subsequently protected me from the more dangerous aspects of this adventure, giving me a compass and something of a map for this wild territory.

On his radio show, Watts initially characterized his LSD experience as more "aesthetic" than mystical, but he realized its mystical potential after being coached through a few more sessions.[13] In 1960, Watts's station, KPFA, broadcast an hour-long symposium on the clinical and therapeutic uses of LSD that was moderated by Cohen at Napa State Hospital.[14] Watts subsequently integrated the drug experience into his larger mystical canvas in a popular book, *The Joyous Cosmology: Adventures in the Chemistry of Consciousness,* published simultaneously in paperback and hardcover in 1962. Cohen and Ditman also provided LSD for several sessions with Bill Wilson, the founder of Alcoholics Anonymous, who compared its effects to the religious experience that had caused him to quit drinking.[15]

Another media luminary initiated to LSD by Cohen and Heard was Clare Boothe Luce, an accomplished writer and political operator and the wife of *Time* and *Life* publisher Henry Robinson Luce. "Oh, sure, we all took acid. It was a creative group—my husband and I and Huxley and [novelist Christopher] Isherwood," Clare said on the April 9, 1982, Dick Cavett show.[16] Born in 1903, she was first an editor at *Vanity Fair* and then author of four successful Broadway plays in the 1930s, a two-term U.S. congresswoman in the 1940s, and ambassador to Italy from 1953 to 1956, among other accomplishments. A front-page obituary in the *New York Times* in 1987 said that she had often been placed on lists of the world's ten most admired women.[17] But in an "informal, and very private report" to Heard and Cohen, she described herself as deeply unhappy her entire life, prone to migraines and gastric upset, and, at times, paralyzed by indecision. Recent events had made things worse: Henry Luce had announced that he planned to leave her for a twenty-four-year-old English woman.[18] The love affair was in the gossip columns.[19] Perhaps worse, Clare was forced to recognize that her husband had not been telling the truth when he had claimed to be impotent twenty-three years earlier. The lie helped Clare gain the Catholic church's blessing for her conversion to that faith while remaining married to a devout Presbyterian. "For almost 58 years—all my conscious life—until last spring—I felt certain that I would be deserted, rejected, 'let down,' denied by everyone or anyone I came to love, or even respect, sooner or later," she wrote.[20]

Clare took LSD with Heard and another friend for the first time in her Phoenix home on March 11, 1959. In a report to Cohen describing her first three experiments, she described seeing the world through the eyes of "a happy and gifted child," full of bliss and contentment, without fear, in joyous acceptance of the good-and-evil duality of nature, and at one with the world. "Whatever the effects of LSD on the body, the effects on the psyche—my psyche—in any event, were at the time altogether good," she wrote. She credited her new peace of mind for the strength to negotiate continued marriage to Henry and to turn down a prestigious job that she said she did not want, as ambassador to Brazil.[21] Her personal journal noted that while on one of these trips she refused a telephone call from "Nixon"—presumably Richard Nixon, vice president at the time—telling her aide that she would return the call.[22]

Over the next several years, she took acid at least fourteen times, with companions including Heard, her husband, and Father John Murray, a noted theologian who was helping the couple work through marital problems.[23] Clare's writings while on LSD suggest that for her, the drug invested somewhat mundane activities and observations with cosmic import. She described gazing through a kaleidoscope and marveling at the taste of jam during one trip in 1959.[24] During another in 1960, she discussed nuclear war with her friends and came to the conclusion that "life like a bell has many resonances—work, children, the copper-brass amalgam—friendships—but faith is the clapper that strikes and makes the resonances."[25] She spent part of one acid trip in 1961 sorting mosaic glass by her swimming pool.[26] In an undated account of an acid trip with her husband, Clare describes Henry examining plants in the garden, then coming back into the house to talk. They discussed the drug: "We agree this could never be taken like alcohol 'Just for kicks.'"[27]

Still, use of the drug in the Luce home had an increasingly recreational feel. In 1960, Clare explored purchasing supplies of the drug directly from an Italian pharmaceutical distributor, and she once received LSD through the mail from Cohen with the note: "Dear Clare—Have you found the enclosed capsule? May it be a glorious day."[28] In one undated journal, she described taking acid by herself before getting in a car for the ride from her New York apartment to her Connecticut estate, where she went for a walk in the autumn woods. "Great beauty, peace, 'reconciliation'—to be alone, mediatory, doing nothing—*not* to be bored, or feel guilty, or even very much alone . . . this is the beauty of the chemical, that it destroys boredom."[29]

From his Beverly Hills office, Janiger ran a series of experiments to study the effect of LSD on creativity that introduced LSD to 848 volunteers between 1955 and 1962, including almost seventy practicing professional artists.[30] The design of the study was simple: Janiger gave participants LSD, offered them art supplies, and encouraged them to create. However, creativity turned out to be as challenging to measure as mysticism. One participant was the diarist Anaïs Nin. Under the influence of LSD in Janiger's Beverly Hills office, she felt surrounded by stunning images and touched by insight. "Without being a mathematician I understood the infinite," she told Janiger while in the throes of the drug. She recalled that he did not act impressed. On further reflection, she realized that most of the images were borrowed from her own published works or the works of others.[31]

The artists who participated in the experiments "invariably commented on the similarity of the LSD-induced state to what they felt might be an essential matrix from which the imaginative process derives," Janiger and a collaborator wrote.[32] About a decade after ending the study, they assessed the results by having an art-history professor review 250 drawings of the same Indian kachina doll, made before and after participants took LSD. The styles of many artists became more abstract when they were on the drug, lines became looser and the compositions became larger on the page. They concluded the LSD art was not ipso facto worse than the artists' usual work, but that they could not determine if it was more creative. "All that can be definitively said about the effect of hallucinogens is that a strong subjective feeling of creativeness accompanies many of the experiences," they wrote.[33]

Innovative theories about LSD that developed in Los Angeles spread through a social network that was thoroughly infused by nonpersonal influences. Although experiments often took place in social settings, it would be the rare subject who had not read *The Doors of Perception* or was unfamiliar with discussions of LSD and hallucinogenic drugs in mass media. Indeed, conversancy with the ongoing media discussion of LSD was likely a prerequisite for membership in a social network that was deliberately woven between individuals based on their potential to contribute. As researchers were increasingly aware, the effect of LSD was deeply influenced by the subject's expectations and external feedback—"set and setting," in the formulation later made famous by Timothy Leary. While the setting of these experiments was accessible to just a sliver of society, the meanings of LSD formulated there were diffused with a much larger audience in mind.

News Coverage of Los Angeles LSD Experiments

It should not be surprising that research exploring the effects of LSD with writers and artists had the collateral effect of inspiring more writing and art about the drug. Many who participated in Cohen's and Janiger's studies subsequently expounded on their meanings in books and magazines. In a 1958 article for the reliably conservative *Saturday Evening Post* (1958 circulation 5.2 million) on "Drugs that Shape Men's Minds," Huxley predicted that drugs offering "self-transcendence and a deeper understanding of the nature of things" would lead to a revolutionary revival of religion.[34] "It will be disturbing; but it will also be enormous fun," he wrote in a 1957 article on the same subject for *Scientific Monthly* (1957 circulation 28,000).[35] The popular nutritionist Adelle Davis sought participation in Janiger's study when she was "overcome with envy" after reading "Seeking the Magic Mushroom" in *Life*.[36] The result of her experience was the pseudonymous 1961 book *Exploring Inner Space: Personal Experiences under LSD-25*, summarized in a seven-page article "Exploring the Soul with LSD" in the pocket-sized magazine *Fate* (1962 circulation 70,000) in 1962. The article concluded by considering whether the drug was "the most important discovery of the twentieth century." A note appended to the end of the article explained, "Neither the author nor *Fate* can help readers obtain LSD."[37] Watts immediately began discussing psychedelic drugs on his San Francisco talk-radio show following his experimentation in 1958, as well as his 1962 book, and in a positive review of Cohen's first popular book about LSD, *The Beyond Within: The LSD Story* (1964) in the *New Republic* (1964 circulation 73,000). In the review, Watts concluded that psychedelic drug use was probably entitled to the same constitutional protections as freedom of worship, but that some degree of regulation was necessary.[38] Heard asked, "Can This Drug Enlarge Man's Mind?" in the bimonthly arts magazine *Horizon* (circulation n.a.) in 1963, concluding that indeed it could.[39]

Heard also advanced his views on the subject in a number of television programs in which he played a role. He moderated an eight-part television series,

Focus on Sanity, which appeared on CBS in 1957. One segment included Cohen interviewing a woman who explained that she was the wife of an employee at the VA hospital where LSD experiments were taking place, and accepted a proffered glass of water spiked with the drug. The documentary picked up three hours later. Cohen and the woman were in the same seats, but she was now gazing around the room in wide-eyed wonder.

> **VOLUNTEER:** It is here, can't you feel it? This whole room, this, this . . . everything is in color and I can feel the air, I can see it, I can see all the molecules. I . . . I . . . I am part of it, can't you see it?
> **COHEN:** I'm trying.
> **VOLUNTEER:** Oh, it is just like you are released, or you're free, or . . . I don't know how I can tell you.
> **COHEN:** How do you feel inside?
> **VOLUNTEER:** Inside? I don't have any inside.
> **COHEN:** Is it all one?
> **VOLUNTEER:** It would be all one if you weren't here.

The woman continued to struggle to express what she was experiencing. "Everything is so beautiful and lovely and alive," she said at one point, and not quite coherently. "I wish I could talk in Technicolor." Cohen also discussed the drug with Heard:

> **COHEN:** Now Gerald, I know you have great personal experience with lysergic acid. What do you think of it?
> **HEARD:** To do this in two minutes, eternity in an hour. . . . It is almost impossible, of course, as all the patients say, to describe it. You can only say "it isn't, it isn't, it isn't," trying to tell people what it is. Well of course, I don't know any of our friends that have taken it, Sid, but haven't said this one thing in common: "Well, I never knew anything like that in the whole of my life." One or two people have said to me, I've said it myself, "That is what death is going to be like. And, oh, what fun it will be!"
> **COHEN:** How do you mean that?
> **HEARD:** Well, I mean that there are the colors, the beauties, the designs, the beautiful way things appear. People themselves, dull people, that I thought dull, appear fascinating, interesting, mysterious, wonderful. But that is only the beginning. A man was saying it this afternoon that was taking it. Suddenly you notice that there aren't these separations. That we are not on a separate island shouting across and to somebody else and trying to hear what they are saying and misunderstanding. You know. You used the word yourself. Empathy. There are things flowing underneath. We are parts of a

single continent. It meets underneath the water. And with that goes such delight. The sober certainty of waking bliss.[40]

Cohen made a number of other television appearances as an LSD expert. In 1957, he served as a technical consultant to a local television special called *The Lonely World.* "It is about LSD," Cohen wrote. "I'm not too proud about the story, but it is not completely incredible. It is the old compromise between fact and drama." In 1958, Cohen again administered LSD in front of television cameras, this time to a twenty-nine-year-old University of Southern California biochemist, for the educational NBC program *Harvest* intended to express "man's achievements in art, literature, public affairs and science."[41] Newspaper reporters invited to the filming described the volunteer giggling and marveling at his surroundings. "It's wild, man, wild," he proclaimed. An article published in advance of the television program in the *Los Angeles Times* dominated the front page of the local section with four photographs of the volunteer wearing a range of expressions. Cohen explained that the drug served important roles in psychiatry by lowering defenses and releasing repressed memories. He also told the reporter that he planned to conduct further experiments with artists to test the drug's effect on creativity. "'We have conditioned ourselves against seeing many beautiful things—things which artists can see for only a moment. Perhaps LSD will allow the artist a more permanent perception while he is affected by the drug," Cohen told the newspaper.[42]

Research presentations by Los Angeles scientists working in this field attracted coverage in the local press. Around the same time as he began working with Heard, Cohen teamed up with Betty Eisner, a young psychologist who volunteered to be one of Cohen's early research subjects after she realized that she would be trying the same drug she had read about in *Look* magazine.[43] Eisner was a student of Eastern religions and a visitor to a Vedanta monastery founded by Heard in Trabuco Canyon outside Los Angeles.[44] While still preparing to experiment with her first official subject, Eisner had a strong sense of what she expected to find. She wrote a friend, "I feel, and I think Sid does too—that the best possible therapeutic LSD experience is one in which a subject glimpses the unity of the cosmos and his own place in it, and then sees and tackles his problems in relationship. And it can be done and that is what we are going to be doing."[45] Their first study tested LSD as an adjunct to psychotherapy on twenty-two volunteers, who spent their trips lying on therapists' couches, discussing family issues and listening to music of their choice. Cohen and Eisner reported that sixteen of the patients improved after one to six LSD sessions, as judged by the researchers, the person closest to the patient, and the patient him- or herself. They attributed the gain to what the researchers called an integrative experience: "[A] state wherein the patient accepts himself as he is. . . . There is a feeling of harmony with his environment, and an upsurge in creativeness." Their formal report about the study went on: "The integrative experience should be described further because it has not been a matter for scientific scrutiny and the semantic difficulties are considerable."[46]

Cohen and Eisner's presentation of this research at the 1958 American Medical Association (AMA) conference in San Francisco landed them on the front page of the *San Francisco Chronicle* the following day. The article began:

A potent chemical that quickly releases long-repressed memories and unconscious emotional conflicts is dramatically speeding the treatment of mental disease.

Unlike the standard sessions of psychoanalysis, which often require hundreds or thousands of hours, and many thousands of dollars, the drug works in a few minutes to expose buried hatreds of parents or spouse, guilt, complexes, death wishes, terrifying experiences from childhood.

The chemical, now available only for research, is known under the code name of LSD-25. It costs about one dollar per treatment.[47]

Following the conference presentation, Cohen and Eisner also appeared on local television in San Francisco to talk about their research. In a letter to a friend, Eisner described appearing on television as fun, but complained that the article was "greatly garbled," making her ambivalent about publicity.[48]

A talk by Janiger at the 1958 California Osteopathic Association annual conference was covered in the *San Diego Evening Tribune* under the headline, "Psychiatrist Lauds Savage Tribe Drugs," with a picture of the doctor captioned, "'Creativity is enhanced.'" In a quotation, he explained, "Only a millionth of a gram [of LSD] on the tongue will induce brilliant hallucinations, enhance creativity, call to memory things believed forgotten."[49]

In the *Los Angeles Times,* a presentation about hallucinogenic drugs by Gordon A. Alles, the pharmacologist credited with developing the amphetamine Benzedrine, was treated even more sensationally:

Life can be beautiful with mescaline drugs, a City of Hope medical conference was told yesterday.

The apparently harmless hallucinatory drugs could be the answer to the thrill-seeker's prayer, said Dr. Gordon A. Alles, UCLA professor of pharmacology. The mind is lofted away in a kaleidoscope of color—a Fourth of July fireworks display in the privacy of the living room.

"And the only after effect we've found is a slight case of indigestion," the professor said.[50]

By 1959, a dozen therapists in the Los Angeles area who had been introduced to LSD through earlier experiments, including Huxley's wife Laura, were charging as much as six hundred dollars to administer LSD to patients in private practice. There were good reasons therapists enjoyed working with LSD. Administered before talk therapy, the drug seemed to increase patients' comfort in talking about their problems and their acceptance of their therapists' explanations. "Under LSD the fondest theories of the therapist are confirmed by the patient," Cohen explained at a conference years later. Whether or not this was a problem was largely a philosophical question. If a patient's belief that he had achieved a psychological insight made him feel better, must it be objectively true? From this "nihilistic" perspective, Cohen observed that "any explanation of the patient's problems, if firmly believed by both the therapist and the patient, constitutes insight or is as useful as insight."[51] Insights reached under the influence of LSD also seemed invested with greater significance by patients and were remembered even after the drug wore off. The effect was described as "portentousness" in a 1972 study of recreational drugs: "[T]he sense that something—even a trivial platitude—is fraught with a cosmic significance too profound to be adequately communicated. Whether or not LSD does in fact enable users on occasion to grasp significant new insights into themselves or the world about them—a much debated issue—the drug certainly gives many users a feeling that they have achieved profound new insights."[52]

One prolific practice run by the psychiatrist Arthur Chandler and the radiologist Mortimer Hartman claimed a success rate approaching 70 percent for routine psychological complaints using a course of treatment that in some cases involved weekly doses of LSD. Both doctors came from the city's psychedelic set. Chandler was part of the coterie of doctors and literary figures around Huxley and Heard, while Hartman participated in an LSD study group founded by a volunteer in one of Cohen's early experiments on psychologists. Members puzzled over evidence of reincarnation, astral projection, and ESP from LSD trips until the group flew apart amid angry denunciations. With the blessing of Sandoz, Chandler and Hartman launched a five-year therapeutic study from a Beverly Hills office that targeted the stereotypically neurotic denizens of Hollywood's movie colony as clients.[53]

The national attention to LSD reached new heights in 1959 when the movie star Cary Grant, previously known for his personal reticence, suddenly became willing—eager, even—to expound at length about personal insights he reached through weekly LSD sessions with Chandler and Hartman. LSD therapy, he told gossip columnists and magazine reporters, allowed him to achieve a degree of happiness that had previously eluded him, despite all his success. The *New York Herald Tribune* gossip columnist Joe Hyams broke the story in the United States, with three nationally syndicated columns that consisted almost entirely of direct quotes. The fifty-five-year-old movie star, at the crest of a decades-long career, described feeling "born again" to Hyams and explained how the new self-knowledge made him a better husband, actor, and man:

"All the sadness and vanities were torn away. I was pleased with the hard core of the strength I found inside of me. I think I've always been a pretty fair actor. Now I know I'm going to be the best actor there is.

"I've had my ego stripped away. A man is a better actor without ego, because he has truth in him. Now I cannot behave untruthfully toward anyone, and certainly not to myself.

"I'm no longer lonely and I am a happy man. I am not saying this to convince myself. It is a fact.

"They told me that this happiness would get greater and greater. Already, I feel I am too happy to stand any more. My saddest moment of today is better than my happiest moment of yesterday."[54]

Hyams said that he was barraged by telephone calls and nearly eight hundred letters when the columns appeared. "Friends wanted to know where they could get the drug. Psychiatrists called, complaining that their patients were now begging them for LSD. Every actor in town under analysis wanted it," he recalled.[55]

The series sparked a feud between Grant and Hyams—not because of the sensitivity of the topic, but because Hyams's articles scuttled a potentially lucrative deal for Grant to sell the exclusive story of his LSD experience to *Look*. According to Hyams's account, Grant initially asked the reporter to hold off publishing about his LSD experimentation, which they discussed during a tape-recorded interview on the set of *Operation Petticoat*. A few weeks later, Grant visited a UCLA journalism class co-taught by Hyams and the *London Daily Mirror* reporter Lionel Crane and regaled the students with psychological insights he credited to LSD therapy. After reviewing the students' papers, Hyams learned that Crane had already shared these tales with his readers across the Atlantic. Hyams said that he then got permission from Grant to run similar quotes to those that had already appeared in the *Daily Mirror*. "Cary's LSD experiments gave the story a strong news peg," he explained. "In addition, I felt the articles were the most revealing ever published about him in New York."[56]

Grant's attempt to kill the series on the eve of publication, Hyams's legal defense of his reputation, and an unusual out-of-court settlement made the story even bigger. The day that Hyams's articles on Grant were announced, the actor called him to demand that the series, scheduled to begin the following day, be pulled. When Hyams refused to act, Grant denied that the conversations on which they were based had ever taken place. The *Los Angeles Times* ran Hyams's column prefaced with Grant's denial. Louella Parsons, the doyenne of Hollywood gossip columnists, sided with the movie star, huffing in her column that when she was a girl, "things were different in the newspaper business." Hyams fretted that the spat was becoming a "cause célèbre" for journalists who relished the opportunity to repeat the sensational quotes. Angered by the damage to his reputation, Hyams filed a five-hundred-thousand-dollar suit against his source for slander, a development reported in the gossip press. Stranger still, after Hyams produced his tape recording of the *Operation Petticoat* interview during depositions, Grant settled the case by giving the reporter the opportunity to ghostwrite his life story. Grant sat for dozens of interviews with Hyams over the course of a year and eventually rewrote the final version of his story, which the *Ladies' Home Journal* (1963 circulation 7.1 million) purchased for $125,000. To keep peace with the star, Hyams shared this windfall by purchasing Grant a twenty-two-thousand-dollar Rolls-Royce.[57]

Other magazines did not wait for this authorized account before publishing their own articles. *Look* (1959 circulation 5.6 million) made up for its lost exclusive with a long piece by Laura Bergquist that turned an unusually critical eye on the popular Hollywood star. "The Curious Story behind the New Cary Grant" warmed to its subject by discussing seemingly queer aspects of the actor's "mysterious" and "fey" personality, including his confession to the classroom of journalism students, his serial marriages, perfectionism, and unique nylon underpants ("a product of his own design"). Bergquist explained that she had spent thousands of hours puzzling over the "new" Cary Grant, interviewing the star and his friends, to reach her conclusion that the changes were indeed real. The final page of the article attributed his transformation, and newfound happiness, to LSD. "All my life I've been searching for peace of mind," he told Bergquist. "I'd explored yoga and hypnotism and made attempts at mysticism. Nothing really seemed to give me what I wanted until this treatment."[58] The article's circumspection aggravated the acid-tongued gossip columnist Hedda Hopper, who fired off a letter to the editors of *Look* the day before the issue was dated to appear. "The article you ran on Cary Grant was the damnedest mish-mash I have ever read. Whom does he think he is fooling? This will probably surprise you: He started with boys and now he has gone back to them." According to one Grant biography, Hopper was mad because she too had hoped to tell the actor's life story.[59]

The many articles that discussed Grant's enthusiasm for LSD stuck to the celebrity's script. A 1960 article on Grant in the *Washington Post*'s Sunday magazine, "Cary Grant—Ageless Idol," ran with a subhead that read, "At 56—and after three unsuccessful marriages—he believes that a drug called L.S.D. has made it possible for him to 'fall in love for the first time.'" It went on to offer glowing descriptions of LSD therapy and a sidebar, "What Is L.S.D. and How It Works."[60] Later that year, the text accompanying a photo spread about the star in *Good Housekeeping* (1960 circulation 4.4 million) explained,

[B]y courageously permitting himself to be one of the subjects of a psychiatric experiment with a drug that eventually may become an important tool in psychotherapy, Grant has become a radically different man. He has become something that few stars have ever become: a healthy, reasonably well-adjusted, mentally fit human being, more dynamic, more dashing than he himself would have believed possible. At fifty-six, he seems literally to be living a second youth of physical and emotional resurgence.

Grant's friends are amazed at the change in him. Some were skeptical at first, but none are now. Clifford Odets, the writer-director, told me in Hollywood last spring, "The changes in him as a result of the treatment have been extraordinary. He's bloomed. He's lost his reticence and shyness. The barricades have been swept away, it seems, and he's now free and spontaneous. He's got a freshness, an alertness, an awareness of things he never had before. Why, he's almost like a kid."[61]

When it finally appeared in 1963, the Grant autobiography for the *Ladies' Home Journal* held few surprises. In the three-part, chronological account of the actor's life, Grant's promise to describe his LSD experiences and their "beneficial results" first appeared as a cliffhanger at the end of part two. In the final pages of the account, he described how revelations achieved under the influence of LSD led him to acceptance of personal responsibility for his happiness. "I learned that all the clichés prove true," he explained.[62]

Over the following decades, Grant stood by his assessment of LSD therapy, describing the benefits he found in the drug in numerous interviews until his death in 1986, including a 1967 interview with the *National Police Gazette* (1967 circulation 190,000) that prominently featured the actor's discussion of the drug (see figure 7).[63] However, the marriage to Betsy Drake that Grant often credited LSD with saving broke up in 1962. At divorce proceedings in 1968, his next wife, the actress Dyan Cannon, accused Grant of erratic, sometimes violent behavior, which she blamed on a weekly LSD habit.[64]

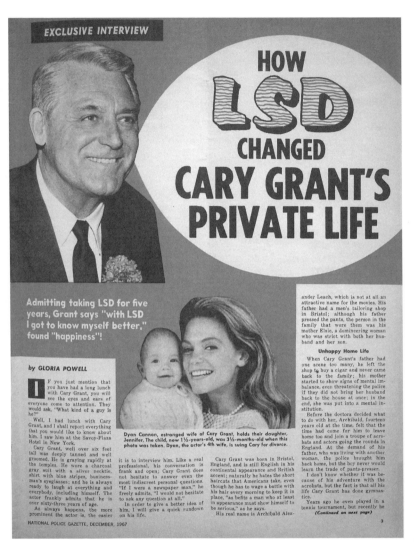

Figure 7. Although Grant's revelation that he used LSD was eight years old, it made the headline of a 1967 interview with the actor in the *National Police Gazette*. Gloria Powell, "How LSD Changed Cary Grant's Private Life," *National Police Gazette,* December 1967, 3. Image courtesy of National Police Gazette Enterprises, LLC. Copyright © 1967 National Police Gazette Corp. Used by permission.

Grant's revelation in 1959 prompted several national magazines to publish articles exploring the sensational new therapy. "In Hollywood, it was only natural that psychiatric patients undergoing analytic treatment should have visions in wide screen, full color, and observe themselves from cloud nine," began a 1960 article in *Time* (1960 circulation 2.4 million) that described the style of therapy conducted by Grant's doctors, Chandler and Hartman, said to result in the "accelerated recovery" of about half their patients. *Time* described an LSD trip as colorful visions and fantasies, mixed with real memories, in some cases going back to the first year of life. "Family conflicts may be projected onto the LSD screen in puppet shows, acted out by Disney characters," the magazine explained. "Whatever the visions' content, most important is the fact that the patient seems able to stand aside and report vividly observed conflicts, dredged from his deepest unconscious and acted out before him." The article did not reflect the casual attitude toward LSD in its publisher's home. The value of the drug was strictly in conjunction with psychotherapy, preferably with a psychiatrist who had experienced the drug twenty to forty times himself. "By itself, it cures nothing," *Time* explained. As for Cary Grant, he "emerged from therapy to give a confused account of what ailed him during a long and successful career, but he was convinced that he had at last found 'a tough inner core of strength.'"[65]

Seven months after breaking the Grant story, Hyams reported on a 1959 conference on LSD in Princeton, New Jersey, for *This Week* magazine (1959 circulation 11.7 million), a Sunday supplement to thirty-seven newspapers nationwide. Illustrated with a kachina-doll drawing by one of Janiger's patients, "How a New Shock Drug Unlocks Troubled Minds" explained that LSD "has rescued many drug addicts, alcoholics and neurotics from their private hells—and holds promise for curing tomorrow's mental ills." The article opened with a bulleted list of findings discussed at the conference: the drug was "of utmost value in psychotherapy," responsible for "remarkable improvement" in drug and alcohol addicts, and provided the cure for a New York man's lifelong stutter.[66] Despite its New Jersey dateline, the sources all came from Los Angeles, Hyams's home base. He summarized Huxley and Cohen's descriptions of acid trips, described Ditman's use of the drug with alcoholics, explained Chandler and Hartman's therapeutic technique, and provided unattributed quotes about the experience that, in other articles, were attributed to Cary Grant. The critical evidence offered by the article came from an as-yet-unpublished study by Cohen, which combined data from forty-four researchers, encompassing twenty-five thousand administrations of hallucinogenic drugs to almost five thousand patients. In 70 percent of these cases, the patient's condition improved, Hyams wrote.[67]

Wire-service articles described other bizarre research with LSD in 1959 and 1960, including laboratory madness experiments on prison inmates and research conducted at the University of California medical school in San Francisco that appeared to show that LSD made lab rats immune to cancer.[68] A 1960 headline in the *Chicago Tribune* asked,

> The Ecstasy Drugs: New Powers for Us All?
> Excited Users Report:
> 1. SHARPER THINKING
> 2. GREATER CREATIVITY
> 3. STRANGE MENTAL ABILITIES
> Should We Start Celebrating?

The article's answer, it seemed, was maybe. Beyond offering hope for a cure for mental illness, the study of LSD "could provide the key to that enigma known as the total personality."[69]

The use of drugs to access fantastic mystical realms was not without detractors. "Beware of LSD," was the headline over a 1960 article in *This Week* (1960 circulation 13 million), six months after the magazine published Joe Hyams's laudatory "Shock Drug Unlocks Troubled Minds." After reviewing the remarkable claims about the drug published in articles from the previous year and the indications that the drug was becoming a "cocktail party fad," the author, a physician, warned that it seemed inconceivable that a drug that "breaks the fetters of our disenchanted existence" could do so without somehow damaging both body and soul. "[B]y giving man by drugs what he ought to earn through moral efforts, we may have committed the one unforgivable sin, the sin against the meaning of his earthly existence," the writer concluded.[70]

The enthusiastic journalism about LSD's unlimited potential relied on research, mostly conducted on the West Coast, which was increasingly isolated from the scientific consensus. The article in *This Week* by Hyams that relied on an unpublished study by Sidney Cohen particularly galled Louis Lasagna, a leading expert in clinical pharmacology and drug-trial design:

> It is quite possible that the author of the article was accurately quoting his informants; LSD-25 has a few enthusiastic boosters in this and other countries. But it is unlikely he tried to check the accuracy of these claims with other psychiatric authorities. Most psychiatrists have *not* found use for LSD-25 in any important respect, for either the diagnosis or therapy of mental illness, and it is unlikely that they will. . . . The agent produces disturbing mental reactions which are extremely upsetting to many subjects, and the benefits from its use are generally held to be

insufficient to justify such use. The drug is a fascinating one, for many reasons, and the article made good reading, but its title and message were misleading and ill-advised.[71]

Jaw-dropping results from West Cost studies with LSD mystified researchers in other parts of the country, where volunteers had less consistent, and often more negative, experiences. "Either LSD is the most phenomenal drug ever introduced into treatment in psychiatry, or else the results were evaluated by a criteria imposed by enthusiastic, if not positively prejudiced, people," a researcher commented at a 1960 conference.[72] Another wrote that California researchers' anomalous outcomes resulted from "therapist-induced mystical experience similar to religious conversion."[73]

Indeed, the drug experiments in literary Los Angeles, in which volunteers selected for their prior attitudes were warned what to expect and coached to find it, allowed for the influence of all sorts of variables beside the chemical itself on the results. Cohen, in particular, was sensitive to concerns that his collaborators' "unscientific" enthusiasm for LSD could tarnish the research. He declined to participate in a second round of psychotherapy experiments with Eisner and separated himself from Heard, in part because of their willingness to accept that experiences on LSD could provide evidence of reincarnation or ESP.[74]

Other reporters did approach the fantastic claims with more skepticism. An Associated Press report distributed to newspapers across the country in 1961 observed that after fifteen years of study, scientists were still no closer to isolating the physical changes caused by the LSD, or even using it to get the same response twice. The reporter noted the expert ambivalence toward the fantastic vision of evolution toward paradise described in Davis's *Exploring Inner Space.* "What does it prove? Nothing. That woman could just as easily have gone from paradise to evolution under LSD," one scientist told the reporter. A vice president of Sandoz agreed. "Oh, these subjects are always reporting cosmic experiences and inner and outer worlds. But how is it that real scientists, taking these drugs in the laboratory and then measuring their reactions carefully, don't have these cosmic results?"[75]

Another Associated Press reporter describing a magic-mushroom demonstration held for the press at a Northridge, California, pharmaceutical research facility struck a similarly skeptical note:

It was like a Hollywood cocktail party, except:
1. The scene was a sprawling, austerely white medical laboratory instead of a studio, and

2. I was gulping mushrooms, not martinis
But I was higher than a kite in a 40-knot wind.
All, of course, in the name of science.

Ultimately, he concluded that the mushrooms caused hallucinations, "although I imagine you could get the same effect with a rubber mallet."[76] The purpose of the press junket that produced the article was to promote an upcoming episode of the half-hour horror/paranormal television program *One Step Beyond*, aired January 1961, that depicted the journey of a team of scientists and philosophers to Mexico, hoping to learn more about mushrooms' power to enhance telepathic ability. As it was originally edited, the program consisted primarily of footage shot in Mexico, including a mushroom ceremony in which several of the researchers got high. When the program's sponsor, Alcoa, backed off because the show seemed too bizarre, it was hastily reedited with footage that appeared to demonstrate how hallucinogenic mushrooms improved the host's ability to guess numbers randomly generated by a computer in a laboratory experiment. The new version passed muster with Alcoa and became the program's highest-rated episode.[77] The Associated Press reporter invited to participate in the experiment was less impressed. He reserved news that the mushrooms appeared to increase his score on the ESP test to the last few paragraphs of the article, which in one paper ran under the headline, "A Second Mushroom, Then—Wham!"[78]

The extent that news coverage of LSD prompted readers to actually try the drug is difficult to gauge, particularly considering that the drug was largely unavailable except through researchers and psychiatrists supplied by Sandoz.[79] Some researchers did worry that the media attention to LSD was inducing volunteers to participate in drug experiments and exerting undue influence on their results. In 1956, the authors of a study published in the *Archives of Neurology and Psychiatry* noted that reports about LSD in newspapers and national magazines had made it more difficult to recruit unbiased subjects. "There was an increased amount of curiosity and willingness to experience the bizarre effects of this drug, which were rather sensationally treated in the press, and the prospects required more reassurances about the safety and reliability of these experiments than their earlier colleagues," the researchers complained.[80] At a meeting of the American Psychiatric Association in 1960, three psychiatrists described concerns that troubled individuals were self-selecting for LSD trials in the hope of treating psychological problems ranging from insecurity to sexual inhibition. After questioning fifty-six volunteers for a study of the drug in New York, they found that many had previously read news accounts of the drug's weird effects. Not quite half of the volunteers had psychiatric problems severe enough to warrant psychiatric treatment.[81]

In 1961, Myron Stolaroff, an electrical engineer who was introduced to LSD by Heard, opened an LSD research center with operations in Los Angeles and the San Francisco Bay area. Stolaroff's International Foundation for Advanced Study administered hundreds of doses of LSD and mescaline to volunteers who paid six hundred dollars a pop.[82] The following year, a group that included the pediatrician John Beresford and the psychologist Jean Houston opened the Agora Scientific Trust in Manhattan, which conducted LSD experiments on normal volunteers to "detail means by which the average person may pass through new dimensions of awareness and self-knowledge to a 'transforming experience' resulting in actualization of latent capacities, philosophical reorientation, emotional and sensory at-homeness in the world, and still other changes beneficial to the person," according to the book they published to describe their work, *The Varieties of Psychedelic Experience.*[83] The FDA began its first investigation into the misuse of LSD in 1961, focusing on Southern California physicians and psychologists who were not authorized to use the drug and culminating in raids on several Los Angeles therapists in 1962.[84] By the end of the year, California legislators were calling for investigations into the "hush-hush" goings-on at Stolaroff's foundation and a ban on recreational use of the drug, the *Los Angeles Times* reported.[85] The paper also covered a drug raid on a Los Angeles church after a parishioner sued the pastor for inducing him to try LSD. The parishioner claimed that he attempted suicide as a result.[86]

An influx of LSD casualties to local emergency rooms caused Cohen to revise his earlier conclusions about the safety of the drug. In 1961, he and Ditman published a study in the *Journal of the American Medical Association* reporting "an increasing number of untoward events in connection with LSD-25 administration," including five cases in which LSD appeared to cause what they described as a prolonged psychotic break. In each case, underlying psychiatric problems were exacerbated through use of the drug and "unskillful therapeutic management." One patient was given LSD more than three hundred times by a "nonmedical practitioner" without medical supervision. Another troubling case was that of a child who inadvertently swallowed an LSD-impregnated sugar cube and was still in a "partial disassociated state" a month later. It was a story with special resonance; an identical incident four years later would result in a flurry of national magazine coverage. "The use of LSD-25 can be attended with serious complications," Cohen and Ditman concluded. "This is especially true now that a black market in the drug exists."[87] The *Los Angeles Times* and the *New York Times* reported on the journal article but were unable to unearth further evidence of a black market in LSD.[88]

Near the end of 1962, the Southern California Psychiatric Society called for a ban on LSD in light of its use by unqualified people at "parties" where it was taken for "kicks," the *Los Angeles Times* reported. The newspaper article cited the society's concern that the drug's uncontrolled use could precipitate schizophrenic reactions, bizarre behavior, and even suicide among these recreational users. The article concluded by weighing these concerns against a statement by a pharmacologist at Stolaroff's foundation that undue restrictions on LSD, peyote, and magic mushrooms "may ultimately hamper and limit explorations into the range of man's consciousness and the structure of his brain."[89]

The *Los Angeles Times* described similar concerns voiced by Timothy Leary at a press conference prior to a 1962 lecture to the Los Angeles Society of Clinical Psychiatrists, shortly before wild tales about his behavior at Harvard put him on a national stage. The reporter repeated Leary's most sensational statements without editorializing. LSD, mescaline, and magic mushrooms were described in Leary's words as "natural chemical foods" offering "transcendency [*sic*] from the game of life into an exhilarating understanding of the rich potentialities beyond it." Leary further explained "that most world religions were first derived, probably accidentally, through the intake of such substances, and that the setting of church was invented to recapture the ecstatic experience of living in a world beyond." The article began and ended with Leary's prediction: "This control of the mind through drugs, which we call internal politics, will be the leading civil liberties issue in coming decades."[90]

LSD research surfaced on the news agenda of local newspapers in California initially by way of typical newsroom routines: a science or general-assignment reporter went to a conference or public lecture, latched onto the one thing that they presumed would be most interesting to readers, and made it the focus of a story for the next day's paper, with little or no additional research. Faced with the typical conference offerings, it is easy to imagine why reporters from local papers gravitated toward the presentation about LSD that described mind-blowing results. Other articles in the *San Francisco Chronicle* that emerged from the 1958 AMA conference that featured Cohen and Eisner's paper included a call for greater investigation of car crashes and a description of freebies available in the convention hall.[91] Observers, such as Lasagna, could fault reporters for not conducting more extensive research, speaking to additional experts, or getting a feel for the general pulse of the field. Likely, they felt that they were accurately describing what an expert said at a news event and allowing readers to decide how to interpret it. They might have felt ill-trained to investigate more deeply this topic so far removed from the usual newspaper fare of crime, official pronouncements, and government activity.[92] It might not have seemed their job.

As a result, most newspaper coverage of this research was strictly informational, alerting the audience to a particular scientific byway but—for the most part—not taking them down that path. In the most enthusiastic articles, LSD was now a wonder drug: mystical, personally transformative, therapy-in-a-pill. In the late 1950s, the drug was new enough that providing even basic information about it would have aided its diffusion, simply by alerting the audience to its existence and what it was now supposed to do. Reporters' attraction to dramatic statements and desire for simplification resulted in articles that were more enthusiastic about LSD than the published writings of the drug's supporters. Apart from the few therapists and centers offering the drug commercially, use of the drug still moved through social circles, but the news coverage could only have lubricated its spread.

The surprising advocacy of LSD by Grant spread news of the innovation to a broader circle, while associating the drug with one of the most popular Hollywood stars of the era. Grant was subject to so much news and gossip attention that many who followed his career no doubt felt a personal attachment to the star. His earnest endorsement seemed bizarre—hence the heavy media attention—but it also seemed a clear reflection of what the leading man experienced as a profound and positive element in his life. It seems unlikely that readers of *Good Housekeeping* or *Ladies' Home Journal* subsequently filled the ranks of 1960s acid trippers, but the coverage was nevertheless part of an educational process that introduced them to the possibilities of spiritual growth and self-realization outside of traditional channels. Scientific theories were presented as futuristic and tentative, while Grant's testimony was concrete, from a well-known and widely liked source.

While most newspaper articles were primarily informational, television specials that showed volunteers in the throes of LSD trips offered gratifications beyond the programs' informational value. The scenes were plainly sensational, not least because scenes like these were banned in entertainment programming, and had been for three decades. Watching a volunteer wig out on LSD would have been exciting and entertaining for many viewers, and more than a little transgressive. It may have been hard for viewers to identify with the subjects of the experiments, but easy to feel the parasocial gratification of standing alongside the fascinated interviewer asking questions. While the programs did not quite take viewers inside the LSD experience, they offered a front-row seat.

A reporter who tried to take the audience deeper was George Dusheck of the *San Francisco Call Bulletin,* remembered as one of the first dedicated science reporters in the country, who claimed to have been drawn to the specialty from the conviction that newspaper editors were blind to the significance of scientific developments.[93] During the first week of 1963, the *San Francisco Call Bulletin* published a four-part series of above-the-fold, front-page features by Dusheck describing local people's successful experiences with LSD. The first installment was promoted with a two-line banner above the paper's masthead:

"SWEET DREAM" THERAPY HERE
The Mindquake Drug

"The use of vision-inducing drugs, which yield a kind of instant Zen, has broken through the frontiers of psychiatry and is spreading through the suburbohemia of the Bay Area," the first article in the series began. A few paragraphs later, it continued,

In the drugged state they experience terrifyingly beautiful hallucinations, break through the sensory bounds of the workaday world, have the illusion of being all-knowing, all-powerful, godlike.

Many believe they have achieved permanently higher levels of awareness and deeper levels of self-understanding.

A few have suffered temporary toxic madness. All have experienced, under the influence of LSD-25, mescaline, and psilocybin, an ineffable emotional and spiritual mindquake that reverberates through their lives for months afterward.

The believers believe with the intensity of Saul after he encountered an invisible Christ on the road to Damascus. The unbelievers denounce the LSD "experience" as mere chemical mysticism, and argue that these potent and possibly dangerous drugs should be used only for medical purposes.

The first installment in Dusheck's series described the discovery of LSD by Albert Hofmann and the use of magic mushrooms by Robert Graves and R. Gordon Wasson. It also included a description of mescaline intoxication from Huxley's *Doors of Perception* and an explanation of the Buddhist concept of Zen.[94]

The second and third installments highlighted experiences of clients who received LSD treatment at Stolaroff's clinic. In the second article, "In a Drug-Filled Chalice, Total Love," a woman described as "a beautiful Menlo Park wife and mother" testified, "There has opened a pipeline to myself, clean and pure, freed of false values, unfounded fears, self-created restrictions, repressed feelings."[95] The next day, a twenty-nine-year-old book editor declared that he found the inner strength to solve his own problems and fired his psychiatrist after two five-hundred-dollar LSD sessions.[96] The final installment, with headlines "On a Pin-Head—Revelations" and "Psychiatry in a Bottle," included more descriptions of LSD trips and attempts by psychiatrists to explain them. It ended with a quote from a Stanford researcher: "This thing is very big. There will be repercussions in psychiatry for years to come. We may have a tool here which can literally liberate people in the way that Buddhists have talked about for centuries." This final installment also included a note from the editor that contrasted with the circumstances of the LSD experiences it described:

> The *News Call Bulletin* has no wish to give the impression that the use of LSD-25 and other vision-inducing drugs is endorsed by most psychiatrists and other physicians.
>
> On the contrary, it would seem that the majority view at this time is that these chemicals are powerful, potentially dangerous and should only be used by qualified investigators in a research hospital setting.[97]

Four days after the series' conclusion, the newspaper ran letters it had received in response. Most praised the articles, but one charged, "[T]he glowing articles on LSD and mescaline give undeserved free advertising." The writer continued, "It is appalling that a newspaper should work so flagrantly against the interests of the community. When is your series on marijuana and heroin running?"[98]

At the time, the nation was fixated on another investigational drug: thalidomide, a pill prescribed to pregnant women in Europe and other parts of the world as a cure for morning sickness and a sleeping aid. An application from the Cincinnati-based William S. Merrell Company to market the drug in the United States was pending before the Food and Drug Administration (FDA), as reports of deformed babies born to women who took the drug began arriving from Europe.[99] The *New York Times* published more than a hundred articles about thalidomide in the last eight months of 1962, including reports on the successive waves of birth defects from around the world and speculation about the scope of potential disaster here. During the same period, nearly fifty articles on the subject were published in magazines indexed by the *Reader's Guide.* The young, female FDA doctor who held up the thalidomide application, Dr. Frances Kelsey, enjoyed brief celebrity, with profiles in the *New York Times, Time, U.S. News and World Report, Good Housekeeping, Reader's Digest,* and *Parents,* and was awarded the highest presidential honor given civil servants.[100] In response to the averted disaster, Congress passed legislation severely limiting physicians' access to experimental drugs. The Kefauver-Harris Drug Amendments, which went into effect in January 1963, required the FDA to certify not only that new drugs were safe but also that they were effective for a particular condition.

The requirement that drugs not only be proven safe but also effective posed a particular problem for LSD. Its safety was debatable; by most accounts, the incidence of long-term negative reactions from a single use by patients who were in good mental health was very low. But even after decades of study, it remained a cure in wait of a condition. The new regulatory provisions did not envision drug use for nonmedical goals like personal growth, mystical exploration, or the relief of boredom. Because LSD was categorized as investigational, it could no longer be used as part of a general psychiatric practice. When the law was enacted, Sandoz immediately restricted access to the drug to psychiatrists who received funding from the National Institute of Mental Health, the Veteran's Administration, or a state mental-health commission, cutting the number of LSD researchers from a few hundred to about seventy.[101]

Many psychiatrists greeted tightened restrictions on LSD with a cheer. In May 1963, Cohen and Ditman published yet another set of case studies in which LSD appeared to trigger prolonged adverse reactions in the *Archives of General Psychiatry*. The cases included a woman who, for two years after her first LSD experiences, was preoccupied with "pseudo-philosophic abstractions about 'truth, beauty, love and life.'" After seeking a second psychiatric LSD experience, she developed the belief that she was in the Garden of Eden and appeared nude in public. After ten days, her husband put her into a mental hospital, where she experienced partial improvement after electroshock therapy and medication. Other cases included a thirty-two-year-old secretary who experienced sporadic panic attacks after three LSD sessions with a psychotherapist; a psychoanalyst who went into a depression after taking LSD; and a woman with a long history of family and mental health problems who abandoned her family and children to live a "beat" lifestyle.[102]

Cohen and Ditman noted that in some cases, the "transcendental" aspect of the LSD experience appeared to incorporate paranoia and, more frequently, megalomania, along with users' desire to share with others their LSD-inspired insight. The tendency was demonstrated by the final case study, of a psychologist who, after three LSD administrations, hatched a number of grandiose plans. "One was to take over Sandoz Laboratories in order to secure a world supply of the drug. He threatened his wife with a gun, then left her, wrote some songs and plays of minor merit, and went off to live in the desert. He recovered gradually after a number of months without specific treatment," the psychiatrists reported. They also noted that while the actual incidence of negative reaction was unknown, it was infrequent; that patients with prior emotional problems were most at risk, and also most likely to seek LSD treatment; and that in a majority of cases wherein complications developed, the drug had been obtained on the black market.[103]

A strongly worded editorial in the journal's same issue summarized the history of LSD, starting with model psychosis, then continued:

> LSD-25 was then used as an adjunct to psychotherapy, presumably loosening defenses and facilitating "insight." The affective release interested many psychiatrists who administered the drug to themselves, and some, who became enamored with the mystical hallucinatory state, eventually in their "mystique" became disqualified as competent investigators. [...]
>
> Here again is the story of ill-results from the ill-advised use of a potentially valuable drug, due to unjustified claims, indiscriminate and premature publicity, and lack of professional controls. Indeed, this is a warning to the psychiatric profession that greater morbidity, and even mortality, is in store for its patients unless controls are developed against the unwise use of LSD-25.[104]

The following year, an editorial in the *Journal of the American Medical Association* argued that nonmedical explanations for the "therapeutic process" with LSD "[tend] to make serious investigators discount this whole area as a delusional belief shared by a group of unstable clinicians and lay enthusiasts."[105]

CHAPTER 5

Luce, Leary, and LSD, 1963–1965

The hardening scientific consensus against LSD might have seemed to signal an end to glorious descriptions of LSD trips in news media. That fact that it did not—and indeed, media descriptions of lavish drug trips multiplied, particularly in magazines—was the result of a number of factors internal and external to news media. Foremost was Timothy Leary. Extensive news coverage transformed Leary into "Mr. LSD," conferring a degree of celebrity that eventually prompted Richard Nixon to label him "the most dangerous man in America."[1] Articles about Leary in "most of the major U.S. magazines" in the months following his dismissal from Harvard "doubtless spurred the growth of the psychedelic underground," according to the most thorough history of the drug.[2]

While most of the news media were skeptical, the reporting in *Time* and *Life,* in particular, offered a hopeful and explicitly Christian twist on Leary's extreme views. Henry Luce, the deeply establishment publisher of *Time, Life,* and a handful of other media properties, had an interest in LSD stemming from his own experimentation and the will to shape his publications' content to reflect his perspective. By respectfully covering psychedelic drugs—the only aspect of the 1960s counterculture that *Time* did treat with respect, according to one biographer[3]—Luce and his magazines prolonged the public debate and lent legitimacy to Leary's research. "I've always maintained that Henry Luce did more to popularize acid than Timothy Leary," wrote the 1960s provocateur Abbie Hoffman, who in one account claimed that he first tried LSD "just about the time a *Life* magazine cover story was touting LSD as the new wonder drug that would end aggression."[4]

Luce was an unlikely advocate of LSD. He had an earnest attachment to mainstream Protestantism and an idealized vision of the American heartland stretching back to his childhood in Chinese missionary schools. Born in 1898 to an American missionary family, Luce came to the United States at age fifteen as a scholarship student at Hotchkiss, an elite Connecticut boarding school, where his background earned him the nickname Chink.[5] Half a century later, he claimed that the thing he "missed most in life" was having an honest-to-goodness American hometown like Oskaloosa, Iowa, which has a population of about eleven thousand and no obviously distinguishing features. (City officials extended Luce honorary citizenship in 1966 after learning of his wish.[6]) In a letter from Hotchkiss, Luce told his father that he aspired to missionary life, but he diligently pursued a career in journalism. Luce worked at the daily newspaper in Springfield, Massachusetts, before following his father's footsteps to Yale, where he earned an appointment along with Hotchkiss's chum Briton Hadden to the *Yale Daily News.* After graduation and a stint together at the *Baltimore News,* the pair founded *Time* as a magazine willing to express an opinion.[7] According to its prospectus, *Time* would differ from the weekly *Literary Digest,* a bestselling magazine of the time, in that "the *Digest,* in giving both sides of a question, gives little or no hint as to which side it considers to be right. *Time* gives both sides, but clearly indicates which side it believes to have the stronger position."[8]

When *Time* and *Life* were at the apex of their influence in the 1960s, Luce was widely blamed by liberal critics for setting the publications' conservative tone. "Because Luce's publications sought to create and control a national consensus, he chose his causes more carefully than some detractors have admitted," one scholar observed.[9] Luce stepped down as editor-in-chief of all of his publications in 1964, but he retained the title of editorial chairman until his death. At the time of his retirement, the official *Time* corporate history had Luce confiding to an old associate, "I do reserve the human right to talk to managing editors and writers and correspondents without going through channels."[10]

Following Luce's death in 1967, the essayist Joseph Epstein wrote in *Commentary* (1967 circulation 55,000):

> Up to the day of his death, then, Henry Luce exercised a pervasive influence over *Time.* This is not to say that he dictated every item that appeared in the magazine, from a review of a biography of Marcel Proust to the latest Jerry Lewis movie (though one may well wonder how many peripheral items were written to please the Boss). But every substantive stand that *Time* ever took was, above all, the

stand of Henry Luce. In a way that applies to few other recent publishers, Luce turned his magazines into personal diaries.[11]

Biographers have described two of Luce's drug experiences. Ralph G. Martin wrote that, during one, Luce conducted an imaginary orchestra in his backyard and admired a squat, hairy cactus he had never before liked. "Did you ever see anything more beautiful?" he asked Father John Courtney Murray, soliciting a laugh.[12] Murray was a Catholic priest and theologian who offered marital counseling to Henry and his second wife, Clare Boothe. During the other, "he claimed to have talked to God on the golf course, and found that the Old Boy seemed to be on top of things and knew pretty much what he was doing," in the words of the writer Wilfred Sheed.[13] For Luce, LSD-induced spiritual epiphanies did not rebut conventional beliefs but rather confirmed them in a direct and visceral way.

Years later, associates recalled several incidents in which Luce expounded his interest in LSD. The rambling speech at the annual banquet for the staff of *Life* during which Luce segued from discussing the changes taking place in the modern world to talking about his and Clare's experiments with LSD was legendary among old *Time-Life* hands.[14] A few years later, during a visit to the former *Time* writer and Pulitzer Prize winner John Hersey at Yale in 1966, the sixty-eight-year-old publisher met with students and later surprised his old friend by delivering a paean to the drug:

> After [the students] had left, he had a scotch, and said, "Oh, John, I've been experimenting with LSD, and it's the most wonderful thing! You look at that glass on the table, and see shimmering colors on either side of it."
>
> This was a time when LSD was ruining lives at Yale. I thanked my stars that he didn't say that when the kids were there![15]

In a brief discussion of Luce's involvement with LSD, biographer W. A. Swanberg wrote that the publisher was so impressed with the drug that "he turned up in New York to present the managing editors of *Time, Life,* and *Fortune* with copies of a book on psychedelic drugs along with an enthusiastic talk about the subject's story possibilities."[16] The story could not be independently verified. However, in 1964, *Time* (1964 circulation 2.9 million) heralded the publication of *The Beyond Within: The LSD Story,* by Sidney Cohen, the psychiatrist who supplied the Luces with the drug, as the first "impartial appraisal by a competent scientist writing in lay language" about LSD.[17] The 1,300-word article (long by *Time*'s standards) recounted several blissful trips, mentioned the possibility of horrible ones, and labeled the drug "definitely dangerous" for borderline psychotics. Of primary concern, however, was that recreational use would tarnish the reputation of a vital tool for scientific inquiry. "But the responsible hopes raised by serious and cautious research have been matched by wildly visionary claims. Irresponsible misuse of the drug has led to both scares and scandals," the lead paragraph ended.[18] This point was picked up in the article's conclusion:

Antics and Reaction: In the last few years, Dr. Cohen and other reputable researchers have been disturbed by what he calls the "beatnik microculture" and its abuses of LSD and other hallucinogens. The danger, he said, is that the public reaction against oddball antics may set back serious research for many years.

It is tempting, he suggests, to say that one gets from the LSD encounter what one deserves, but he quotes Aquinas for a more accurate summation: "*Quidquid recipietur secundum modum recipiientis recipietur*"—our nature determines what we receive. But mankind will not always know its present mental limits. "The mind's surmised and still unknown potential," says Dr. Cohen, "is our future. The experience called hallucinogenic will play a role in leading us to the future."[19]

Apparently, the Aquinas quote was a favorite. Cohen included a version of it in an extraordinarily warm inscription to Clare Booth Luce on the front leaf of a gift copy of the book.[20]

Cohen, who remained head of psychosomatic medicine at a Veterans Administration hospital in Los Angeles, was a moderate voice in the debate over LSD: concerned about the casualties of LSD but still awed by its promise to reduce pain, treat alcoholics, and tap the human mind's full potential. LSD "opened a door from which we must not retreat merely because we feel uncomfortably unscientific at the threshold," he wrote in 1959.[21] Luce would almost certainly have agreed.

Timothy Leary's Trip

Leary and Luce could not have been more different in outlook. Both were visionaries, but while Luce idealized conservative values, Leary was an iconoclast with a lifelong aversion to authority. Luce's father was a missionary; Leary's was abusive and a drunk. And while Luce followed the well-trod path through Hotchkiss to Yale to business success, Leary spent much of his early life fleeing trouble of his own making. At his Catholic high school, Leary sabotaged his mother's plans for his Ivy League education with a rebellious editorial in the school newspaper. After a year at Holy Cross College in Worcester, he won appointment to West Point and promptly abandoned classwork, dedicating himself instead to poker and illicit nights on the town, one evening burglarizing a liquor store to stock beer for a dorm-room party. He didn't last long at

West Point. Caught drunk after a boozy train ride back from the Army-Navy football game in Philadelphia, Leary claimed that other cadets had provided the whiskey. It was a lie, in violation of the academy's honor code. After weathering nine months of silent treatment from other cadets, Leary resigned from West Point and enrolled in the first university to accept him, the University of Alabama. Despite stellar grades, in November 1942 he was expelled for spending the night in a women's dormitory.[22]

His wartime deferment from military service reaching an end, Leary endured basic training and entered a program for psychology majors that involved three months studying at Georgetown University, followed by six months at Ohio State. A patron from the University of Alabama, the head of the psychology department who Leary claimed made him a "surrogate son" after failing to seduce him, interceded with the military to have him transferred to a hospital for deafened soldiers in Butler, Pennsylvania. There he met his first wife, Marianne Busch. As the war drew to a close, Leary successfully petitioned the University of Alabama for reinstatement and was allowed to transfer credits and fulfill remaining requirements for a bachelor's degree by correspondence. After discharge as a sergeant, Leary matriculated at Washington State University, earning a master's degree in psychology. In 1947, Marianne gave birth to their first child, Susan, and Timothy began doctoral studies in psychology at the University of California, Berkeley. Their son, Jack, was born in 1949, and the following year Leary defended a doctoral dissertation, based on observations of hundreds of hours of group therapy, that explored the measurement of personality change. The following year, he helped found the psychology department at Kaiser Permanente Hospital in Oakland.[23]

Leary's research reflected his rebellious attitude. The study that brought him notice, published in 1955 with his colleague Frank Barron, compared the rate of improvement of patients on a waiting list for psychotherapy at Kaiser with those who actually received treatment. Both groups improved, but "the therapy patients did not improve significantly more than the waiting-list controls," the study concluded.[24] The lesson, he explained in a 1983 autobiography, was that "[f]or all its efforts, psychology still hadn't developed a way of significantly and predictably changing human behavior. I had found myself practicing a profession that didn't seem to work."[25] Leary's next major accomplishment was a scheme to interpret multiple-choice personality-test scores by plotting them on a two-dimensional circular grid. Leary laid out his model, based on analysis of six years' data collected by Kaiser, in *The Interpersonal Diagnostic of Personality*, which was praised in the *Annual Review of Psychology* as "the most important book on psychotherapy of the year."[26]

Academic success, with an attendant government research grant and pleasant home in the Berkeley hills, masked a tumultuous personal life. Timothy and Marianne drank heavily at once- or twice-weekly cocktail parties for a group of professionals he nicknamed the "International Sporting Set." In a lightly fictionalized account, Leary reminisced that the alcohol fueled "[s]tage dramatics, coarse, oversimplified Shakespearean dialogues. Tipsy sexual histrionics."[27] Drunk, Marianne was wild and angry, provoked by the open secret of her husband's philandering. By 1955, Leary was renting an apartment on Telegraph Avenue to accommodate trysts with a hospital secretary. Marianne sought psychotherapy and initiated her own affair with a married friend. Finally, on the eve of Leary's thirty-fifth birthday, following a night of heavy drinking and a discussion about the state of their marriage, Marianne killed herself by running the car in their closed garage after Timothy went to bed. Less than a year later, Leary married the woman with whom he was having an affair. That ended in divorce two years later, but not before Leary's nose was broken in one domestic brawl, and the cops showed up for another. He suffered other blows. Leary's dissertation advisor was arrested for soliciting sex at a public restroom a block from the hospital. Leary and his advisor had been involved in a sexual relationship after his degree was finished, and Leary was terrified that he would be found out after the arrest made the local papers. On top of it all, his grant money was running out. Twice, inspectors documenting Leary's compliance with his National Institute of Mental Health grant had found him absent from the job. In 1958, Leary packed up his kids, abandoned his position, and, with another girlfriend briefly at his side, left for Spain with a trunk full of psychological test results that he hoped would be the foundation of a new book.[28]

The book did not progress quickly. Moving through a procession of apartments and rented rooms, Leary fell into depression. One night, sick in a filthy Spanish hotel room, his children back with relatives in the United States, he hit bottom and his depression broke. By early 1959 he had moved on to an apartment in Florence, where he completed a draft of his new book, *The Existential Transaction,* on a rented typewriter. The manuscript, which proposed "new, humanistic methods for behavior change," according to Leary's 1983 autobiography,[29] was never published and has not been located by biographers. One person who read it was Leary's former colleague and LSD researcher Frank Barron, who visited Leary in Florence. "It was marginal," he remembered. While in Florence, Barron told Leary about his recent creativity experiments with hallucinogenic mushrooms, in which Leary had little interest, and introduced him to David McClelland, a Harvard professor on sabbatical, who was charged with revitalizing the university's struggling Department of Social Relations.[30] Leary recalled telling McClelland about *The Existential Transaction* over pale Chianti:

I explained that by *existential* I meant that the psychologist should work with people in real-life situations, like a naturalist in the field, observing behavior in the trenches. "We should treat people as they actually are and not impose the medical model or any other model on them." [. . .]

By *transaction* I mean that psychologists shouldn't remain detached from their subjects. They should get involved, engaged in the events they're studying. They should enter each experiment prepared to change as much or more than the subjects being studied.[31]

McClelland offered the hotshot young professor a one-year appointment to Harvard.

When he got to Harvard, Leary's first cause was promoting the existential transaction. (He considered research with mescaline "foolishness" and was against drug treatment, in general, as a tool of authoritarian control.[32]) He dispatched his graduate students to do their research on skid row, in prisons, and at community centers. He quickly became popular with students but aggravated colleagues by answering any question with an exegesis of his personal theory. Near the end of his first year, McClelland warned, "Above all, you have got to stop using slogans and waving banners, because they seem to me to only confuse matters."[33]

That summer, while vacationing with friends in Mexico, Leary overcame his reservations about drugs and tried magic mushrooms for the first time. The decision to do so was prompted, in part, by mundane concerns about the declining vitality of a man on the cusp of his fortieth birthday. He described lying with his lover on a beach chair, realizing that there was no difference between their skins, watching fantastic displays of jeweled landscapes and exotic settings. He told two friends, "I learned more in the six or seven hours of this experience than in all my years as a psychologist."[34] Several decades and many hundreds of trips later, Leary recollected, "[L]ike almost everyone who has had the veil drawn, I came back a changed man." Leary generalized that the expansion of perception and experience causes the taker to confront the fact that their previous perspective was fragile, subjective, and incomplete. "We discover abruptly that we have been programmed all these years, that everything we accept as reality is just social fabrication," he later concluded.[35] Back at Harvard, Leary resolved to get his hands on more mushrooms, so he and others could take them and write what they saw. He sent a note requesting psilocybin pills from Sandoz Laboratories and, on the advice of a graduate student, read *The Doors of Perception*. As it happened, its author was in Boston for a visiting professorship at MIT.[36]

Over the course of "many" meetings with Huxley in October and November 1960, Leary imagined a program of group self-experimentation with LSD that transcended all conventions of experimental design and control. He foresaw collaboration between experimenter and subject, each with full control of experiments that would take place not in laboratories, but the world: "From these meetings grew the design for a naturalistic pilot study, in which the subjects would be treated like astronauts—carefully prepared, briefed with all available facts, and then expected to run their own spacecraft, make their own observations, and report back to ground control. Our subjects were not passive patients but hero-explorers."[37] Leary's research followed a spontaneous, casual approach. The first experiment was conducted on the evening that four small, grey pillboxes of psilocybin arrived in the mail from Sandoz. Leary was having a small party in his apartment. After working on a bottle of burgundy and some whiskey and soda, Leary was enjoying "a fine alcoholic stupor," when an undergraduate couple who lived upstairs stopped by. Another friend of Leary's, a scientist, suggested, "the hell with all this phony talk and measurement business, let's get mushrooms and start swinging."[38]

> I had been lecturing all year on research philosophy and ethics and how you should be collaborative and not use your position as a scientist to get an unfair advantage and about sharing information and sharing the power to make decisions with the subjects. And this was the way we had set up the mushroom research. Collaborative all the way. No pulling rank. Everyone taking turns giving mushrooms and taking them. . . . Besides, it would be a useful pilot study.[39]

Leary and his guests took psilocybin that night. And the following night too, while Leary's thirteen-year-old daughter Susan held a slumber party upstairs.

Leary reached out to the poet Allen Ginsberg, who stayed at Leary's sprawling Cambridge house not long after receiving a frosty reception to the poems "Laughing Gas," "Mescaline," and "Lysergic Acid" from the Group for the Advancement of Psychiatry, a Boston professional organization for psychiatrists. After a psilocybin trip, Ginsberg opened his address book and offered to guide Leary through the world of Beats, publishers, artists, and musicians to spread what Ginsberg took to be the holy, mystic experience. Soon, Leary was being introduced around New York, delivering pills from a seemingly bottomless supply to figures including Jack Kerouac, Dizzy Gillespie, Thelonious Monk, Robert Lowell, and others, many of whom already had long-standing relationships with marijuana, mescaline, and other drugs.

Experiences were not all positive. One young woman, the girlfriend of Grove Press founder Barney Rosset, attempted suicide the day after taking some of Leary's mescaline, and a guest at one of Leary's first psilocybin sessions had a violent reaction that could be described as a bad trip.[40] Leary did not mention the suicide attempt in his 1983 autobiography. It seemed that the professor's insistence on recognizing others' internal freedom and his refusal to "pull rank" overrode any sense of responsibility for providing drugs. Through the lens of Leary's existential transaction, prudence was made the enemy of virtue.

Leary's attitude enhanced his popularity with graduate students in the Department of Social Relations, who flocked to participate in his research studies and gatherings at his rented house. Richard Alpert, a thirty-year-old tenure-track professor in Leary's department, threw in with Leary too after a mind-blowing trip at Leary's house in February 1961. "I was ready to devote my life to Timothy because I felt, 'Now here is a man who is a real visionary. He sees through the system and can truly stand back and look,'" Alpert recalled.[41] Leary and Alpert became parental figures to a close group of graduate students, among the best in the department, who shared their taste and excitement for psilocybin. In March 1961, Leary initiated their most ambitious study. Felons with three to five months remaining before parole from the Massachusetts Correctional Institution in Concord would take psilocybin three times in group-therapy sessions with members of Leary's staff, who would also take the drug. Standardized personality tests would be administered before and after therapy. Leary recalled: "We made it clear to the prisoners that this was nothing *we* were doing to them. There was no doctor-patient game going here. We would take the drugs along with them. We were doing nothing to them that we weren't happily doing ourselves."[42] The felons were trained to take over the experiment by administering tests, recruiting volunteers, and delivering lectures. The team also followed up with members of the experimental group after release, creating a nonprofit foundation to coordinate post-release efforts.[43]

Leary's team initially reported that post-release, participants in the study were returned to the correctional system at about half the rate as the general prison population. Although subsequent follow-ups did not find this improvement in recidivism, Leary claimed that participating prisoners committed dramatically fewer new crimes (as opposed to parole violations) than the general population.[44] "It seemed that two major factors were bringing about changes in the convicts: first, the perception of new realities helped them recognize that they had alternatives beyond the cops and robbers game; then, that the empathetic bonding of group members helped them sustain their choice of a new life," Leary wrote in 1964.[45] The reported degree of improvement in recidivism varied among his half-dozen scholarly articles describing the experiment, but Leary promoted it as a great success. "We had halved the crime rate," he claimed in 1968.[46]

After his introduction to LSD in December 1961, Leary expanded his research to include that drug, too. Leary's attachment to personal theories deepened with his involvement with drugs. That summer, he and Alpert shocked the audience at a major international psychology conference in Copenhagen by abandoning academic reserve and delivering talks that amounted to paeans to drug experience. Leary praised psychedelic drugs as the most efficient way to "cut through the game structure of Western life," while Alpert delivered an homage to the visionary experience as an end to itself. "The overall reaction that I heard to Tim's talk was that it was a kind of incoherent rambling," recalled Herbert Kelman, another Harvard psychology professor in the audience. "Basically a paean to the drug experience. I couldn't find anything of substance there. It was rather shocking. I am not prone to making diagnoses but I remember one Danish psychologist there saying it sounded like the talk of someone who had been on drugs for a long time."[47]

In 1962, Leary and Alpert's activities caught the attention of university officials and the student press. During the spring semester, the *Harvard Crimson* ran a steady stream of articles in which Leary and Alpert described the amazing potential of their research, while others voiced misgivings over their casual, unscientific methods. The *Crimson*'s coverage began with an article by Andrew Weil, who became a bestselling health writer whose bearded face was twice featured on the cover of *Time* magazine, in 1997 and 2005.[48] The article leaned heavily on Huxley's rapturous descriptions of mescaline to introduce Leary and Alpert's work, mentioning plans for an interdisciplinary "mushroom seminar" in which graduate students would take monthly trips and apply the insights to their respective fields.[49] In a letter to the editor in response, Leary and Alpert stressed how seriously they took their ethical and professional responsibilities, claiming that their attitude was not unbounded enthusiasm but "unbounded concern . . . concern for the many problems created by the consciousness-expanding drugs. Problems of conceptualization. Problems of measurement. Problems of application and follow-up. Problems of interpretation. Problems of control."[50]

But it was their neglect of these issues that bothered colleagues in the Department of Social Relations. The following month, the student paper reported on a raucous departmental meeting where other faculty charged that conventions of scientific experimentation were being ignored and the drug was being administered in a nonchalant and irresponsible manner. Leary and Alpert claimed that it would be impossible to warn subjects of the effects of the drugs in advance without imposing effects and influencing the experience. That was also why it would be inappropriate to conduct experiments in a hospital, they explained. It was necessary for the experimenters to take drugs with their subjects so they could follow their reactions. "But no staff member," Leary was quoted as saying in the student paper, "has ever been in a situation when he couldn't handle any eventuality."[51] The controversy was replayed in the *Boston Herald,* a Hearst tabloid, the following day, with an account describing the faculty debate and some of Leary and Alpert's more conventional research under an explosive headline: "Hallucination Drug Fought at Harvard."[52]

The Massachusetts Department of Public Health launched an investigation that concluded before the end of the semester.[53] Leary and Alpert were found to have done nothing wrong, but the health department required that in the future psilocybin be administered by a physician.[54] Leary turned over his supply of psilocybin to the university's health services, where it was to be kept under lock and key. But while access to psilocybin was now somewhat limited, Leary's group still had a virtually unlimited supply of LSD and, thanks to publicity in the *Crimson,* a growing supply of eager volunteers. At off-campus gatherings, the circle of hero-explorers grew to include a number of professors and graduate students from the Divinity School, several of whom were deeply impressed by the experience.[55]

One of them, a divinity doctoral student named Walter Pahnke, conducted probably the most widely discussed study about LSD under Leary's tutelage. Journalists variously referred to it as the Good Friday Experiment, the Marsh Chapel Experiment, and the "Miracle at Marsh Chapel."[56] Pahnke, who was also a physician, gave ten seminary students psilocybin pills, while another ten were given nicotinic acid, an active placebo that caused a tingling sensation but no cognitive effects. The seminarians were taken to a Boston University chapel, where they listened to religious services piped from another part of the building. Following the service, they completed a 147-item questionnaire. The volunteers under the influence of psilocybin had statistically higher scores on indices designed to measure nine categories of mystical experience.[57] Leary, who had resisted Pahnke's proposal to subject psychedelics to the kind of conventional experiment that he abhorred, embraced the experiments' results as "a systematic demonstration of the religious aspects of the psychedelic experience."[58] A psychotherapist interested in psychedelic experiences praised it as "of especial importance because of its careful methodological controls."[59] It seemed a rare piece of objective evidence for something that had so often been described in purely subjective terms.

While reporters frequently cited the Good Friday and Concord Prison experiments to explain the effects of psychedelic drugs, reanalysis decades later concluded that they were tainted, in one case by selective reporting and in the other by fraud. In Pahnke's thesis and subsequent reports on the Good Friday Experiment, which documented mystical reactions from psilocybin, negative aspects of the seminary students' experiences appeared to be "significantly underemphasized," Rick Doblin's 1991 reanalysis found.[60] Particularly troubling was the failure to mention that one participant was tranquilized with Thorazine after he left the chapel and ran madly through the streets. Of the seven members of the original study's experimental group who were reinterviewed by Doblin, five recalled experiencing moments when they feared going crazy or dying, or that they were too weak to survive the ordeal, details left out of the original study.[61] Still, all members of the experimental group who participated in the followup "considered their original experience to have made a uniquely valuable contribution to their spiritual lives," Doblin found.[62] Although the double-blind design of the study almost certainly failed—experimenters and volunteers likely realized very quickly who was on psilocybin and who was not—the reanalysis concluded that the results "strongly support the hypothesis that psychedelic drugs can help facilitate mystical experiences when used by religiously inclined people in a religious setting," a hypothesis also supported by a 2006 Johns Hopkins study.[63] Pahnke died in a scuba-diving accident in 1971.

Problems with the Concord Prison Experiment were worse. Doblin's 1998 critique of that study found Leary's claim that psychedelic therapy led to a short-term decline in criminal behavior to be "false" because it was based on flawed comparisons between participating and nonparticipating prisoners. Leary's distinctions between the new crimes and parole violations were also specious.[64] Ralph Metzner, a graduate student who was Leary's second author on the original study, wrote that it was "disconcerting, of course, to discover, 35 years after the fact, that a research project I was involved in and wrote about, made quantitative errors and reported erroneous conclusions."[65] Metzner went on to recall how disappointed group members where when, nearly a year into the project, they discovered that the convicts involved in the psilocybin experiments were doing no better than the control group, despite personality-test performances that suggested they would. Metzner wrote that he had no idea how Leary concluded that the subjects committed fewer new crimes:

> This "finding," which has now turned out to be erroneous, was of course the kind of result we wanted to find. It enabled us to maintain a positive, enthusiastic attitude in talking about the project. We fell victim to the well-known "halo effect," by which researchers tend to see their data in as positive a light as possible. I have myself, in later years, sometimes forgotten the basically negative result we reported in the study, and talked about the project as if we lowered the recidivism rate. . . . Whether Leary made these mistakes consciously, faking the results that he wanted, or whether they were unconscious mistakes of carelessness, motivated by over-enthusiasm is impossible to say at this point.[66]

In October 1962, Leary and Alpert announced plans to form an independent research association, the International Federation for Internal Freedom (with the propitious acronym IFIF), ostensibly to avoid the university's infringement on their academic freedom. "The rumors of the past two years, culminating with the publicity of last spring, have made it clear that these materials are too powerful and too controversial to be researched in a university setting," they told the *Crimson*.[67] In December, university officials issued a warning that Harvard was developing a black market in hallucinogenic drugs.[68] The issue broke into the *New York Times* in a front-page article quoting a Harvard dean's charge that "intellectual promotion" of "mind-distorting" drugs by unnamed experimenters was increasing their use among undergraduates.[69] Although not named in the warning, Leary and Alpert responded to its assertion that psychedelic drugs pose "a serious hazard to the mental health and stability even of apparently normal people" in a letter to the student paper. "While these statements are conservative from the administrative point of view, they are reckless and inaccurate from the scientific. . . . What is in question is the freedom or control of consciousness, the limiting or expanding of man's awareness," they wrote. In the letter to the editor, Leary and Alpert argued that all stimuli are processed chemically in the brain, and that "artificial" and "natural," "dangerous" and "beneficial" are semantic distinctions. "There is, however, no factual evidence that consciousness-expanding drugs are uniquely dangerous and considerable evidence they are safe and beneficial," they concluded, and on these two points they cited an early, optimistic survey of negative consequences by Sidney Cohen and Leary's own work.[70] The *New York Times* reported on Leary and Alpert's letter to the *Crimson,* repeating their warning that baseless restrictions on psychedelic research were creating a "scientific underground."[71] The same week, a brief in *Newsweek* (1962 circulation 1.5 million) reported that Leary had founded IFIF to conduct drug experiments aimed at transcending ego and identity. "The group ostensibly is serious, but its offbeat dilettantism (much like some of the interest in hypnotism) has caused concern among university officials," the two-hundred-word item concluded. *Newsweek* also mentioned "disturbing reports" that Harvard students trafficked LSD for one dollar per dose.[72]

The entire issue received less attention in the *Boston Globe,* which largely neglected the scandal at Harvard beyond an inside article in December 1962 that identified the "key dispute" as whether nonmedical personnel should be permitted to conduct drug experiments.[73] In March, the paper ran a feature in which an artist described taking psilocybin in an informal group experiment organized by Leary the previous year. The artist, head of the design department at the Massachusetts Institute of Art, said he was "disappointed" that he did not experience the out-of-this-world results described by Huxley but credited the experience with inspiring him to create a slideshow teaching students how to get "high on color" and see paintings with the focused perception of an artist. The article was accompanied with a photograph of him and his work.[74]

Midway through Harvard's spring semester in 1963, Leary decamped for California, instructing a secretary to hand out reading lists to his classes, one unfortunate student's honors thesis gathering dust on his desk. Superiors learned secondhand of his departure when he appeared in the West Coast media.[75] In Los Angeles, Leary announced to local reporters at a press conference at the Statler Hilton that he was starting an LSD research institute in Mexico to continue his work. Harvard, he said, had told him to give up his experiments or leave.[76] Sources at Harvard told the *Boston Globe* that this was "an exaggeration" and that Leary had in fact abandoned his job.[77] When Harvard actually fired Leary at the end of May for leaving his job, and Alpert for giving drugs to an undergraduate, newspapers including the *New York Times* and *Chicago Tribune* ran inside stories about the university's announcement and Alpert's rebuttal that Harvard acted in bad faith.[78] The *Boston Globe* published a longer inside article explaining Leary's Mexican project by quoting extensively from an IFIF mailing that described the group's plan to lease a remote Mexican hotel "as a center for study, retreat, recreation and experimentation on consciousness expanding" year-round. "Several scientists . . . said its contents revealed what they had been contending, that the organization headed by Alpert and Leary is more interested in a group experiment with cult overtones than in scientific research."[79] The final dismissal of Leary and Alpert was not a major national news story. Other papers, including the *Washington Post* and *Los Angeles Times,* didn't cover the announcement at all.

In 1963, most major newspapers had little interest in Leary or his wild claims about LSD. When he and twenty followers were ejected from Mexico just a few days after he was fired from Harvard, the *Boston Globe, New York Times, Washington Post,* and *Los Angeles Times* all ran brief wire-service stories explaining little more than the Mexican government's complaint that they "had entered the country as tourists and were engaged in unauthorized activities."[80] The short item was the only mention of Leary in the *Washington Post* prior to 1965. The *Chicago Tribune* overlooked the development. The rare newspaper to cover Leary's Mexican venture more thoroughly was the *San Francisco News Call Bulletin,* which ran two stories by George Dusheck based on an interview with a "top Mateo County psychiatrist and LSD researcher" who went on the retreat, for which participants paid two hundred dollars a month. The psychiatrist said that life at the disbanded LSD colony was "lovely, casual and open" but that he did not agree with the group that LSD should be freely available to all.[81]

The failure of newspapers to explore new territory opened by LSD was noted in an essay on "LSD and the Press" by William Braden, author of the 1967 book *The Private Sea: LSD and the Search for God*. "Since 1963, the newspapers had had almost nothing to say about the potential benefits of psychedelics in psychotherapy and related fields," complained Braden, a *Chicago Tribune* reporter.[82] He chalked this up to newspapers' lack of expertise with a subject that overlapped science with theology, sociology, and psychology, the fact that a remarkable drug trip did not mesh with what was typically considered "news," and an affinity for concrete thinking that seemed at times to make newspaper journalists deliberately obtuse. "The press has often groped to understand anything radically new and complex—including nuclear energy, space flight, and now psychedelic drugs." Furthermore, he surmised, newspaper editors had no wish to print something that would encourage readers to try a drug.[83] With a few exceptions, he found the topic of psychedelic drugs absent from television and radio. "It is painful to admit that the major magazines have done a better job than newspapers in reporting on LSD, and that *Time* and *Life* between them have possibly done the best job of all."[84]

The *New York Times* paid more attention to LSD and Leary than other major papers, although still without stepping into the alternative reality proposed by the professor and his favored drug. Five months after Leary was expelled from Mexico, a *Times* reporter checked in with him and Alpert at their communal home in Millbrook, New York.[85] He reported that they had good relationships with their neighbors and had restricted their drug experiments to eating hallucinogenic morning-glory seeds, although there is reason to doubt that was actually the case.[86] The *New York Times* published two more articles about Leary in 1963—one about a lecture in Philadelphia in which he described using LSD to induce religious experiences, and another about a conference discussion of the Concord Prison Experiment—and several other articles describing mounting evidence of LSD's danger. Although research with the drug was curtailed after 1963, the paper wrote more about what research there was, with reports about its successful use on mentally ill children,[87] a large-scale trial of LSD on normal subjects at New York University,[88] the promising results achieved by Canadian scientists using LSD to treat alcoholism,[89] the results of the Harvard Good Friday Experiment that had been supervised by Leary,[90] and the creation of glass etched with concentric circles that "create the effects of hallucination-producing drugs without the drugs."[91] Still, the coverage seemed sufficiently sparse that in a 1966 *Times* article explaining Leary's campaign for recognition of a religious right to use psychedelic drugs, the reporter commented that "the increasing use of LSD poses social, medical and religious questions that do not seem to be receiving the attention they deserve."[92]

Newspapers in Los Angeles, Chicago, Boston, and Washington, D.C., were less enthralled. Days before Leary and Alpert were fired from Harvard, the *Washington Post* ran a front-page story, "Drugs that set Brain Aflame Herald Awesome Age of Plastic Personality," describing research suggesting the "awesome possibilities for good or evil" of mescaline, LSD, and psilocybin:

> They have been credited with wiping out alcoholism with a single treatment, and cleansing the mind of neurotics. There have been strong warnings against using them on psychotics. In vision production, their effects have been likened by William James, the American psychologist-philosopher, to the dramatic conversion of Saul of Tarsus from a rabid anti-Christian to St. Paul, the Apostle.
>
> They have been blamed for at least one suicide; murderous impulses in another taker, and the causing of a respectable married secretary to take to appearing nude in public. They have been administered to homosexuals, with controversial results.[93]

The article went on to describe "the experience" and its use as a cure for alcoholism. The *Post* then said little more about LSD for the next two years. The *Los Angeles Times,* publishing from what had been the epicenter of LSD use, ran a few articles mentioning academic symposia and research involving LSD, and several more expressing concern over its use among youth, but seemed no longer interested in exploring the drug effect. In 1963, Paul Coates, the host of the *Confidential File* television program that stirred controversy by showing a man on LSD in 1955, urged lawmakers to crack down on the drug in his *Times* column.[94] "LSD—Delusions of Grandeur Plague the Wonder Drug," was the headline over one 1964 article that urged skepticism toward Leary's "dramatic" claims and "evangelical and cultish" approach.[95] The *Chicago Tribune* and *Boston Globe* hardly mentioned LSD at all outside of its appearance in syndicated medical-advice columns and a testimonial for the drug's beneficial results in an interview with Cary Grant.[96] When the *Globe* ran a twelve-part series on the "Dope Menace" at the start of 1965, LSD was mentioned only once, and then only in a list of new drugs about which parents needed to worry.[97]

In the absence of widespread abuse, the idea of hallucinogenic drug use did not trigger the knee-jerk antipathy toward narcotics that had been often observed in the past, and journalists were apparently less concerned that their reporting could play a role in diffusing the practice. In July 1963, when the FDA announced that it would analyze whether morning-glory seeds cause hallucinations after reports that seed distributors in Boston, New York, and California were having trouble keeping them on the shelves, the *New York Times* helpfully cited a study published by the International Foundation for Advanced Study: "If 50 to 100 seeds were chewed and swallowed, there was little effect. Eating 100 to 150 produced some hallucination, and 200 to 500 made the subjects act as if they received a high dose of LSD."[98] *San Francisco Chronicle* columnist Herb Caen devoted a column to the run on morning-glory seeds, syndicated to papers including the *Los Angeles Times*. "If you happen to have a pack around the house, chew a few and let me know what happens. If it's Hallucination City, I'll be right over."[99]

Exploring LSD Experience

Whether the prospect of exploring a realm of inner experience that intersected with sociology, philosophy, and metaphysics was overwhelming, distasteful, or simply too far out for hard-bitten daily-newspaper reporters, many magazine writers accepted the challenge. A rush of magazines explained the backstory to Leary's historic dismissal with articles that frequently lingered over the glory and meaning he ascribed to LSD experience and apparent cultural antecedents from Indian religion to Aldous Huxley. While newspaper reporting focused on incremental, real-world events, the magazines were more interested in their connection to the world of culture and ideas. Magazines did not discover the story of Leary and Alpert directly, but rather refracted through the lens of earlier news reports, and made sense of it through connection to previous discussions in media and literature. Indeed, LSD's relationship to the media, celebrities, and deep ideas often was the story. Recreational use of LSD was still exceedingly small, but the emergence of a flamboyant spokesperson seemed to signal to many magazines that its cultural moment had arrived. The media attention was disproportionate to real-world use of LSD and generated primarily in reaction to other media, characteristics of "media hype" described by Stephen D. Reese and Lucig H. Danielian.[100]

While fascinated by Leary, some magazines were squeamish about describing the drug experience he embraced. After Leary and Alpert were fired, *Newsweek* (1963 circulation 1.5 million) ran a second article recapping their activities at Harvard and their plans to open the retreat center in Mexico and IFIF "joy and happiness centers" in the United States that contained no mention of Huxley and said little about the drug's reputed effect.[101] Weil reprised the back-and-forth that played out in the *Harvard Crimson* in a feature for *Look*

(1963 circulation 7.1 million), "The Strange Case of the Harvard Drug Scandal." Weil, who as an undergraduate was denied participation in Leary and Alpert's psychedelic studies,[102] thoroughly described the history and context of experiments at Harvard but did not delve deeply into the drugged state. "Descriptions of the drugs stressed such effects as heightened perceptions, increased awareness of one's surroundings, tremendous insights into one's own mind, accelerated thought processes, intense religious feelings, even extrasensory phenomena and mystical rapture," he explained. He criticized Leary and Alpert for having a commitment to the value of drug experience before their formal experiments even began.[103] The reporter who covered the campus controversy for the *Boston Herald* added context and a more distanced perspective for an article in *The Reporter* (1963 circulation 163,000), a respected biweekly. His article, "The Hallucinogenic Drug Cult," related the history of Leary's and Alpert's LSD research, including the Concord Prison Project and "Miracle at Marsh Chapel," followed more briefly by the concerns of Harvard and American Psychological Association officers and the evidence of a spreading black market. Ultimately, the article concluded that current laws were inadequate to permit scientific research while discouraging uncontrolled use.[104] Leary lambasted the article in a letter to the editor of *The Reporter* for its concern with drug control and failure to look more deeply into the experience. Despite misgivings over what he called "shock-scare techniques, lurid innuendoes, salacious gossip, the breathless, pious exposé style," Leary allowed, "the article does contain a conscientious summary of the research on religious implications and deserves thoughtful rereading. Exactly what happened with those religious students and hardened convicts who experienced spiritual revelation?"[105]

Other magazines, however, luxuriated in the psychedelic space that advocates said the drug opened. Leary was even more outraged by an article in *Esquire* (1963 circulation 874,000) that reproduced his and Alpert's proselytizing tone as well as their astounding conclusions. No viewpoints besides those of the LSD advocates were explored in "Getting Alienated with the Right Crowd at Harvard," which began: "The nervous system . . . is a completely adequate, completely efficient, ecstatic organ. . . . Trust your inherent machinery. Be entertained by the social game you play. Remember, man's natural state is ecstatic wonder, ecstatic intuition, ecstatic accurate movement. Don't settle for less." This pitch doesn't come from "some bright lads in an advertising agency, but rather assistant professor Richard Alpert and lecturer Timothy Leary of the Harvard Social Research Department," Martin Mayer went on to explain. The magazine described their beliefs in another passage that began, "Leary and

Alpert consumed quantities of the drugs and found that as a result they could understand the Mysteries of Life."[106] The tone was sarcastic, but the editors of *Esquire* clearly understood that the sales pitch was the article's appeal. Five years later, the magazine published an article by Leary himself, describing the psilocybin trip during which he and Allen Ginsberg determined "to turn on the world."[107]

Leary defended against what he perceived as attacks on his character in the article by expounding on the importance of his work. In an extended response to *Esquire,* he cataloged and dismissed what he described as the charges leveled by Mayer (for example, that he and Alpert were "like laxative salesmen" and "promoting drug consumption") as libelous and defamatory distractions from the "awesome" power of psychedelic drugs. In the response, Leary emphasized the seriousness of his research, the respectability of his collaborators, and the safety of LSD. And he pointed to a raft of research, including his own, indicating that the drug had great value. The subhead over one section was "It Makes You Feel So Good." The subhead for another section was "LSD Turns You On to God."[108]

Leary was happier with the three-story package on psychedelic drugs in *Playboy* (1963 circulation 1.3 million). "A Reporter's Objective View" was a lengthy history of hallucinogenic drug use and research, lingering on its possible sexual effects and culminating with the work at Harvard. The article telegraphed their enthusiasm while downplaying the concerns of university officials. The other pieces were an essay by Huxley, in which he dreamed of a utopian future in which drugs would help individuals overcome the mental limits imposed by language and ideology; and the novelist Alan Harrington's first-person description of an LSD trip with Leary and Alpert at IFIF headquarters.[109] Leary, Alpert, and Metzner congratulated the magazine for writing the most thorough and accurate of ten articles they said had recently appeared in national magazines. "Yours was the only attempt to make an objective appraisal of this new and complex form of neurological energy," they wrote in a published letter to the editor.[110]

Even articles that condemned Leary and LSD use generally were fascinated by the drug experience he described. In "The Dangerous Magic of LSD," the *Saturday Evening Post* (1963 circulation 6.6 million) offered a portrait of Leary and Alpert, who by that time had been thrown out of Mexico after some weeks at their psychedelic retreat at a remote beachfront hotel, as leaders of a "band of dedicated cultists" who "wander the hemisphere like misplaced lotus-eaters, seeking the freedom to drug themselves with hallucinogens and to study and enjoy the unearthly raptures they call The Experience." The "dangerous magic" in the article's title was conveyed in the opening paragraph with a cascade of images from Adelle Davis's *Exploring Inner Space.* Deep in the article, "The Experience" was explained this way:

> In general, earthly realities evaporate. Conscious memory, reasoning power, time and space perceptions stop functioning normally. During the early stages, sensory perceptions are almost unbearably acute. . . . As the effects reach deeper levels, the subject grows detached from his own ego; he undergoes a kind of psychological death. Then, reborn, he may believe that he has penetrated the ageless imponderables of who-am-I?, what-is-the-meaning-of-life? A number of painters, writers and musicians say LSD enables them to understand their own creative processes and thus improve their work. Many subjects testify to mystical revelations. God, they maintain, appeared to them; they heard Him and talked to Him. Others are pervaded by an awareness of the unity of all things, of identification with the cosmos and a boundless, ego-dissolving love for mankind. And still others, struggling against the loss of their egos, suffer hideous torment.[111]

The article gave a history of the psychedelic movement by way of Los Angeles, where Dr. Mortimer Hartman, one half of the LSD therapy practice that treated Cary Grant, had been suspended from medical practice after being picked up by police in a Ritalin-induced stupor behind the wheel of a parked car. The magazine found his partner, Dr. Arthur Chandler, lounging by a swimming pool surrounded by young men and women with the appearance of "starlets" that he described as patients. "The trouble is, LSD attracts unstable therapists as much as it does the neurotic patient. It gives them an intoxicating sense of power to bestow such a fabulous experience on others," Sidney Cohen told the magazine.[112] The article included an arresting picture of an LSD "cultist" in a meditation room of IFIF headquarters outside Boston (see figure 8).

Fascination with the LSD experience and its star-studded history infused a 1963 article in *Cosmopolitan* (1963 circulation 885,000) titled "LSD: Hollywood's Status Symbol Drug," that began with a scene from *Alice in Wonderland,* where "the extraordinary properties of the vision-producing drug, LSD-25, would seem almost commonplace." The article touched on concerns that the drug could prove harmful for some users, but its primary focus was to let readers in on what it described as a Hollywood and high-class fad.

> Suddenly, LSD has become the sophisticated "fun thing" to try among the smart set, the fast set and the beat set, and if you haven't got a buddy who can run down to his friendly neighborhood LSD bootlegger and buy and ampule of those little blue pills, you are simply not *in,* my friend. . . . Like winter colds and Asian flu, LSD is sweeping the nation, and its eager exponents assure us it will soon be as much a part of the American culture and diet as Mom's apple pie.[113]

In If-If's Newton Center, Mass., meditation room, reachable only by ladder from the basement, a cultist squats amid incense fumes.

Figure 8. The caption on this photo published in the *Saturday Evening Post* reads, "In If-If's Newton Center, Mass., meditation room, reachable only by ladder from the basement, a cultist squats amid incense fumes." Other photographs with the story included portraits of Leary, Alpert, and Metzner, as well as several shots of spaced-out IFIF acolytes. John Kobler, "The Dangerous Magic of LSD," *Saturday Evening Post,* November 2, 1963, 30. Photograph © SEPS licensed by Curtis Licensing Indianapolis, Ind. All rights reserved.

As with *Esquire,* the tone was knowing and sarcastic, but hardly discouraging. The article discussed the history of LSD by way of Los Angeles, describing the excitement over Cary Grant's 1959 admission of using the drug, the advocacy of Aldous Huxley, Alan Watts, and Allen Ginsberg, and the sprouting of "cultist groups" in San Francisco and Hollywood, "where it has now virtually become a status symbol among the cocktail-party set." The article explained the scandal at Harvard but was uncertain in its judgment of Leary. The reporter quoted an anonymous LSD researcher: "I think Leary's done a lot of harm to the cause of psychedelic medicine, but I give him credit for having the guts to stick his neck out. He's convinced he's right and he's willing to jeopardize his career for those ideas. Only time will tell whether he's right." The most extensive description of the drug effect came from the folk singer Ronnie Gilbert of the Weavers, who said that LSD therapy helped her beat "a deep, aching depression."[114]

While the *Ladies' Home Journal* (1963 circulation 7.1 million) did not judge Cary Grant's use of LSD, it was troubled by psychedelic drug use when considered in the abstract. An October 1963 article on "Instant Happiness" presented LSD use as irresponsible and unnecessary. Amid descriptions of drug trips and misbehavior by Timothy Leary, the article included anecdotes about unnamed people who "flipped" on LSD: a Chicago housewife who took LSD on a dare and was then hospitalized for months at the Illinois State Institute, and a "brilliant young graduate student in physics" who "took the stuff on a sugar cube and went wild. He tore off his clothes in the street, fought policemen and had to be handcuffed, straightjacketed and hospitalized, perhaps for years." A doctor at the mental hospital offered the story's moral: "'Apparently, LSD appeals greatly to people who think it is not enough to be alive, awake and running around,' says Dr. Jackson Smith, institute clinical director. 'LSD is dangerous as hell.'"[115]

The first article in *Time* (1963 circulation 2.7 million) about the scandal at Harvard, published before Leary and Alpert were formally severed from the university, was no more accepting of psychedelic drug use than the *Ladies' Home Journal.* The news magazine's scathing, dismissive tone seemed an exaggerated version of its more routine putdowns of liberal politicians and disfavored causes:

> For a couple of freewheeling years, two young Harvard psychologists have carried on wide-ranging experiments with mind-altering drugs. At the university's Center for Research in Personality, they sent their graduate-student subjects floating off into other-worldly visions of new and fantastic forms of "reality" and a new meaning of life. Now the cosmic ball is over. Timothy Leary and Richard Alpert, both Ph.D.s, are being dropped from the Harvard faculty because university authorities agree with the medical profession that the drugs they use

are too dangerous for campus experiments. But the two psychologists are acting blithely unconcerned.

The article stated, "psychiatrists and other physicians in general are solidly arrayed against non-medical applications of such potent drugs."[116]

In subsequent articles the magazine changed its position and tone. When *Time* returned to LSD in October 1963, it was with a religion-department article that included a catalog of endorsements by academics, ministers, and psychologists, each describing use of the drug to achieve religious experiences. The possibility of serious negative consequences was not mentioned. The article, titled "Instant Mysticism," began:

> In every age, men have struggled to perceive God directly rather than as a tenuously grasped abstraction. Few succeed, and the visions of the world's rare mystics have normally come only after hard spiritual work—prayer, meditation, ascetic practice. Now a number of psychologists and theologians are exploring such hallucinogenic drugs as mescaline, psilocybin and LSD-25 as an easy way to instant mysticism.
>
> In large enough doses, these drugs can simulate the effects of certain forms of psychosis—to the point, in some cases, of permanent derangement. But in controlled, minute doses the drugs produce weird and wonderful fantasies of sight and feeling; in Greenwich Village and on college campuses, they seem to be replacing marijuana as the hip way to get kicks. Some investigators who have tried the drugs claim to have undergone a profound spiritual experience, and these men are seriously, if gingerly, studying the undefined relationship between drug-induced visions and the classic forms of mystical ecstasy.[117]

The article mentioned Leary only in passing, en route to describing his findings, including the results of a survey of sixty-nine "religious professionals" in which more than half described experiencing the deepest spiritual experiences of their lives while on LSD or psilocybin. Two paragraphs were also devoted to describing the results of the Good Friday Experiment, which was not linked to the tarnished professor. The concern over nonmedical drug use that was voiced in the previous article in *Time* was replaced with the possibility that the drugs could someday rival, rather than supplement, conventional religion. "The drugs make an end run around Christ and go straight to the Holy Spirit," the president of a Presbyterian seminary said. Another religious scholar claimed that the drug experience was actually different from that of genuine mystics. Supportive theologians and scholars were given the final word. According to an MIT instructor who took LSD as a divinity student at Harvard: "The pity is that our everyday religious experience has become so jaded, so rationalized that to become aware of the mystery, wonderment and confusion of life we must resort to the drugs. Nevertheless, many of us are profoundly grateful for the vistas opened up by the drug experience. It remains to be seen whether this experience is to be interpreted in religious language."[118]

The same month that *Time* published "Instant Mysticism," *Life* (1963 circulation 7.1 million) ran the second article in a two-part series on "Control of the Brain" titled "The Chemical-Mind-Changers," focusing extensively on LSD. Clare Boothe and Henry Luce took special interest in the series; a rough draft, initialed by Henry with a handwritten note to Clare, is preserved in her papers. The first part, which dealt with electronic stimulation of the brain using electrodes, underwent few changes between review by the Luces and publication in *Life*. Several paragraphs were lightly rewritten, and 250 words discussing the brain's architecture were added.[119]

Changes to the installment dealing with LSD were more dramatic after review by the Luces. As well as getting a new lead and five-hundred-word introduction, the section of the story dealing with LSD was thoroughly revised and expanded. The rough draft of the story reviewed by the Luces described the general effects of LSD and contemporary psychiatric research with the drug in about four hundred words, with no attribution. The published story devoted about 1,600 words to contemporary LSD research and included expert comment by two psychiatrists, including Cohen, who was cited as the primary source for "some landmarks that will aid the reader in reaching a rational opinion" on what had lately become a matter of controversy. The article said Cohen had found that "the evidence indicates that with proper precautions, they [LSD and mescaline] are safe when given to a selected healthy group," and "for 'normal' people, the hallucinogens can give a rewarding esthetic, philosophical or religious experience—such as a sudden sense of comprehension of the nature of God."[120] Leary's name was not mentioned in the article, which included two pages of photographs of LSD subjects in contemplative poses (see figure 9). The following year, *Time* (1964 circulation 2.9 million) published the long article about "The Pros and Cons of LSD" that was likely prompted by Luce.[121]

Cohen was also the chief authority for a six-page 1965 article about LSD in the *New York Times Magazine* (1965 circulation 1.4 million), which opened with quotes from one user who said that she could hear smells, and another who discovered that God is love. "As Dr. Sidney Cohen, chief of psychosomatic medicine at the Veterans Administration Hospital in Los Angeles, and a leader in LSD research in America, recently put it, today's powerful hallucinogens are to all other psyche-altering drugs 'as a Himalayan peak is to a sand hill,'" the article

Figure 9. The *Life* article "The Chemical Mind Changers" opened with John Loengard's photograph of Barbara Dunlap, "a Cambridge, Mass. housewife," studying a lemon rind under the influence of LSD during an experiment conducted by IFIF. Leary's name does not appear in the article. See Robert Coughlan, "The Chemical Mind Changers," *Life*, March 15, 1963, 81. © John Loengard/Time Life Pictures/Getty Images

explained. "Typical evidence" of the drug's "astonishing positive psychological effects" was the Good Friday Experiment, described over several paragraphs without mention of Leary's name. After a few pages of drawings and descriptions of psychedelic experiences, the writer blamed the public interest in LSD on Huxley's *Doors of Perception* and the activities of Leary and Alpert. "Such publicity . . . might have the final unhappy result of making the whole subject taboo," he complained. "Are hallucinogens, particularly LSD, really revolutionary drugs which can expand man's consciousness and lead him toward new horizons of health and happiness? Only further controlled experiments can answer the question finally."[122]

A stream of articles drawing all sorts of weird connections to LSD reflected the drug's growing salience, at least to journalists. The *Saturday Review* (1963 circulation 298,000), which nine years earlier published excerpts from *The Doors of Perception* excised of discussions of mysticism or drug fantasy, in 1963 offered a first-person account of an LSD trip without any mention of LSD advocates' startling claims. Following a reasonably pleasant hallucinogenic experience, the author said that he experienced several days of depression and apathy, followed by weeks of jumpiness and occasional hallucinations. After months of relying on barbiturates for sleep, the writer said that he recovered. "But if the condition I had was schizophrenia, my sympathy for those so afflicted has been increased many times," the article, "They Split My Personality," concluded.[123] At the opposite extreme was Gerald Heard's 1964 article in the arts magazine *Horizon* (circulation n.a.) that answered the question, "Can This Drug Enlarge Man's Mind?" with an unambiguous yes.[124] There was no mention of Leary in that article, either. In 1964, *Sports Illustrated* (1964 circulation 1 million) talked about a marine biologist's proposal to drop LSD in lakes so researchers could count the confused fish that surfaced. In 1965, *Newsweek* (1965 circulation 1.7 million) introduced an item about an architect who took LSD to design a "better" mental institution with doggerel from Huxley and Humphry Osmond, a story also covered in the *New York Times*,[125] while *Harper's* (1965 circulation 279,000) published an article by Sidney Cohen about the use of LSD to ease the pain of dying.[126] *Missiles and Rockets* (1965 circulation 45,000) reported that scientists gave LSD to monkeys to replicate the disorientating sensations of space travel.[127]

An increasing number of television and radio appearances of LSD also reflected its growing prominence in mass culture. In September 1963, guests on David Susskind's nationally syndicated late-night talk show *Open End* discussed the benefits and drawbacks of LSD and hypnosis.[128] In 1963, Leary and Alpert were booked to appear on a television show, *Tonight in Saint Louis,* on station KSD-TV, but their appearance was cancelled at the last minute by station management.[129] In 1964, Leary and another psychologist appeared on a late-morning radio talk show in New York to discuss the controversy over LSD.[130] Leary and Metzner appeared on an afternoon talk show, *For Your Information,* on WTOP in Washington, D.C., in 1965 to discuss the effects of LSD.[131] The following month, another psychologist appeared on a different Washington radio station, WMAL, to discuss LSD as "medicine's first mental x-ray."[132] In 1965, Peter Stafford, a writer sympathetic to the psychedelic movement, was interviewed on the New York radio station WBAI for the second broadcast in a series titled "The Age of Involvement."[133]

Around this time, LSD also made early appearances on entertainment television. In a 1965 episode of the socially conscious courtroom drama *The Defenders* titled "Fires of the Mind," father-and-son attorneys defend a Leary-like therapist accused of murder after one of his clients commits suicide. The elder attorney drops the case in disgust, while the son becomes interested, tries LSD, and is impressed by the experience of expanded consciousness. The film historian Stephen Bowie notes that the episode was remarkable "in its unwillingness to take as a given the idea that psychotropic drugs are harmful" and in its characters' descriptions of benefiting from them.[134] LSD also played a role in a 1965 episode of the CBS drama *The Doctors and the Nurses* titled "Last Rites for a Rag Doll," in which "experimentation with the new hallucinatory drug LSD leads to dramatic events."[135]

That same year, *March of Time,* the Time-Life arm that by this point was making documentaries for television, sponsored an hour-long program that covered much of the same territory as the *Life* series "Control of the Brain" two years earlier, but with less emphasis on LSD. "Frontiers of the Mind," aired in 1965, described contemporary research into brain science using electronics, with abundant footage of humans and animals reacting to stimulation from electrodes implanted in their brains. A five-minute segment in the second half of the show was devoted to LSD, including footage of three subjects describing their sensations while under the influence of the drug. "Similar, but less potent hallucinating drugs have been used for thousands of years," the voiceover by William Conrad explained. "To some, it is an experience of transcendental, even religious beauty. To others, it is a journey into hell." Cohen appeared in the documentary supervising the administration of LSD to two of the subjects. He warned:

> LSD is one of the most potent chemicals we know. It can unhinge a mind, it can cause depression which can culminate in suicide, prolonged psychotic reactions, paranoid states and so forth. We are finding that LSD and other drugs like it are coming onto the black market and that people who shouldn't have the drug are taking it under conditions that they shouldn't take it under and we are finding that a few of them are running into trouble. It would be as dangerous as driving a car blindfolded along one of our local freeways to use LSD casually and without proper precautions.

The next section of the documentary discussed military research with drugs that could someday be dropped in water supplies or sprayed from the air, but did not specify that LSD was being tested in this regard.[136] Cohen also provided commentary on a 1965 episode of the television program *Through the Looking Glass* about the reactions of an alcoholic patient undergoing LSD treatment.[137]

LSD was on the media agenda in the early 1960s, but as a cultural and scientific phenomenon rather than a political problem that called for a governmental response. While television was relatively slow to cover LSD, and newspapers were relatively restrained, popular magazines offered detailed portraits of the drug and the people using it. The activities of Leary, Alpert, and their small band of supporters were interesting and hardly seemed a threat to the public at large. Government officials rarely appeared in coverage. And while Leary was clearly controversial—his termination from Harvard, the first time a Harvard faculty member had been fired in at least a decade, was evidence of that—he did not seem like a criminal. Possession of LSD was not illegal. To many reporters, the fate of LSD seemed undecided, and psychedelic drug use seemed to introduce new problems for science, the humanities, and religion, as well as the law. *Time* and *Life,* in particular, presented LSD as a religious and scientific breakthrough, describing Leary's philosophy while avoiding his name and sidestepping the issue of LSD cultism that his behavior raised. By offering a seemingly responsible, mainstream alternative to Leary's proselytizing, coverage in *Time* and *Life* discouraged the impression that LSD was a problem demanding government action.

In the early 1960s, drug control in general barely registered on Americans' list of concerns. When Gallup asked Americans to name the most important problems facing the nation in a 1964 poll, the most common responses were "racial problems" and "international problems," unsurprising in the midst of the civil-rights movement and the cold war. Even when asked to name the cause for "the lack of respect for the law and the increased crime in the United States today," 41 percent of respondents cited "parents, home life." Only 2 percent mentioned drugs.[138] On the federal level, even in regard to drug control LSD was largely an afterthought. The only drugs specifically mentioned in the Drug Abuse Control Amendments of 1965, which created a Bureau of Drug Abuse Control within the FDA to license the sale and distribution of dangerous drugs, were amphetamines and barbiturates, although the bill was written to allow the secretary of the FDA to extend the law's reach to other stimulants, tranquilizers, and drugs with "hallucinogenic effect." Newspaper articles on the bill mentioned LSD only in passing, if at all.[139] Possession of drugs for personal use was specifically permitted under the law.[140]

Beyond the marvelous characteristics attributed to psychedelic experience, more than anything else it was probably the name "Timothy Leary" that became many Americans' first association with the drug. His stature as a foremost expert on LSD was sustained by media interest in his remarkable studies, and he offered reporters a clear vision where other researchers provided only tentative hopes and qualifications. While critical of Leary's behavior, journalists often allowed him to define the meaning and significance of the drug itself. The media fascination with Leary—and Leary's courting of media—made a celebrity of the former professor. Whether this helped or hindered the cause of "inner freedom" that he espoused is open to debate. Leary's prophetic manner, odd-ball behavior, and reckless prescriptions probably turned off more people than he turned on. "He's a very nice fellow. But no single individual can dominate a situation without rubbing many people the wrong way," Braden wrote.[141] Others were less charitable. "Some of the best friends of LSD are its worst enemies," Cohen wrote in the preface to a 1966 book in which Cohen debated the merits of LSD with Alpert, illustrated with the *Time* and *Life* photographer Lawrence Schiller's pictures of tripping volunteers. "In their way they have aborted much of the careful study of this most important agent. They have managed to shock the citizenry to the point that all hope of safely, cautiously and gradually introducing the psychedelics into our culture is lost."[142] An exasperated Huxley complained, "I am very fond of Tim—but why, oh why, does he *have* to be such an ass?"[143]

In 1965, newspaper and magazine articles about increasing drug use on college campuses and by middle-class youth obliquely raised the issue of LSD in a more threatening context. Near the start of the year, articles in the *New York Times* relayed official concerns that youthful marijuana use would lead to narcotics addiction and that university administrators were quietly fretting about expanding drug use.[144] Attention increased as the year went by. "As students return to colleges and universities across the nation, investigators from the Federal Bureau of Narcotics and of the Food and Drug Administration will try to head off what some fear is becoming the latest student craze: drug taking," wrote the *Washington Post*'s Leonard Downie Jr. in a front-page article picked up by newspapers across the nation in September.[145] "College Crowd Going to Pot," the *Boston Globe* headlined a November 1965 column by the syndicated columnist Jack Anderson that also described the results of a Narcotics Bureau survey of the situation at fifty universities.[146] In 1965, the *Los Angeles Times* published two articles in which Cohen warned that the increasing use of LSD by college and high-school students was resulting in instances of long-term, negative psychological consequences, one on the front page.[147]

But to most reporters, LSD seemed like a small aspect of a larger youth drug problem. In December 1965, a five-page *Saturday Evening Post* (1965 circulation 6.6 million) report on "The Thrill Pill Menace," subtitled "Illicit Drugs Are Hooking the Nation's Youth and Creating a Vast New Industry in the Underworld," included only a one-sentence mention of LSD.[148] One journalist who deeply explored the phenomenon of collegiate drug use was the nonfiction stylist Michael Herr, who in 1965 visited colleges across the country to grapple, not entirely successfully, with the reasons for the casual pot, psychedelic, and amphetamine use he observed. Herr reported in *Mademoiselle* (1965 circulation

605,000) an "authentic underground" of students who took drugs for serious inquiry, and "a religion of LSD," but the students he talked to either knew little about drugs or considered them a casual escape.[149]

While the transcendental and mystical aspects of LSD had preoccupied many magazine writers, the actual motives of many LSD users were not all that lofty. Just as the serious and scholarly experiments with LSD by intellectuals in Los Angeles degenerated into increasingly recreational use, the same motives emerged as the drug spread to other groups. According to one study published in 1964, most patients who took LSD at a "religious-medical center" described their motivation as "self-knowledge," but the younger, black-market users, who characteristically took LSD with other drugs in party settings, appeared to have been mostly looking for a good time. Among black-market users, "one finds the most cited motive the desire for aesthetic enhancement, coupled with self-enhancement, curiosity, and, implicit but not always explicit, the search for a new kind of 'high,' 'kicks,' or euphoria," a team of sociologists observed.[150] Similarly, Todd Gitlin wrote that the 1960s counterculture claimed ideological motives in its embrace of psychedelic drugs, but they soon became just another substance used for recreation, relaxation, and escape, a "chemical form of instant gratification, reproducing the larger culture's reliance on tranquilizers, alcohol and other sanctioned drugs."[151]

If the mystical and transcendental drug experiences depicted in media were not replicated by drug users, they still seemed to be effective advertising. In 1966, a group of LSD researchers conducted a survey to measure the impact of "sensational" publicity in such magazines as *Playboy, The Reporter,* and the *Saturday Evening Post* on recruitment of volunteers for experiments. Most of the nineteen researchers who responded to the survey disclosed that volunteers were at least as numerous following the publicity, but the number of "appropriate" volunteers had declined. Many now volunteered in hope that the drug would help them solve personal problems, and more viewed their participation as potentially dangerous. The survey also indicated that many who stepped forward since the spate of publicity were lured by a "promise of nirvana."[152]

CHAPTER 6

Moral Panic and Media Hype, 1966–1968

Drugs seemed to be on everyone's mind in the late 1960s. Marijuana, not LSD, was the drug of choice in college dorms and hippie pads across the country. A new familiarity with marijuana budding from its new popularity with upper- and middle-class youth undermined the legacy of antimarijuana campaigns of the 1930s. There was a growing acceptance by journalists and the public that pot was mild in effect, nonaddictive, and problematic chiefly to the extent that it could lead to more dangerous drugs. No longer did marijuana seem to invariably lead to antisocial behavior, violence, and mental deterioration, and the momentum of the federal government was swinging toward reduced penalties for marijuana use. In 1967, articles in *Life* (circulation 7.4 million), *Newsweek* (circulation 1.9 million), *Look* (circulation 7.7 million), *The Nation* (circulation 29,000), and the *New Republic* (circulation 120,000) questioned the wisdom of marijuana prohibition, reportedly leading to the paranoid hippie complaint, "Man, are you aware there's a *conspiracy* in the magazines to make pot legal?"[1] Even Harry Anslinger, who retired as narcotics commissioner at the age of seventy in 1962, conceded that the criminal penalties for marijuana use were too severe for young offenders.[2]

A number of factors encouraged journalists to look toward LSD, rather than marijuana, to explain the youthful fascination with illicit drugs. Hundreds of mental-hospital admissions vividly demonstrated that drug's danger, and there was by now a thick stack of newspaper and magazine articles demonstrating its appeal. In contrast to the relatively mundane effects reported by pot smokers, conveying the otherworldly significance of an LSD trip still remained an artistic and literary opportunity. The existence of a philosophy and star-studded cultural history also encouraged journalists wishing to explain the larger phenomenon of drug use to look toward LSD. As in the old joke about the drunk found searching under a lamppost for the keys he dropped across the street—"The light is better here"—reporters who wanted to understand illicit drug use often looked at LSD because the experience was so well illuminated.

And no other drug was promoted by as colorful and quotable an advocate as Timothy Leary. He was constantly in the news in the spring of 1966, not always in the manner of his choosing. Since December 1965, he had faced drug charges after being caught with a small amount of marijuana while crossing the border to Texas. Articles about his trial and conviction the following March were in newspapers from coast to coast.[3] In April, a police force led by the Dutchess County assistant prosecutor (and future Watergate "plumber," federal inmate, and talk-show host) G. Gordon Liddy raided the Millbrook, New York, estate where Leary and assorted long- and short-term guests lived, and Leary was again arrested. "The ensuing media coverage of the bust went far beyond any press agent's wildest dream," Leary's biographer Robert Greenfield wrote.[4] As well as chronicling legal battles, newspapers published articles specifically explaining—or rebutting—Leary's claims. "LSD Ties with Happiness Declared Hokum," declared the *Los Angeles Times* in the headline over a 1966 front-page article contrasting Leary's assertions with those of "serious scientists."[5] An article in the *New York Times,* also illustrated with a photograph of Leary, declared, "LSD: A Fascinating Drug and a Growing Problem."[6]

Despite the controversy surrounding him—or because of it—journalists remained interested in what Leary had to say. He was constantly on television and radio in the spring of 1966. A week before he testified in front of a U.S. Senate subcommittee investigating marijuana and LSD use on college campuses in May, WKCR radio in New York carried a half-hour press conference with Leary.[7] The next day, Leary participated in a twenty-five-minute "news close-up" on New York radio WNEW featuring him and two other LSD users.[8] Days after testifying to the senators, Leary was on an episode of the nationally syndicated talk show *Open End,* "The Thrill and the Threat of LSD," with a panel that included Humphrey Osmond and a physician concerned about the drug's risks.[9] In June he was interviewed for a documentary, *The Kick Seekers ... Washington's Drug Problem,* that aired in Washington, D.C.[10] He was familiar enough to parody. At the end of June, an LSD prophet who had to employ a "reality sitter" during infrequent periods of clarity appeared in a sketch on Mort Sahl's Los Angeles television show.[11]

Outside of the talk format, LSD made only occasional appearances in broadcast news and entertainment programming in the late 1960s.[12] A 1966 *CBS Reports* documentary, narrated by Charles Kuralt, explored LSD therapy at a Maryland mental hospital. "The potential scientific uses of lysergic acid diethylamide were vividly demonstrated . . . in a way that also underscored the hazards of the drug," according to one reviewer.[13] In 1967, WGBH in Boston aired a debate between Leary and the MIT professor Jerome Lettvin over the merits of LSD. Leary sat cross-legged in front of the packed hall of MIT students, lit a candle, and sermonized that LSD brought individuals to a more profound understanding of the world and that dropping out was a rational response to a "menopausal" society, while colorful, disjointed imagery was displayed on the screen at his back.[14] In an article about the debate that appeared about a week before it was broadcast, the *Boston Globe* declared that Lettvin's rebuttal that LSD diminished reason won the day, trumpeting his one-word retort to Leary's claim that druglike hallucination was the hallmark of the visionary mystic: "Bull . . . !!"[15]

That journalists were outwardly skeptical about Leary was less surprising than the fact that they were willing to air his views at all. In contrast to the tradition in reporting on narcotics and other drugs, outright advocacy for psychedelic drug use and exaltation of psychedelic experience remained within the realm of permissible public discourse. Literary and philosophical musings about LSD that percolated through mass media over the previous decade established precedent for discussing this drug in ways that would have been simply unacceptable for others. Although LSD was increasingly described in a context of law enforcement and black-market, recreational use, the regular appearance of LSD advocates in the news and the continued discussion of their views sustained the impression that the use of LSD was still up for debate.

Leary hit the front pages of newspapers from coast to coast on May 14, 1966, after he told the U.S. Senate subcommittee investigating campus drug use that one-third of all college students were using the drug, certainly an exaggeration. LSD had "eerie power to release ancient energies from the brain, I would say even sacred energies," Leary told the subcommittee. He prescribed college courses instructing students in the safe psychedelics use, predicting that such classes "would end the indiscriminate use of LSD and be the most popular and productive courses ever offered." The senators seemed baffled. "I've been continually confused by your testimony," Senator Edward M. Kennedy complained following Leary's opening statement.[16] Confusion did not immediately translate into official hostility. In the session featuring Leary's testimony, the subcommittee consultant who helped direct questioning allowed that the drug advocates were earnest in their convictions. "He did not think 'we want to criticize the drug out of existence,'" the *New York Times* reported, along with Leary's testimony.[17] Ten days later, the head of the FDA urged the senators not to change the law to make LSD illegal. "It would automatically place maybe 10 percent or hundreds of thousands of college students in the category of criminals," newspapers reported Dr. James L. Goddard as saying. "I would hate to see them charged with a crime."[18]

In April 1966, Sandoz, still the only legal manufacturer of LSD, announced that it would cease distribution of the drug and recalled all supplies from investigators. Even studies approved by the FDA were brought to a halt. The announcement took place a week after a highly publicized case in which a New York man named Stephen Kessler claimed that LSD made him kill his mother.[19] Within days of each other in May 1966, California and New York passed laws making possession of LSD a crime.[20] Apparently satisfied by assurances that the new Bureau of Drug Abuse Control would clamp down on illegal manufacture and distribution of LSD, the senators did not amend federal law to make possession of LSD a federal crime.[21]

Shortly after testifying to the Senate subcommittee, Leary consulted with the communications theorist Marshall McLuhan over lunch at the Plaza Hotel in New York for a critique of his performance. McLuhan had achieved an unlikely degree of celebrity for gnostic prophesies such as "The medium is the message," contained in his 1964 bestseller *Understanding Media.* Although many found McLuhan's aphoristic writing exasperating, on Madison Avenue he was revered as a prophet.[22] There was an affinity between Leary's view of drugs as mind-expanding and McLuhan's view that media operates as an extension of human consciousness. Both perceived that society was in the midst of transformation. For McLuhan, it was the eclipse of over-rational print culture by the immersive, sensory experience of television.[23] For Leary, it was mind-expanding drugs triggering "a revolution of consciousness" by exposing the shallowness of social roles and expectations imposed by the older generation.[24] Both were attuned to Leary's role as a product pitchman.

In a 1983 book, Leary recalled McLuhan's advice:

"Dreary Senate hearings and courtrooms are not the platforms for your message, Tim. You call yourself a philosopher, a reformer. Fine. But the key to your work is advertising. You're promoting a product. The new and improved acceler-

ated brain. You must use the most current tactics for arousing consumer interest. Associate LSD with all the good things that the brain can produce—beauty,
fun, philosophic wonder, religious revelation, increased intelligence, mystical
romance. . . .

"To dispel fear you must use your public image. You are the basic product
endorser. Whenever you are photographed, smile. Wave reassuringly. Radiate
courage. Never complain or appear angry. It's okay if you come off as flamboyant and eccentric. You're a professor, after all. But a confident attitude is the best
advertisement. You must be known for your smile."[25]

Leary listened. As the journalist Don Lattin pointed out, countless news photographs taken in the three decades since show Leary with a radiant smile,
regardless of circumstances.[26]

McLuhan also gave Leary the inspiration, and almost certainly the actual
words, for a catchphrase to market his idea. In his 1983 book, Leary wrote
that he spent several days thinking about McLuhan's advice, including an acid
trip analyzing "the packaging of American revolutions: 'Give Me Liberty or
Give Me Death,' 'A Nation Cannot Exist Half Slave and Half Free,' 'We Have
Nothing to Fear but Fear Itself.' 'Lucky Strike Means Fine Tobacco.'" Leary
wrote that one morning in the shower, the phrase "turn on, tune in, drop out"
came to mind.[27] But in an undated interview with the journalist Neil Strauss,
Leary explained: "I actually didn't invent that. That slogan was given to me by
Marshall McLuhan. I was having lunch with him in New York City. He was
very much interested in ideas and marketing, and he started singing something like, 'Psychedelics hit the spot / Five hundred micrograms, that's a lot,'
to the tune of a Pepsi commercial. Then he started going 'Turn on, Tune in,
Drop out.'"[28] There were obvious reasons why Leary, who frequently ignored
inconvenient facts and was prone to self-mythologizing, might assume credit
for the phrase, and why McLuhan, a working academic, might not. McLuhan,
who died in 1980, did not appear to have written about the meeting with Leary.
"Turn on, tune in, drop out" also appeared to echo the headline to a January
31, 1966, article in *The Nation* (1966 circulation 28,000), "Drugs on Campus:
Turned on and Tuned out."[29]

The phrase was in tune with the times. Turning on and tuning in, with radios
and televisions, were activities with which Americans had become increasingly familiar. The phrase was consistent with McLuhan's vision of humans
extending their consciousness by accessing new types of experience offered
by technology, and his conviction that this cultural shift should be embraced.
Like McLuhan's other famous catchphrase, "The medium is the message," the

LSD slogan emphasized the impact of engagement with the technology without commenting on the messages it ostensibly contained.

Like many LSD-inspired pronouncements, "turn on, tune in, drop out" seemed to capture a great thought that under closer examination seemed so vague or general as to be meaningless. As with other great advertising slogans—think Nike's "Just do it" or "Be a Pepper"—meaning was entirely dependent on context. And like other slogans, it sank deeply into the American lexicon. Leary professed to be flattered that in the 1960s, Squirt soda advertised, "turn on to flavor, tune in to sparkle, and drop out of the cola rut," while the evangelist Billy Graham announced a crusade with the theme, "turn on to Christ, tune in to the Bible, and drop out of sin." In April 1968, *Mad* magazine lampooned hippies in an issue titled "Turn on, Tune in, Drop Dead," the third phrase being a signature *Mad* expression.[30]

As Leary expounded on the slogan over the following decades, he often claimed that "turning on" did not exclusively refer to using drugs. His first public use of the phrase may have been at a lecture in Boston about a week after his Senate subcommittee testimony. The *Boston Globe* reported that "Leary explained that he wanted people to set an example to their 'old Auntie Mamie' by 'turning on' and 'tuning in' to the nobler aspects of life without using drugs. They should also 'drop out' or detach themselves from meaningless living and senseless conflict with the older generation."[31] In what biographer Robert Greenfield dismissed as "a calculated strategy designed to curry favor with the establishment," Leary also called for a one-year moratorium on LSD to allow young people and their elders to work out their differences.[32]

This conciliatory, non-drug interpretation of "turn on, tune in, drop out" was not how it typically was received. According to the *Oxford English Dictionary*, "turn on" entered the lexicon as "a drug-taker's 'trip'" around 1969, a few years after the slogan was introduced.[33] The religious scholar Huston Smith, whom Leary had introduced to psychedelic drugs a few years earlier, criticized the slogan, and "drop out" in particular, for encouraging people to leave jobs and school while failing to present an alternative to the status quo. "The slogan is too negative to command respect," he wrote.[34] Leary perceived otherwise, writing in his 1983 book, "*Drop Out* suggested an active, selective graceful process of detachment from voluntary and involuntary commitments."[35] But again, this was probably not what his audience heard. In January 1967, Leary riffed on the slogan from the stage of the Gathering of Tribes for a Human Be-In in San Francisco, a signature event of the hippie counterculture for which Leary received top billing. "Drop out of high school. Drop out of college," the High Priest said. "Drop out, junior executive. Drop out, senior executive. Turn on, tune in, drop out."[36]

Moral Panic

As the Senate subcommittee held hearings on campus drug use, legislatures in New York and California rushed to institute anti-LSD laws, and government and health officials issued statements and calls for action. Journalists covered it all with avid fascination. In the atmosphere of heightened concern about LSD, even minor arrests or injuries that could be related to LSD seemed newsworthy. As in the 1930s, law enforcement opened its files to journalists, offering a diet of violence and mayhem. "If you changed a few nouns in any of the anti-marijuana stories of the thirties, you ended up with a reasonable facsimile of the standard 'LSD madness' story as it began appearing in the spring of 1966," wrote the journalist and social historian Jay Stevens.[37] Fraught warnings about medical side effects from LSD began appearing in 1967, following the publication in the journal *Science* (1967 circulation 121,000) of a poorly designed study that linked LSD with birth defects. "Within twenty-four hours, news of the study had swept the country like wildfire," wrote a pair of sociologists who studied the episode as a moral panic.[38]

In retrospect, the concerns were overblown. The most widely repeated horror stories were false or misleading, and none of the medical side effects associated with LSD materialized. To this day, no physiological side effects from LSD have been found. Hospital admissions as a result of LSD use have been relatively rare since the 1970s, when the federal government began systematically collecting statistics.[39] Bad LSD freak-outs may have been more common in the 1960s than in subsequent decades because drug users and medical first responders were less familiar with how to manage the drug effect. Freak-outs certainly *seemed* more common, with headlines such as "Mystery of a Nude Coed's Fatal Fall," "Naked in a Rose Bush," and "Strip Teasing Hippie Goes Wild in Lakespur on LSD," turning up in one author's survey of articles about LSD in a newspaper morgue.[40] Searches of electronic archives revealed that in New York, Boston, Chicago, and Los Angeles, LSD was in newspapers nearly every day in the spring of 1966, in articles about crime, legislation, culture, or medicine.

Sensational and exaggerated stories about LSD seemed true because they had the aura of what Stephen Colbert might call "truthiness": even while collapsing under close examination, they seemed true because they felt right. Erich Goode and Nachman Ben-Yehuda rooted this feeling in the moral expectation that those who broke society's rules would be punished:

> The media reported these stories—irresponsibly we now know, and probably should have known then—because they knew these stories were newsworthy, both from their professional judgment and what they surmised the public's reaction would be, and not because they were trying to force them on the public's

attention. They were news because they corresponded to the media representatives' definition of what's news (tell a good story, introduce the human interest angle, tell a story with a specific audience in mind) and because publishers, editors and journalists realized the public would find these stories interesting. They didn't check their sources; they assumed these claims to be true because of the prevailing sentiment of the times. Both media representatives and the public should have been able to look around them and see that these claims were bogus. These stories were appealing and credible because they corresponded with what these new, and newly deviant, drugs were supposed to do. . . . These now classic drug-related stories took on an energy not merely from their putative material threat but also from the fact that they introduced a moral dimension to their subjects and topics.[41]

The most popular stories contained aspects of poetic justice. It seemed particularly suiting that college students who took drugs to see mystical wonders would come to ruin by staring at the sun, or that the terrific effects claimed of LSD would come at a terrible cost. As they hyped LSD, journalists echoed and amplified stories that appeared to convey these larger truths, even while the particular details of the stories might often have seemed, as the newsroom expression goes, "too good to check."

The stories that had the greatest currency were not products of journalistic enterprise but rather were created (in some cases out of whole cloth) by political figures and officials of professional groups seeking to capitalize on the widespread public interest. Officials who promoted these stories, like the journalists who covered them, may have been earnest in their concern, but the histories of several of the most prominent LSD horror stories illustrate how they also advanced personal agendas. One public official who capitalized on the media interest in LSD was the Brooklyn district attorney Aaron E. Koota, remembered for a "penchant for publicity and controversy" in his *New York Times* obituary, who in 1966 was in the middle of his first term.[42] "I know I have been criticized, called a headline-hunter," said Koota, whose background was in prosecuting organized crime, "but I am convinced there are times when a District Attorney must use the newspapers to awaken the community to a menace in its midst, even before he has collected enough evidence to prosecute anybody."

In April 1966, days after calling on legislators in Albany to pass a law banning LSD, Koota invited reporters to his Brooklyn office to announce that his office was investigating reports that the drug was being made in city schools. The district attorney had set up a tip line and a special post-office box to take complaints. "If [the schools] need any help, any expert guidance or advice so as to prevent the possibility of students using the facilities of the school for the manufacture of LSD, we stand ready to help or guide them," Koota told the *New York Times,* and repeated in an appearance on local TV.[43] City principals and the presidents of the three city colleges in Brooklyn said that they were aware of no evidence to back the charge, which Koota said was based on letters from parents.[44] The charge was never substantiated.

Koota simultaneously advanced two prosecutions that were widely reported at the time and lingered for years in magazine articles about LSD: the case of five-year-old Donna Wingenroth, a Brooklyn girl who ate an LSD-impregnated sugar cube left in the house by her eighteen-year-old uncle and was rushed to the hospital; and of Stephen Kessler, a thirty-year-old medical student who claimed not to remember killing his mother-in-law because he was on LSD. As in the earlier stories of marijuana-induced murder, the responsibility of LSD for these tragedies was ambiguous: children eat all sorts of poisons left around their homes, and Kessler had been in and out of mental institutions for years. His claim that LSD had caused a three-day bout of amnesia was unprecedented in scientific literature about the drug. At trial, it emerged that Kessler's LSD use took place a month before the murder, and he claimed to be drunk on sleeping pills and alcohol at the time of the crime.[45] A jury eventually found Kessler not guilty by reason of insanity, and Koota dropped charges against Wingenroth's uncle because the poisoning was clearly unintentional.[46]

The *New York Times* covered these episodes extensively—more than a half-dozen articles about Kessler's arrest and trial, and three articles about Wingenroth— because they seemed to engage with moral concerns about LSD, and because the Brooklyn district attorney was making the announcements. Because they did seem such vivid demonstrations of the horrors of LSD, the stories of Kessler and Wingenroth were covered in other newspapers and repeated in magazine articles that hammered on the moral themes. *Newsweek* (1966 circulation 1.8 million) made "pitiful" five-year-old Donna's ordeal the primary subject of two stories, one leading to warnings about increasing LSD use on campus, the other informing readers that "the case against LSD steadily mounts."[47] *Newsweek* also ran two stories primarily about Kessler, one a description of the crime that led to a call for greater regulation of LSD, and a shorter piece about the New York jury's verdict.[48] In *Time* (1966 circulation 3.1 million), both Kessler and Wingenroth were introduced in a single 1966 story on "The Dangers of LSD" that also led to a brief discussion of the need for more effective LSD control.[49] The *New York Times Magazine* (1966 circulation 1.4 million) and *Reader's Digest* (1966 circulation 15.6 million) included the episodes as in the LSD cabinet of horrors.[50] They were described in the *New Republic* (1966 circulation 108,000) as well, but in a context critical of Koota's role in whipping up interest in both cases.[51]

Among the newspaper articles describing freak-outs and mental-hospital admissions related to LSD, there was a special place for articles about college students getting so high they went blind from staring at the sun. In May 1967, newspapers across the country published an Associated Press article, date-lined Santa Barbara, that said four such cases were brought to the attention of the local ophthalmological society.[52] The episode caught the attention of *Time* (1967 circulation 3.5 million). "Under LSD they could do this for three or four minutes, hardly squinting and feeling no pain, so their eyes were wide open to the sun's infra-red rays, and the macula, the point of clearest vision in the retina, was badly burned," explained the magazine in a brief article, titled "More Bad Trips on LSD," that also described two cases of LSD-DUI in Los Angeles.[53] The anecdote appeared a few months later in the classroom magazine *Senior Scholastic* (circulation n.a.) in an article that quoted "most medical authorities" as saying that "LSD is 'one of the most dangerous drugs on the illicit market—more dangerous than heroin—because a single dose can cause permanent mental derangement.'"[54]

The blindness story surfaced again in January 1968, when the Associated Press moved a similar account, published in newspapers across the country, this time about six students from a college in eastern Pennsylvania.[55] *Newsweek* (1968 circulation 2.1 million) reported:

> "It's a real tragedy," Norman M. Yoder of Pennsylvania's state welfare department said sadly. "And the parents are asking, 'How can something like this happen?'" It can, and it did, happen this way. Six young men—all college juniors studying for nice careers in engineering, all "nice kids, not hippies"—slipped out into a woodland clearing a half-mile from their campus in western Pennsylvania and tripped out on LSD. Then the six nice kids flopped on their backs in the grass and each, in a trance roughly akin to a fit of catalepsy, gazed unblinkingly up into a blazing springtime sun. Though each had sampled LSD at least once before, classmates got worried and went looking for them. Six hours after the trip began, they found the six kids, all still in the clearing—and all totally, permanently, and helplessly blind.[56]

Except that they weren't. Three days before *Newsweek* published the item, the governor of Pennsylvania declared the report a hoax perpetrated by Yoder out of apparent concern for youthful LSD use. Newspapers covered the retraction, as did *Time,* sharing ophthalmologists' doubts that LSD could really overcome the reflexive urge to blink.[57] *Newsweek* ran a scolding letter to the editor. "As you must be painfully aware by now, the entire affair was the ill-conceived hoax of individuals who possibly share your zealotry for evoking before the public's terror-charged eyes the many perils presumably awaiting the hallucinogenic traveler," the letter read.[58] The California and Pennsylvania cases are now judged to be hoaxes, but at least two articles in peer-reviewed journals subsequently described treatment of individuals who appear to have suffered ocular damage from bright sunlight while under the influence of LSD.[59]

Along with repeating horrific anecdotes, monthly magazines offered vague and exaggerated assessments of LSD's danger. "Until an enormous number of disturbing mysteries are unraveled by scientists, LSD will remain about as safe as a do-it-yourself brain-surgery kit for amateurs," a 1966 article in *Reader's Digest* (1966 circulation 15.6 million) concluded after a series of credible anecdotes about LSD tragedies, including a Los Angeles student who got hit by a motor vehicle and a forty-two-year-old woman who committed suicide after coworkers slipped the drug into her drink.[60] In other articles emphasizing risks from LSD, journalists seemed less concerned with factual accuracy than dramatically pressing a point. "There was a report, for example, of a man hospitalized after he had drilled a hole into his skull with a dentist's drill while under the influence of LSD, believing that this would cause him to break out of ordinary time and enter into another dimension," offered a 1967 article in *Parent's Magazine and Better Homemaking* (1967 circulation 2 million) titled "LSD: A Growing Menace to Teenagers."[61] A critical editor might wonder how a confused acidhead got his hands on a dental drill. That no names, dates, or locations were included contributed to the apocryphal feel. The urge to use anti-LSD evidence that was just beyond verification infected even Edward M. Brecher, the celebrated science writer and later author of the levelheaded *Consumers Union Guide to Licit and Illicit Drugs* (1972), which advocated for drug-law reform.[62] To make a case about the danger of LSD in a 1967 article for *McCall's* (1967 circulation 8.6 million) titled "LSD: Danger to Unborn Babies," Brecher included unpublished research by a college junior purporting to demonstrate that the drug caused birth defects in rats.[63]

Concrete evidence against LSD seemed to emerge early in 1967, when the State University of New York in Buffalo geneticist Maimon Cohen decided to examine the chromosomes of LSD users after wandering through the Haight-Ashbury neighborhood of San Francisco. In 1967, he published a study in the peer-reviewed journal *Science* (1967 circulation 121,000) reporting that when human blood cells were placed in a culture containing LSD, some of the chromosomes within the blood cells seemed to break. As well, blood cells of a single schizophrenic patient who had been given LSD fifteen times were found to have more broken chromosomes than normal. The man had also been treated with Librium and Thorazine.[64]

The possibility that the drug caused genetic damage revived memories of the thalidomide disaster, which unfolded over eight months in 1962 with waves of reports of women giving birth to deformed babies from countries where the sedative was widely used. Major newspapers across the country published the news that LSD had been linked to birth defects in March 1967, and over the following months reported on subsequent studies that seemed to confirm the effect. *Time* (1967 circulation 3.5 million) covered studies suggesting that LSD could cause chromosomal damage and birth defects, although qualifying the findings as preliminary.[65] Other publications projected more certainty. A story about the research in *U.S. News and World Report* (1967 circulation 1.5 million) ran under the subhead, "The Truth about LSD Is Coming Out, and It Is a Tragic Story."[66] With a psychedelic cover showing a young woman's blank face over a swirl of indigo and blue (see figure 10), the *Saturday Evening Post* (1967 circulation 6.9 million) revealed "The Hidden Evils of LSD" in an article that began with a list of unnamed people with horrible medical conditions—a deformed baby, incurable bone cancer, bone-breaking epileptic seizures—allegedly caused by the drug. "If you take LSD even once, your children may be born malformed or retarded," warned a pullout from the main text.[67] The *Washington Post* published an article linking a baby born with "faulty intestines and a misshapen head" to LSD, crediting the information to the *Saturday Evening Post* article. "Worse Deformities Feared in LSD than Thalidomide," was the headline. "To the hippies such cases are accidents best not to report, since they may close off the sources of LSD," the article explained.[68] Three months later, newspapers across the country published an Associated Press article about "the first documented case of a baby born with birth defects after her mother had taken LSD during pregnancy," prompted by the publication of a case study in the British medical journal *The Lancet*.[69] Fears that the drug triggered mental breakdowns and caused birth defects were sensationalized to melodramatic effect in a 1968 story in *Modern Romances* (1968 circulation 760,000), "One Taste of Evil . . . One Taste of LSD; That Wild and Sickening Night at the Party Led to Months of Fear and Agony" (see figure 11).[70]

Within four years of the publication of the first study of the effect of LSD on chromosomes in *Science,* nearly one hundred scientific studies were published examining links between LSD and chromosomal damage. The flurry of studies about LSD and chromosomes had several flaws in common: inadequate control over factors known to result in chromosome breakage; failure to conduct before-and-after observation in human subjects; the use of far higher amounts of LSD

Figure 10. While the background is entrancing, the blank expression on the young woman's face suggests danger beyond the bliss. The August 12, 1967, edition of the *Saturday Evening Post* included the article by Bill Davidson, "The Hidden Evils of LSD." Photograph © SEPS licensed by Curtis Licensing Indianapolis, Ind. All rights reserved.

for the test-tube experiments than would normally be consumed; and lack of proof that damage to cells in a test tube translates to negative health effects. Also suspicious was the absence of a significant number of deformed babies.[71] While researchers did report six cases of birth defects that may have been associated with LSD use, the number is unsurprising considering that the Centers

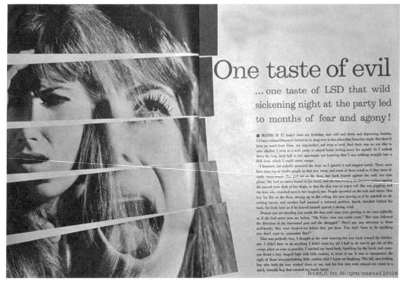

Figure 11. After eating an LSD-laced cookie at a party, the anonymous writer of the first-person story was hospitalized for two weeks in a state mental institution and tormented by fear that she would give birth to a deformed child. "One Taste of Evil . . . One Taste of LSD; That Wild and Sickening Night at the Party Led to Months of Fear and Agony," *Modern Romances,* September 1968, 26–27. Copyright © 1968, 2014 by Broadlit, Inc. All Rights Reserved.

for Disease Control estimates that 3 percent of infants born in America have some significant birth defect.[72] A review of the research published in *Science* in 1971 concluded that "pure LSD ingested in moderate doses does not produce chromosomal damage detectable by available methods."[73]

To sociologists who examined news-media coverage of LSD, reasonable concerns were overtaken by a moral reaction against what the drug represented. "Turn on, tune in, drop out" and boasts that psychedelic drugs would upend the status quo directly assaulted conservative social mores and, taken literally, society itself. LSD encapsulated beliefs that directly conflicted with social norms. "What with the supposed threat of cosmic revelations and an alternative world-view—which never panned out to begin with—the use of LSD seemed to possess a *distinctly deviant potential,*" Goode and Ben-Yehuda wrote.[74] News coverage at times took on a moral tone. As in the 1920s and 1930s, the words "evil" and "menace" appeared in magazine headlines. Magazines attributed hereditary physiological damage to LSD that, generations earlier, could have been described as damage to the "race."

Concern over negative reactions from LSD spread beyond those with moral qualms about drugs. In the summer of 1967, the *East Village Other,* an underground newspaper sympathetic to the "head" camp of 1960s counterculture,[75] ran a three-part series discussing the emerging evidence of chromosome damage linked to LSD. The articles each began by warning readers who actually *were* tripping to save their reading for later. Chromosomal damage was not "absolutely proven," one of the articles read. "Please do not conclude, however, that it is unlikely." It continued by informing women they could be tested for damage at Bellevue Hospital and provided a phone number. As for men, "that quota is nearly filled."[76] Each article ended with the author's affirmation of his belief in the value of psychedelic experience and a reminder that there were other psychedelic drugs, mescaline in particular. "Obviously, we need psychedelics as strong as LSD that are free of chromosomal side-effects. Obviously also, we who believe in the use of psychedelics must gather ourselves into some kind of chemical laboratory for research and experimentation. (If you are interested in such a project, contact PRL at EVO.)," concluded the last article in the series, a detailed review of the chromosome studies.[77] At nearly the same time, an article in the alternative *L.A. Free Press,* reprinted in the *Boston Avatar,* had a psychologist describing the psychodynamics resulting in immature "acid-heads" seeking psychological help. Psychological dangers aside, "[hallucinogens] should not be taken until we know much more about the later effects of their use on our bodies, especially the reproductive system," wrote the psychologist Arthur Janow, who became the author of the bestselling *The Primal Scream* (1970) and the best-known practitioner of a style of therapy of the same name.[78]

While widespread, the impact of the negative publicity on LSD use was short-lived and quickly overwhelmed by increasing numbers of first-time users. Observers wrote that the scare caused some LSD users to seek abortions, and caused others to temporarily quit LSD or switch to other drugs.[79] There were no systematic surveys of recreational drug use in the 1960s, and estimates of the prevalence of LSD were uncomfortably speculative and vague. However, an attempt to retroactively estimate hallucinogen use in the 1960s from responses on surveys conducted decades later indicated a generally upward trend.[80] In 1967, Woodstock, the iconic music festival that marked the furthest extension of hippie culture and featured entertainer Wavy Gravy's warnings to avoid the brown acid, was still two years away. After the acute fears died down, a more persistent effect on drug users may have been to discredit mass media as a source of information about their use.

Psychedelic Hype

In 1967, a physician who studied LSD complained, "[O]ver and over, [the communications media] have emphasized the ecstasies and hedonistic values of

LSD and underemphasized its enormous dangers."[81] Often, journalists sensationalized the benefits and dangers of LSD in the same article. In contrast with the tradition in reporting on the abuse of narcotics and illegal drugs, journalists did not feel compelled to omit potentially enticing information about LSD or avert readers' eyes from its allure. In earlier reporting on illicit drugs, publications typically demonstrated restraint by turning away at the moment the spike entered the vein or the smoke was inhaled. Not so with LSD. As well as describing the personal experiences of drug-trial volunteers and recreational users, journalists frequently reprised literary descriptions of drug trips from the 1950s and, less often, described their own experiences. Art was also frequently used to convey the drug experience. According to an article in *U.S. Camera* (1967 circulation 199,000), a magazine dedicated to photo hobbyists:

> Psychedelic experiences have been getting a lot of publicity of late. Almost every national publication has devoted at least part of an issue to discussion of the "hippie" movement and its experimentation with various mind-expanding or hallucinogenic drugs. Many thousands of words have been expended in an effort to describe the effects of LSD on the human mind, yet very few of these descriptions have done more than scratch the surface. The written word is simply too limited to explore fully the agonies and ecstasies of an acid joy-ride that are principally visual in effect.[82]

A photo feature on psychedelic art in *Horizon* (1968 circulation 154,000) similarly explained, "What a psychedelic artist tries to represent is the intense, ecstatic superdream in supertechnicolor that he has undergone through the use of a hallucinogenic drug—the inner landscape of the deeper self."[83]

Many magazines were also skeptical that prohibition was the correct response to the LSD fad. In 1966, the *New Republic* (1966 circulation 108,000), a generally left-leaning journal of opinion, published articles questioning the evidence of psychological damage from LSD use and the thin factual basis behind the hysteria raised by the Kessler and Wingenroth cases.[84] The magazine, which had published Alan Watts's conclusion that psychedelic drugs were "basically a religious problem, entitled to the same constitutional protection as freedom of worship" in 1964,[85] printed a commentary in 1967 by another former associate of Leary, Lisa Bieberman, who bemoaned the irresponsibility of Leary and his "corruption" of the term "psychedelic" from its serious philosophical and religious roots. "If the future of LSD is to be more wholesome than its past, it must be squarely recognized that the most publicized advocates of the psychedelic are its worst enemies. We cannot rely on them to fight our battles for us, whether it be for religious freedom, the right to do research, or the dissemination of accurate information. Flower power is no substitute for integrity."[86] While critical of Leary, the *New Republic* published articles critical of LSD prohibition in 1966 and again in 1968.[87]

The *Atlantic Monthly* also held hope that far-out promises of LSD might still be realized. In 1966, the magazine (1966 circulation 285,000) proposed that research with LSD might still bridge the "two cultures gap" between science and humanities bemoaned by prominent thinkers:

> Man is unique by virtue of being possessed by intuitions concerning the scope of the mysterious universe he inhabits. He has devised for himself all manner of instruments to probe the nature of this universe. Now at last, with the molecule of this strange acid, he has found an instrument which opens the inner eye of the mind and which may hopefully allow him to explore the vast interior spaces where the history of millions of years of memories lie entangled among the roots of the primordial self. Through it we may find a means of understanding more clearly the roots of madness and of helping the insane to return to the world of commonplace reality.[88]

The large-format family magazine *Look,* a direct competitor with *Life* and the *Saturday Evening Post,* viewed the growing use of psychedelic drugs within the context of a larger social movement as embodying a positive impulse to broaden human experience. While cautionary in its discussion of LSD, the magazine embraced the possibility that changes in human consciousness could evoke profound cultural change. In June 1966, the *Look* (1966 circulation 7.6 million) editor and writer George Leonard described a three-day Trips Festival in San Francisco, which attracted about ten thousand "students, businessmen, SNCC workers, fraternity boys, [and] motorcyclists" for an overwhelming sensory experience of music, lights, noise, and projected images that was billed as a simulation of an LSD trip. "The festival was meaningless in any terms today's culture can conjure up. It was a clumsy turning away from the past toward no one knows what. You could call it a failure, but you would have to call it a huge, splashy, California-style failure, shared by thousands of people. It is clear that all this reaching out toward an unknown future . . . adds up to a risk-filled business, evoking cautionary questions: Where is the California game taking us? Do we want to go there? Is there any way to stop it?"[89] Leonard, credited with being one of the first journalists to predict the 1960s counterculture, was thrilled by the possibilities, ultimately deciding that he would rather be a part of the movement than to merely report it. Leonard became a central figure at Esalen, a spiritual retreat and learning center outside of San Francisco, and a founder of the Human Potential movement. "We believe that all men somehow possess a divine potentiality; that ways may be worked out—specific, systematic ways—to help, not the few, but the many towards a vastly expanded capacity to learn, to love, to feel deeply and create," he and Esalen cofounder Michael Murphy wrote in 1968 for the *San Francisco Oracle*.[90] The *Oracle* was a frankly pro-LSD underground newspaper, founded out of a head shop in 1966 "to provide guidance and archetypes for the journey through the states of mind that the LSD experience had opened up; and to invent and examine the new social and cultural forms and institutions that needed to align the world with vision."[91]

The month after Leonard explored the California game, *Look* published a one-page article, "The Other Side of LSD: The Promise and the Peril," describing psychiatrists' hopes for a drug that "exerts fantastic effects upon man's most vital organ" and, in the author's view, the hopelessness of controlling a substance that was colorless, odorless, easily synthesized, and potent in miniscule amounts. The article was critical of new laws in New York and California prohibiting LSD and approved of federal authorities' judgment that prohibiting possession of the drug would make it more difficult to track down suppliers and less likely victims of bad LSD reactions would seek help. "What many of the world's leading authorities on LSD and other 'mind-affecting' drugs feared most has finally happened. A mood of public—and to an extent, professional—hysteria has been generated and is blocking legitimate scientific research on these substances," the article began. After discussing the effects of the drug and recent legal developments, the article went on, "If the current trend continues, vital discoveries bearing on the mind and its control may be left to scientists elsewhere."[92]

The following year, *Look* (1967 circulation 7.7 million) published a seventeen-page examination of "The Mounting Menace of Drug Abuse" whose title encompassed the nation's seemingly bottomless appetite for amphetamine and barbiturate pills, as well as the more youthful phenomena of marijuana and LSD. "Contrary to the claims of indescribable delights by some drug takers," most of those who abuse drugs do so to relieve some inner pain, the main article explained. "Fundamentally, drug abuse is a health and social problem, not a police problem. . . . The solution is education, not punishment," it concluded.[93] Another article in the package, by the senior editor Jack Shepard, described marijuana and LSD use at the University of Missouri in a tone that was generally sympathetic to the young drug users.[94] To better understand the college drug scene, Shepherd also took LSD himself, describing his trip in an off-campus college apartment in a page-long, chronological account of thoughts and sensations. "I wanted to take LSD. I wanted to see what it is like," Shepard explained by way of introduction. He found it profoundly disorienting, with delightful visual effects and moments of fear and alienation. Reflecting back on the experience, he wrote, "I'm more aware now of colors and patterns, of the way people get frightened and cut themselves off from each other. I think I know better what love is. I was alone and far from people I trust and love. I got cut off from everyone, including myself. College students take risky trips all the time. What's happening to them?"[95]

To *Look,* Leary had made himself a sideshow to the genuine social changes that were taking place. *Look*'s 1967 package on drug use included a visit to Leary at Millbrook, where he was living with about twenty-five disciples. It was titled "The Visions of Saint Tim":

> My own square's-eye view is that his impulses are sometimes deplorably rooted in vanity, a sad corruption of his considerable natural charm. (Impressionable adherents have confessed to experiencing a "contact high" without drugs, just from being in his presence.) However, Leary's intentions as a social critic, and even as a self-inspired chemical Moses, are probably sincere. And he cannot be blamed for inventing the drop-out phenomenon. Nevertheless, he can be taxed with silly, anti-adult broadsides, shamelessly seductive of a troubled-enough youth ("the wisest and holiest generation in history"). He is also both reckless and contradictory in his pushing of LSD. . . .
>
> In sum, I would say that like the Great Oz, Leary is not a bad man; just not a very good wizard.[96]

For the previous year, Leary had been pressing his message about the sacramental use of LSD with multimedia stage shows billed as psychedelic celebrations, featuring the former professor sermonizing over projected images and audio effects. Booked for a weekly three-month engagement in a former vaudeville theater in New York in 1966, it was described as a failure by *Look,* losing money at the box office, eliciting responses such as "fraud," "atrocious ham," and "unmitigated bore," and turning off even hippies who were predisposed to the message. Nevertheless, the theatrical efforts provided arresting images for *Look's* investigation of drugs, with color photographs conveying the former professor's fantastic depictions of psychedelic experience (see figure 12).[97]

Reviewers for other magazines, even magazines that were open to the "fruitful potentialities" of psychedelic drug use, in the words of the *New Yorker* (1966 circulation 467,000), were not impressed with Leary's off-Broadway show. The *New Yorker's* October 1966 "Notes and Comment" column observed, "Psychopharmacology is very much with us, and the business of altering states of feelings and awareness by the controlled use of drugs is, or ought to be, accepted as an imminent prospect," but deplored its careless and exaggerated description. "Before the present mumbo-jumbo about the utopiates grows any more turgid or gains any more hysterical momentum, the responsible and authoritative findings on them ought to be aired," concluded the commentary.[98] It was followed by a "Talk of the Town" item describing Leary's first celebration that quoted heavily from

Drugs and Mysticism

THE VISIONS OF "SAINT TIM"

By J. M. Flagler LOOK SENIOR EDITOR
Photographed by James H. Karales

Is TIMOTHY LEARY "the most evil man in America to-day," as some critics see him, or "a saint," as I have heard goggle-eyed adherents intone? To put the scene in-to perspective, in 1963, Leary was fired by Harvard Uni-versity after using students in controversial experiments with LSD, which causes hallucinations, not an advertised feature of the Harvard prospectus. Leary surfaced on a friendly estate in Millbrook, N.Y., proclaimed LSD a new kind of "sacrament," and went on to found the League for Spiritual Discovery, the first psychedelic religion. The cult has 25 resident disciples at Millbrook.

Recently, Leary hit the glory trail, combining "ser-mons" with mixed-media "light shows" in what he called "celebrations" of the drug's God-finding proper-ties. The coast-to-coast tour was not a triumph. While the light shows intrigued, Leary's own breathy preach-ments often evoked such responses as "fraud," "atro-cious ham," "unmitigated bore," and even disenchanted many predisposed hippies. The celebrations lost Leary $10,000 at the box office.

On the face of it, then, Leary seems but puny men-ace or paper savior. However, he enjoys unique visibil-ity in the LSD picture. Scientists charge his notoriety with thwarting serious LSD research. Heartbroken parents blame his "turn on, tune in, drop out" dictum for luring good students from school. Conversely, on campuses, even the nonalienated sentimentally defend "Uncle Tim's" right to hallow LSD and his attacks on society's soul-strangulating "tribal games." (The "academic game" is perhaps the renegade psychology teacher's pet peeve, after the "psychiatric game.") And a 30-year U.S. rap (now being appealed) for trying to spirit a few grains of marijuana across the Mexican border last year has given Leary the added appeal of martyr.

When I last saw Leary, a few weeks ago, he had just emerged—barefoot, serene and, as always, personally engaging—from the woods near his Millbrook head-quarters. He was wearing not the Hindu *dhoti* ensemble that he affects in public appearances, but simply a pair of earth-stained chinos. As we sat on steps before the many-towered, 60-room mansion—a Hudson River Gothic curiosity, its walls adorned with cabalistic Orien-tal art—that houses his cadre of League disciples, he ex-plained that he and his flock were all spending the sum-mer outdoors, "turning on." "The woods are very sen-sual," he confided. Having myself on occasion been an invited occupant of the mansion, the interior of which is most charitably described as an amiable but unhy-gienic shambles, I was inclined to see the move as salu-tary. I had once found myself dining off a kitchen side-board there along with two ravenous pussycats.

"I've dropped out completely myself," Leary went on to announce, plucking a leaf from his uncombed mane of curling hair. "I'm already an anachronism in the LSD movement, anyway. The Beatles have taken my place. That latest album—a complete celebration of LSD!"

Leary smilingly gave me his "the-whole-world-is-turning-on" look, with which I was by now familiar, but for which I had not always discovered substantiation. In fact, reports indicate that even marijuana-defending college youths are becoming —what else?—leery of LSD, as demonstrable horror stories accrue. Still, Leary—whose own 300-odd trips with LSD have seemingly left him with nothing worse clinically than an incurable case of optimism—can say that in ten years, not only will LSD be legal, but that its celebrants, through "public acts of beauty and humor," will be well on the way to having totally revamped society. My inclination is to respond, "Lots of luck." Society could certainly stand a lot of re-vamping. Reflecting upon the pastoral and dizzily dilap-idated home grounds of the League, though, I can't help but question whether lounging on old floor mattresses,

18 LOOK 8.8.67   continued

Wolf meets girl in Leary drama. Mix of slides, movies, strobe lights gives illusion of psychedelic "trip."

Figure 12. The 1967 article in *Look* takes a dim view of Timothy Leary's crusade to make a religion of LSD, but includes five pages of arresting images by James H. Karales of Leary's upstate New York retreat and his theatric show. The image on the left page shows a girl encountering a wolf in Leary's psychedelic drama. J. M. Flagler, "T Visions of Saint Tim," *Look,* August 8, 1967, 18–19. Photo by James Karales, copyright/courtesy: Estate of James Karales.

Prophet or phony?
An exotic scholar
makes a
religion of LSD.

scorner of limelight or candlelight, Leary does star turn in play. Here, with distaff disciples, he rehearses shadow sequence of episode titled, "All Girls Are Mine."

rling slide effects blur filmed dancers.

evangelist, Leary advises L.A. audience: "Turn on."

Symbolic of LSD, "magic" potion is raised by actor. Play was based on novel, Steppenwolf, a psychedelic source book.

Leary's mumbo-jumbo to unflattering effect.[99] Leary's second celebration was attended by *Life* (1966 circulation 7.3 million) for a one-page review titled, "Is This Trip Really Necessary?" that described "quite beautiful visual effects" combined with disjointed commentary from Leary. "After a half hour it was obvious the whole performance was a travesty," assistant editor Roger Vaughn wrote.[100] Earlier in 1966, *Mademoiselle* published a reporter's account of participating in a forty-dollar group psychedelic session with Leary in Chicago, during which he talked about drugs and led meditations but left most participants disappointed by the lack of a genuine psychedelic experience.[101] Despite giving the impression that they saw through him, the cumulative effect of the journalists' efforts was to keep Leary in the public eye.

While *Look* saw LSD in the context of a larger social movement, *Popular Science* (1967 circulation 1.4 million) professed to take a purely pragmatic approach. In 1967, the magazine known for elaborate home-workshop projects and features on futuristic vehicles offered "My LSD Trip: A Non-Cop, Non- Hippie Report of the Unvarnished Facts," describing a trip taken under medical supervision. An editors' note introducing the feature explained, "Many lawmakers seem to have adopted the same dogmatic approach that gave us the unenforceable prohibition laws. They've shown little interest in exploring more effective ways of controlling LSD use. *Popular Science* assigned its dare-anything reporter, Bob Gannon, to experience an LSD 'trip' under responsible supervision. He participated in one of the most respected scientific research projects. The data from his experience now forms a useful part of the scientific literature."[102] Armed with pre-trip advice from Timothy Leary, who suggested that he focus his mind on his wedding ring should he feel confused and "flipped out," Gannon had an overwhelming, enjoyable LSD experience. "Under LSD I found myself in a swirling, whirling maelstrom, my mind a kaleidoscope," he explained. He wrote that toward the end of the trip, "I became aware of a deep, newly revealed disenchantment with the values of my generation, an awareness that the principal drive is that of greed, and that our affluence comes from the mass cult of selfishness and bigotry and duplicity. Is this what the flower children see, I wondered; is this why they switch to open, simple, idealistic ways? Is theirs a revolution against the fast buck, the tyranny of company-think, the demands of status, the immoral killing in wars?" The following day, he was relieved to find that "things again matter," but that as he tried to put himself back together again, there were things that no longer quite fit.[103]

Two magazines targeting hip, pleasure-seeking men, *Playboy* and *Esquire,* also explored LSD absent of moral concerns. The editorial mix of *Esquire* at this time blended interest in prep-school fashion with long-form, narrative New Journalism and sometimes jarring iconoclasm. Under the art director George Lois, provocative *Esquire* covers depicted Mohammed Ali as a saint, Sonny Liston as Santa, and

Lt. William Calley, convicted for war crimes for his role in the My Lai massacre in Vietnam, as an all-American family man.[104] In 1963, the magazine had enraged Leary by mocking his salesmanlike pitch when reporting on his dismissal from Harvard. In September 1966, *Esquire* (1966 circulation 924,000) included an article about a young man's visit to a mental hospital to grasp the ramifications of going too far out with LSD in a package about "How Our Red-Blooded Campus Heroes Are Beating the Draft."[105] Two years later, the magazine (1968 circulation 1.1 million) published a first-person account by Leary of a trip with the poet Allen Ginsberg in 1960 and their subsequent decision to "turn on the world."[106]

The proudly libertine lifestyle magazine *Playboy* also turned over space for Leary to explain his views. In 1967, the magazine (1967 circulation 3.6 million) conducted a lengthy Q and A with Leary "to present his side of the psychedelic story." Over the course of the thirteen-page interview, Leary described the LSD experience, offered advice to those considering trying the drug, extolled its influence on society, and dismissed concerns about mental-health risks. The material that made the biggest splash had to do with sex. "There is no question that LSD is the most powerful aphrodisiac ever discovered by man," Leary explained to readers of the magazine best known for its erotic centerfolds. "I'm saying simply that sex under LSD becomes miraculously enhanced and intensified." Two pages of the interview dwelled on the alleged aphrodisiac power of LSD. "In a carefully prepared, loving LSD session, a woman will inevitably have several hundred orgasms," Leary further explained, although he declined to give a comparable number for men.[107]

Like stories about LSD blindness and medical side effects, Leary's assertion that the drug was a potent aphrodisiac echoed across the media and became part of the hype. Publications including the *New York Times Magazine* and *Mademoiselle* repeated the claim made in the *Playboy* interview in order to dispute it.[108] Also prompted by the *Playboy* article, the psychedelic-loving *San Francisco Oracle* published a three-page article on "Sex, Religion, and LSD," discussing what it characterized as pagan views on the continuity of humanity and nature and reverence of fertility. "Those who studied religion and mysticism are aware that the ultimate religious and ultimate sexual experiences are identical," the *Oracle* explained.[109]

Pulp publishers were also fascinated by drug-fueled sex, although they were more interested in the wild passion that LSD was said to unleash and the supposed danger of the drug than these feelings of spiritual fulfillment. In 1964, *Man's Illustrated* described a poolside LSD orgy to begin its "sizzling exposé of America's latest sex drug," which included stark antidrug warnings as well as descriptions of a number of other group-sex scenes.[110] A 1968 article in *Man's Story*, "Psyching Out—Our National Disgrace," was introduced with a full-page picture of a scantily clad couple cavorting in bed. "She munches LSD-coated sugar cube for what she thinks will give her greater sexual pleasure," the caption read. "The 'high' she will experience, however, may end in death."[111] The LSD freak-outs described in the story were decidedly less erotic than the picture advertised. Pulp paperback books published in the late-1960s included *LSD Orgy, Acid Orgy*, and *Trip'N'Trade*.[112]

Even articles in more respectable publications that included dubious horror stories about LSD and frightening warnings incorporated artwork and vivid descriptions of drug trips that were calculated to telegraph the drug's allure. In *Newsweek* (1966 circulation 1.8 million), a 1966 cover for "LSD and the Mind Drugs" showed the blissed-out face of a young man, eyes closed, face turned upward, against an unfocused background of purple and yellow flowers. The article inside began with a twenty-nine-year-old Yale graduate's description of an acid trip in which he felt as though he was becoming a plant. It continued:

> Largely unknown and untasted outside the researcher's laboratory until recently, the hallucinogenic drug LSD has suddenly become a national obsession. Depending on who is doing the talking, it is an intellectual tool to explore psychic "inner space," a new source of kicks for thrill seekers, the sacramental substance of a far-out mystical movement—or the latest and most frightening addition to the list of mind drugs now available in the pill society being fashioned by pharmacology. "Every age produces the thing it requires," says psychiatrist Humphrey Osmond of the New Jersey Neuro-Psychiatric Institute in Princeton. "This age requires ways of learning to develop inner qualities."[113]

The paragraphs about Kessler and Wingenroth were dwarfed by the discussion of the history of psychedelic drugs and its prominent advocates, including Leary, Ginsberg, and Huxley. Alongside a double-exposed inside photograph depicting two half-naked "turned-on dancers," the text explained that LSD's "alluring patina of pseudo-intellectuality and adventure" proved "particularly attractive to certain affluent members of today's pop society—students from multiversities, young professionals in the big cities, artists and self-proclaimed creative types, and fringe people of all kinds." While the tone was skeptical, the article included sufficient material to allow readers to understand the pro-drug perspective and perhaps to feel its allure. "'The LSD people I know,' says Jack Margolis, a 31-year-old Hollywood scriptwriter, 'are doctors, lawyers, psychiatrists. Talk about trips. Well, taking LSD is more enriching than going to Europe.'"[114]

Many times, magazines found sensational descriptions of the benefits of LSD to be compatible with sensational declarations of its dangers. In 1966, the digest-sized magazine *Pageant* (1966 circulation 541,000) introduced a lengthy Q and A with the Leary disciple Arthur Kleps with a full-page warning, printed on a black page in reverse type, reminiscent of the exaggerated warnings at the start of exploitation films that offered nudity in the name of sex education:

DANGER!

The article that begins on the next page will shock you. It is about worshipers who take the controversial, fantasy-causing drug LSD for religious reasons. The statements made by the author, a leader of the LSD-using Neo-American Church, constitute strong medicine that should not be swallowed whole—at least not without the appropriate antidotes.

After a bulleted list of cautionary statements from the FDA and physicians, the introduction concluded: "WARNING: PROCEED WITH CAUTION." [115] In the interview that followed, Kleps described how LSD could serve as agent for spiritual fulfillment.

Increasing black-market use of LSD did not escape the attention of the editors of *Time* magazine in the spring of 1966. When J. R. R. Tolkien's *Lord of the Rings* topped the paperback bestseller list, *Time* (1966 circulation 3.1 million) noted, "[T]he hobbit habit seems to be almost as catching as LSD." [116] Reporting "An Epidemic of 'Acid-Heads'" in another 1966 article, *Time* declared that "everywhere the diagnosis is the same: psychotic illness resulting from unauthorized, nonmedical use of the drug LSD-25," which, according to another 1966 article, was reportedly causing Los Angeles city hospitals to care for up to two hundred victims of bad trips a day. [117] The article quoted Sidney Cohen saying, "LSD can kill you dead—by making you feel that you can walk on water, or fly."

Despite these concerns, *Time* and *Life* continued to elaborate the putative benefits of psychedelic drug use and the hope that the drugs could be used to provide law-abiding citizens with mystical experiences, envisioned in familiar Christian terms. Yet another 1966 *Time* article began:

St. Paul was converted while riding on the road to Damascus by a sudden vision of the Risen Christ, who appeared to him in the form of a blinding light that struck him to the ground.

Teresa of Avila, the 16th Century saint, had poetic visions of "pure water running over crystal, the sun reflecting it and striking through it." Simone Weil, the lonely Jewish girl who turned into a Christian mystic, tells how the recitation of lines by George Herbert, such as, "Love bade me welcome, yet my soul drew back," acted on her intuitive conscious like prayer. "Then it happened," she recalled. "Christ himself came down, and he took me."

Deep within myself: Most experiences of mystical consciousness have come only after hard work—spartan prayers, meditation, fasting, mortification of the flesh. Now it is possible, through the use of LSD and other psychedelic drugs, to induce something like mystical consciousness in a controlled laboratory environment. [118]

Quoting an article in the *Journal of Religion and Health* describing the Good Friday experiment, *Time* reported that LSD mystics sense "deeper purposes in life, lose their anxiety of death and guilt." The article did not mention Leary or the drug's increasing recreational use. Two months later, *Time* reported on a small study that found that mental patients who were tense and withdrawn had lackluster experiences on LSD, while the experience of those who were outgoing, friendly, and talkative universally enjoyed their experience. That article began, "What kind of person is likely to enjoy a trip on LSD? Only the extrovert," reporting a presentation at a regional meeting of the National Association for Mental Health.[119]

Life (1966 circulation 7.3 million) published its most comprehensive treatment of LSD in March 1966, as the efforts of Leary, Koota, and the Senate subcommittee were poised to catapult the drug to even greater prominence. *Life*'s LSD cover story (see figure 13), inside headlined, "A Remarkable Mind Drug Suddenly Spells Danger: LSD," balanced concerns and hopes for LSD in a five-article package. The package was cautionary in parts, offering the *Life* science editor Albert Rosenfeld's opinion that LSD was "emphatically not" for everyone and that for some it may be "a one way ticket to an asylum, a prison or a grave."[120] A two-page photo spread showed a young woman sobbing in the throes of a bad trip, while elsewhere it warned of LSD being dropped in girls' drinks and an unnamed mother's claim that she put LSD in her children's orange juice and sent them to the woods when she and her husband needed some time to trip together.

Despite these risks, however, *Life* ultimately came down against prohibition of LSD. As well as the scare stories, the package included two pages of testimonials on the potential of LSD to induce religious experiences under the headline, "Scientists, Theologians, Mystics Swept Up in a Psychic Revolution." And along with the story about the teenage girl's bad trip, the package included a first-person account by a "hard-headed, conservative, Midwestern, Republican businessman" who discovered an understanding of God while using LSD.[121] The package left no doubt that the psychedelic experience as described by Leary and Alpert was real, for better or worse, and genuinely significant. "It is frightening to think what will happen if this awesome drug is only available to those willing to risk jail for it," the main article concluded. In an editorial the following month, *Life* suggested that lawmakers should take a lesson from Prohibition and find a way to discourage LSD "cultism" while still "making LSD available, under controlled conditions, to researchers and citizens who have good reason to try LSD and who can pass the necessary physical and mental tests."[122]

Five months later, LSD was again on the cover of *Life* (see figure 14), this time with a photo feature that conveyed the drug experience through art. "From LSD and fascination with mind-expanding visions comes the drugless trip," read the

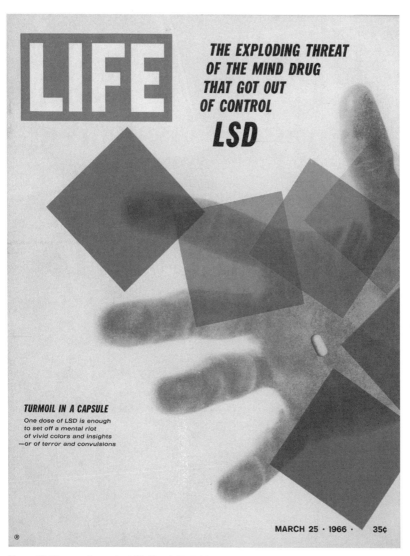

Figure 13. The cover image for *Life*'s March 25, 1966, feature on LSD. The ten-page article featured a number of photographs of people intoxicated by LSD, including five photographs headlined "A Teen-Age LSD User Meets Terror on a Bad Trip." *Life* logo and cover treatment © Time Inc. Image by Lawrence Schiller. Photograph by Lawrence Schiller © Polaris Communications, Inc. All Rights Reserved.

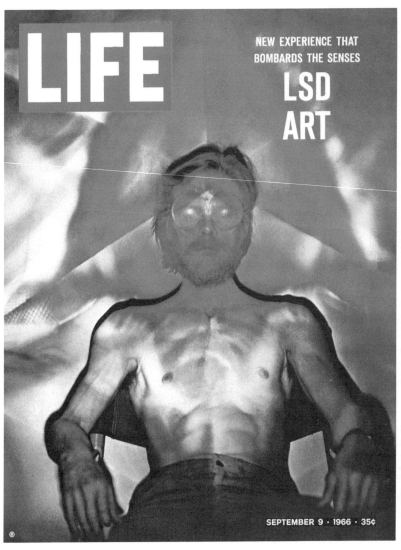

Figure 14. The text accompanying the 1966 *Life* feature on LSD art explained that psychedelic art was intended to convey the "hallucinatory effects and intensified perceptions" of LSD and other mind-expanding drugs, but without requiring the user to indulge. The feature included six pages of color photographs of psychedelic artworks inside. "Psychedelic Art," *Life,* September 9, 1966, 19. © The LIFE Premium Collection/Getty Images.

lead-in to *Life*'s "LSD Art" cover story, which included ten inside photographs of artwork "aimed at inducing the hallucinatory effects and intensified perceptions that LSD, marijuana and other psychedelic (or mind-expanding) drugs produce."[123]

Time and *Life* lost interest in LSD following the death of the publisher Henry Luce from heart blockage on February 28, 1967, one day after checking into St. Joseph's Hospital in Phoenix. For reading material, he had brought a detective novel, his Bible, and a work of theology.[124] After four articles about LSD in 1966, the subject was dropped from the pages of *Life*. *Time* published four articles dealing with LSD in 1967 and two in 1968, but without lingering on the benefits or theological implications of LSD trips.

The year following his death, New York newspapers ran gossipy headlines about the revelation in a Luce biography that Henry and Clare had used LSD. The biography, by John Kobler, who had described "The Dangerous Magic of LSD" for the *Saturday Evening Post* in 1963, included only a paragraph and a footnote about LSD, but the nugget was the focus of publicity surrounding the book's publication.[125] "LSD Gave Luces the Time of Their Life," was the headline in the *New York Post*.[126] The coverage in the *New York Times* was more restrained in tone, if not in focus: "Luce's Experiments with LSD Reported."[127]

When asked, Clare, who had ended her use of LSD years earlier, after taking more than a dozen trips that she credited at the time with transforming her psychological outlook, consistently downplayed the extent of her involvement with the drug. The Yippie radical Abbie Hoffman claimed that he confronted Clare with his view that "Henry Luce did more to popularize acid than Timothy Leary" when he bumped into her in the lobby of the Eden Roc Hotel at the 1972 Republican National Convention in Miami. "She did not disagree with this opinion," Hoffmann wrote in a 1980 book. "America's version of the Dragon Lady caressed my arm, fluttered her eyes and cooed, 'We wouldn't want everyone doing too much of a good thing.'"[128] What is almost certainly a more accurate version of the meeting was recorded by the journalist and true-crime writer Joe McGinniss, who witnessed the conversation and described it in the *New York Times Magazine.*

> We ride down the elevator with Clare Boothe Luce. She has a friendly chat with Abbie Hoffman in the lobby. He says good-by to her and starts toward the door. Then he stops and turns.
>
> "Hey," he says, "have you ever dropped acid?"
>
> "I beg your pardon?"
>
> "Have you ever taken LSD?"

"Oh, LSD. Why yes, as a matter of fact, I have. But I must tell you, it was only once and quite some time ago. And it was under very controlled circumstances."

"Did you like it?"

"Well, yes, I did. Oh, it didn't change my life or anything dramatic like that, but it was a good experience. I must say, though, I never was tempted to do it again."

"Maybe you didn't have the right setting."

"Oh, no. The setting was marvelous. It's just that I think once was enough. And of course it was only 100 milligrams, and I understand now people are taking something like a thousand."

Abbie Hoffmann shakes his head and laughs. "Too much," he says. Clare Boothe Luce smiles warmly. "Good-by. It was delightful to have met you."

"So long," Abbie Hoffmann says. "See you in Nirvana."[129]

Asked about LSD again in a 1973 Q and A published in the *New York Times Magazine,* she told the interviewer "we only took it once or twice" and allowed the interviewer's question, "But it was part of a medical research project, wasn't it?" to stand uncorrected.[130]

Many journalists were interested the possibilities of LSD even in the late 1960s, as the drug's recreational potential was becoming clear, and its use was increasingly being made a crime. The coverage in *Time* and *Life* was particularly notable because of the contrast between the magazines' interest in psychedelics and the views of the Main Street audience they cultivated. Even as recreational psychedelic drug use was expanding, Luce's magazines described the benefits of LSD in an explicitly Christian context and depicted users including businessmen, academics, and others outside of the hippie mold. *Time* and *Life* challenged their audiences to suspend easy condemnation of LSD and consider its possibilities for people like themselves.

As with the horror stories, talk of the marvelous potentialities of LSD were less materially real than media hype. Individuals had mystical or religious experiences they considered personally transformative under the influence of LSD, but this was not reliably the case, and there was no evidence that outside clinical environments the drug produced any positive, persistent effect. None of the society-wide transformations predicted by LSD advocates materialized. LSD use was certainly growing in the late 1960s, but it was most often being consumed in a casual and recreational manner, not unlike the other substances in growing circulation.[131]

The news media's pro-LSD homilies and anti-LSD horror stories were both based on occurrences that were magnified by journalists and repeated until they took on a life that was divorced from the real world. With the negative hype, this took place quickly, as newspaper wire services moved stories about arrests and misbehavior that were picked up by publications in faraway places, and magazines distilled them for curios in a cabinet of LSD horrors. The broader scope and context that distinguished magazine reporting from newspaper journalism was often a product of time spent combing through previously published accounts. Before the Internet, when access to out-of-town newspapers was scarce, back issues—even bound collections—of magazines were vital tools for researching current topics. Many reporters' first stop in researching the LSD story would have been their organization's own publications library.

The journalists who hyped the philosophy of LSD also echoed ideas that were developed and lived largely in previous media reports. As with the concerns over side effects, pro-LSD hype was seeded by work of academics and scholars, but exaggerated in mass media far beyond the limits of what responsible scholarship could support. This process began earlier and took longer. Over the course of a decade, views about psychedelic drugs that were introduced by Huxley and elaborated by Leary became familiar through repetition. Even to journalists who saw Leary as a fraud, he seemed relevant primarily because he was so well known for expressing these views. While attuned to the exaggerations, contradictions, and reckless behavior that eroded Leary's credibility, journalists continued to turn to him for the colorful quotes and far-out predictions that had made him famous. The fact that reporters who closely examined drug use among young people found scant evidence of the importance of his psychedelic philosophy was not enough to dislodge what had become a ready-made, easily accessible, intellectual-sounding explanation.

As with the horror stories, hype over the importance of LSD attracted journalists because it resonated with larger themes. By connecting psychedelic drugs to larger narratives about the progress of science, social change, and even (in an ironic reversal of age-old fears about drug use damaging what was frequently called the "race") human evolution, the use of these drugs seemed more interesting than simple pleasure-seeking or escapism. High-minded philosophy and the interest of literary figures gave journalists a fig leaf for nakedly titillating descriptions of interior drug experience, material normally restricted to the least respectable backwaters of the media landscape.

The unavoidable presence of psychedelic drugs on the media agenda in the late 1960s brought the subject to the attention of many Americans who would have been unlikely to attend one of Leary's lectures, buy an album offering a guided LSD trip, or encounter an underground newspaper. Psychedelic motifs and the use of the word itself were seeping into many aspects of popular culture, but usually without any sort of explanation of what it was supposed to mean or represent. "Psychedelic now means gaudy illegible posters, gaudy unreadable tabloids, loud parties, anything paisley, crowded noisy discotheques, trinket shops and the slum districts that patronize them," Lisa Bieberman complained in the *New Republic* in 1966.[132] Even the Beatles were singing about LSD, although most who heard the songs on the radio were not sure what they were saying. "Day Tripper" peaked at number five on the Billboard Hot 100 chart in January 1966. The following year, the band released an album that came to define the psychedelic rock style, *Sgt. Pepper's Lonely Hearts Club Band,* including the song "Lucy in the Sky with Diamonds." Although the band denied it at the time, Paul McCartney confirmed decades later that both songs were indeed about LSD.[133]

For the average American with only minimal personal contact with the drug culture, the news media were the outstanding source of explicit explanation of the cultural phenomenon. To those in the know, mainstream media's attempts to explain what was going on within a youthful subculture that self-consciously rejected it often seemed clumsy or exploitative. Reflecting on 1960s culture generally, Bob Dylan's "Ballad of a Thin Man" (1965) offered a biting portrait of a journalist as someone who knew that something was happening, but was unable to grasp what it was. Maybe the journalists at *Popular Mechanics, Look,* or *Esquire* did not really understand what the drug experience was all about, but they surely tried to make readers feel that they did.

By putting the issue of LSD before the public, the mass media contributed to a public impression that use of the drug was a problem, which easily translated into support for government action of some sort. While the discussion of pro-LSD views in news coverage kept the drug's future open to debate, even mainstream news outlets friendly toward psychedelics shared the broad consensus that some form of government action was required. In both the media and the U.S. Senate subcommittee hearings, deliberation ranged only from control to prohibition, not the full gamut to inaction or greater liberalization. Momentum for greater controls against LSD had been building since 1963, when Congress, with the support of the medical profession, raised regulatory barriers choking research with the drug. States began imposing laws against LSD possession in 1966, although federal legislators initially declined to do so out of reluctance to label a large number of young people as criminals. At the height of the side-effects scare in 1967, the National Institute of Mental Health terminated its last LSD research project on human subjects. In 1968, Congress passed a bill modifying the Drug Abuse Control amendments to make possession of LSD and other "depressant or stimulant drugs" a misdemeanor offense and the sale of these drugs a felony. Finally, in the Comprehensive Drug Abuse and Control Act of 1970, Congress classified LSD with heroin, marijuana, and a few other drugs as a "Schedule 1," indicating that it had a potential for abuse and no current medical use.[134] As with marijuana, the political decision that LSD and other psychedelic drugs had no medical value remains subject to debate and appears to be contradicted by studies demonstrating beneficial uses of LSD and similar drugs, particularly in treating the anxiety accompanying life-threatening illness. In 2006, the British medical journal *The Lancet* called for revision of the legal structure that hinders research "largely based on social and legal, as opposed to scientific, concerns."[135] Critics also point out that stiff legal penalties for LSD possession are disproportionate to the health risks the drug poses. In this sense, anti-LSD laws do not seem to be rational, but the implementation certainly was not rash. To opponents of the concept of moral panic, the incremental prohibition of LSD indicated a deliberative process involving a range of social actors that contradicted the idea of a "panic."[136] On the federal level, LSD was only one aspect of larger drug-control bills, and its treatment was consistent with that of other black-market, recreational drugs. Quite likely, state and federal officials would have acted in the same way against LSD even had it not been discussed so frequently and at such length in the news.

With talk of crime, abuse, and legislation, LSD was increasingly brought to the media agenda with the attributes of an illegal drug. The historian David Musto observed that Americans have reliably exhibited a reflexive revulsion to drugs when mass media has brought the subject to their attention.[137] This disgust was highly situational. It certainly was not the public's initial reaction to LSD when it was introduced in the late 1950s, or to other new drugs magazines presented as "pharmaceutical miracle cures," as one researcher described the coverage.[138] Sales of the prescription minor tranquilizer trade-named Miltown seemed to boom as a result of attention in the press. "Indeed, based on the first rash of popular media coverage, most Americans could have been forgiven for assuming that Miltown and other 'happy pills' were fashionable new consumer goods, available to anyone who wanted them," the historian David Herzberg observed.[139]

As the media began discussing LSD in terms of recreational use, black markets, and even drug addiction and crime, it was elevated to the public's attention within the framework of illegal dope rather than legitimate medication. The sociologist Jock Young argued that society was antagonistic primarily to drugs taken for "hedonistic reasons," which contravened social expectations of work and responsibility. "It is when drug use is seen as unrelated to productivity, when it leads to 'undeserved' pleasures, when it gives rise to experiences which question the taken-for-granted 'reality,' that the forces of condemnation are brought into play."[140] A simpler explanation could be that individuals who felt bound to follow the law felt little sympathy for those who broke it.

Media hype over psychedelic drugs probably did little to alter audience members' fundamental attitudes toward illegal drug use. The news media brought the subject of LSD to all of America's attention, but individuals with different opinions and prior beliefs reacted in different ways. Many Americans, particularly those with no interest in drugs and no patience for drug users, were turned off by what they saw. Sociologists who made LSD a textbook case of moral panic perceived a hostile reaction rooted in fear, superficially in response to the drug's physiological effects on users, and more deeply anchored in the threat that Leary and psychedelic philosophy seemed to pose to the social status quo. Young perceived that public outrage was rooted in envy. "For if a person lives by a code of conduct which forbids certain pleasures, which involves the deferring of gratification in certain areas, it is hardly surprising that he will react strongly against those whom he sees as taking shortcuts," he wrote.[141]

Others worried about an opposite reaction among the people who were not morally opposed to drug use and actually inclined to try it. In drawing attention to LSD, the mass media in the late 1960s continued to seed curiosity in something that still relatively few had encountered firsthand. Sensational description of the allure of LSD was a regular component of mass media coverage, particularly in magazines and newspapers. "The news media, by reporting this drug, has reported the attractiveness of the drug, and as such has become attractive to our teenagers and our youth of today," a Los Angeles police captain complained to the Senate subcommittee in 1966.[142] The allure of LSD was clinically explained, dramatized in testimonials and narrative accounts, and shown through pictures. Many early print articles and television reports included images of people *on* LSD. Magazine coverage, in particular and with increasing frequency, also included eye-popping imagery *as seen by* people on LSD. The opportunity to vicariously experience a psychedelic trip through a trustworthy reporter, or even with Leary himself, was the primary attraction of the many articles offering detailed, first-person accounts of drug experiences. Even articles that took a dim view of LSD use overall were accompanied by trendy art, repeating patterns, and swirling colors that signified the psychedelic trip.

The most profound influence of the hype over LSD might have been from the informational effect of this material, rather than any influence on attitude. Scholars of the diffusion of innovation describe the acquisition of an understanding of the uses and benefits of a new technology as a precondition for its eventual adoption. News media since the 1950s explained the use and benefit of LSD quite explicitly, and with greater sustained interest than any popular-entertainment medium. To a surprising extent, the cultural conversation over psychedelic drug use was conducted in the media, rippling from magazine accounts in which psychedelic pioneers including Huxley, Wasson, Watts, and Leary published their views. The mass media instructed all Americans, teetotalers and potential users alike, about a powerful personal experience outside their everyday worlds. The intellectual justifications for LSD use ultimately may have been beside the point for many who used the drug, but the news coverage opened the eyes (and indeed, expanded the minds) of Americans to the possibility of direct spiritual and personally meaningful encounters that few before would have considered possible.

By informing a broad cross section of the country of the existence and desirability of psychedelic experience, news reporting on the subject played an important early role in the diffusion of the recreational use of LSD, which appears to have increased even after the end of the 1960s. The coverage probably did little to counter the revulsion of those who had a knee-jerk reaction against drug use. However, given the widespread use of legal drugs, including amphetamines and barbiturates, it seems likely that the revulsion observed by drug historians had as much to do with a particular substance's legal status as with drug use itself. Even as legal prohibition of LSD was becoming a reality, journalistic accounts continued to explain the benefits of LSD as well as potential costs. In demonstrating these possibilities, the news coverage introduced America to the very existence of experiences rarely encountered in contemporary life, including direct mystical encounters, heightened personal insight, and emotionally resonant visions. Awareness of these experiences would not have been the final step in the process by which an individual drug user came to try LSD, but it may well have been the first.

For the fraction of the audience that subsequently tried LSD, the hype over the drug in the media potentially influenced what they ultimately experienced. More than other substances, reactions from LSD seemed notoriously subject to the expectations and situation of the drug user—"set and setting," in Leary's famous formulation. In the late 1960s, several observers worried that the discussion of bad trips and permanent health damage in the news media triggered anxiety among hypersuggestible LSD users, actually causing some of the freak-outs that were described. The enthusiastic descriptions of psychedelic experience may have influenced some audience members in this way as well, by suggesting the kind of reaction they should strive for and expect. The coverage included justification for taking an LSD trip, instructional details, and a framework for interpreting the confusing drug effect.

But for many, awareness of psychedelic experiences led down other paths. In 1968, the *Ladies' Home Journal* (1968 circulation 6.9 million) published an article listing thirteen "psychedelic exercises," including meditating and using a kaleidoscope, that promised to send readers on mind-expanding trips without the use of drugs.[143] New religions, such as the New Age movement and Neopaganism, and very old ones, like Buddhism, grew with an influx of people seeking personal spiritual and mystical encounters, while yoga and meditation took off as secular exercises to expand consciousness, in many cases divorced from the religious contexts that created them.[144] Of course, all these practices required more work and commitment than simply taking LSD, the drawbacks of which were becoming well known. As the Summer of Love turned to fall, the most common means for pursuing psychedelic sensations, and certainly the easiest, would continue to be through media.

Postscript

Psychedelic Media

In 1968, Richard M. Nixon successfully campaigned for the U.S. presidency on a promise to restore law and order to a nation jolted by riots, political protests, and the assassinations of Martin Luther King Jr. and Robert F. Kennedy. Nixon positioned himself as the voice of Americans who were frustrated by the counterculture and nostalgic for a more conformist, more traditional America. In a special message to Congress in 1969, at the start of a fifteen-month push to overhaul drug regulation and enforcement, Nixon identified the growing use of illegal drugs as a "serious national threat to the personal health and safety of millions of Americans."[1] In public remarks, Nixon emphasized direct threats to society posed by drugs, blaming drug use for increasing crime rates and ruining the lives of drug users. In private conversation, he was also outraged by the "immorality" of drugs and the disregard for law that their use implied. In a conversation with the television personality Art Linkletter, preserved by the White House's secret tape-recording system, Nixon explained, "Believe me, it is true, the thing about the drug [marijuana], once people cross that line from [unintelligible] straight society to the drug society, it's a very great possibility they are going to go further. You see, homosexuality, dope, immorality in general. These are the enemies of a strong society. That's why the communists and left-wingers are pushing the stuff, they are trying to destroy us." The antiwar protesters, Nixon believed, were "all on drugs."[2]

Nixon's war on drug abuse was to be fought not only through legislation and law enforcement, but also through the media. At a meeting with East Coast newspaper and broadcasting executives in Rochester, New York, in 1971, he explained:

> We can prosecute the pushers; we can treat the addicts. But in the final analysis, unless we establish a new attitude among our people—and here you have got to start with young people at high school, even grammar school, age—it means that the traffic will continue to grow. So education—education by the media, by the newspapers and the television and the radio, by the teachers, by all leaders of opinion—is an absolute essential or our program will fail.
>
> So we ask for your help in this. We are going be sending a lot of materials out. Please don't treat it as boilerplate. It is, in my view, as I have indicated, drug traffic is public enemy number one domestically in the United States today, and we must wage a total offensive, worldwide, nationwide, governmentwide, and if, I might say so, media wide.[3]

The Nixon administration pressed the media war aggressively, on multiple fronts. In October 1969, he recruited Linkletter, perhaps best remembered as the host of *Kids Say the Darndest Things,* to address cabinet and legislative leaders on the topic of narcotics and dangerous drugs two weeks after his daughter Diane threw herself from the window of her Los Angeles apartment. Linkletter was convinced that his daughter jumped out the window because of a flashback from an LSD experience six months before, although police collected no direct evidence that this was the case. A few weeks later, Nixon dispatched Air Force One to deliver Linkletter to Washington to reprise his talk at a conference of state governors, which was briefly excerpted in *U.S. News and World Report.*[4] A few months after that, Linkletter contributed an article to *Reader's Digest* that echoed the administration line:

> Drug abuse has become a national plague, an epidemic of monstrous proportions. Ten years ago, if you were an average American teenager or parent, you were almost immune. The problem existed, but it was far away—in ghettos, in slums, in the twilight of the criminal world. Even five years ago it seemed remote. Not anymore. Today the shadow of the tragedy that struck us looms over every family regardless of educational level, wealth or position, regardless of anything. If you have a child in college or high school, in junior high or even elementary school, it is no longer a question of his possible exposure someday to illicit drugs. He is being exposed to them at this moment, *now.* To assume otherwise is wishful thinking at its blindest.[5]

While he did not have quite the star power of Cary Grant, government-sponsored appearances elevated Linkletter as a celebrity spokesperson against the rising tide of drug use. Over the next few years, he delivered his message to the United Nations General Assembly and called for a war on drugs in *Good House-keeping* and for antidrug school programs in *Education Digest.*[6]

In 1970, Nixon instructed his chief domestic advisor John Ehrlichman to "further utilize television in the fight against drug abuse."[7] The following month, the White House hosted a highly choreographed event for executives of the six major television-production companies, network television executives, advertising executives, and "the producers of select programs which can accommodate anti-narcotic themes" to enlist support in the fight against drugs.[8] Attendees represented at least 90 percent of primetime shows, according to a White House official. The daylong event included screenings of antidrug films in the White House theater, a demonstration of drug-sniffing dogs, a speech by the attorney general, and a surprise meeting with Nixon, who exhorted, "If this nation is going to survive, it will have to depend to the great extent on how you gentlemen help to raise our children."[9] In a memorandum, the deputy director of the White House Office of Communications Jeb Stuart Magruder explained that the goal of the program was "to make available to the television industry information on anti-drug themes that could be used in a broad expanse of appropriate television programs."[10]

For the Nixon White House, the day was an unambiguous success. Following the event, "at least twenty television programs . . . will have a minimum of one anti-drug theme in it as a result of our conference," Magruder wrote to Ehrlichman. Those shows included *The Name of the Game, Hawaii Five-O, The FBI, Mod Squad,* and *Marcus Welby, M.D.*[11] Through the late 1960s, network television had said little about psychedelic drugs. One notable appearance was in 1967, when the police procedural *Dragnet* returned to television after a seven-year absence. Sgt. Joe Friday's first case was "The LSD Story," in which he and Officer Bill Gannon investigate what is wrong with a young man found with his head buried in the ground. Extracted, his face was shown to be painted blue and yellow. The producers "tried to make the opener a shocker—and did well, especially for viewers with color sets," according to one reviewer.[12] For most of the program, Sgt. Joe Friday was hamstrung by the lack of laws against LSD, finally enacted in time to break up an LSD party at which they found the young man, "Boy Blue," dead. "The theme of the story enabled 'Dragnet' to show the young swingers on Sunset Strip in Los Angeles and also an LSD party in a weird color TV suggesting hallucinogenic visions. It was all a shade corny," another reviewer wrote.[13] On CBS, the Smothers Brothers managed to sneak jokes about smoking marijuana past network censors before getting pulled from the air for criticizing the Vietnam War in 1969.[14] Responding to what the journalist Edward

Jay Epstein described as "continual White House pressure," television stations and sponsors donated thirty-seven million dollars worth of commercial time for administration antidrug messages by 1971.[15]

The Nixon administration took an even more aggressive stance with radio broadcasters. In 1969, the White House invited leading disc jockeys to a White House event and entreated them to join an antimarijuana campaign, but they demurred. Vice President Spiro Agnew took aim at drug-themed music in a speech the following year in Los Vegas. "We should listen more carefully to popular music, because at its best it is worthy of more serious application, and at its worst it is blatant drug culture propaganda. . . . I may be accused of advocating 'song censorship' for pointing this out, but have you really heard the words of these songs?" In particular, he pointed to the Beatles' "With a Little Help from My Friends," the Byrds' "Eight Miles High," and Jefferson Airplane's "White Rabbit." A month after the session for television executives, the White House held a similar day of meetings for radio executives at which FCC chairman Dean Burch suggested that the commission would look favorably on stations that provided time for antidrug commercials when broadcast licenses came up for renewal.[16]

In 1971, the FCC issued a public notice that, in light of complaints about rock lyrics promoting or glorifying illegal drugs "such as marijuana, LSD, 'speed,' etc.," radio broadcasters would now be responsible for making a judgment "whether a particular record depicts the dangers of drug abuse or, to the contrary, promotes such illegal drug use." Not knowing the content of songs "raises serious questions as to whether the continued operation of the station is in the public interest," the notice continued. The FCC statement suggested that a station's decision to air drug-themed songs could jeopardize its broadcasting license. The FCC softened its stance the following month, clarifying that at renewal time, "our function is solely limited to a review of whether a licensee's programming efforts, on an overall basis, have been in the public interest." In 1973, the Supreme Court reasoned that requiring radio stations to keep track of all the drug-themed music they played did not violate the First Amendment because it did not prohibit the airing of content and because a station must have knowledge of what it is broadcasting to serve the public interest.[17]

The Nixon administration's aggressive antidrug rhetoric reflected growing public distress. The most detailed quantitative study of the relationship between news media and presidential and public agendas regarding the drug issue during this period concluded that the public's concern over drug abuse influenced Nixon's agenda, rather than the other way around. Using a path-analysis model, the communication scholars Thomas J. Johnson and Wayne

Wanta found that in this case, real-world conditions, represented by numbers of drug arrests, appeared to influence the amount of attention to drug abuse in four major newspapers and the level of concern registered in public-opinion polls. News attention appeared to further increase public concern. With this issue, Nixon appeared to capitalize on existing public fears.[18]

News-media interest in exploring the wonders of LSD and psychedelic experience cooled after 1968. The exceptional circumstances that initially opened the door to depictions of LSD in the media—the legal ambiguity, the laboratory settings, and the serious scientific and academic interest—no longer applied. After years of attention, the experience no longer seemed so novel, newsworthy, or cutting-edge. Psychedelics had become stained by a hippie counterculture that, for many Americans, had lost its initial mystery and allure. As the use of LSD was prohibited, it was increasingly discussed in the context of other illegal drugs, in terms of crime, legislation, and abuse. Reporters, editors, and producers could hardly fail to notice the revulsion toward law-breaking and illicit drug use that contributed to Nixon's presidential victory and increasingly registered in public-opinion polls. For news outlets that catered to those whom Nixon in 1969 referred to as the "silent majority," there was little advantage in continued rhapsodizing over LSD. Even for outlets that cultivated a hipper audience, attainment of psychedelic experiences through LSD was no longer news. The *Readers' Guide to Periodical Literature* indexed only eleven magazine articles under "LSD" in 1969, including five in the science-oriented publications *Science* and *Chemistry,* half the number as the year before, and one-third as many as the year before that, when coverage was near its peak.

But while news interest in psychedelic experience faded, it was a continuing fascination for filmmakers, who attempted to engross audiences with visual effects that simulated the drug trip itself.[19] Although the drug-trip chronicles by Aldous Huxley and R. Gordon Wasson borrowed inspiration from the world of letters, drug experience was frequently analogized to an immersive experience of film watching, with volunteers describing visual effects that seemed like Technicolor and hallucinations that resembled cartoons. Sidney Cohen compared closed-eye hallucinations of LSD to avant-garde film, "those futuristic motion pictures they experimented with some years ago," playing on the tripper's personal screen. By the mid-1960s, Timothy Leary promised theatergoers a psychedelic experience from multimedia shows that blended lecture with music and projected imagery. For filmmakers, as for magazine editors, exploring psychedelic experiences provided an outlet for experimentation with visual special effects and imaginative storytelling that tried to communicate in an immediate, abstract way.

LSD emerged as a subject for exploitation films in 1965 and 1966, with the release of movies including *The Love Statue: LSD Experience* (1965); *Movie Star, American Style*, also released as *LSD, I Hate You* (1966); and *Hallucination Generation* (1966), which *Variety* critiqued as failing to live up to its billing as "a cinematic substitute for LSD, with the filmgoer promised something new in experiences." As in *The Tingler* (1959), the effect of LSD was indicated by the selective use of color in the predominantly black-and-white picture. In many of these early films, use of the drug led to outrageous sexual adventures, regrettable crime, or both. The same company responsible for *Hallucination Generation* released Roger Corman's more expensive 1967 film *The Trip*, which showed the fantasies and impressions of a television director played by Peter Fonda as he wandered Los Angeles in the throes of LSD. Corman, who experimented with LSD in preparation for directing the film, said that it would accomplish "total cinema" by taking the audience through the emotions and experiences of an LSD trip. "More than plot, I wanted an impressionistic, free-form trip in every sense," Corman explained. "The audience will know the terror, the exhilaration, the loneliness and the ecstasy of a trip by the time Fonda finishes with them." Criticized by the film critic Judith Crist as "an hour and a half commercial for LSD," the film was denied a certificate by the British film censor. In 1967, Columbia Pictures also released the hastily produced *The Love-Ins*, which depicted a Leary-like figure who leads young people to drugs and dissolution, a common plot within the short-lived "LSD film subgenre" identified by one film historian. *Columbia* changed the tagline in advertisements for the film from "Take a trip into the psychedelic world of the hippies" to "Take a look into the swinging world of the hippies" after media outlets, including the *Los Angeles Times*, complained.[20]

In the late 1960s, the government at various levels had less influence over the motion-picture industry than over broadcasting, which was subject to regulation through the FCC. The ability of local and state governments to censor films was eroded by a series of Supreme Court decisions, beginning with *Burstyn v. Wilson* (1952), which finally acknowledged that films convey ideas and are entitled to the same First Amendment protection as books, newspapers, and speech. In a series of decisions over the next five years, the Court reversed the decisions of censorship boards in Ohio, New York, and Kansas for attempting to ban films that were "harmful" (*Superior Films Inc. v. Dept. of Education of Ohio*), "immoral" (*Commercial Pictures Corp. v. Board of Regents of New York*), or "obscene, indecent and immoral, and as such tend to debase or corrupt morals" (*Holmby Productions Inc. v. Vaughn*). After 1956, the only standard that remained clearly permissible for the censorship of films was obscenity. Developed in cases over censorship of dirty books, the court confirmed that obscenity was also a valid standard for local censorship boards in the 1961 case *Times Film Corp. v. Chicago.* While obscenity was itself notoriously difficult to define, it was clearly and narrowly about sex.[21]

Faced with declining ticket sales and changing audiences, in 1968 the movie studios abandoned the Motion Picture Production Code in favor of a system of ratings more permissive toward mature themes, including drugs. Under the production code, depictions of drug use, as well as sex and other potentially offensive material, were prohibited from films bearing the code authority's stamp of approval, which many first-run theater owners required. (Many of these theaters were actually owned by the studios.) Rather than certifying the acceptability of films for all audiences, the Motion Picture Association of America's new system acknowledged the audience's desire for mature content by labeling movies as appropriate for general audiences ("G"), more mature audiences ("M," a designation that in 1970 became "GP," then in 1972 "PG," or parental guidance suggested), restricted ("R," requiring parents accompany children under age seventeen), and adults only ("X"). No longer strictly prohibited, drug sequences were a sure ticket to an R rating, even when the drug use was shown in a negative light.[22]

The major film studios exercised their new freedom with an onslaught of films exploring drugs. "There should be little doubt that at this stage the moviemakers are involved in the *in* world of LSD," the *New York Times* wrote in a 1968 roundup of movies under production. Otto Preminger's *Skidoo* (1968), a musical comedy with an overtly pro-LSD message starring Jackie Gleason, Carol Channing, and Frankie Avalon, tanked at the box office despite television ads featuring Sammy Davis Jr. and Timothy Leary. Preminger took LSD in preparation for directing the film. "What you saw in the film was really based on my experiences," he told the press. "I mean the physical symptoms that you see there, or what Gleason sees, are very much based on my 'trip.'" The movie received terrible reviews and failed to connect with the fans of LSD or of its aging stars. Other 1968 films that year widely recognized as psychedelic included the Beatles' animated *Yellow Submarine* and the Monkees' surreal stream-of-consciousness *Head,* with a screenplay that cowriter Jack Nicholson reportedly structured while on LSD.[23]

Other films more successfully conveyed the sensations of nonrational profundity, emotional resonance, and symbolic meaning associated with LSD. One of the more successful psychedelic movies of 1968 was Stanley Kubrick's *2001: A Space Odyssey,* which had nothing to do with drugs. The film won an Oscar for special visual effects, including a twenty-three-minute-long final act depicting alien contact and human evolution through a sequence of rapidly shifting lights and unexplained images of seemingly cosmic importance. Much like an LSD trip, the film trafficked in sensations of awe and significance absent of logical explanation. "Let the Awe and Mystery of a Journey Unlike Any Other Begin," was one of the film's taglines. To many, including young fans laid on their backs in front of the first row of theater seats for the film's final act, it seemed to offer a drug experience. MGM recognized this appeal in advertising that promoted the film as "the ultimate trip."[24] The incessant drug use in *Easy Rider* (1969), starring Peter Fonda and Dennis Hopper, horrified some critics, but the film earned two Oscar nominations and became the largest-grossing general-release film in the history of Columbia Pictures. Marijuana smoke wafted through theaters showing the film in 1969, the film critic Roger Ebert remembered, and its paranoid vision of the straight world closing in on its countercultural heroes struck a note with young audiences.[25] A horrible, mind-blowing LSD trip in a New Orleans graveyard was only a small part of the picture, but the movie itself seemed like an idealized drug trip, rife with images (such as the discarding of a wristwatch and the juxtaposition of motorcycle riders and cowboys) that practically demanded symbolic interpretation. The same year, three Oscars went to *Midnight Cowboy,* which contained no direct references to LSD but established the protagonist's character with trip-like montages of emotionally resonant imagery.

As with the music of the Grateful Dead and Jefferson Airplane, forged for drug-addled audiences at West Coast acid tests, LSD films seemed particularly well suited for viewing while on psychedelic substances. Movie advertisements appealed to this practice, dubbed "enhanced cinematic viewership" by the film historian Harry M. Bentoff, even for films that initially had nothing to do with drugs. Disney promoted 1960s rereleases of *Fantasia* (1940) and *Alice in Wonderland* (1951) with notoriously trippy advertising campaigns, featuring dancing mushrooms, hookah-smoking caterpillars, and psychedelic lettering, attracting turned-on audiences and helping films that had been box-office failures turn profits for the first time.[26] The merger of drugs and media seemed momentarily complete, as audiences used media-simulated drug experiences to shape actual drug experiences in real time. Aside from pornography and, perhaps, golf instructional videos, it is hard to imagine a more perfect collision of bodily and media experience.

The idea of a psychedelic world was inextricably tangled with its representation in media. The first generation of literary experimenters, led by Aldous Huxley, developed the idea of an artistic and mystical drug experience with reference to romantic literature and Eastern religious texts. Beginning in the mid-1950s, popular magazines elaborated what had amounted to a minor literary fad by combining sensational first-person accounts, visual representations, and far-fetched scientific claims. Over the following decades, the vivid imagery and special effects with which writers, musicians, filmmakers, and artists stocked their descriptions of psychedelic drugs became embedded in the public imagination, defining the potential of drug experience for the vast majority of audience members who would never try, or who had not yet actually tried, the drugs. The media attention groomed potential drug users to expect a media experience.

Much of this book has been dedicated to explaining why journalists peered into the new psychedelic experience so intently. The novelty of LSD, the interest in it among celebrities and literary thinkers, and a powerful belief that this experience would help solve mysteries of science and the human mind all contributed to the topic's appeal. Descriptions of LSD intoxication were further sensational because they pushed against boundaries of propriety, because they were intensely personal, and because they carried the whiff of the illicit even while the legal status of the drug was ambiguous. News accounts appeared to illuminate a realm of experience that had been systematically excluded from mass media. For decades, federal officials who perceived advantage in portraying the nation's drug problem as small and under control had used the levers at their disposal to squelch the media conversation about drugs. The coverage of psychedelic drugs allowed readers to peer into a forbidden realm.

The coverage was also sensational in the sense that it strove not only to engage the intellect but to convey the sensory and emotional experience of the drug trip. While magazines began this period decidedly oriented toward literary, print culture, part of the appeal of LSD to magazine editors and writers was the opportunity it provided to experiment with the more immersive, sensory experiences the new forms of media—especially television—were said to provide.[27] The subject challenged journalists to experiment with rich description, first-person, stream-of-consciousness writing, trick photography, and photo manipulation to explain experiences considered beyond the usual capacity of language to describe. By the early 1970s, the use of mass media to convey this type of experience was relatively common. Psychedelic experience was fodder for popular music and film, while television producers, with the encouragement of federal officials, dramatized its dangers. Set against the near absence of drugs from mass media a few decades before, drugs seemed to be everywhere.

The magazines ushered in not only a new use of drugs but also a new use of media. Coverage of LSD and other hallucinogenic drugs during the 1950s and 1960s shows how media was used to achieve a previously unrecognized set of gratifications, including sensations of mystical insight and phantasma-goric escape. Over the years, mainstream audiences became accustomed to accessing these sensations first through magazines, then music and moving pictures, until ultimately psychedelic experience was associated as much with its expression through media as the drugged state that had been its inspiration. Through intensive hype of LSD and psychedelic phenomena, the news media demonstrated the transporting, mind-expanding power not only of drugs, but also of journalism.

Notes

Introduction

1. See Stephen Siff, "Henry Luce's Strange Trip: Coverage of LSD in *Time* and *Life*, 1954–68," *Journalism History* 34 (Fall 2008): 126–33. While the magazines' flattering coverage of LSD was noted only in passing by Luce biographers, it was used as ammunition by the Church of Scientology in a series of full-page advertisements in *USA Today* responding to an unfavorable 1991 *Time* story about the church. The church accused *Time* of being wrong in its coverage of LSD, Prozac, Hitler, and Mussolini, as well as Scientology. See Scott Donaton and Steven W. Colford, "Scientology Fires Ad Barrage at *Time*," *Advertising Age*, June 3, 1991, 50.

2. Loudon Wainwright, *The Great American Magazine* (New York: Alfred A. Knopf, 1986), 285.

3. "Oral History of Andrew Heiskell (1987)," Columbia University Libraries Oral History Research Office, Interview 1, Session 5, 264–65, accessed July 2, 2013, http://www.columbia.edu/cu/lweb/digital/collections/nny/heiskella/index.html.

4. Stephen D. Reese and Lucig H. Danielian, "Intermedia Influence and the Drug Issue: Converging on Cocaine," in *Communication Campaigns about Drugs: Government, Media, and the Public,* ed. Pamela J. Shoemaker (Mahwah, N.J.: Lawrence Erlbaum Associates, 1989), 31, 33.

5. Lucig H. Danielian and Stephen D. Reese, "A Closer Look at Intermedia Influences on Agenda Setting: The Cocaine Issue of 1986," in *Communication Campaigns about Drugs: Government, Media and the Public,* ed. Pamela J. Shoemaker (Mahwah, N.J.: Lawrence Erlbaum Associates, 1989), 57.

6. "The *Playboy* Interview: Marshall McLuhan," *Playboy*, March 1969, 63.

7. David F. Musto and Pamela Korsmeyer, *The Quest for Drug Control: Politics and Federal Policy in a Period of Increasing Substance Abuse, 1963–1981* (New Haven, Conn.: Yale University Press, 2002), 12.

8. Susan L. Speaker, "'The Struggle of Mankind against Its Deadliest Foe': Themes of Counter-Subversion in Anti-Narcotic Campaigns, 1920–1940," *Journal of Social History* 34 (Spring 2001): 591–96.

9. Jimmie L. Reeves and Richard Campbell, *Cracked Coverage: Television News, the Anti-Cocaine Crusade, and the Reagan Legacy* (Durham, N.C.: Duke University Press, 1994).

10. Philip Jenkins, *Synthetic Panics: The Symbolic Politics of Designer Drugs* (New York University Press, 1999).

11. LSD was included on a list of "contemporary innovations" by the diffusion theorist Everett M. Rogers, but not discussed in any depth. See Rogers with F. Floyd Shoemaker, *Communication of Innovations: A Cross-Cultural Approach* (New York: Free Press, 1971), 17.

12. Allen H. Barton, "Paul Lazarsfeld and Applied Social Research: Invention of the University Applied Social Research Institute," *Social Science History* 3 (Spring–Summer 1979): 4–16.

13. Paul F. Lazarsfeld, Bernard Berelson, and Hazel Gaudet, *The People's Choice: How the Voter Makes Up His Mind in a Presidential Campaign* (New York: Duell, Sloan, and Pearce, 1944), 120, 125.

14. Ibid., 151–52.

15. Edward M. Brecher and the editors of *Consumer Reports, Licit and Illicit Drugs: The Consumers Union Report on Narcotics, Stimulants, Depressants, Inhalants, Hallucinogens, and Marijuana—Including Caffeine, Nicotine, and Alcohol* (Boston: Little, Brown, 1972), 366.

16. Everett Rogers and Arvind Singhal, "Diffusion of Innovations," in *An Integrated Approach to Communication Theory and Research*, ed. Michael Brian Salwen and Don W. Stacks (Mahwah, N.J.: Lawrence Erlbaum Associates, 1996), 419.

17. James S. Coleman, Elihu Katz, and Herbert Menzel, *Medical Innovation: A Diffusion Study* (Indianapolis: Bobbs-Merrill, 1966), 19; and Herbert Menzel and Elihu Katz, "Social Relations and Innovation in the Medical Profession: The Epidemiology of a New Drug," *Public Opinion Quarterly* 19 (Winter 1955–56): 339.

18. Christophe Van den Bulte, "*Medical Innovation* Revisited: Social Contagion versus Marketing Effect," *American Journal of Sociology* 106 (March 2001): 1415–16; Charles Winick, "The Diffusion of Innovation among Physicians in a Large City," *Sociometry* 24 (December 1961): 384–96.

19. Coleman, Katz, and Menzel, *Medical Innovation*, 61.

20. The authors of the reanalysis surmised that the Landmark Bureau researchers might have failed to adequately measure media content and drug marketing in *Medical Innovation* because the study was originally undertaken as commercial research to evaluate the effectiveness of an advertising newsletter the pharmaceutical company Pfizer inserted in the *Journal of the American Medical Association*. The initial focus on

this narrow question prompted the *Medical Innovation* researchers to collect detailed data on physicians' exposure to their client's newsletter and to *JAMA,* but less about exposure to other advertising, journals, or visits by drug-company representatives. An erroneous conclusion may have also reflected a lack of detailed knowledge of the research setting by the primary researchers, none of whom actually visited the cities where the study took place. See Van den Bulte, "*Medical Innovation* Revisited," 1409, 1429–30.

21. Everett M. Rogers, *Diffusion of Innovations,* 5th ed. (New York: Free Press, 2003), 18, 205, 305.

22. Jenkins, *Synthetic Panics,* 18.

23. Maxwell E. McCombs and Donald Shaw, "The Agenda-Setting Function of Mass Media," *Public Opinion Quarterly* 36 (Summer 1972): 177, 184.

24. Pamela J. Shoemaker, Wayne Wanta, and Dawn Leggett, "Drug Coverage and Public Opinion, 1972–1986," in *Communication Campaigns about Drugs: Government, Media, and the Public,* ed. Pamela J. Shoemaker (Mahwah, N.J.: Lawrence Erlbaum Associates, 1989), 97.

25. McCombs and Shaw, "Agenda-Setting Function of Mass Media," 177.

26. Todd Gitlin, "On Drugs and Mass Media in America's Consumer Society," in *Youth and Drugs: Society's Mixed Messages,* Office for Substance Abuse Prevention Monograph 6, ed. Hank Resnik (Rockville, Md.: U.S. Department of Health and Human Services, 1990), 49; and George Gerbner, "Stories That Hurt: Tobacco, Alcohol, and Other Drugs in the Mass Media," in *Youth and Drugs: Society's Mixed Messages,* 111.

27. Charles Atkin, "Promising Strategies for Media Health Campaigns," in *Mass Media and Drug Prevention: Classic and Contemporary Theory and Research,* ed. William D. Crano and Michael Burgoon (Mahwah, N.J.: Lawrence Erlbaum Associates, 2002), 38–39.

28. Danielian and Reese, "Closer Look at Intermedia Influences on Agenda Setting," 47–48.

29. Maxwell McCombs and Amy Reynolds, "News Influence on Our Pictures of the World," in *Media Effects,* 2d ed., ed. Jennings Bryant and Dolf Zillmann (Mahwah, N.J.: Lawrence Erlbaum Associates, 2002), 6, 8–9.

30. Pamela J. Shoemaker and Stephen D. Reese, *Mediating the Message: Theories of Influences on Mass Media Content,* 2d ed. (White Planes, N.Y.: Longman, 1996), 205–9.

31. Ibid., 225–28.

32. Gitlin, "On Drugs and Mass Media in America's Consumer Society," 40.

33. Jock Young, "The Myth of the Drug Taker in the Mass Media," in *The Manufacture of News: Social Problems, Deviance, and the Mass Media,* ed. Stanley Cohen and Jock Young (London: Constable, 1973), 315.

34. Erich Goode and Nachman Ben-Yehuda, *Moral Panics: The Social Construction of Deviance,* 2d ed. (Malden, Mass.: Wiley-Blackwell, 2009), 79.

35. Young, "Myth of the Drug Taker in the Mass Media," 316.

36. McCombs and Reynolds, "News Influence on Our Pictures of the World," 10–12.

37. Rogers and Shoemaker, *Communication of Innovations,* 127.

38. Gitlin, "On Drugs and Mass Media in America's Consumer Society," 32.

39. Goode and Ben-Yehuda, *Moral Panics,* 2d ed., 81.

40. Elihu Katz, Michael Gurevitch, and Hadassah Hass, "On the Use of Mass Media for Important Things," *American Sociological Review* 38 (April 1973): 164.

41. Elihu Katz, Jay G. Blumler, and Michael Gurevitch, "Uses and Gratifications Research," *Public Opinion Quarterly* 37 (Winter 1973–74): 510–12.

42. Denis McQuail, *Mass Communication: An Introduction,* 3d ed. (Thousand Oaks, Calif.: Sage, 1994), 320.

43. Ibid., 12.

44. The most thorough general history of LSD is Martin A. Lee and Bruce Shlain, *Acid Dreams: The CIA, LSD, and the Sixties Rebellion* (New York: Grove Weidenfeld, 1985). For a discussion of the influence of LSD on American culture, see also Jay Stevens, *Storming Heaven: LSD and the American Dream* (New York: Atlantic Monthly Press, 1987).

45. See in particular Robert Greenfield's scholarly biography of Leary, *Timothy Leary: A Biography* (New York: Harcourt, 2006), and the journalist Don Lattin's narrative history, *The Harvard Psychedelic Club: How Timothy Leary, Ram Dass, Huston Smith, and Andrew Weil Killed the Fifties and Ushered in a New Age for America* (New York: HarperOne, 2010).

46. Erika Dyck, *Psychedelic Psychiatry: LSD from Clinic to Campus* (Baltimore: Johns Hopkins University Press, 2008), 13–15.

47. Sociologists have opened the *Readers' Guide to Periodical Literature,* a library staple that indexed about one hundred popular magazines during this period, to estimate the level of magazine attention to LSD. Between 1950 and 1970, the *Guide* indexed 155 articles about LSD, compared to 111 about marijuana and 203 about narcotics, which encompassed everything from abuse of opiate drugs to legislative and law-enforcement attempts to control the international production of opium. There were only thirty-one articles about barbiturates, forty-two about amphetamines, both of which had known dangers and were in extremely widespread use, and ninety-two articles about the new and wildly popular minor tranquilizers including Miltown and Valium. See Erich Goode, *Drugs in American Society,* 5th ed. (Boston: McGraw-Hill College, 1993), 254–55; and Erich Goode and Nachman Ben-Yehuda, *Moral Panics: The Social Construction of Deviance* (Cambridge, Mass.: Blackwell, 1994), 54–55.

48. Max Rinkel et al., "Clinical and Physio-Chemical Observations in Experimental Psychosis," *American Journal of Psychiatry* 111 (June 1955): 881; Six Staff Members of Boston Psychopathic Hospital, "Experimental Psychoses," *Scientific American,* June 1, 1955, 39; and Robert M. Goldenson, "Step into the World of the Insane," *Look,* September 21, 1954, 30.

49. Albert Hofmann, *LSD, My Problem Child,* trans. Jonathon Ott (New York: McGraw-Hill, 1980), 58–59.

50. Jonathon O. Cole and Martin M. Katz, "The Psychotomimetic Drugs: An Overview," *Journal of the American Medical Association* 187 (March 7, 1964): 758.

51. Richard Blum, "Background Considerations," in *Utopiates: The Use and Users of LSD-25,* ed. Richard Blum and Associates (New York: Atherton Press, 1964), 4.

52. Frank Barron, "Motivational Patterns in LSD Usage," in *LSD, Man, and Society,* ed. Richard C. DeBold and Russell C. Leaf (Middletown, Conn.: Wesleyan University Press, 1967), 4.

53. Thalidomide, few may recall today, in 1962 caused severe birth defects to ten thousand babies worldwide. See W. V. Caldwell, *LSD Psychotherapy: An Exploration of Psychedelic and Psycholytic Therapy* (New York: Grove Press, 1968), 24–25.

54. Goode, *Drugs in American Society,* 254–55; and John R. Neill, "'More than Medical Significance': LSD and American Psychiatry, 1953 to 1966," *Journal of Psychoactive Drugs* 19 (January–March 1987): 41.

55. Late-1960s media coverage of LSD, particularly by popular magazines, was the basis of extended illustrations of moral panic in Goode and Ben-Yehuda's books on the theory. Skeptics of moral-panic theory, who argue that it mischaracterizes as panic a social response that should instead be viewed as the result of careful and deliberate efforts by social actors, have also illustrated their point through the representative example of LSD. See Goode and Ben-Yehuda, *Moral Panics,* 2d ed., 77–81; and Benjamin Cornwell and Annulla Linders, "The Myth of 'Moral Panic': An Alternative Account of LSD Prohibition," *Deviant Behavior* 23 (July 2002): 325–26.

56. Brecher and the editors of *Consumer Reports, Licit and Illicit Drugs,* 375; and William Braden, "LSD and the Press," in *The Manufacture of News: Social Problems, Deviance, and the Mass Media,* ed. Stanley Cohen and Jock Young (London: Constable, 1973), 202.

57. Goode, *Drugs in American Society,* 254–55.

58. See Timothy Leary, *Psychedelic Prayers and Other Meditations* (Berkeley, Calif.: Ronin, 1997), 35, originally published as *Psychedelic Monograph II* in 1966. Government and medical antidrug statements bracketing the drugs together as "hallucinogens" also encouraged confusion between marijuana and LSD. See Brecher and the editors of *Consumer Reports, Licit and Illicit Drugs,* 369.

59. Sarah M. Pike, *New Age and Neopagan Religions in America* (New York: Columbia University Press, 2004), 84; and Gary Laderman, "LSD," freq.uenci.es (blog), November 1, 2011, accessed August 25, 2013, http://freq.uenci.es/2011/11/01/lsd/.

60. Robert S. Ellwood, *The Sixties Spiritual Awakening: American Religion Moving from Modern to Postmodern* (New Brunswick, N.J.: Rutgers University Press, 1994), 324.

Chapter 1. Early Restrictions on Drug Speech, 1900–1956

1. Sidney Cohen, "The Cyclic Psychedelics," *American Journal of Psychiatry* 125 (September 1968): 393.

2. [William James], Rev. of *The Anaesthetic Revelation and the Gist of Philosophy, Atlantic Monthly,* November 1874, 627.

3. William James, *Varieties of Religious Experience* (1902; reprint, Cambridge, Mass.: Harvard University Press, 1985), 307–8.

4. James H. Leuba, "Professor William James' Interpretation of Religious Experience," *International Journal of Ethics* 14 (April 1904): 330.

5. Although mescaline was considered less potent than LSD, both drugs were used in the 1950s for basic research on schizophrenia, as treatment for alcoholism, and in psychotherapy. See Gary M. Fisher, "Some Comments Concerning Dosage Levels of Psychedelic Compounds for Psychotherapeutic Experiences," in *The Psychedelic Reader: Selected from the Psychedelic Review,* ed. Gunther M. Weil, Ralph Metzner, and Timothy Leary (New Hyde Park, N.Y.: University Books, 1965), 145.

6. Havelock Ellis, "Mescal: A New Artificial Paradise," *Contemporary Review,* January 1898, reprinted in *Wildest Dreams: An Anthology of Drug-Related Literature,* ed. Richard Rudgley (London: Little, Brown, and Co., 1999), 286, 288. See also Havelock Ellis, "Mescal: A Study of a Divine Plant," *Popular Science Monthly,* May 1902, 65, 71.

7. David F. Musto, *The American Disease: Origins of Narcotic Control,* expanded ed. (New York: Oxford University Press, 1999), x–xii.

8. Susan L. Speaker, "Creating a Monster: Newspapers, Magazines, and the Framing of America's Drug Problem," *Molecular Interventions* 2 (July 2002): 201–2.

9. An Act for the Suppression of Trade in, and Circulation of, Obscene Literature and Articles of Immoral Use, 42nd Cong., 3rd sess. (March 3, 1873), Statutes at Large of the United States of America, 1789–1873, ch. 258, 598.

10. Frederick F. Schauer, *The Law of Obscenity* (Washington, D.C.: Bureau of National Affairs, 1976), 13.

11. Richard F. Hixson, *Pornography and the Justices: The Supreme Court and the Intractable Obscenity Problem* (Carbondale: Southern Illinois University Press, 1996), 9.

12. *Regina v. Hicklin,* qtd. in Marjorie Heins, *Not in Front of the Children: "Indecency," Censorship, and the Innocence of Youth* (New York: Hill and Wang, 2001), 28.

13. Jack Hafferkamp, "Un-Banning Books," in *Porn 101: Eroticism, Pornography, and the First Amendment,* ed. James Elias et al. (Amherst, N.Y.: Prometheus Books, 1999), 401.

14. Dan Streible, "Children at the Mutoscope," *Cinémas: Journal of Film Studies* 14 (Autumn 2003): 92, 98.

15. Michael Starks, *Cocaine Fiends and Reefer Madness: An Illustrated History of Drugs in the Movies* (New York: Cornwall Books, 1982), 13.

16. Daniel Czitrom, "The Politics of Performance: Theater Licensing and the Origins of Movie Censorship in New York," in *Movie Censorship and American Culture,* ed. Francis G. Couvares (Washington, D.C.: Smithsonian Institute Press, 1996), 16–42.

17. Starks, *Cocaine Fiends and Reefer Madness,* 54.

18. Garth S. Jowett, "'A Capacity for Evil': The 1915 Supreme Court *Mutual* Decision," in *Controlling Hollywood: Censorship and Regulation in the Studio Era,* ed. Matthew Bernstein (New Brunswick, N.J.: Rutgers University Press, 1999), 21–25.

19. Jill Jonnes, *Hep-Cats, Narcs, and Pipe Dreams: A History of America's Romance with Illegal Drugs* (New York: Scribner, 1996), 61.

20. Ibid., 62–71.

21. Laura Wittern-Keller, *Freedom of the Screen: Legal Challenges to State Film Censorship, 1915–1981* (Lexington: University Press of Kentucky, 2008), 53.

22. Starks, *Cocaine Fiends and Reefer Madness,* 55.

23. Susan L. Speaker, "Demons for the Twentieth Century: The Rhetoric of Drug Reform, 1920–1940," in *Altering American Consciousness: The History of Alcohol and Drug Use in the United States, 1800–2000,* ed. Sarah W. Tracy and Caroline Jean Acker (Amherst: University of Massachusetts Press, 2004), 216.

24. David Nasaw, *The Chief: The Life of William Randolph Hearst* (New York: Houghton Mifflin, 2000), 386.

25. Annie Laurie, "Drug Evil Invades Cities, Towns as Ruthless Ring Coolly Recruits Victims," *San Francisco Examiner,* October 10, 1921.

26. Editorial, "Aroused Public Must Fight Spread of Drug Menace by Stamping Out Dope Peddler," *San Francisco Examiner,* October 10, 1921.

27. Annie Laurie, "'Paradise Alley' Is Fetid Hell-Hole of Lost Souls in Grip of Deadly Drug," *San Francisco Examiner,* October 12, 1921; and Annie Laurie, "'Street of Living Dead' Harbors Dope Sellers in San Francisco," *San Francisco Examiner,* October 11, 1921.

28. "Drug Traffic Is Menace to Society; It Must Be Attacked at the Root," editorial, *San Francisco Examiner,* October 27, 1921. Speaker estimates that the number of addicts was actually declining from a peak of around three hundred thousand people two decades earlier. See Speaker, "Creating a Monster," 204.

29. Annie Laurie, "Youth of Land Being Poisoned by Narcotics, Declares Annie Laurie," *San Francisco Examiner,* January 21, 1923.

30. "Dope Must Go!" editorial cartoon, *San Francisco Examiner,* January 18, 1923; and "Face to Face," editorial cartoon, *San Francisco Examiner,* January 23, 1923.

31. Advertisement for *Hearst's International Magazine, Indianapolis News,* January 19, 1923.

32. Sidney Howard, "The Inside Story of Dope in this Country," *Hearst's International,* February 1923, 15.

33. Ibid., 14; and "Dope Traffic Grips Whole Nation; Addicts Increasing in Every Town," *Lewiston (Maine) Evening Journal,* March 5, 1923.

34. Speaker, "Demons for the Twentieth Century," 211–13.

35. Richmond P. Hobson, "One Million Americans Victims of Drug Habit," *New York Times,* November 19, 1924.

36. Speaker, "Demons for the Twentieth Century," 213.

37. Richmond P. Hobson, "The Struggle of Mankind against Its Deadliest Foe" (radio transcript), *Narcotic Education* 1 (April 1928): 51–54.

38. Annie Laurie, "Dope Habit Traps College Girls, Evil Robs Woman of Mate, Home," *San Francisco Examiner,* February 24, 1928.

39. Annie Laurie, "Marijuana Causes New Peril, Weed Drives Fiends to Murder," *San Francisco Examiner,* February 25, 1928.

40. William Randolph Hearst, "Dope Crusade Is Nation's Crusade," *San Francisco Examiner,* January 28, 1923.

41. Qtd. in Speaker, "Demons for the Twentieth Century," 222, n. 29.

42. Conspiracy theorists have proposed that Hearst campaigned against marijuana because he worried that cheap paper produced from hemp would decrease the value of

his timber holdings, but there is no direct evidence to back this up, and skeptics point out that the publisher would have benefited from cheap paper. See Steven Wishniak, "Debunking the Hemp Conspiracy Theory," Alternet, February 20, 2008, accessed July 29, 2014, http://www.alternet.org/story/77339/debunking_the_hemp_conspiracy _theory.

43. Nasaw, *The Chief,* 35–36, 44.

44. "The So-Called Dope Evil," *Chicago Daily Tribune,* September 8, 1935.

45. "The Campaign against Narcotics," *Chicago Daily Tribune,* January 30, 1928.

46. "War on Narcotics," *Los Angeles Times,* January 9, 1923.

47. Alma Whitaker, "The Narcotic Bogey," *Los Angeles Times,* January 20, 1929.

48. Jonnes, *Hep-Cats, Narcs, and Pipe Dreams,* 154.

49. Harry J. Anslinger, "Marijuana, Assassin of Youth," *American,* July 1937, 19, 150.

50. John C. McWilliams, "Through the Past Darkly: The Politics and Policies of America's Drug War," in *Drug Control Policy: Essays in Historical and Comparative Perspective,* ed. William O. Walker III (University Park: Pennsylvania State University Press, 1992), 16–17 (quote on 17).

51. Jonnes, *Hep-Cats, Narcs, and Pipe Dreams,* 159.

52. Harry J. Anslinger, "Marijuana More Dangerous than Heroin or Cocaine," *Scientific American,* May 1938, 293.

53. Jonnes, *Hep-Cats, Narcs, and Pipe Dreams,* 159.

54. Larry Sloman, *Reefer Madness: A History of Marijuana* (New York: St. Martin's Griffin, 1998), 207.

55. Alfred R. Lindesmith, "'Dope Fiend' Mythology," *Journal of Criminal Law and Criminology* 31 (July–August 1940): 208.

56. John F. Galliher, David P. Keys, and Michael Elsner, "*Lindesmith v. Anslinger*: An Early Government Victory in the Failed War on Drugs," *Journal of Criminal Law and Criminology* 88 (Winter 1998): 667–69.

57. Rufus King, *The Drug Hang-Up: America's Fifty-Year Folly* (New York: W. W. Norton and Co., 1972), 82–85, 161–75.

58. Galliher, Keys, and Elsner, "*Lindesmith v. Anslinger,*" 670–78 (quote, from a 1950 letter to Motion Picture Association of America president Eric Johnson, on 673).

59. Eric Schaefer, *"Bold! Daring! Shocking! True!" A History of Exploitation Films, 1919–1959* (Durham, N.C.: Duke University Press, 1999), 242–43 (quote on 243).

60. John C. McWilliams, *The Protectors: Harry J. Anslinger and the Federal Bureau of Narcotics, 1930–1962* (Newark: University of Delaware Press, 1990), 102.

61. Ibid., 101.

62. Starks, *Cocaine Fiends and Reefer Madness,* 55.

63. Indeed, Anslinger wrote two books filled with hard-boiled accounts of derring-do by federal agents. See Harry J. Anslinger with Will Oursler, *The Murderers: The Story of the Narcotic Gangs* (New York: Farrar, Straus and Cudahy, 1961); and Harry J. Anslinger with J. Dennis Gregory, *The Protectors: The Heroic Story of the Narcotics Agents, Citizens and Officials in Their Unending, Unsung Battles against Organized Crime in America and Abroad* (New York: Farrar, Straus, and Co., 1962).

64. Starks, *Cocaine Fiends and Reefer Madness,* 55–56.

65. Jonnes, *Hep-Cats, Narcs, and Pipe Dreams,* 159.

66. Gerard Peil, "Narcotics," *Life,* July 19, 1943, 83–84.

67. National Association of Radio and Television Broadcasters, "Code of Practices for Television Broadcasters," adopted December 6, 1951, accessed August 21, 2012, http://www.tvhistory.tv/SEAL-Good-Practice.htm.

68. John C. McWilliams, *The Protectors,* 101.

69. Schaefer, *"Bold! Daring! Shocking! True!"* 1–2, 43–95, 235–37.

70. "The Boom in Paperback Books," *Fortune,* September 1953, 123. For a taste of the lurid cover art used to market these books, see Stephen J. Gertz, *Dope Menace: The Sensational World of Drug Paperbacks, 1900–1975* (Port Townsend, Wash.: Feral House, 2008).

71. House Select Committee on Current Pornographic Materials, Investigation of Literature Allegedly Containing Objectionable Materials: Hearings before the Select Committee on Current Pornographic Materials, 82nd Cong., 2nd Sess., December 1–5, 1952, 69–70.

72. Hixson, *Pornography and the Justices,* 11–12.

73. The introduction to the 1977 edition of *Junky* is reprinted in Allen Ginsberg, *Deliberate Prose: Selected Essays 1952–1995* (New York: HarperCollins, 2000), 382–85 (quote on 384).

74. Thomas Newhouse, *The Beat Generation and the Popular Novel in the United States, 1945–1970* (Jefferson, N.C.: McFarland and Co., 2000), 98.

75. The case against Ginsberg's *Howl* is discussed in Edward de Grazia, "How Justice Brennan Freed Novels and Movies during the Sixties," *Cardoza Studies in Law and Literature* 8 (Winter 1996): 260; Michael Barry Goodman reviews the case against Burroughs's *Naked Lunch* in *Contemporary Literary Censorship: The Case History of Burroughs' Naked Lunch,* (Metuchen, N.J.: Scarecrow Press, 1981), 2, 4; and the case against the first issue of *Big Table,* a literary magazine with objectionable works by Burroughs, Kerouac, and Gregory Corso, is discussed in Jonathon Green and Nicholas J. Karolides, *Encyclopedia of Censorship,* new ed. (New York: Facts on File, 2005), 370–71.

76. Jerold Simmons, "Challenging the Production Code: *The Man with the Golden Arm," Journal of Popular Film and Television* 33 (Spring 2005): 42.

77. Starks, *Cocaine Fiends and Reefer Madness,* 56.

78. Musto, *American Disease,* 230.

79. "Law for Isolation of Addicts Urged," *New York Times,* July 2, 1951.

80. Richard J. Bonnie and Charles H. Whitebread II, "Forbidden Fruit and the Tree of Knowledge," *Virginia Law Review* 56 (October 1970): 1073–75.

81. Musto, *American Disease,* 232.

82. Ibid., 231.

83. Kathleen McLaughlin, "Russian Says G.I.'s Buy up Narcotics," *New York Times,* May 6, 1952.

84. "On Television," *New York Times,* June 26, 1951.

85. Bonnie and Whitebread, "Forbidden Fruit and the Tree of Knowledge," 1064, n. 5.

86. "The Rise of Senator Legend," *Time,* March 24, 1952, 22.

87. Special Committee on Organized Crime in Interstate Commerce, Notable Senate Investigations, U.S. Senate Historical Office, Washington, D.C., accessed September 6, 2013, http://www.senate.gov/artandhistory/history/common/investigations/pdf/Kefauver_Committee_fullcitations.pdf.

88. "Hearings to Show Teen-Age Drug Use," *New York Times,* June 7, 1951.

89. "Dewey Approves Narcotics Inquiry," *New York Times,* April 6, 1951.

90. "The Junkies," *Time,* May 25, 1951, 25.

91. Charles Gruntzner, "High School Users of Narcotics Put at 1-in-200 Ratio," *New York Times,* June 13, 1951.

92. "6,000 Children in N.Y. Called Dope Addicts," *Washington Post,* June 13, 1951.

93. "8 Bills at Albany Ask Narcotics War," *New York Times,* January 18, 1951.

94. "Narcotics Arrests Rise," *New York Times,* February 7, 1951.

95. "Buffalo Ring Set to Sell Narcotics," *New York Times,* November 30, 1951; "Narcotics Raiders Strike in Capitol," *New York Times,* November 17, 1951; and "Narcotics Agent 'Enrolls' in High School, Breaks up Wichita Falls Marijuana Ring," *New York Times,* November 22, 1951.

96. "Radio-TV Notes," *New York Times,* July 11, 1951.

97. "On Television," *New York Times,* September 18, 1951; "On Television," *New York Times,* April 25, 1951; and "Law for Isolation of Addicts Urged," *New York Times,* July 2, 1951.

98. "Dope's Flow Said to Have Red's Backing," *Los Angeles Times,* September 18, 1951.

99. Sarah Brady Siff and Stephen Siff, "Red Menace/Drug Menace: Anticommunism and the American War on Drugs," paper presented at Under Control? Alcohol and Drug Regulation, Past and Present, London School of Hygiene and Tropical Medicine, June 22, 2013.

100. Dan Fowler, "Your Child May Be Hooked," *Look,* June 30, 1953, 92.

101. Wenzell Brown, "A Monkey on My Back," *Look,* March 10, 1953, 98–103.

102. Gon Sam Mue with Willam J. Slocum, "They Haven't Killed Me Yet," *Saturday Evening Post,* August 16, 1954, 17.

103. Neil M. Clark, "They're Death on Dope Runners," *Saturday Evening Post,* July 26, 1952, 36.

104. Gledhill Cameron, "Detective Kitty Barry," *Collier's,* November 26, 1954, 32.

105. Thomas A. Wadden Jr., as told to Thomas Drake Durrance, "We Put Heat on Washington Dope Peddlers," *Saturday Evening Post,* October 3, 1953, 134.

106. Lila Leeds with Bill Fay, "Narcotics Ruined Me," *Collier's,* July 26, 1952, 21.

107. Susan L. Speaker, "'The Struggle of Mankind against Its Deadliest Foe': Themes of Counter-Subversion in Anti-Narcotic Campaigns, 1920–1940," *Journal of Social History* 34 (Spring 2001): 596.

Chapter 2. Introducing LSD, 1953–1956

1. "Aldous Huxley Dies of Cancer on Coast," *New York Times,* November 23, 1963.

2. Hofmann, *LSD, My Problem Child,* 15.

3. Ibid., 5.

4. More recent research has proposed mass poisoning from ergot-infected rye as a cause of the hysteria surrounding the Salem witch trials in 1692–93. See Linnda R. Caporael, "Ergotism: The Satan Loosed in Salem," *Science* 192 (April 2, 1976): 21–26.

5. Hofmann, *LSD, My Problem Child*, 14.

6. Ibid., 16–18.

7. Ibid., 24.

8. Lee and Shlain, *Acid Dreams*, 12–13.

9. Text of the product monograph for Delysid is quoted from Hofmann, *LSD, My Problem Child*, 47.

10. Raymond E. Fancher, *Pioneers of Psychology* (New York: W. W. Norton and Co., 1979), 230–33, 238–40.

11. Dyck, *Psychedelic Psychiatry*, 14–15.

12. Erich Guttmann, "Artificial Psychoses Produced by Mescaline," *Journal of Mental Science* 82 (May 1936): 203.

13. Charles Savage and Louis Cholden, "Schizophrenia and the Model Psychoses," *Journal of Clinical and Experimental Psychopathology* 17 (December 1956): 405.

14. Stevens, *Storming Heaven*, 16–18.

15. Dyck, *Psychedelic Psychiatry*, 14–15.

16. Stevens, *Storming Heaven*, 16.

17. David Healy, *The Creation of Psychopharmacology* (Cambridge, Mass.: Harvard University Press, 2002), 182.

18. Erika Dyck, "Flashback: Psychiatric Experimentation with LSD in Historical Perspective," *Canadian Journal of Psychiatry* 50 (June 2005): 383.

19. John R. Neill, "'More than Medical Significance': LSD and American Psychiatry, 1953 to 1966," *Journal of Psychoactive Drugs* 19 (January–March 1987): 39.

20. Hofmann, *LSD, My Problem Child*, 25–27, 46.

21. Healy, *Creation of Psychopharmacology*, 182.

22. Lee and Shlain, *Acid Dreams*, 20.

23. Paul Gahlinger, *Illegal Drugs: A Complete Guide to Their History, Chemistry, Use, and Abuse* (New York: Penguin, 2004), 49.

24. Brecher, *Licit and Illicit Drugs*, 350.

25. Osmond and Smythies qtd. in Dyck, *Psychedelic Psychiatry*, 18.

26. Max Rinkel, Robert Hyde, Harry Solomon, and Hudson Hoagland, "Clinical and Physio-Chemical Observations in Experimental Psychosis," *American Journal of Psychiatry* 111 (June 1955): 892.

27. Now known largely as a result of a mention in Hunter S. Thompson's novel *Fear and Loathing in Las Vegas* (1971), recreational drug aficionados continue to question whether adrenochrome has any psychoactive effects. The effects described do not include hallucinations. See Erowid Adrenochrome Vault, "Adrenochrome," November 28, 2001, accessed August 21, 2012, http://www.erowid.org/chemicals/adrenochrome/adrenochrome.shtml.

28. Steven J. Novak, "LSD before Leary: Sidney Cohen's Critique of 1950s Psychedelic Drug Research," *Isis* 88 (March 1997): 91.

29. Ibid., 90–92.

30. Qtd. in Stevens, *Storming Heaven,* 24.

31. Jeff Sigafoos, Vanessa A. Green, Chaturi Edrisinha, and Guilio E. Lancioni, "Flashback to the 1960s: LSD in the Treatment of Autism," *Developmental Neurorehabilitation* 10 (January–March 2007): 79–80.

32. Ibid., 77–80.

33. Lee and Shlain, *Acid Dreams,* 57.

34. Ibid., 63.

35. Rinkel, Hyde, Solomon, and Hoagland, "Clinical and Physio-Chemical Observations in Experimental Psychosis," 882–83.

36. Lee and Shlain, *Acid Dreams,* 63.

37. Ibid., 70.

38. For some studies, the institutional review boards charged with overseeing research ethics have required that volunteers be drawn from hospital staff and medical students for this reason. See Lawrence Altman, *Who Goes First? The Story of Self-Experimentation in Medicine* (Berkeley: University of California Press, 1998), 209, xv.

39. Roy R. Grinker Sr., "Bootlegged Ecstasy," *Journal of the American Medical Association* 187 (March 7, 1964): 768.

40. "Hint Chemical in Body Cause of Insanity," *Chicago Tribune,* May 8, 1954; and Alton L. Blakeslee, "Adrenalin Seen as Insanity Cause," *The (Newport, R.I.) News,* May 7, 1954.

41. "New Drug Returns Adults to Childhood," *Washington Post and Times Herald,* June 18, 1954.

42. Walter C. Alvarez, "New Light Being Shed on Mind Ills," *Los Angeles Times,* March 24, 1954; Walter C. Alvarez, "Research Sheds New Light on Mental Ills," *Los Angeles Times,* January 22, 1956; Walter C. Alvarez, "Changes Required in Modern Psychiatry," *Los Angeles Times,* June 7, 1956; Walter C. Alvarez, "Brain-Action Drugs Help Psychosis Study," *Los Angeles Times,* September 2, 1956.

43. "Scientists Pondering over Human Brain and What Makes It Operate," *Los Angeles Times,* December 30, 1956.

44. "For a Fee, Prisoners Become Human Guinea Pigs to Aid Insanity Tests," *Los Angeles Times,* March 13, 1957.

45. "Science Notes," *New York Times,* December 1, 1957; and Nate Haseltine, "'Artificial Insanity' Aids Mental Research," *Washington Post and Times Herald,* March 18, 1956.

46. Sammye Johnson and Patricia Prijatel, *The Magazine from Cover to Cover: Inside a Dynamic Industry* (Chicago: NTC Publishing Group, 1999), 5.

47. Marcel C. LaFollette, *Making Science Our Own: Public Images of Science 1910–1955* (Chicago: University of Chicago Press, 1990), 3.

48. Jonathan Metzl, "'Mother's Little Helper': The Crisis of Psychoanalysis and the Miltown Resolution," *Gender and History* 15 (August 2003): 240–41.

49. See the introduction, n. 6.

50. Aline Mosby, "Controversial Series on TV Specializes in Real Life," *Clovis (N.M.) News Journal,* December 18, 1955.

51. Robert M. Yoder, "Help for the Living Dead," *Saturday Evening Post,* October 22, 1955, 42–43, 64–65, 71.

52. Lillian Pompian, "Experimental Insanity," *Today's Health,* August 19, 1956, 38–39, 58–59; and Rinkel, Hyde, Solomon, and Hoagland, "Clinical and Physio-Chemical Observations," 882.

53. William Engle, "Alice-in-Wonderland Drug," *American Weekly,* September 26, 1954, 15.

54. "Mescal Madness," *Newsweek,* February 23, 1953, 92.

55. Robert M. Goldenson, "Step into the World of the Insane," *Look,* September 21, 1954, 30.

56. Ibid., 32.

57. "Experimental Psychoses," *Scientific American,* June 1, 1955, 35, 39.

58. Dyck, *Psychedelic Psychiatry,* 18–19, 35–36.

59. Sidney Katz, "My Twelve Hours as a Madman," *MacLean's,* October 1, 1953, 9.

60. Robert H____, as told to William Michelfelder, "I Went Insane for Science," *Man's Magazine,* August 1956, 17. The story appears under the same headline in *Man's Magazine,* December 1961, 38–41, 84–85.

61. Paul Terrell, as told to Ted Levine, "I Went Experimentally Insane," *Argosy,* October 1959, 25, 66.

62. Harry M. Benshoff, "The Short-Lived Life of the Hollywood LSD Film," *The Velvet Light Trap* 47 (Spring 2001): 34.

63. Howard Becker, "Exploration of the Social Bases of Drug-Induced Experiences," *Journal of Health and Social Behavior* 8 (September 1967): 166.

64. Keith L. Justice, *Bestseller Index: All Books, by Author, on the lists of* Publishers Weekly *and the* New York Times *through 1990* (Jefferson, N.C.: McFarland and Co.: 1998). *The Doors of Perception* did not make *New York Times* or *Publishers Weekly* lists.

65. Dyck, *Psychedelic Psychiatry,* 59.

66. Ibid., 58–64, 74.

67. Humphry Osmond and J. R. Smythies, "The Present State of Psychological Medicine," *Hibbert Journal* 52 (January 1953): 136.

68. One teacher's guide recommended Huxley's *Brave New World* on a year-long twelfth-grade curriculum containing thirteen other authors, including Jane Austen, Joseph Conrad, and Herman Melville. See Dwight L. Burton, *Literature Study in the High Schools* (New York: Holt, Rinehart and Winston, 1959), 135.

69. David King Dunaway, *Huxley in Hollywood* (London: Bloomsbury, 1989), 284–85.

70. Aldous Huxley, *Letters of Aldous Huxley,* ed. Grover Smith (New York: Harper and Row, 1969), 670.

71. Humphry Osmond, "May Morning in Hollywood," in Aldous Huxley, *Moksha,* ed. Michael Horowitz and Cynthia Palmer (Los Angeles: J. P. Tarcher, 1977), 36.

72. Qtd. in Novak, "LSD before Leary," 93.

73. Aldous Huxley, *Brave New World* (New York: Harper and Brothers, 1962), 52.

74. Huxley, *Letters of Aldous Huxley,* 669.

75. Aldous Huxley, *The Doors of Perception* (New York: Harper and Brothers, 1954), 33–34.

76. Ibid., 73.

77. Aldous Huxley, *Heaven and Hell,* in *The Doors of Perception and Heaven and Hell* (New York: HarperPerennial, 2004), 87, 155.

78. Lee and Shlain, *Acid Dreams,* 55.

79. Marvin Barrett, "Aldous Huxley, Merchant of Mescalin," *The Reporter,* March 2, 1954, 46.

80. Ibid., 47.

81. "Dream Stuff," *Time,* June 28, 1954, 66; and Huxley, *Doors of Perception,* 18, 22.

82. Aldous Huxley, "Mescalin—An Answer to Cigarettes?" *Saturday Review,* February 6, 1954, 14; and James S. Slotkin, "The Anthropologist," *Saturday Review,* February 6, 1954, 15.

83. "Huxley Samples New Drug," *Tuscon Daily Citizen,* February 20, 1954.

84. Berton Roueche, "Shimmering Hours," *New York Times Book Review,* February 17, 1954, 6.

85. Leonard Wibberly, "Aldous Huxley Opens the Door," *Los Angeles Times,* March 7, 1954.

86. Sterling North, "Aldous Huxley Describes Intoxication on Mescalin," *Washington Post,* February 7, 1954.

87. Delos Avery, "Bookman's Holiday," *Chicago Tribune,* January 31, 1954.

88. "Exclusive! *People Today* Reports on the Sensational Drug Mescalin," *People Today,* April 7, 1954, 5, 3.

89. "Is It a New Source of Addiction," editorial, *(Beckley, W.Va.) Raleigh Register,* March 30, 1954.

90. "'Genius' Draws Term in Jail," *San Mateo (Calif.) Times,* October 12, 1955.

91. John Dollard, "In the Eden of the Mind," *New York Times,* April 8, 1956.

92. Hans Meyerhoff, "In the Mind's Antipodes," *New Republic,* May 14, 1956, 17–18.

93. Richard Eberhart, "The Other Side of the Mind," *The Nation,* April 14, 1956, 309–10.

94. Rogers and Shoemaker, *Communication of Innovations,* 265.

95. "Artificial Psychoses," *Time,* December 19, 1955, 60, 63.

96. Harold A. Abramson qtd. in the transcript of a discussion following Kenneth E. Godfrey, "The Metamorphosis of an LSD Psychotherapist," in *The Use of LSD in Psychotherapy and Alcoholism,* ed. Harold A. Abramson (Indianapolis: Bobbs-Merrill Co., 1967), 475.

Chapter 3. Creating a Psychedelic Past, 1954–1960

1. The term "American Voodoo" is used in Laura Bergquist, "Peyote: The Strange Church of Cactus Eaters," *Look,* December 10, 1957, 36.

2. See "magic mushroom," *Oxford English Dictionary,* 3d ed.

3. "2nd Commercial—Mushrooms," transcript for live commercial on *Person to Person*, May 6, 1957, Tina and R. Gordon Wasson Archives, Harvard University Herbaria (hereafter Wasson Archives), series 4, *Life* folder.

4. Omer C. Stewart, *Peyote Religion: A History* (Norman: University of Oklahoma Press, 1987), 17–41, 213–22.

5. "Peyote Used as Drug in Indians' 'Cult of Death,'" *New York Times*, January 14, 1923.

6. Ibid.

7. Stewart, *Peyote Religion*, 226–30.

8. Ibid., 232–38, 274.

9. Elizabeth X. Green, "Peyote Cult," *Hobbies*, March 1950, 142.

10. Vincent H. Gaddis, "The Cult of the Sacred Cactus," *Travel*, November 1948, 17, 33.

11. "Button, Button . . .," *Time*, June 18, 1951, 82.

12. "The Church and the Cactus," *Time*, August 9, 1954, 49.

13. Alice Marriott, "The Opened Door," *New Yorker*, September 25, 1954, 80, 89.

14. Laura Bergquist, "Peyote: The Strange Church of Cactus Eaters," *Look*, December 10, 1957, 36, 38.

15. Philip H. Wootton Jr. to R. Gordon Wasson, March 6, 1956, Wasson Archives, series 4, *Life* folder; and R. Gordon Wasson, "Seeking the Magic Mushroom," *Life*, May 13, 1957, 102.

16. Valentina P. Wasson, "I Ate the Sacred Mushrooms," *This Week*, May 19, 1957, 1, 8–10, 36; and Henry Raymont, "This Week Magazine Ends Publication Nov. 2," *New York Times*, August 14, 1969.

17. "Extract from Radio Newsreel," stamped "checked as broadcast" by BBC, transmitted May 9, 1957, Wasson Archives, series 4, *Life* folder.

18. See press clippings, Wasson Archive, series 4, Magazine Articles/Mentions folder.

19. "Road to Endsville," *Newsweek*, February 9, 1959; and Sanka Knox, "Mushroom Ritual Recreated Here," *New York Times*, January 30, 1959.

20. See press clippings, Wasson Archive, series 4, Magazine Articles/Mentions folder.

21. Wasson to Allan Richardson, July 21, 1957, Wasson Archives, series 2, Richardson folder.

22. "The Quest for the Magic Mushroom," *The (Mexico City) News*, November 4, 1960.

23. E. A. Wasson, *Religion and Drink* (New York: Burr, 1914), 293.

24. Donald H. Pfister, "R. Gordon Wasson—1898–1986," *Mycologia* 80 (January–February 1988), 11–13; Christopher Brown, "R. Gordon Wasson, 22 September 1898–23 December 1986," *Economic Botany* 41 (October–December 1987), 469–73; and "R. Gordon Wasson, a Mushroom Expert and Banker, Is Dead," *New York Times*, December 26, 1986.

25. "Dr. V. P. Wasson, Pediatrician, 57," *New York Times*, January 2, 1959.

26. Wasson, "Seeking the Magic Mushroom," 113. This story is also recounted in Valentina Pavlovna Wasson and R. Gordon Wasson, *Mushrooms, Russia, and History,*

vol. 1 (New York: Pantheon, 1957), 4–5; and Jonathan Ott and Steven H. Pollock, "Interview: R. Gordon Wasson," *High Times,* October 1976, 24.

27. Wasson, "Seeking the Magic Mushroom," 113.

28. Andy Letcher, *Shroom: A Cultural History of the Magic Mushroom* (New York: HarperCollins, 2006), 93.

29. Wasson, "Seeking the Magic Mushroom," 114.

30. Qtd. in Letcher, *Shroom,* 233–34.

31. Ott and Pollock, "Interview," 26.

32. Valentina Pavlovna Wasson and R. Gordon Wasson, *Mushrooms, Russia, and History,* vol. 2 (New York: Pantheon, 1957), 245.

33. This definition is furnished by Richard Conniff, *The Species Seekers: Heroes, Fools, and the Mad Pursuit of Life on Earth* (New York: W. W. Norton and Co., 2011), 35–36. The controversy over the existence of hallucinogenic mushrooms is reviewed in Letcher, *Shroom,* 69–80.

34. Wasson and Wasson, *Mushrooms, Russia, and History,* vol. 2, 245–65.

35. Wasson to Allan Richardson, July 3, 1954, Wasson Archives, series 2, Richardson folder.

36. Entry for August 12, 1955, Wasson Archives, Field notebooks, box 1.

37. Wasson to Roger Heim, July 18, 1955, Wasson Archives, series 2, Heim folder.

38. Wasson to Robert Graves, August 26, 1955, Wasson Archives, series 2, Graves folder.

39. Letcher, *Shroom,* 193–95.

40. Pfister, "R. Gordon Wasson," 12.

41. Phillip H. Wootton to Wasson, March 6, 1956, and Wasson to Wootton, February 27, 1956, Wasson Archives, series 4, *Life* folder.

42. Wasson to Graves, September 12, 1956, Wasson Archives, series 1, Graves folder.

43. Wootton to Wasson, March 6, 1956.

44. "2nd Commercial—Mushrooms," Wasson Archives, series 4, *Life* folder.

45. Wasson, "Seeking the Magic Mushroom," 101–2, 109.

46. Ibid., 109.

47. Ibid., 110.

48. Ibid., 117; and Huxley, *Doors of Perception,* 13–14.

49. Wasson, "I Ate the Sacred Mushrooms," 9, 36.

50. Wasson to Richardson, July 7, 1956, Wasson Archives, series 2, Richardson folder.

51. Valentina P. Wasson and R. Gordon Wasson, "The Hallucinogenic Mushrooms," *Garden Journal,* January–February 1958, 1–6.

52. Stephen R. De Borhegyi, as told to Thor Goodman, "Quest for the Sacred Mushrooms," *Fate,* October 1957, 42–43.

53. Ibid., 43.

54. "Mushroom Madness," *Time,* June 16, 1958, 44.

55. Wasson, "Seeking the Magic Mushroom," 101.

56. Wasson to Richardson, Nov. 28, 1956, Wasson Archive, series 2, Richardson folder.

57. "Mycophile," *New Yorker,* May 18, 1957.

58. "Extract from Radio Newsreel," Wasson Archives, series 4, *Life* folder.

59. Paul Bird, "There Is More to a Mushroom than Meets the Eye," *New York Times,* July 14, 1957.

60. Robert Graves, "How to Avoid Mycophobia," *Saturday Review,* May 11, 1957, 21–22, 47; and Robert Graves, "Mushrooms, Food of the Gods," *The Atlantic,* August 1957, 73–77.

61. Willis Harrison, "Mushrooms: Gourmet's Delight or Devil's Tool," *Toledo Blade Sunday Pictorial,* January 19, 1958.

62. Clipping from *Daily Nebraskan,* March 11, 1958, series 4, Wasson Archive, series 4, Articles about RGW folder.

63. Stephen C. Pelletiere, "Ex-Banker Feels Asia Holds Key to Mushroom Paradise," *Milwaukee Journal,* May 25, 1963.

64. William D. Cole, "The Vegetable that Drives Men Mad," *True, the Man's Magazine,* December 1959, 56.

65. Letcher, *Shroom,* 93–94, 101.

66. Ibid., 88–113.

67. Letters to the editors, *Life,* June 3, 1957, 16.

68. Ibid.

69. Peter Stafford, *Psychedelics Encyclopedia,* 3d ed. (Berkeley, Calif.: Ronin, 1992), 116.

70. R. Gordon Wasson, "Drugs: The Sacred Mushroom," *New York Times,* September 26, 1970.

71. Letcher, *Shroom,* 98; and Allen Hughes, "Mexican Cult of 'Maria Sabina' Is a Poetic Premiere at Carnegie," *New York Times,* April 18, 1970.

72. Ward Meade, "Virility and those 'Magic' Mushrooms," *Uncensored,* March 1958, 32, 33.

73. George W. Herald, "Curse or Cure? The Truth about the 'Devil's Drugs,'" *Real for Men,* February 1958, 16.

74. Ed Gallivan, "The Poison Eaters," *True Crime,* November 1960, 6.

75. Alex Severus, "Drugs and the Mind's Hidden Powers," *Cosmopolitan,* January 1960, 43, 45.

76. Robert Graves, "Journey to Paradise," *Holiday,* August 1962, 37.

77. Robert Graves, "The Sacred-Mushroom Trance," *Story* 36.3, no. 140 (May–June 1963): 6–13.

78. Budd Schulberg, "The Night We Ate Magic Mushrooms," *Esquire,* December 1961, 316.

Chapter 4. Research at the Intersection of Media and Medicine, 1957–1962

1. Coleman, Katz, and Menzel, *Medical Innovation,* 42–44, 48, 156.

2. Lazarsfeld, Berelson, and Gaudet, *People's Choice,* 151–52.

3. Richard Blum, Eva Blum, and Mary Lou Funkhouser, "The Natural History of LSD Use," in *Utopiates: The Use and Users of LSD-25,* ed. Richard Blum and Associates (New York: Atherton Press, 1964), 62–63.

4. Lee and Shlain, *Acid Dreams*, 51–52.

5. Ibid., 90.

6. Steven J. Novak, "LSD before Leary: Sidney Cohen's Critique of 1950s Psychedelic Drug Research," *Isis* 88 (March 1997): 88.

7. Ibid., 109.

8. Cohen included the narrative of his first LSD trip as the account of an unnamed doctor in *The Beyond Within: The LSD Story* (New York: Atheneum, 1968), 106–11 (quote on 107). Novak identified the origin of this passage through comparison with Cohen's initial record of his reactions. See Novak, "LSD before Leary," 92, n. 16.

9. Novak, "LSD before Leary," 92.

10. Sidney Cohen qtd. in ibid., 95.

11. Oscar Janiger qtd. in Stafford, *Psychedelics Encyclopedia*, 42.

12. Timothy Leary, *Flashbacks: A Personal and Cultural History of an Era* (New York: G. P. Putnam's Sons, 1990), 44.

13. Alan Watts, *In My Own Way: An Autobiography, 1915–1965* (Novato, Calif.: New World Library, 1972), 323.

14. "Clinical and Therapeutic Uses of L.s.d.," KPFA, broadcast October 15, 1960, Pacifica Radio Archives, accessed August 7, 2013, http://pacificaradioarchives.org/recording/bb0155a.

15. Novak, "LSD before Leary," 97.

16. Lee and Shlain, *Acid Dreams*, 71.

17. Albin Krebs, "Clare Boothe Luce Dies at 84: Playwright, Politician, Envoy," *New York Times*, October 10, 1987.

18. Clare Boothe Luce kept a transcript of a conversation she held with her husband concerning this episode in their marriage and discussed her reaction in other personal writings. See "Conference between HRL and CBL," and "Imaginary Interview," Clare Boothe Luce Collection, Library of Congress, Washington, D.C., (hereafter Clare Booth Luce Collection), box 796, container 4.

19. W. A. Swanberg, *Luce and His Empire* (New York: Charles Scribner's Sons, 1972), 403.

20. She discussed her psychological state in a letter addressed to Heard but with instructions for him to pass it along to Cohen. See Clare Boothe Luce to Gerald Heard, November 20, 1959, Clare Boothe Luce Collection, box 796, container 12.

21. Ibid.

22. Clare was active in the Republican party and served as national co-chair for Barry Goldwater's 1964 presidential run. See "Experiment with LSD 11 Mar. 1959, Phoenix, Arizona," Clare Boothe Luce Collection, box 793, container 4.

23. In her LSD journals, Luce typically listed those present with initials only. However, correspondence with Murray and Heard confirms that they took LSD together. Gerald Heard to Clare Boothe Luce, February 13, 1960, Clare Boothe Luce Collection, box 766, container 3; John Murray to Clare Boothe Luce, March 12, 1960, Clare Boothe Luce Collection, box 766, container 9; John Murray to Clare Boothe Luce, August 1,

1962, Clare Boothe Luce Collection, box 795, container 8; and "Conference between HRL and CBL," Clare Boothe Luce Collection, box 796, container 4.

24. Journal dated December 8, 1959, Clare Boothe Luce Collection, box 793, container 4.

25. Journal dated August 6, 1960, Clare Boothe Luce Collection, box 793, container 4.

26. Journal dated February 14, 1961, Clare Boothe Luce Collection, box 793, container 4.

27. "A.M. 11:45 HRL took 100 gamma of lsd . . .," n.d. Clare Boothe Luce Collection, box 793, container 4.

28. Sidney Cohen to Clare Boothe Luce, n.d., Clare Boothe Luce Collection, box 795, container 3.

29. "11:30 A.M. Took 75 micrograms LSD 25 at Waldorf . . .," n.d., Clare Boothe Luce collection, box 973, container 4.

30. Oscar Janiger and Marlene Dobkin de Rios, "LSD and Creativity," *Journal of Psychoactive Drugs* 21 (January–March 1989): 129, 131.

31. Anaïs Nin, *The Diary of Anaïs Nin, Volume 5: 1947–1955* (New York: Harcourt, Brace, Jovanovich, 1974), 255–60 (quotes on 257 and 259).

32. Marlene Dobkin de Rios and Oscar Janiger, *LSD, Spirituality, and the Creative Process* (Rochester, Vt.: Park Street Press, 2003), 81.

33. Janiger and Dobkin de Rios, "LSD and Creativity," 133, 132.

34. Aldous Huxley, "Drugs that Shape Men's Minds," *Saturday Evening Post,* October 18, 1958, 113.

35. Aldous Huxley, "History of Tension," *Scientific Monthly,* July 1957, 9.

36. Jane Dunlap [Adelle Davis], *Exploring Inner Space: Personal Experiences under LSD-25* (New York: Harcourt Brace and World, 1961), 11.

37. Jane Dunlap [Adelle Davis], "Exploring the Soul with LSD," *Fate,* June 1962, 31.

38. Alan Watts, "Who Will Run Your Nervous System," *New Republic,* November 28, 1964.

39. Gerald Heard, "Can This Drug Enlarge Man's Mind?" *Horizon,* May 1963, 115.

40. Thanks to the *Harvard Psychedelic Club* author Don Lattin for posting footage of the 1957 documentary on the Internet. See "LSD Research," accessed August 28, 2012, http://www.youtube.com/watch?v=V5d4wWGK4Ig.

41. Novak, "LSD before Leary," 101. *Harvest's* mission is quoted in an article about its host, Frank Baxter. See David Stewart, "Frank Baxter, Television's First Man of Learning," *Current,* January 29, 1996, accessed August 13, 2013, http://www.current.org/1996/01/frank-baxter-televisions-first-man-of-learning/.

42. Harry Nelson, "Fantastic Sensations Gained with New Drug," *Los Angeles Times,* March 13, 1958.

43. Betty Eisner, "Remembrances of LSD Therapy Past," self-published memoir, August 7, 2002, 5–6, accessed August 1, 2014, http://www.erowid.org/culture/characters/eisner_betty/remembrances_lsd_therapy.pdf.

44. Ibid., 12.

45. Ibid., 20–21.

46. Betty Grover Eisner and Sidney Cohen, "Psychotherapy with Lysergic Acid Diethylamide," *Journal of Nervous and Mental Disease* 127 (December 1958): 531, 533, 535–36.

47. Milton Silverman, "Drug 'Purges' Mind of Old Repressions," *San Francisco Chronicle*, June 26, 1958.

48. Eisner, "Remembrances of LSD Therapy Past," 91.

49. Palmer Chase, "Psychiatrist Lauds Savage Tribe Drugs," *San Diego Evening Tribune*, May 12, 1958.

50. "Hallucinatory Drugs Defended by Doctor," *Los Angeles Times*, February 21, 1958.

51. Sidney Cohen, "Psychotherapy with LSD: Pro and Con," in *The Use of LSD in Psychotherapy and Alcoholism*, ed. Harold A. Abramson (Indianapolis: Bobbs-Merrill, 1967), 578.

52. Brecher, *Licit and Illicit Drugs*, 351.

53. Stevens, *Storming Heaven*, 63–65.

54. Joe Hyams, "What Psychiatry Has Done for Cary Grant," *New York Herald Tribune*, April 20, 1959.

55. Hyams qtd. in Bob Gains, "LSD: Hollywood's Status Symbol Drug," *Cosmopolitan*, November 1963, 79.

56. Joe Hyams, *Mislaid in Hollywood* (New York: Peter H. Wyden, 1973), 90.

57. Ibid., 78–98; and Charles Higham and Roy Moseley, *Cary Grant: The Lonely Heart* (New York: Harcourt, Brace, Jovanovich, 1989), 248–54.

58. Laura Bergquist, "The Curious Story behind the New Cary Grant," *Look*, September 1, 1959, 50, 57.

59. Marc Eliot, *Cary Grant* (New York: Harmony Books, 2004), 325–26; and Higham and Moseley, *Cary Grant*, 254.

60. Amos Coggins, "Cary Grant—Ageless Idol," *Washington Post*, February 14, 1960; and Herman Goodman, "What Is L.S.D. and How It Works," *Washington Post*, February 14, 1960.

61. Richard Gehman, "The Ageless Cary Grant," *Good Housekeeping*, September 1960, 66.

62. Cary Grant, "Archie Leach (Part I)," *Ladies' Home Journal*, January–February 1963, 50–53, 133–42; Cary Grant, "Archie Leach (Part 2)," *Ladies' Home Journal*, March 1963, 23–24, 35–42; and Cary Grant, "Archie Leach (Conclusion)," *Ladies' Home Journal*, April 1963, 86–87, 148–52 (quotes are from "Part 2," 42, and "Conclusion," 152).

63. Gloria Powell, "LSD Changed Cary Grant's Private Life," *National Police Gazette*, December 1967, 3–4, 25. See also Mae Tinee, "Cary Grant Suave Fielder of Questions on Many Topics," *Chicago Tribune*, December 13, 1964; Warren Hodge, "The Other Cary Grant," *New York Times*, July 3, 1977; Betty White, "Cary Grant Today," *Saturday Evening Post*, March 1978, 46; Gene Siskel, "The Real Cary Grant," *Chicago Tribune*, December 7, 1986.

64. "Cary Took LSD, Mrs. Grant Says," *Washington Post*, March 21, 1968.

65. "The Psyche in 3-D," *Time*, March 28, 1960, 83.

66. Joe Hyams, "How a New Shock Drug Unlocks Troubled Minds," *This Week*, November 8, 1959, 7.

67. Ibid., 7, 9–10.

68. See, for example, "16 Prisoners 'Go Crazy' in Humanity's Behalf," *Washington Post*, January 13, 1957; "Scientist Finds Clew to Cancer's Growth," *Chicago Tribune*, March 29, 1959; and Nate Haseltine, "New Cancer Drug to be Tested," *Washington Post*, March 28, 1960.

69. Norma Lee Browning, "Ecstasy Drugs: New Powers for Us All," *Chicago Tribune*, October 2, 1960.

70. Franz E. Winkler, "Beware of LSD," *This Week*, May 15, 1960, 15.

71. Louis Lasagna, *The Doctors' Dilemmas* (New York: Harper and Brothers, 1962), 207–8.

72. Louis Jolyon West qtd. in Harold A. Abramson, ed., *The Use of LSD in Psychotherapy* (New York: Macy Foundation, 1960), 185.

73. Jonathan O. Cole, "Drugs and Control of the Mind," in *Man and Civilization: Control of the Mind*, ed. Seymour M. Farber and Roger H. L. Wilson, (New York: McGraw-Hill, 1961), 117.

74. Novak, "LSD before Leary," 100–101.

75. "Has Science Met Defeat," *Sandusky (Ohio) Register*, August 18, 1961.

76. Ralph Dighton, "A Second Mushroom, Then—Wham!" *Asheville (N.C.) Citizen-Times*, December 11, 1960.

77. John Kenneth Muir, *An Analytical Guide to Television's* One Step Beyond, *1959–1960* (Jefferson, N.C.: McFarland, 2001), 188–92.

78. Dighton, "Second Mushroom, Then—Wham!"

79. Brecher, *Licit and Illicit Drugs*, 366.

80. Nicholas Bercel et al., "Model Psychoses Induced by LSD-25 in Normals," *Archives of Neurology and Psychiatry* 75 (1956): 590.

81. Nate Haseltine, "Doctors Cite Mental Quirks of Drug-Test Volunteers," *Washington Post*, May 13, 1960.

82. Novak, "LSD before Leary," 106.

83. Stafford, *Psychedelics Encyclopedia*, 49; and R. E. L. Masters and Jean Houston, *The Varieties of Psychedelic Experience* (New York: Dell, 1966), 1.

84. Novak, "LSD before Leary," 108.

85. Howard Kennedy, "Legal Curb Urged on 'Thrill Drugs,'" *Los Angeles Times*, December 31, 1962.

86. "Drugs Seized in Raid on Church Analyzed," *Los Angeles Times*, June 15, 1962.

87. Sidney Cohen and Keith Ditman, "Complications Associated with Lysergic Acid Diethylamide (LSD-25)," *Journal of the American Medical Association* 181 (July 14, 1962): 161–62.

88. Harry Nelson, "Doctors Reveal Traffic in Hallucinations Drug," *Los Angeles Times*, July 14, 1962; and Donald Janson, "Doctors Report a Black Market in Drug that Causes Delusions," *New York Times*, July 14, 1962.

89. Harry Nelson, "Restrictions Urged on Hallucinatory Drug," *Los Angeles Times*, December 14, 1962.

90. "Use of Mind-Changing Drugs Seen as Issue," *Los Angeles Times*, November 30, 1962.

91. Elmont Waite, "Medical Study of Drivers Who Have Accidents Urged," *San Francisco Chronicle*, June 26, 1958; and Arthur Hoppe, "Physicians Sample the Pitchmen's Wares," *San Francisco Chronicle*, June 26, 1958.

92. William Braden argued in 1973, "Newspapers in recent years have produced their experts on outer space, as well as education, labour, politics, urban planning, and human relations, to the point where major city rooms have come to resemble mini-universities. As yet, however, they have not developed any comparable authorities on inner space." See Braden, "LSD and the Press," 197.

93. Alex Barnum, "George Dusheck—Pioneering S.F. Science Reporter," *San Francisco Chronicle*, June 4, 2005.

94. George Dusheck, "Visions . . . a Drug on the Market," *San Francisco News Call Bulletin*, January 2, 1963.

95. George Dusheck, "In Drug-Filled Chalice, Total Love," *San Francisco News Call Bulletin*, January 3, 1963.

96. George Dusheck, "A Man and His Dream Drugs . . . Fires his Psychiatrist," *San Francisco News Call Bulletin*, January 4, 1963.

97. George Dusheck, "On a Pin-Head—Revelations," *San Francisco News Call Bulletin*, January 5, 1963.

98. "Pulse of the Public: A Rare Psychic Adventure," *San Francisco News Call Bulletin*, January 9, 1963.

99. "Thalidomide Disaster," *Time*, August 10, 1960, 80.

100. "Vigilant Doctor Gets a Medal," *U.S. News and World Report*, August 20, 1962, 13; Morton Mintz, "'Heroine' of FDA Keeps Bad Drug off the Market," *New York Times*, July 15, 1962; Morton Mintz, "The Doctor Said No," *Reader's Digest*, October 1962, 86–89; J. L. Block, "Doctor Kelsey's Stubborn Triumph," *Good Housekeeping*, November 1962, 12; and "*Parents* Magazine Honors Dr. Frances Oldham Kelsey for Outstanding Service to Family Health," *Parents*, October 1962, 64.

101. Novak, "LSD before Leary," 108.

102. Sidney Cohen and Keith Ditman, "Prolonged Adverse Reactions to Lysergic Acid Diethylamide," *Archives of General Psychiatry* 8 (May 1963): 476–79.

103. Ibid., 479.

104. Roy R. Grinker Sr., "Lysergic Acid Diethylamide," *Archives of General Psychiatry* 8 (May 1963): 425.

105. Jonathon O. Cole and Martin M. Katz, "The Psychotomimetic Drugs: An Overview," *Journal of the American Medical Association* 187 (March 7, 1964): 758.

Chapter 5. Luce, Leary, and LSD, 1963–1965

1. Laura Mansnerus, "Timothy Leary, Pied Piper of Psychedelic 60's, Dies at 75," *New York Times*, June 1, 1996.

2. Lee and Shlain, *Acid Dreams,* 88.

3. Robert E. Herzstein, *Henry R. Luce, Time, and the American Crusade in Asia* (New York: G. Putnam's Sons, 1991), 240.

4. Abbie Hoffman, *Soon to Be a Major Motion Picture* (New York: G. P. Putnam's Sons, 1980), 73.

5. Alan Brinkley, *The Publisher: Henry Luce and His American Century* (New York: Alfred A. Knopf, 2010), 34.

6. "Luce Had Missed U.S. Hometown," *Lawrence (Kans.) Journal-World,* March 1, 1967.

7. Brinkley, *The Publisher,* 52–53.

8. Alden Whitman, "Henry R. Luce, Creator of Time-Life Magazine Empire, Dies in Phoenix at 68," *New York Times,* March 1, 1967.

9. James L. Baughman, *Henry R. Luce and the Rise of the American News Media* (Baltimore: Johns Hopkins University Press, 1987), 7.

10. Curtis Prendergast with Geoffrey Colvin, *Time Inc.: The Intimate History of a Changing Enterprise,* vol. 3 (New York: Atheneum, 1986), 195. W. A. Swanberg reports that at the time of his retirement, Luce was asked by the editor of *McCall's,* "But if the editors now decide to support candidate A for President, and you are for candidate B, which candidate will the magazines support?" Luce responded: "That's simple. They will support candidate B." See W. A. Swanberg, *Luce and His Empire* (New York: Charles Scribner's Sons, 1972), 443.

11. Joseph Epstein, "Henry Luce and His *Time,*" *Commentary,* November 1967, 40.

12. Ralph G. Martin, *Henry and Clare: An Intimate Portrait of the Luces* (New York: G. Putnam's Sons, 1991), 401. This trip is also described in Herzstein, *Henry R. Luce, Time, and the American Crusade in Asia,* 240.

13. Wilfred Sheed, *Clare Boothe Luce* (New York: E. P. Dutton, 1982), 124. Both trips are also briefly mentioned in Baughman, *Henry R. Luce and the Rise of the American News Media,* 193. The origins of these accounts and the dates when these episodes took place are not clear, but correspondence between Clare Boothe Luce and Gerald Heard indicate that they took place sometime between March 1959 and February 1960.

14. Loudon Wainwright, *The Great American Magazine* (New York: Alfred A. Knopf, 1986), 285.

15. John Hersey qtd. in Martin, *Henry and Clare,* 401. The episode is also described in Swanberg, *Luce and His Empire,* 476.

16. Swanberg, *Luce and His Empire,* 463.

17. "The Pros and Cons of LSD," *Time,* December 18, 1964, 63.

18. Ibid.

19. Ibid., 64.

20. The inscription reads, "Clare, if 'What is received is received according to the nature of the recipient'—I am both the finest and the worst of men—the finest for having known you—the worst for having lost that greatest of opportunities. It is to you—of course—to whom the book was written—a poor enough offering—but with it goes my love to the end." See Clare Boothe Luce Collection, box 715, container 14.

21. Novak, "LSD before Leary," 100.

22. Greenfield, *Timothy Leary*, 17–61.

23. Ibid., 62–75.

24. Frank Barron and Timothy F. Leary, "Changes in Psychoneurotic Patients with and without Psychotherapy," *Journal of Counseling Psychology* 19 (August 1955): 245.

25. Leary, *Flashbacks*, 16. The evolution of Leary's psychological thought is also described in Thomas J. Riedlinger, "Existential Transactions at Harvard: Timothy Leary's Humanistic Psychotherapy," *Journal of Humanistic Psychology* 33 (Summer 1993): 6–18.

26. Qtd. in Stevens, *Storming Heaven*, 128.

27. Qtd. in Greenfield, *Timothy Leary*, 76.

28. Ibid., 76–97.

29. Leary, *Flashbacks*, 16.

30. Greenfield, *Timothy Leary*, 101–4 (quote on 103).

31. Leary, *Flashbacks*, 17.

32. Greenfield, *Timothy Leary*, 115.

33. Qtd. in ibid., 106.

34. Qtd. in ibid., 113.

35. Leary, *Flashbacks*, 33.

36. Greenfield, *Timothy Leary*, 15–18.

37. Timothy Leary, *High Priest*, new ed. (Berkeley, Calif.: Ronin, 1995), 67.

38. Ibid., 69.

39. Ibid., 69–70.

40. Greenfield, *Timothy Leary*, 125–42.

41. Ibid., 144.

42. Leary, *Flashbacks*, 85.

43. Ibid., 88.

44. Rick Doblin, "Dr. Leary's Concord Prison Experiment: A 34-Year Follow-Up Study," *Journal of Psychoactive Drugs* 30 (October–December 1998): 420–21.

45. Timothy Leary, Ralph Metzner, Madison Presnell, Gunther Weil, Ralph Schwitzgebel, and Sarah Kinne, "A New Behavior Change Program Using Psilocybin," *Psychotherapy* 2 (July 1965): 71.

46. Leary, *High Priest*, 209.

47. Qtd. in Greenfield, *Timothy Leary*, 159.

48. See the *Time* covers "Can This Guy Make You Healthy," May 12, 1997; and "Living Better Longer," October 17, 2005.

49. Andrew Weil, "'Better Than a Damn' from the Bottle," *Harvard Crimson*, February 20, 1962.

50. Richard Alpert and Timothy Leary, "Mescaline Reaction," *Harvard Crimson*, February 21, 1962.

51. Robert E. Smith, "Psychologists Disagree on Psilocybin Research," *Harvard Crimson*, March 15, 1962.

52. Noah Gordon, "Hallucination Drug Fought at Harvard," *Boston Herald*, March 16, 1962.

53. "State Will Investigate Research on Psilocybin," *Harvard Crimson*, March 21, 1962.

54. Bruce L. Paisner, "State Allows Drug Studies at University; Officials Will Require Attendance of Doctor," *Harvard Crimson*, April 16, 1962.

55. Greenfield, *Timothy Leary*, 179–80.

56. Timothy Leary, *The Politics of Ecstasy* (Berkeley, Calif.: Ronin Publishing, 1998), 15.

57. Walter N. Pahnke, "Drugs and Mysticism," in *Psychedelics: The Uses and Implications of Hallucinogenic Drugs*, ed. Bernard Aaronson and Humphry Osmond (Garden City, N.Y.: Anchor, 1970), 145–65.

58. Timothy Leary, "The Religious Experience: Its Production and Interpretation," in *The Psychedelic Reader*, ed. Gunther M. Weil, Ralph Metzner, and Timothy Leary (New Hyde Park, N.Y.: University Books, 1965), 192.

59. Joseph Havens, "Working Paper: Memo on the Religious Implications of the Consciousness-Changing Drugs (LSD, Mescaline, Psilocybin)," *Journal for the Scientific Study of Religion* 3 (Spring 1964): 218.

60. Rick Doblin, "Pahnke's 'Good Friday Experiment': A Long-term Follow-up and Methodological Critique," *Journal of Transpersonal Psychology* 23 (August 1991): 21.

61. Ibid., 21–22.

62. Ibid., 23.

63. Ibid.; and R. R. Griffiths, W. A. Richards, U. McCann, and R. Jesse, "Psilocybin Can Occasion Mystical-Type Experiences Having Substantial and Sustained Personal Meaning and Spiritual Significance," *Psychopharmacology* 187 (August 2006): 268.

64. Doblin, "Dr. Leary's Concord Prison Experiment," 422.

65. Ralph Metzner, "Reflections on the Concord Prison Experiment and the Follow-Up Study," *Journal of Psychoactive Drugs* 30 (October–December 1998): 427–28.

66. Ibid., 428.

67. Joel E. Cohen, "Drugs and Inner Freedom," *Harvard Crimson*, October 25, 1962.

68. Joseph M. Russin, "Drug Warning Gets Wide Coverage; Source of Drugs Remains Mystery," *Harvard Crimson*, December 1, 1962.

69. Fred M. Hechinger, "Use of 'Mind-Distorting' Drugs Rising at Harvard, Dean Says," *New York Times*, December 11, 1962.

70. Timothy Leary and Richard Alpert, "Letter from Alpert, Leary," *Harvard Crimson*, December 13, 1962.

71. Fred M. Hechinger, "Harvard Debates Mind-Drug 'Peril'" *New York Times*, December 14, 1962.

72. "Hallucinations," *Newsweek*, December 10, 1962, 56.

73. Herbert Black, "Many Issues Involved in Harvard Drug Dispute," *Boston Globe*, December 13, 1963.

74. Jean Dietz, "Artist Reveals Effects of Vision Drug," *Boston Globe*, March 24, 1963.

75. Greenfield, *Timothy Leary*, 194–95.

76. Harry Nelson, "Psychologist Plans Institute on Brain Drugs," *Los Angeles Times*, April 17, 1963.

77. "Leary—I'm Ousted; Harvard—Nonsense," *Boston Globe*, April 17, 1963.

78. "Harvard Fires 2 for Testing a Brain Drug," *Chicago Tribune,* May 29, 1963; "Harvard Ousting Aide in Drug Case," *New York Times,* May 28, 1963; and John H. Fenton, "Ousted Educator Rebuts Harvard," *New York Times,* May 29, 1963.

79. Herbert Black, "Ousted Harvard Researchers Plan 'Retreat' in Mexico," *Boston Globe,* May 29, 1963.

80. The quotation is from a UPI report that ran in the *New York Times, Washington Post,* and *Boston Globe.* See "Mexico Ousts 20 in Drug Research," *New York Times,* June 16, 1963; "Mexico Expels 20 in Psychic Drug Study," *Washington Post,* June 15, 1963; and "Ex-Harvard Doctor Ordered Out of Mexico," *Boston Globe,* June 15, 1963. The *Los Angeles Times* ran a similar item credited to the Associated Press, "Mexico Ousts 21 Researchers in 'Magic' Tests," *Los Angeles Times,* June 15, 1963.

81. George Dusheck, "'Paradise Lost' in a Mexico LSD Colony," *San Francisco News Call Bulletin,* July 2, 1963. See also Dusheck, "LSD 'Paradise' Shut by Mexico," *San Francisco News Call Bulletin,* July 1, 1963.

82. Braden, "LSD and the Press," 199.

83. Ibid., 196–97, 204 (quote on 196).

84. Ibid., 207.

85. "Psychic-Drug Testers Living in Retreat," *New York Times,* December 14, 1963.

86. Greenfield writes that during this period, residents of the Millbrook took LSD weekly in carefully programmed sessions. See *Timothy Leary,* 208.

87. Emma Harrison, "LSD Drug Found to Aid Children," *New York Times,* November 10, 1963.

88. Natalie Jaffe, "Mind Expanding Drug Studied at N.Y.U. Center," *New York Times,* March 12, 1965.

89. John A. Osmundsen, "Mind Drugs Helped Alcoholics to Quit Habit, Scientists Report," *New York Times,* May 11, 1965.

90. John A. Osmundsen, "Harvard Study Sees Benefit in Use of Mind Drugs," *New York Times,* May 15, 1965.

91. John A. Osmundsen, "Device Stimulates Mind-Drug Effects," *New York Times,* December 19, 1964.

92. Thomas Buckley, "L.S.D., for League of Spiritual Discovery," *New York Times,* October 2, 1966.

93. Nate Haseltine, "Drugs that Set Brain Aflame Herald Awesome Age of Plastic Personality," *Washington Post,* May 27, 1963.

94. Paul Coates, "Lawmakers Should Tread Lightly in Hypnosis Field, Heavily on LSD," *Los Angeles Times,* January 3, 1963.

95. Robert R. Kirsch, "LSD—Delusions of Grandeur Plague the Wonder Drug," *Los Angeles Times,* October 25, 1964.

96. Tinee, "Cary Grant Suave Fielder of Questions on Many Topics."

97. Ray Richard, "Parents Didn't Believe Their Kids Were Hooked—Until Too Late," *Boston Globe,* January 26, 1965.

98. "U.S. Studies Morning Glory Seeds as Narcotic," *New York Times*, July 11, 1963.

99. Herb Caen, "Wonderful Morning Glory Whirl," *Los Angeles Times*, July 12, 1963.

100. Reese and Danielan, "Intermedia Influence and the Drug Issue," 31.

101. "No Illusions," *Newsweek*, June 10, 1963.

102. Lattin, *Harvard Psychedelic Club*, 94.

103. Andrew T. Weil, "The Strange Case of the Harvard Drug Scandal," *Look*, November 8, 1963, 43.

104. Noah Gordon, "The Hallucinogenic Drug Cult," *The Reporter*, August 15, 1963, 35–43.

105. Timothy Leary, letter to the editor, *The Reporter*, September 12, 1963, 6.

106. Martin Mayer, "Getting Alienated with the Right Crowd at Harvard," *Esquire*, September 1963, 73.

107. Timothy Leary, "In the Beginning, Leary Turned on Ginsberg and Saw That It Was Good," *Esquire*, July 1968, 83–86.

108. Leary, *Politics of Ecstasy*, 70–86.

109. Dan Wakefield, "A Reporter's Objective View," Alan Harrington, "A Novelist's Personal Experience," and Aldous Huxley, "A Philosopher's Visionary Perspective," in "The Pros and Cons, History and Future Possibilities of Vision-Inducing Psychochemicals," *Playboy*, November 1963, all beginning on 84.

110. Richard Alpert, Timothy Leary, and Ralph Metzner, "Dear Playboy," *Playboy*, February 1963, 5.

111. John Kobler, "The Dangerous Magic of LSD," *Saturday Evening Post*, November 2, 1963, 32.

112. Ibid., 39.

113. Bob Gains, "LSD: Hollywood's Status-Symbol Drug," *Cosmopolitan*, November 1963, 78.

114. Ibid., 79, 80.

115. Robert P. Goldman, "Instant Happiness," *Ladies' Home Journal*, October 1963, 68–69.

116. "LSD," *Time*, March 29, 1963, 72.

117. "Instant Mysticism," *Time*, October 25, 1963, 86.

118. Ibid., 87.

119. Robert Coughlan, "Control of the Brain," *Life*, March 8, 1963, 92–95. The typed rough draft of the article is in the Clare Boothe Luce Collection, box 715, container 14.

120. Robert Coughlan, "The Chemical Mind Changers," *Life*, March 15, 1963, 89; and Clare Boothe Luce Collection, box 715, container 14.

121. "The Pros and Cons of LSD," *Time*, December 18, 1964, 63–64.

122. Leonard Wallace Robinson, "Hearing Color, Smelling Music, Touching a Scent," *New York Times Magazine*, August 22, 1965, 14, 57.

123. Harry Asher, "They Split My Personality," *Saturday Review*, June 1, 1963, 43.

124. Heard, "Can This Drug Enlarge Man's Mind?"

125. "The LSD Blueprint," *Newsweek*, May 24, 1965, 69; and John A. Osmundsen, "Mind Drugs Help Architect's Work: Use of LSD Aids Designer of Mental Hospitals," *New York Times*, May 9, 1965.

126. Sidney Cohen, "LSD and the Anguish of Dying," *Harper's*, September 1965, 69–72, 77–79.

127. "Drugs Studied to Aid Astronauts," *Missiles and Rockets*, March 15, 1965, 33.

128. Arleene MacMinn, "Weekend TV," *Los Angeles Times*, September 7, 1963.

129. B. J. Wander Jr., "Ex-Harvard Psychologists Attempt to Clear Clouds of 'Mind' Drugs," *Edwardsville (Ill.) Intelligencer*, November 5, 1965.

130. "Radio," *New York Times*, October 13, 1964.

131. "Radio Highlights for the Week," *Washington Post*, October 24, 1965.

132. "Selected Highlights on the Radio this Week," *Washington Post*, December 12, 1965.

133. Paul Gardner, "Successor to 'Creative Persons' Listed on N.E.T.'s Fall Line-Up," *New York Times*, August 30, 1965.

134. Stephen Bowie, "LSD," Classic TV History Blog, April 29, 2012, accessed August 13, 2013, http://classictvhistory.wordpress.com/2012/04/29/lsd/.

135. "Television Highlights," *Washington Post*, January 5, 1965.

136. *The March of Time*, "Frontiers of the Mind," originally aired November 29, 1965. The program has been digitized and is available through the HBO Archival Collection, www.hboarchives.com. Military research with LSD is discussed at length in Lee and Shlain, *Acid Dreams*.

137. "Television This Week," *New York Times*, March 28, 1965.

138. Musto and Korsmeyer, *Quest for Drug Control*, 3.

139. "House Votes Stiff Curbs on 'Pep Pills' by 402 to 0," *Washington Post*, March 11, 1965; and "Bill to Control Pep Pill Sales Passed by House," *Los Angeles Times*, March 11, 1965. Coverage in the *New York Times* and *Chicago Tribune* did not mention LSD.

140. *Drug Abuse Control Amendments of 1965*, Public Law 89-74, 89th Cong., 2d Sess. (July 15, 1965).

141. Braden, "LSD and the Press," 206.

142. Richard Alpert and Sidney Cohen, *LSD*, ed. Carol Sturm Smith (New York: New American Library, 1966), 10.

143. Aldous Huxley, *Letters of Aldous Huxley*, ed. Grover Smith (New York: Harper and Row, 1969), 945.

144. Martin Arnold, "Narcotics a Growing Problem of Affluent Youth," *New York Times*, January 4, 1965; and Fred M. Hechinger, "Education: Drug Issue," *New York Times*, February 28, 1965.

145. Leonard Downie Jr., "Drug-Taking Spreads on Nation's Campuses," *Washington Post*, September 9, 1965; and Leonard Downie Jr., "College Craze: Drug Taking Attracts Close Attention of Federal Narcotics, Food Officials," *Boston Globe*, September 11, 1965.

146. Jack Anderson, "The Narcotics Kick: College Crowd Going to Pot," *Boston Globe*, November 25, 1965.

147. Harry Nelson, "Students' Drug Use Stirs Alarm," *Los Angeles Times,* August 5, 1965; and Mal Terence, "LSD: Problem for Both Science and Law," *Los Angeles Times,* November 21, 1965.

148. Bill Davidson, "The Thrill-Pill Menace," *Saturday Evening Post,* December 4, 1965, 27.

149. Michael Herr, "The Drug Puzzle," *Mademoiselle,* August 1965, 246–47.

150. Blum, Blum, and Funkhouser, "Natural History of LSD Use," 31–35, 40.

151. Gitlin, "On Drugs and Mass Media in America's Consumer Society," 44.

152. Charles D. Dahlberg, Ruth Mechaneck, and Stanley Feldstein, "LSD Research: The Impact of Lay Publicity," *Journal of American Psychiatry* 125 (November 5, 1968): 685, 687.

Chapter 6. Moral Panic and Media Hype, 1966–1968

1. Braden, "LSD and the Press," 208.

2. Musto and Korsmeyer, *Quest for Drug Control,* 23–27.

3. Greenfield, *Timothy Leary,* 246–52.

4. Ibid., 263.

5. George Reasons, "LSD Ties with Happiness Declared Hokum," *Los Angeles Times,* July 12, 1966.

6. Bernard Weinraub, "LSD: A Fascinating Drug and a Growing Problem," *New York Times,* April 22, 1966.

7. "Radio," *New York Times,* May 7, 1966.

8. "Radio—Today's Leading Events," *New York Times,* May 8, 1966.

9. "Dr. Leary to Appear on LSD Panel Show," *New York Times,* May 6, 1966; and "Television This Week," *New York Times,* May 15, 1966.

10. "Television Highlights," *Washington Post,* June 30, 1966.

11. Charles Champlin, "Bigger Audiences for a Lonely Voice," *Los Angeles Times,* July 8, 1966.

12. Braden, "LSD and the Press," 207.

13. Jack Gould, "TV: Uses of LSD—A Grim Warning," *New York Times,* May 18, 1966.

14. WBGH Educational Foundation, "LSD: Lettvin vs. Leary," originally aired November 30, 1967, can be streamed from the Web site of WGBH, accessed November 21, 2013, http://openvault.wgbh.org/catalog/7df2a7-lsd-lettvin-vs-leary.

15. Bud Collins, "LSD Lion Loses to M.I.T. Mauler," *Boston Globe,* November 24, 1967.

16. John H. Averill, "Witnesses Tell of LSD Usage, Perils," *Los Angeles Times,* May 14, 1966.

17. "Leary Sees Crisis in the Use of LSD," *New York Times,* May 14, 1966.

18. Marjorie Hunter, "F.D.A. Denies Need for New LSD Law," *New York Times,* May 24, 1966.

19. Murray Schumach, "Distributor of LSD Recalls All Supplies," *New York Times,* April 15, 1966.

20. "The Legislature Controls LSD," *Los Angeles Times,* May 13, 1966; and Sydney H. Schanberg, "Albany Votes Bill to Force Police to Patrol Private Housing Here," *New York Times,* May 12, 1966.

21. Musto and Korsmeyer, *Quest for Drug Control,* 21.

22. Alden Whitman, "Marshall McLuhan, Author, Dies; Declared 'Medium Is the Message,'" *New York Times,* January 1, 1981.

23. Marshall McLuhan, *Understanding Media: The Extensions of Man* (New York: McGraw Hill, 1964), 3–6.

24. Timothy Leary, *Turn On, Tune In, Drop Out* (Berkeley, Calif.: Ronin, 1999), 40–41.

25. Leary, *Flashbacks,* 251–52.

26. Lattin, *Harvard Psychedelic Club,* 123.

27. Leary, *Flashbacks,* 253.

28. Neil Strauss, *Everyone Loves You When You're Dead* (New York: HarperCollins, 2011), 337.

29. Greenfield points out the similarity in *Timothy Leary,* 283.

30. Ibid.

31. "Leary to Disciples: Turn On, Drop Out," *Boston Globe,* May 22, 1966.

32. Greenfield, *Timothy Leary,* 264.

33. See "turn on," *Oxford English Dictionary,* 3d ed.

34. Lattin, *Harvard Psychedelic Club,* 143.

35. Leary, *Flashbacks,* 253.

36. Greenfield, *Timothy Leary,* 283.

37. Stevens, *Storming Heaven,* 277.

38. Goode and Ben-Yehuda, *Moral Panics,* 2d ed., 203.

39. Ibid., 202–4.

40. Braden, "LSD and the Press," 201.

41. Goode and Ben-Yehuda, *Moral Panics,* 2d ed., 79.

42. Peter Kerr, "Aaron E. Koota, 78, Is Dead; Former Judge and Prosecutor," *New York Times,* July 23, 1984.

43. Bernard Weinraub, "Koota Is Studying School-Made LSD," *New York Times,* April 20, 1966; and "3 Colleges Named in Study of Drugs," *New York Times,* April 25, 1966.

44. "Principals Deplore Koota's LSD Charge," *New York Times,* May 15, 1966; and "3 City Colleges Defended on LSD," *New York Times,* April 26, 1966.

45. Stafford, *Psychedelics Encyclopedia,* 62.

46. F. David Anderson, "Jury Acquits Kessler in LSD Murder," *New York Times,* October 26, 1967, and "Koota Seeks to Free Youth Whose Niece Ate LSD Cube," *New York Times,* May 18, 1966.

47. "Donna's Long Trip," *Newsweek,* September 25, 1967, 98; and "Donna and the Sugar Cube," *Newsweek,* April 18, 1966, 100.

48. "Murder by LSD?" *Newsweek,* April 25, 1966, 29; and "High Ground," *Newsweek,* November 6, 1967, 37.

49. "Dangers of LSD," *Time,* July 22, 1966, 52.

50. Leonard Wallace Robinson, "Hearing Color, Smelling Music, Touching a Scent," *New York Times Magazine*, August 22, 1965, 52; and Warren R. Young, "The Truth about LSD," *Reader's Digest*, September 1966, 59.

51. Thomas Buckley, "LSD Trigger," *New Republic*, May 14, 1966, 15.

52. "Four Students under LSD Hurt Eyes by Sun-Gazing," *New York Times*, May 19, 1967.

53. "More Bad Trips on LSD," *Time*, May 26, 1967, 70.

54. "New Light on LSD," *Senior Scholastic*, September 28, 1967, 22.

55. "6 Youths on LSD 'Trip' Blinded by Sun," *New York Times*, January 13, 1968; "Blame LSD and Sun for Blinding 6," *Chicago Tribune*, January 13, 1968; "6 College Men Take LSD, Blinded by Sun," *Los Angeles Times*, January 13, 1968.

56. "Darkness at Noon," *Newsweek*, January 22, 1968, 24, 28.

57. "Another LSD Hallucination," *Time*, January 26, 1968, 66.

58. Letters, *Newsweek*, February 5, 1968, 4.

59. D. G. Fuller, "Severe Solar Maculopathy Associated with the Use of Lysergic Acid Diethylamide (LSD)," *American Journal of Ophthalmology* 81 (April 1976), 413–16; and H. Schatz and F. Mendelblatt, "Solar Retinopathy from Sun-Gazing under the Influence of LSD," *British Journal of Ophthalmology* 57 (April 1973), 270–73.

60. Young, "Truth about LSD," 59.

61. William W. Zeller, "LSD: Growing Menace to Teenagers," *Parents' Magazine and Better Homemaking*, November 1, 1967, 145.

62. *Licit and Illicit Drugs* was praised as "a towering work of scholarship" in a *New York Times* editorial on the same day as his obituary in 1989. See "Drugs and Edward Brecher," *New York Times*, April 25, 1989.

63. Edward M. Brecher, "LSD: Danger to Unborn Babies," *McCall's*, September 1967, 71.

64. Goode, *Drugs in American Society*, 251–52.

65. "Cell Damage from LSD," *Time*, March 24, 1967, 46; and "Drugs and Chromosomes," *Time*, September 15, 1967, 84–85.

66. "A New Report on LSD: Threat to Unborn Children," *U.S. News and World Report*, October 9, 1967, 66.

67. Bill Davidson, "The Hidden Evils of LSD," *Saturday Evening Post*, August 12, 1967, 22.

68. Nate Haseltine, "Worse Deformities Feared in LSD than Thalidomide," *Washington Post*, August 1, 1967.

69. "Trace Baby's Deformity to Mother's LSD," *Chicago Tribune*, November 24, 1967; "First Birth Defect Attributed to Use of LSD by Mother," *New York Times*, November 24, 1967; and "Birth Deformity Laid to LSD," *Washington Post*, November 24, 1967.

70. "One Taste of Evil . . . One Taste of LSD; That Wild and Sickening Night at the Party Led to Months of Fear and Agony," *Modern Romances*, September 1968, 26–29, 70–75.

71. Goode, *Drugs in American Society*, 252–53; and Andrew Weil, *The Natural Mind* (New York: Houghton Mifflin, 2004), 44–45.

72. "Birth Defects," Centers for Disease Control and Prevention, accessed October 27, 2013, http://www.cdc.gov/ncbddd/birthdefects/index.html.

73. Norman I. Dishotsky, William D. Loughman, Robert E. Mogar, and Wendell R. Lipscomb, "LSD and Genetic Damage," *Science* 172 (April 30, 1971): 440.

74. Goode and Ben-Yehuda, *Moral Panics*, 2d ed., 81.

75. Abe Peck, "Abe Peck on Why EVO Mattered," The Local East Village Blog, February 25, 2012, accessed October 28, 2013, http://eastvillage.thelocal.nytimes.com/2012/02/25/abe-peck-on-why-evo-mattered/.

76. Simon Galubara, "Micro Come Down," *East Village Other*, June 1, 1967.

77. Joel Meltz, "Acid Burned a Hole in My Genes," *East Village Other*, August 8, 1967. See also Simon Galubara, "Acid Chromosomes," *East Village Other*, May 15, 1967.

78. Art Janow, "Treating Acid Indigestion," *Boston Avatar*, August 4, 1967.

79. Weil, *Natural Mind*, 44–45; and Brecher, *Licit and Illicit Drugs*, 373–74.

80. Joseph Gfroerer and Marc Brodsky, "The Incidence of Illicit Drug Use in the United States, 1962–1989," *British Journal of Addiction* 87 (September 1992): 1348.

81. Donald B. Louria, "The Abuse of LSD," in *LSD, Man, and Society*, ed. Richard C. DeRold and Russell C. Leaf (Middletown, Conn.: Wesleyan University Press, 1967), 41.

82. "The Camera Takes a Trip," *U.S. Camera*, December 1967, 49.

83. "Psychedelic Art," *Horizon*, April 1, 1968, 28–31.

84. Tom Buckley, "The LSD Trigger," *New Republic*, May 14, 1966, 19–20; and Leszek Ochota, "What Is the Clinical Evidence," *New Republic*, May 14, 1966, 21–22.

85. Alan Watts, "Who Will Run Your Nervous System," *New Republic*, November 28, 1964, 15.

86. Lisa Bieberman, "The Psychedelic Experience," *New Republic*, August 5, 1967, 17, 19.

87. "The Kick," *New Republic*, April 16, 1966, 10; and David Sanford, "LSD Crackdown," *New Republic*, March 16, 1968, 11–12.

88. John Bleibtreu, "LSD and the Third Eye," *Atlantic Monthly*, September 1, 1966, 69.

89. George B. Leonard, "Where the California Game Is Taking Us," *Look*, June 28, 1966, 110.

90. George B. Leonard and Michael Murphy, "Esalen," *San Francisco Oracle*, February 1968, 6.

91. Allen Cohen, ed., *The San Francisco Oracle, Facsimile Edition: The Psychedelic Newspaper of the Haight-Ashbury, 1966–1968* (Berkeley, Calif.: Regent, 1991), xxvii.

92. John A. Osmundsen, "The Other Side of LSD: The Promise and the Peril," *Look*, July 26, 1966, 78.

93. Roland H. Berg, "Why Americans Hide behind a Chemical Curtain," *Look*, August 8, 1967, 13.

94. Jack Shepherd, "Potheads in Missouri," *Look*, August 8, 1967, 14–16.

95. Jack Shepherd, "I Popped in the Pill. I'm Off," *Look*, August 8, 1967, 23.

96. J. M. Flagler, "The Visions of Saint Tim," *Look*, August 8, 1967, 21.

97. Ibid., 18.

98. "Notes and Comment," *New Yorker,* October 1, 1966, 41–42.

99. "Celebration #1," *New Yorker,* October 1, 1966, 42–43.

100. Roger Vaughan, "Is This Trip Really Necessary?" *Life,* November 11, 1966, 24.

101. Rita Hoffmann, "The Psychedelic Game: A Day's Journey into Darkest Inner Space," *Mademoiselle,* March 1966, 179, 220.

102. Robert Gannon, "My LSD Trip: A Non-Cop, Non-Hippie Report of the Unvarnished Facts," *Popular Science,* December 1967, 61.

103. Ibid., 170.

104. *Esquire* published these covers in April 1968, December 1963, and November 1970. Renowned advertising man George Lois's covers for *Esquire* were exhibited at the Museum of Modern Art in New York and subsequently published in *George Lois: The Esquire Covers @ MOMA* (New York: Assouline, 2010).

105. Jacob Brackman, "The End of the Trip," *Esquire,* September 1966, 126.

106. Timothy Leary, "In the Beginning, Leary Turned on Ginsberg and Saw That It Was Good . . .," *Esquire,* July 1968.

107. "*Playboy* Interview: Timothy Leary," *Playboy,* September 1966, 100.

108. Donald Bruce Louria, "Cool Talk about Hot Drugs," *New York Times Magazine,* August 6, 1967, 45–46; and Max Lerner, "LSD Spelled Out," *Mademoiselle,* January 1967, 124.

109. Allan D. Coult, "Sex, Religion and LSD," *San Francisco Oracle,* January 1968, 20.

110. Joseph Andrews, "LSD—The Instant Thrill Pill," *Man's Illustrated,* July 1964, 23.

111. Jim Arthur, "Psyching Out—Our National Disgrace," *Man's Story,* August 1968, 36.

112. Stephen J. Gertz, *Dope Menace: The Sensational World of Drug Paperbacks, 1900–1975* (Port Townsend, Wash.: Feral House, 2008), 148–49.

113. "LSD and the Drugs of the Mind," *Newsweek,* May 9, 1966, 59.

114. Ibid., 60.

115. Arthur J. Kleps and R. E. Miles, "With LSD I Saw God," *Pageant,* August 1966, 57.

116. "The Hobbit Habit," *Time,* July 15, 1966, 48.

117. "Epidemic of 'Acid-Heads,'" *Time,* March 11, 1966, 44; and "LSD," *Time,* June 17, 1966, 30.

118. "Mysticism in the Lab," *Time,* September 23, 1966, 62.

119. "Turning It On with LSD," *Time,* November 25, 1966, 58.

120. Albert Rosenfeld, "The Vital Facts about the Drug and Its Effects," section of "Spread the Perils of LSD," *Life,* March 25, 1966, 30A.

121. "A Hard-Headed Businessman's Vivid Memory," section of "Spread the Perils of LSD," *Life,* March 25, 1966, 30D.

122. "LSD: Control, Not Prohibition," *Life,* April 29, 1966, 4.

123. "Psychedelic Art," *Life,* September 9, 1966, 19.

124. Swanberg, *Luce and His Empire,* 482.

125. John Kobler, *Luce: His Time, Life, and Fortune* (Garden City, N.Y.: Doubleday, 1968), 102.

126. "LSD Gave Luces the Time of Their Life," *New York Post,* March 2, 1968.

127. "Luces' Experiments with LSD Reported," *New York Times,* March 2, 1968.

128. Hoffman, *Soon to Be a Major Motion Picture,* 73.

129. Joe McGinniss, "The Resale of the President," *New York Times Magazine,* September 3, 1972, 20.

130. Martha Weinman Lear, "On Harry, and Henry and Ike and Mr. Shaw; Clare Boothe Luce, She Who Is behind 'The Women' Backstage," *New York Times Magazine,* April 22, 1973, 220.

131. Gitlin, "On Drugs and Mass Media in America's Consumer Society," 44; and Goode and Ben-Yehuda, *Moral Panics,* 2d ed., 81.

132. Bieberman, "Psychedelic Experience," 17.

133. "Sir Paul Reveals Beatles Drug Use," BBC News, June 2, 2004, accessed November 21, 2013, http://news.bbc.co.uk/2/hi/3769511.stm.

134. Lee and Shlain, *Acid Dreams,* 93.

135. "Reviving Research into Psychedelic Drugs," editorial, *The Lancet* 367 (April 15–21, 2006): 1214.

136. Benjamin Cornwell and Annulla Linders, "The Myth of 'Moral Panic': An Alternative Account of LSD Prohibition," *Deviant Behavior* 23 (2002): 325–26.

137. Musto and Korsmeyer, *Quest for Drug Control,* 12.

138. Jonathan Metzl, "'Mother's Little Helper': The Crisis of Psychoanalysis and the Miltown Resolution," *Gender and History* 15 (August 2003): 241.

139. David Herzberg, *Happy Pills in America: From Miltown to Prozac* (Baltimore: Johns Hopkins University Press, 2010), 60.

140. Young, "The Myth of the Drug Taker in the Mass Media," 315.

141. Ibid., 316.

142. Alfred W. Trembly, speaking before the Special Subcommittee of the Committee on the Judiciary, U.S. Senate, The Narcotic Rehabilitation Act of 1966: Hearings before a Special Subcommittee on the Judiciary, U.S. Senate, 89th Cong., January 25, 26 and 27, May 12, 13, 19, 23 and 25, June 14 and 15, July 19, 1966, 219.

143. Severin Peterson and Peggy Peterson, "Something New for Your Peace of Mind," *Ladies Home Journal,* February 1968, 112–14.

144. Sarah M. Pike, *New Age and Neopagan Religions in America* (New York: Columbia, 2004), 84; and Robert C. Fuller, *Spirituality in the Flesh: Bodily Sources of Religious Experience* (New York: Oxford, 2008), 87, 89.

Postscript

1. Richard Nixon, "Special Message to the Congress on Control of Narcotics and Dangerous Drugs," July 14, 1969, the American Presidency Project, ed. Gerhard Peters and John T. Woolley, accessed November 25, 2012, http://www.presidency.ucsb.edu/ws/?pid=2126.

2. Common Sense for Drug Policy, "Nixon Tapes Show Roots of Marijuana Prohibition: Misinformation, Culture Wars, and Prejudice," in *CSPD Research Report,* March 2002, 3–4.

3. Richard Nixon, "Remarks to Eastern Media Executives Attending a Briefing on Domestic Policy in Rochester, New York," June 18, 1971, the American Presidency Project, ed. Gerhard Peters and John T. Woolley, accessed March 3, 2014, http://www .presidency.ucsb.edu/ws/?pid=3049.

4. Edward Jay Epstein, *Agency of Fear: Opiates and Political Power in America,* rev. ed. (New York: Verso, 1990), 152; and Art Linkletter, "'Get Them Turned Back On to Live,'" *U.S. News and World Report,* December 29, 1969, 25.

5. Art Linkletter, "We Must Fight the Epidemic of Drug Abuse!" *Reader's Digest,* February 1970, 56–57.

6. Art Linkletter, "We Must Declare War on Drugs," *Good Housekeeping,* April 1970, 94; and Art Linkletter, "How Schools Can Fight Drug Abuse," *Education Digest,* October 1971, 20.

7. Epstein, *Agency of Fear,* 166.

8. Ibid., 167.

9. Ibid., 169.

10. Ibid., 167.

11. Ibid., 170.

12. Clay Gowran, "Dragnet Turns LSD into a TV Shocker," *Chicago Tribune,* January 13, 1967.

13. Jack Gould, "TV: Frank Exploration on 'Sex in the Sixties' Program," *New York Times,* January 13, 1967.

14. Jon Niccum, "Smothers Brothers Recall TV Censorship Battles," Lawrence.com, March 2, 2007, accessed November 25, 2013, http://www.lawrence.com/news/2007/ mar/02/smothers_brothers_recall_tv_censorship_battles.

15. Epstein, *Agency of Fear,* 170–72.

16. Ibid., 152, 170–71; Eric Nuzum, *Parental Advisory: Music Censorship in America* (New York: HarperCollins, 2001), 141–42; and Fred Powledge, *The Engineering of Restraint: The Nixon Administration and the Press* (Washington, D.C.: Public Affairs Press, 1971), 45–46.

17. Powledge, *Engineering of Restraint,* 46; Nuzum, *Parental Advisory,* 142; and Kenneth C. Creech, *Electronic Media Law and Regulation,* 3d ed. (Boston: Focal Press, 2000), 123.

18. Thomas J. Johnson and Wayne Wanta, with Timothy Boudreau, Janet Blank-Libra, Killian Schaffer, and Sally Turner, "Influence Dealers: A Path Analysis Model of Agenda Building during Richard Nixon's War on Drugs," *Journalism and Mass Communication Quarterly* 73 (Spring 1996): 189–90.

19. Benshoff, "Short Life of the Hollywood LSD Film," 29; and Cohen, *Beyond Within,* 50.

20. Benshoff, "Short-Lived Life of the Hollywood LSD Film," 34–38.

21. Garth Jowett, "'A Significant Medium for the Communication of Ideas': The Miracle Decision and the Decline of Motion Picture Censorship, 1952–1968," in

Censorship and American Culture, ed. Francis G. Couvares (Washington, D.C.: Smithsonian Institute Press, 1996), 258–68. A three-part test in the 1973 case *Miller v. California* established the following guidelines for identifying obscenity: "(a) whether 'the average person, applying contemporary community standards' would find that the work, taken as a whole, appeals to the prurient interest; (b) whether the work depicts or describes, in a patently offensive way, sexual conduct specifically defined by the applicable state law; and (c) whether the work, taken as a whole, lacks serious literary, artistic, political, or scientific value [citations omitted]." *Miller v. California,* 412 U.S. 15(1973): 24–25.

22. Starks, *Cocaine Fiends and Reefer Madness,* 57.

23. Benshoff, "Short-Lived Life of the Hollywood LSD Film," 38–40; and Dorian Lynskey, "The Monkees' Head: 'Our Fans Couldn't Even See It,'" *The Guardian,* April 28, 2011, accessed August 22, 2014, http://www.guardian.co.uk/music/2011/apr/28/monkees-head-jack-nicholson-interview.

24. Benshoff, "Short-Lived Life of the Hollywood LSD Film," 32.

25. Roger Ebert, "Easy Rider (1969)," Octber 24, 2004, accessed August 22, 2014, http://www.rogerebert.com/reviews/great-movie-easy-rider-1969.

26. Benshoff, "Short-Lived Life of the Hollywood LSD Film," 32.

27. McLuhan, *Understanding Media,* 3–6.

Index

Note: Page numbers in *italics* indicate figures.

abortion, 19, 159
Abramson, Harold A., 67
Academy of Canadian Film and Television, 30
acid. *See* LSD
addiction. *See* alcoholism; drug addiction
adrenaline, 47
adrenochrome, 47, 50, 55, 201n27
advertising and advertisements: as approach to LSD advocacy, 148–50; drug prescribing influenced by, 192–93n20; of *Hearst's International Magazine*, 23; of Huxley's *Doors of Perception*, 64; magazine articles on LSD as, 144; magic mushrooms and, 83–84, 107. *See also* antidrug crusades
agenda setting in media: antidrug rhetoric in context of, 27; influences on, 7–9, 28–32; LSD's shift to illegal status in, 177–78; political, official, and professional rhetoric underlying, 152–53; topics' flow from research journals to popular magazines, 57. *See also* media hype
Agnew, Spiro, 184

Agora Scientific Trust (Manhattan), 108
Alcoa, 107
alcohol consumption: Christian defense of, 76; of "International Sporting Set," 120; LSD compared with, 93; in media corporate culture, 1–2; mescaline compared with, 65; mixed messages on, 26; moral attitudes toward, 8
Alcoholics Anonymous, 61
alcoholism: drug research on, 196n5; LSD's promise for treatment of, 61, 104, 129, 130, 141
Algren, Nelson, 33–34
Alice in Wonderland (Carroll), 134
Alice in Wonderland (film), 188
Alles, Gordon A., 98–99
Alpert, Richard: fired from Harvard, 128, 136–37; LSD and other drug experiments of, 123, 124–25, 127, 170; mentioned, 129, 143; popular magazines on, 131–33, 136–37, 139
Alvarez, Walter C., 50
amanita muscaria (mushroom), 78
American Bar Association-American Medical Association joint study, 29
American Journal of Psychiatry, 12, 29, 51
American Journal of Sociology, 5

American magazine, 28, 31
American Medical Association (AMA), 29, 98, 109. See also *Journal of the American Medical Association*
American Municipal Association, 36
American Museum of Natural History (New York), 74
American Psychiatric Association, 46–47, 107–8
American Voodoo: articles on, 68–69, 85; use of term, 204n1. *See also* magic mushrooms
American Weekly, 51–52
amphetamines, 65, 98, 142, 143, 162, 179, 194n47
Anderson, Jack, 143
animal studies, 44, 46, 105
Annual Review of Psychology, 119
Anslinger, Harry J.: anti-drug speech tactics of, 28–32, 34, 39; appointed to head FBN, 27–28; on penalties for marijuana use, 145; as talk show guest, 35, 38
antibiotics. *See* tetracycline
anticommunism, 30, 35, 38
antidrug crusades: boomerang effect of, 7; FBN's role in 1930s, 28–32; government activity's influence on, 7–8; LSD and marijuana confused in, 195n58; media hype of LSD in context of, 3–4; morality clause and, 21–22; mythology of violence in, 28–29; in newspapers, 22–27. *See also* Nixon, Richard M.
antipsychotic drugs, 12, 46, 51
Anti-Saloon League, 24, 70
Arbuckle, Roscoe "Fatty," 21, 22
Archives of General Psychiatry (journal), 113–14
Archives of Neurology and Psychiatry (journal), 107
Argosy (magazine), 57
artists. *See* creativity; visual arts
Associated Press reports: on adrenochrome and LSD research, 50; exaggerated stories about LSD effects, 154, 156; on magic-mushroom experiment, 106–7; skepticism about mystical experiences in, 106–7
Association of Motion Picture Producers, 21

Atkin, Charles, 7
Atlanta (Ga.) penitentiary, 50
The Atlantic, 83
Atlantic Monthly, 17, 161
autism, 48–49
Avalon, Frankie, 187

"Ballad of a Thin Man" (song), 176
Baltimore News, 116
barbiturates, 65, 140, 142, 162, 179, 194n47
Barron, Frank, 119, 120
Barry, Kitty, 39
BBC radio, 74, 83
Beatles (group), 176, 184, 187
Beats and Beat culture, 85, 113, 118, 122–23, 134
Becker, Howard, 60
Bentoff, Harry M., 188
Ben-Yehuda, Nachman, 8, 9, 151–52, 158, 195n55
Benzedrine (amphetamine), 65, 98
Beresford, John, 108
Bergquist, Laura, 73, 101, 204n1
The Beyond Within (Cohen), 95, 117–18, 208n8, 213n20
Bicycle Day, 10, 43–44
Bieberman, Lisa, 160, 176
Big Table (magazine), 199n75
birth control, 13, 19
birth defects: CDC statistics on, 157–58; LSD alleged as cause of, 13, 151, 155–58, *157, 158*; thalidomide as cause of, 13, 112, 156, 195n53
Black, Winifred (a.k.a. Annie Laurie), 22–23, 25–26
black-market drugs: at Harvard, 127; LSD as, 108, 114, 169; spread of, 132, 144
Blake, William, 81
blindness hoax, 154–55
Boggs Act (1951), 35, 37
Boston Avatar, 159
Boston Globe: on antidrug crusade, 27; as case study, 11; on drug use in universities, 127, 143; on Leary-Lettvin debate, 147; on Leary's departure from Harvard, 128; limited attention to drugs (1963–1968), 130; medical column in, 50; on "turn on, tune in, drop out" phrase, 150

Boston Herald, 125, 132
Boston Psychiatric Hospital, 46–47, 49, 51, 53–54, 55
Boston University, Marsh Chapel experiment, 125–26, 129, 132, 137–38, 139
Bowie, Stephen, 141
Braden, William, 129, 143, 212n92
brain: animal studies of electrical stimulation of, 46; documentary on, 141; popular magazines on, 138, *139*. *See also* human consciousness; mental illness; unconscious mind
Brave New World (Huxley), 61, 62, 203n68
Brecher, Edward M., 155
British Mental Hospital, 50
Browning, Elizabeth Barrett, 17
Buddhism, 111, 112, 180
Burch, Dean, 184
Bureau of Indian Affairs, 70–71, 72
The Burning Question (a.k.a., *Reefer Madness*, film), 32
Burroughs, William S., 33–34, 199n75
Burstyn v. Wilson (1952), 186
Burton, H. Ralph, 32
Busch, Marianne, 119, 120
Byrds (group), 184

Caen, Herb, 131
California: anti-LSD law of, 151; Trips Festival in, 161. *See also* Los Angeles LSD experiments
California Osteopathic Association, 98
Canada: drug documentary produced in, 30; film awards in, 30; LSD research at Saskatchewan Mental Hospital, 55–56, 61
Cannon, Dyan, 102, *103*
Catholic Church, 69–70, 93
Cavett, Dick, 92
CBS radio, 38
CBS Reports (television), 147
CBS television: LSD discussed on, 96, 141, 147; magic mushrooms discussed on, 69, 80
CDC (Centers for Disease Control), 157–58
celebrity culture: alleged cocaine use in, 21; anti-drug trafficking tactics in, 29–31; drug scandals in, 22–23; LSD experience

linked to, 134, 136. *See also* film; Grant, Cary; Leary, Timothy; television
censorship: decline of book, 32–33; of drug information, 19–22; of films, 186; of television and film depictions of drug use, 12, 14, 18
Centers for Disease Control (CDC), 157–58
Central Intelligence Agency (CIA), 11
Chandler, Arthur, 99–100, 104, 134
Channing, Carol, 187
Chaplin, Charlie, 62
Chemistry (journal), 185
Chicago: Leary's psychedelic sessions in, 166
Chicago Tribune: antidrug laws opposed by, 26–27; as case study, 11; enthusiasm for LSD's potential in, 105; on Huxley's *Doors of Perception*, 66; on Leary and Alpert, 128; limited attention to drugs (1963–1968), 130
children and teens: alleged drug involvement of, 34–35, 36–38, 152–55; LSD research on, 48–49, 129; magazines' depictions of addiction of, 39–40. *See also* youth and college students
China: drug exports of, 35
chlorpromazine (Largactil or Thorazine), 46, 51, 126, 156
Christianity: Huxley's *Doors of Perception* linked to, 63–65; Leary's views in context of, 115; LSD mystical experiences in, 71, 117, 133–34, 137, 138, 169–70, 174; peyote use in, 70, 72. *See also* Catholic Church; mystical and spiritual experiences; religion
CIA (Central Intelligence Agency), 11
civil rights: free speech (*see* First Amendment); LSD as right under religious freedom, 130; psychedelic drug use as issue in, 109
Coates, Paul, 51, 130
cocaine: antidrug crusades against, 4, 18–19; criminal penalties for, 30; films about, 20–21; Freud's use of, 49; marijuana linked to, 29, 35, 52; media hype in 1980s, 3, 7; mescaline compared with, 52, 63; naiveté about, 14; sources of, 25

Cohen, Bernard, 6
Cohen, Maimon, 155–56
Cohen, Sidney: background and position of, 90; book inscribed for C. Luce, 118, 213n29; cautions about LSD, 106, 108, 113, 134, 141, 143, 169; on drug trip testimonies, 17, 99; as expert, 96–97, 98, 138, 141; film and hallucinations compared by, 185; on LSD advocacy, 143; LSD research and diffusion by, 90–95, 97–98, 104, 105, 117, 127; on LSD to ease pain of dying, 140; WORK: *The Beyond Within*, 95, 117–18, 208n8, 213n20
Colbert, Stephen, 151
cold war, 35
Cole, William D., 83
Coleman, James, 5, 89, 192–93n20
Coleridge, Samuel Taylor, 17
Collier's (magazine), 39, 40
Columbia Pictures, 186, 188
Columbia University Bureau of Applied Social Research, 4, 9–10
Commentary (magazine), 116–17
Comprehensive Drug Abuse and Control Act (1970), 176–77
Comstock, Anthony, 19–20
Comstock Law (1873), 19–20
Confessions of an English Opium-Eater (De Quincey), 17, 90
Confidential File (television), 51, 130
congressional hearings: Anslinger's testimony for, 28, 35; Current Pornographic Materials (House), 32; marijuana and LSD (Senate), 146, 147–48, 176, 178; Organized Crime in Interstate Commerce (Senate), 35–37
Conrad, William, 141
conspiracy theories, 197–98n42
Consumers Union, 47
Consumers Union Guide to Licit and Illicit Drugs (Brecher), 155
Contemporary Review (periodical), 18
cops. *See* law enforcement
Corman, Roger, 186
corporate culture, 1–2
Cosmopolitan (magazine), 87, 134, 136
Costello, Frank, 36

Crane, Lionel, 100
creativity: experiments on LSD's effect on, 94–95, 122, 134; measurement problem and, 48, 67; unlocking of, 82, 98, 105, 134, 140. *See also* visual arts
criminal activities: Anslinger's testimony on drug-induced, 28–29; assumptions about peyote and, 71–72; hearings on organized crime, 35–37; LSD-DUI reported, 154; LSD linked to deviancy, 158; number arrested for narcotics use, 37; rhetoric on drug users, 22, 25–26. *See also* laws and statutes; murder; sexual violence; violence
Crist, Judith, 186
cultist groups, *135*, 136, 170. *See also* Leary, Timothy
culture: "psychedelic" as circulating in, 175–76; psychedelic drugs and potential for changing, 161–62; "turn on, tune in, drop out" phrase in, 149–50. *See also* celebrity culture; moral beliefs; public opinion; social beliefs

Danielian, Lucig H., 3, 7, 131
Darwin, Charles, 62
Davies, Marion, 26
Davis, Adelle (pseud. Jane Dunlap), 95, 106, 134
Davis, Sammy, Jr., 187
"Day Tripper" (song), 176
The Defenders (television), 140–41
Delysid, 44–45. *See also* LSD
De Quincey, Thomas, 17, 90
Dewey, Thomas E., 36
Dickson, W. K. Laurie, 19
diffusion theory: LSD, research, and social circles in, 10–11, 89–98, 104, 105, 108, 117, 127, 208–9n23; on media influence, 4–6; media's informational role in, 50–51, 85, 109–12, 178–79; tetracycline studied in, 5, 89, 192–93n29
Disney Corp., 188
Ditman, Keith, 92, 104, 108, 113
Doblin, Rick, 126
doctors. *See* physicians
The Doctors and the Nurses (television), 141

Dole, Vincent, 29

The Doors of Perception (Huxley): ideas in, 63–66; Leary's reading of, 121; media's informational reporting on, 111; public discourse sparked by, 14, 60, 68–69, 72, 139; readers' responses to, 81, 85, 90; as well-known text, 94

Dope (Laurie), 26

Dopokoke, 20

Downie, Leonard, Jr., 143

Dragnet (television), 31, 183

Drake, Betsy, 102

Drug Abuse Control Amendments (1965), 142, 176

The Drug Addict (documentary), 30

drug addiction: call for education not punishment, 162–63; feared as weakness, 35; literature on, 32–34; LSD's promise for treatment of, 104; magazines' depictions of children and teens, 39–40; medical research on, suppressed by government, 29; morphine, 23, 33–34; sympathetic portraits of female addicts, 25, 30, 32

drugs: attributes applied to, 9; black market for, 108, 114, 127, 132, 144, 169; influences on prescribing of, 5–6, 192–93n20; influences on use of illegal, 6–7; investigational category, 90; laws on physicians' access to experimental, 112–13; limited concern about control, 142; Schedule 1 (no medical use), 176–77. *See also* alcohol consumption; fear of drugs —SPECIFIC: amphetamines, 65, 98, 142, 143, 162, 179, 194n47; antipsychotic, 12, 46, 51; barbiturates, 65, 140, 142, 162, 179, 194n47; chlorpromazine (Largactil or Thorazine), 46, 51, 126, 156; morphine, 23, 33–34, 52; Ritalin, 134; tetracycline, 5, 89, 192–93n20; thalidomide, 13, 112, 156, 195n53; tranquilizers, 51, 177, 194n47. *See also* cocaine; LSD; mescaline; narcotics; opium; peyote; psilocybin (and psilocin)

drug speech: approach to, 14; difficult to prosecute, 33; early drug trip testimonies as, 17–18; in early film and television, 19–22; FBN and Anslinger's tactics against, 28–32, 33; media's exclusion of, 39–41; newspaper antidrug crusades and, 22–27; in novels, 32–34; post-WWII narcotics scare and, 34–40. *See also* antidrug crusades

drug trafficking: FBN campaign against, 28–32, 33; as murder, 23–24, *24*; Nixon's war on, 181–85; televised hearings on, 35–37. *See also* laws and statutes

drug use: as analogy for rejection of society, 33–34; black market availability and, 127; increases in, 143–44; moral attitudes toward, 8; Nixon's war on, 181–85; popular magazines blamed for promoting, 12–13. *See also* recreational drug use; universities

drug users: criminalization of, 22, 25–26; drug-reform rhetoric on, 22–23; estimated number of, 23, 197n28; motivations of, 162–63; sympathetic depictions in film, 20–21. *See also* drug addiction; LSD experiences; psychedelic experiences

DUI (driving under the influence), 154

Dunlap, Barbara, *139*

Dusheck, George, 110–12, 128–29

dying, LSD to ease pain of, 140

Dylan, Bob, 176

East Village Other (newspaper), 158–59

Easy Rider (film), 188

Eberhart, Richard, 66

Ebert, Roger, 188

educational curriculum, 61, 203n68

Education Digest, 183

Ehrlichman, John, 183

"Eight Miles High" (song), 184

Eisner, Betty, 97–98, 106

elites: allegedly better able to describe experience, 63, 90–92; experimentation and hope of, 87; meaning of psychedelic experiences constructed by, 11, 42, 60, 62, 64

Ellis, Havelock, 18, 41, 52, 85

Ellwood, Robert S., 14

entertainment industry. *See* celebrity culture; film; television

Epstein, Edward Jay, 183–84

Epstein, Joseph, 116–17
ergot (grain fungus): effects of poisoning
from, 43, 201n4; LSD synthesized from,
12, 42. *See also* LSD
Esalen (spiritual center), 161–62
ESP (telepathy or extra sensory perception), 99, 106, 107
Esquire: controversial covers of, 166,
223n104; on Leary and Alpert's drug experiments, 132–33, 136; Leary's article
in, 133, 167
Ethnomycological Studies (journal), 80
The Existential Transaction (Leary, unpublished), 120–21
Exploring Inner Space (Davis under pseud.
Dunlap), 95, 106, 134

Fairbanks, Douglas, Sr., 20–21
Fantasia (film), 188
Fate (monthly), 82, 95
The FBI (television), 183
FBN. *See* Federal Bureau of Narcotics
FCC (Federal Communications Commission), 184, 186
FDA. *See* Food and Drug Administration
Fear and Loathing in Las Vegas (Thompson),
201n27
fear of drugs: mushrooms and sex linked
in, 86–87; peyote and sex linked in, 72;
as reflexive public reaction, 4, 177–78;
spike in use and, 31; youth drug problem
in, 143–44. *See also* moral panic
Federal Bureau of Narcotics (FBN): antidrug trafficking tactics of, 28–32, 33;
challenges for, 35; drug taking concerns
of, 143; founding, 27–28; glamorized
lives of agents in, 39; post-WWII concerns about drug trafficking, 34–35
Federal Communications Commission
(FCC), 184, 186
federal government. *See* congressional
hearings; government activism; laws
and statutes
film: drug depictions blocked from, 12, 14,
18, 20, 21–22, 30–31, 110; drug use depicted in (early 1900s), 19–21, 30; drug
use depicted in (early 1960s), 185–89;
exploitation type, 31–32, 186; FBN and
Anslinger's influence on, 29–31; LSD's

first appearance in, 60; as psychedelic
experiences, 185, 187–88. See also *specific films*
First Amendment (free speech): drug-
themed music lists not covered in, 184;
films not included in, 20; films protected
under, 186; ways to work around, 7–8
Flynn, Errol, 30
Focus on Sanity (television), 96
Fonda, Peter, 186, 188
Food and Drug Administration (FDA): Bureau of Drug Abuse Control in, 142, 148;
drug approval requirements of, 112–13;
drug taking concerns of, 143; LSD warnings from, 169; misuse of LSD investigated by, 108; morning-glory seeds
investigated by, 130–31; opposed to
criminalizing LSD, 148
Foote, Edward Bliss, 19
For His Son (film), 20
Fortune (magazine), 2, 32, 117
For Your Information (radio), 140
Frazer, James, 77
Freud, Sigmund, 45, 49

Gaddis, Vernon H., 71
Gannon, Bob, 166
Garbo, Greta, 62
Garden Journal, 82
Gathering of Tribes for a Human Be-In
(San Francisco), 150
Geiges, Leif, *53*
genetics: chromosomal damage and birth
defects linked to LSD use, 13, 151, 155–
58, *157, 158*; countercultural warnings
about, 158–59
Gilbert, Ronnie, 136
Gillespie, Dizzy, 122
Ginsberg, Allen: on Burroughs's *Junky*, 33;
circle of, 122, 167; LSD advocacy of, 136,
168; prosecuted for obscene language,
34, 199n75; psilocybin trip of, 133
Gitlin, Todd, 9, 144
Gleason, Jackie, 187
Goddard, James L., 148
The Golden Bough (Frazer), 77
Goldstein, Nathaniel, 36, 37
Goode, Erich, 8, 9, 151–52, 158, 195n55
Good Housekeeping, 102, 110, 112, 183

government activism: agenda setting influenced by, 7–8, 28–32; drug effects depictions blocked from television and film, 12, 14, 18, 20, 21–22, 30–31, 110; "LSD as problem" for, 176–80; regulatory issues in, 95; war on drug abuse, 181–85. See also *specific agencies*

Graham, Billy, 150

Grant, Cary: doctor of, suspended, 134; LSD experiences discussed by, 15, 99–102, *103*, 104, 110, 130, 136

Grateful Dead (group), 188

Graves, Robert, 77, 78, 80, 83, 87, 111

Great Britain: LSD experiments in, 50; mescaline research in, 45, 52; obscenity defined in, 19

Greenfield, Robert, 146, 150, 216n86

Griffith, D. W., 20

Group for the Advancement of Psychiatry, 122

Gynergen (drug), 43

Hadde, Briton, 116

Hallucination Generation (film), 186

hallucinogenic drugs. *See* psychedelic drugs

hallucinogenic mushrooms. *See* magic mushrooms; psilocybin (and psilocin)

"halo effect," 126

Hamilton (Ohio) Evening Journal, 24

Hansen, Jim, 54

Harding, Warren G., 21

Harper's (magazine), 140

Harrington, Alan, 133

Harrison Narcotic Act (1914), 18–19

Hartman, Mortimer, 99–100, 104, 134

Harvard Crimson (newspaper), 124, 125, 127, 131

Harvard University: black-market drugs at, 127; Leary dismissed from, 115, 128, 136–37; Leary's appointment in Dept. of Social Relations, 120–21, 123, 124; Leary's LSD and other drug experiments and, 121–28, 136–37; popular magazines on, 132, 136; psilocybin experiment with seminary students of, 125–26, 129, 132, 137–38, 139. *See also* Boston Psychiatric Hospital

Harvest (television), 97

hashish. *See* marijuana

Hawaii Five-O (television), 183

Hays, Will H., 21–22

Head (film), 187

Healy, David, 46

Heard, Gerald: circle of, 62, 91, 99; Cohen's disagreement with, 106; LSD experiments and diffusion by, 91, 92–93, 95, 108, 208–9n23; C. Luce and, 213n13; popular magazine essay of, 140; television appearances of, 95–97; Vedanta monastery of, 97

Hearst, William Randolph, 26

Hearst newspapers: anti-marijuana campaign of, 25–26, 197–98n42; drug-reform rhetoric in, 22–24; editorial stance of, 26; on LSD research, 51–52; on moving-picture arcades, 19; narcotics as monstrous hyena in, 23–24, *24*

Hearst's International Magazine, 23–24, *24*

Heaven and Hell (Huxley), 63, 66

Heffter, Arthur, 18

Heim, Roger, 79–80

Heiskell, Andrew, 2

Herbert, George, 169

heroin: crime linked to, 39; criminal penalties for, 36; dream of, 40; imports of, 25, 35; LSD compared with, 154; marijuana compared with, 29; as Schedule 1 (no medical use) drug, 176–77

Herr, Michael, 143–44

Hersey, John, 117

Herzberg, David, 177

Hibbert Journal, 61–62

hippie counterculture: antidrug campaign against, 181–85; chromosomal damage discussed in, 158–59; key event of, 150; marijuana as drug of choice in, 145; music of, 176; Trips Festival, 161; "turn on, tune in, drop out" phrase and, 149–50. *See also* psychedelic devotees; psychedelic experiences

Hobbies (magazine), 71

Hobson, Richmond P., 24–25, 27

Hoffer, Abram, 56, 61

Hoffman, Abbie, 115–16, 173–74

Hofmann, Albert: as first to experience LSD, 10, 42–44; LSD first synthesized by, 12, 111; mushroom studies of, 80, 82; on self-experimentation, 49

Holiday (magazine), 87
Hollywood studios, 31–32. *See also* celebrity culture; film; industry codes; television; *and entries under Motion Picture*
Hoover, J. Edgar, 30
Hopper, Dennis, 188
Hopper, Hedda, 101–2
Horizon (magazine), 95, 140, 160
Houston, Jean, 108
Howard, Sidney, 23–24, *24*
Howl (Ginsberg), 199n75
human consciousness: early research on, 11–14, 46, 50; hopes for understanding via LSD, 12, 50–57, *53, 54, 58–59,* 60, 160–61; introvert's vs. extrovert's experiences with LSD, 170. *See also* brain; mental illness; unconscious mind
Human Potential movement, 161–62
Hunt, George, 2
Hunt Ball (New York), 2
Huxley, Aldous: background, 61–62; circle of, 90, 91, 99; Leary and, 121–22, 143; LSD advocacy of, 89–90, 91–92, 95, 104, 136, 168, 179; narrative power of, 87–88, 188; psychedelic experiences of, 42, 60, 62–63, 68, 72, 81, 128, 185; readers of, 11, 85; student newspaper referencing, 124
—WORKS: Brave New World, 61, 62, 203n68; Heaven and Hell, 63, 66; "A Philosopher's Visionary Perspective" (in *Playboy*), 133. See also *The Doors of Perception*
Huxley, Andrew, 62
Huxley, Julian, 62
Huxley, Laura, 99
Huxley, Thomas, 62
Hyams, Joe, 100–101, 102, 104, 105
Hyde, Robert, 53–54
hype. *See* media hype; psychedelic hype

I, Claudius (Graves), 77
Ickes, Harold, 71
IFIF. *See* International Federation for Internal Freedom
inadvertent social norming concept, 7
Indianapolis Star, 24
Indian ritual drug use: approach to studying, 15; educational side of stories about, 86; history of, 69–70; mush-room use in, 78–79; neglected in psychedelic discourse, 87–88; outsiders' interests and participation in peyote use, 68–69, 71–73; recording of ritual, 74, 107. *See also* magic mushrooms; peyote
industry codes (television and film): adoption of, 21–22; audience designations in, 187; drug effects depictions blocked by, 12, 14, 18, 20, 21–22, 30–31, 110. *See also* obscenity; Production Code Administration; *and entries under Motion Picture*
insanity. *See* mental illness
International Federation for Internal Freedom (IFIF): drug experiments at, 133, *139*; founding, 127, 128; meditation room of, 134, *135*; plans for, 131
International Foundation for Advanced Study (Calif.), 108, 131
International Narcotics Education Association, 27
The Interpersonal Diagnostic of Personality (Leary), 119
Isherwood, Christopher, 62, 92

James, William, 17–18, 130
Janiger, Oscar, 91, 94, 95, 98, 104
Janow, Arthur, 159
Jansen, William, 37
Jefferson Airplane (group), 184, 188
Jenkins, Philip, 6
Johnny Stoolpigeon (film), 30
Johnson, Thomas J., 184–85
Johnson-Cartee, Karen S., 10
journalists: antidrug beliefs embraced by, 18–19; as arguably best LSD researchers, 50, 55–57; Dylan's song about, 176; Leary's appeal for, 146–47; limited expertise of, 129; LSD introduced to public by, 11–14; LSD in wider issues for, 175–76; participation in Indian ritual drug use, 72–73; routine practices of, 7–8; special effects deployed by, 10; "too good to check" expression of, 152. *See also* media; *and specific journalists*
Journal of Criminal Law and Criminology, 29
Journal of Mental Science, 45, 52
Journal of Religion and Health, 170

Journal of the American Medical Association
(*JAMA*): drug advertising in, 192–93n20;
on LSD experiments, 49, 108, 114; popular
magazines blamed for promoting drug
use, 12
Joyce, James, 32–33
The Joyous Cosmology (Watts), 92
J. P. Morgan and Company, 68, 75–77, 80
Junky (Burroughs), 33
"Just Say No" campaigns, 4

Kaiser Permanente Hospital, 119
Kansas: censorship board of, 20
Karales, James H., *164–65*
Katz, Elihu, 5, 89, 192–93n20
Katz, Sidney, 55–56
Kefauver, Estes, 35
Kefauver Committee, 35–37
Kefauver-Harris Drug Amendments
(1962), 112
Kelman, Herbert, 124
Kelsey, Frances, 112
Kennedy, Edward M., 147–48
Kerouac, Jack, 34, 122
Kessler, Stephen, 148, 153, 160, 168
The Kick Seekers (documentary), 146
Kids Say the Darndest Things (television), 182
Kleps, Arthur J., 48, 168–69
Kobler, John, *135*, 173
Koota, Aaron E., 152–54, 170
Korsmeyer, Pamela, 4
KPFA (radio), 92
"Kubla Khan" (Coleridge), 17
Kubrick, Stanley, 187
Kuralt, Charles, 147

Ladies' Home Journal, 101, 102, 110, 179–80
L.A. Free Press, 159
LaGuardia, Fiorello, 29
The Lancet (British journal), 156, 177
Landmark Bureau, 5, 192–93n20
Lang, Gladys Engle, 6
Lang, Kurt, 6
Largactil (chlorpromazine), 46
Lasagna, Louis, 105–6, 109
Lattin, Don, 149, 209n40
laughing gas, 17–18
Laurie, Annie (a.k.a. Winifred Black),
22–23, 25–26

law enforcement: journalists' access to files
of, 151; magazine's glamorization of lives
in, 39; on media coverage of drugs, 178;
television's depiction of, 31–32, 183
laws and statutes: accessibility problem
in, 132; FBN campaign for uniformity
in, 28–32; opposition to tough antidrug
laws, 26–27; on physicians' access to
experimental drugs, 112–13; sentences
for drug convictions, 35, 145, 146. *See also*
censorship; criminal activities; government activism; industry codes; obscenity; prohibition of LSD
—SPECIFIC: Boggs Act (1951), 35, 37; Comprehensive Drug Abuse and Control Act
(1970), 176–77; Drug Abuse Control
Amendments (1965), 142, 176; Harrison
Narcotic Act (1914), 18–19; Kefauver-
Harris Drug Amendments (1962), 112
Lazarsfeld, Paul F., 4–5
Leary, Jack, 119
Leary, Marianne Busch, 119, 120
Leary, Susan, 119, 122
Leary, Timothy: background and career,
118–21; celebrity status and LSD advocacy of, 11, 15, 115, 142–43, 168, 175; on
civil rights, 109; fired from Harvard, 115,
128, 136–37; on Huxley, 91–92; ideas
more than name in media, 128–31, 142–
43; as irresponsible sideshow, 160–61,
163; LSD and other drug experiments of,
121–28, 129, 170, 216n86; magazine articles about, 131–33; magazine writing of,
133, 167; McLuhan's advice for, 148–49;
Mexico's ejection of, 128–29; movie role
of, 187; popular magazines on, 131–33,
136–37, 139; psychedelic celebrations of,
163, *164–65*, 166, 185; radio and television appearances of, 140, 146–47; Senate
testimony of, 146, 147–48; on set and
setting for taking LSD, 49, 95, 179; "turn
on, tune in, drop out" phrase of, 149–50
—WORK: *The Existential Transaction* (unpublished), 120–21; *The Interpersonal Diagnostic of Personality*, 119
Lee, Martin A., 48, 218n136
Leeds, Lila, 30, 40
Leggett, Dawn, 6
Leonard, George, 161–62

letters to the editor: on LSD articles, 112; on magic mushrooms, 84–85; on *Playboy*'s coverage, 133

Lettvin, Jerome, 147

Librium, 156

Liddy, G. Gordon, 146

Life (magazine): alcohol consumption in corporate culture of, 1–2; competition of, 161; covers of, *171, 172*; editorial stance of, 7, 116–17; on fears of spike in drug use, 31; instructions for peyote use in, 85; letters to editor about magic mushrooms, 84–85; magic mushroom story in, 69, 73, *74*, 74–75, 77, 79–83; marijuana prohibition questioned in, 145
—LSD COVERAGE: brain chemistry and, 138, *139*, 141; decline of, 173; Leary's psychedelic celebrations, 166; prohibition opposed, 170; pros/cons in, 169, 170, *171, 172*, 173, 174; psychedelic art as alternative to LSD trip, 170, *172*, 173; respectfully written, 115, 129, 142; sensationalization in, 3, 191n1

Lindesmith, Alfred, 29, 30

Linkletter, Art, 181, 182–83

Linkletter, Diane, 182

Literary Digest (weekly), 116

literature (fiction), 32–34, 168

lobotomy patients, 46, 55

Loengard, John, *139*

Lois, George, 166, 223n104

London Daily Mirror, 100

The Lonely World (television), 97

Look (magazine): on American Voodoo, 68; on drug use, 162–63; on Huxley's *Doors of Perception*, 73; marijuana prohibition questioned in, 145; on psychedelics and potential for cultural change, 161; on teenage addicts, 39
—LSD COVERAGE: clinical trial findings, 12; experience depicted, 53–55, *54*; Grant's story, 100, 101–2; Leary and Alpert's experiments, 132; Leary's psychedelic celebrations, 163, *164–65*, 166; prohibition opposed, 162

Lorre, Peter, 30

Los Angeles LSD experiments: cautions about LSD in, 105–7, 108–9, 113–14; decline of attention to, 128–31; enthu-siasm for LSD's potential in, 104–7; Grant's role in, 15, 99–102, *103*, 104, 110, 130; media as influence on volunteers in, 107–8; physical and mental complications in, 108–9, 113; scientific research and therapeutic uses discussed, 97–100; writing and television appearances about, 95–97. *See also* celebrity culture; Cohen, Sidney; Heard, Gerald; measurement issues

Los Angeles Society of Clinical Psychiatrists, 109–12

Los Angeles Times: antidrug rhetoric in, 27; as case study, 11; drug research reported in, 98–99; on drug use in universities, 143; on FDA investigation, 108; on Huxley's *Doors of Perception*, 65; on imported drugs, 38; limited attention to drugs (1963–1968), 130; on *The Love-Ins*, 186; medical column in, 50; on morning-glory seeds, 131
—LSD COVERAGE: call for ban, 109; Grant's story, 101; Leary, 128, 146; television taping of drug trip, 97

The Love-Ins (film), 186

The Love Statue (film), 186

Lowell, Robert, 122

LSD (lysergic acid diethylamide): access to, 90–91, 125; *Alice in Wonderland* linked to, 134; attempt to separate from psychedelic scene, 160–61; attributes applied to, 9; call for ban on, 108, 109; congressional hearings on, 146, 147–48, 176, 178; cost of, 98; demands for, 162, 168; dosage, purity, and safety of, 46, 60, 133; early research on, 11–13; FDA regulations on, 113, 176–77; first human experiences of, 10, 42–44; first shipment to U.S., 46–47; growing salience of, 139–40; history summarized, 114; illicit drug use linked to, 145–46; limited media attention to (1963–1968), 128–31; marijuana confused with, 195n58; media attention as fostering negative view of, 176–80; media's informational reporting on, 111–12; origin of, 10–11; possibilities touted, 130, 137; scientific research on, 42–46; as "therapy-in-a-bottle," 110, 111–12; warnings about, 105–6, 136–37,

151–59, *157, 158*, 167–70. *See also* diffusion theory; Los Angeles LSD experiments; LSD experiences; measurement
issues; prohibition of LSD; therapeutic
use of LSD
LSD, I Hate You (film), 186
LSD experiences: advertising approach to
advocacy of, 148–50; dangers perceived
in, 145–46; drugged research subjects
on, 48; first film appearance of, 60;
freak-outs and hospital admissions due
to (side-effects scare), 151, 154–55, 168,
169, 176, 179; Grant's story of, 15, 99–
102, *103*, 104, 110, 130, 136; Hofmann's
description of, 42–44; Katz's description of, 55–56; C. Luce's description of,
2, 92, 93–94, 117, 173, 213n13; H. Luce's
description of, 2, 92, 93–94, 117–18,
173, 213n13; popular magazines' depiction of, 51–57, *53, 54, 58–59*, 60, 134, *135,*
136–40; psychedelic art as alternative
to, 170, *172*, 173; set and setting of, 49, 95,
174, 179; underground papers and, 162,
175; weakened social prohibitions on,
68–69. *See also* Cohen, Sidney; Heard,
Gerald; Leary, Timothy; Los Angeles
LSD experiments; mystical and spiritual
experiences; psychedelic experiences
Luce, Clare Boothe: background and position of, 92–93, 208n22; Cohen's auto-
graphed book for, 118, 213n20; editorial
role of, 138; A. Hoffman's meeting of,
173–74; LSD experiences and journals
of, 2, 92, 93–94, 117, 173, 208–9n23,
213n13
Luce, Henry Robinson: background, 93,
116, 118; conservative stance of, 1;
death, 173; editorial control by, 115–17,
138, 213n10; LSD experiences of, 2, 92,
93–94, 117–18, 173, 213n13. *See also* Time
Inc.
"Lucy in the Sky with Diamonds" (song),
176
Lumière brothers, 19
lysergic acid diethylamide. *See* LSD

MacLean's (magazine), 55–56
Mademoiselle, 143–44, *166*, 167
Mad magazine, 150

magic mushrooms: Barron's experiments
with, 120; coining of term, 68; discovery
and promotion of, 15, 69, 80, 82; history
and mythology of, 76–78, 81, 83–84;
Indian use of, 69, 79; Leary's first try
of, 121; letters to editor about, 84–85;
media's informational reporting on, 111;
museum exhibit about, 74; pharmaceutical research on, 106–7; recording of
ceremony with, 107; sales and promotion of, 83–84; story and promotion in
Life, 69, 73, *74, 74–75*, 77, 80–83; story
and promotion in *This Week*, 73–74, *75,*
81–82. *See also* psilocybin (and psilocin);
Wasson, R. Gordon
Magruder, Jeb Stuart, 183
Man's Illustrated, 167
Man's Magazine, 57, *58–59*, 83
Man's Story, 167–68
The Man with the Golden Arm (Algren), 33–34
The Man with the Golden Arm (film), 34
March of Time series, 141
Marcus Welby, M.D. (television), 183
Margolis, Jack, 168
marijuana: alleged violence due to use,
25–26, 28–29, 32, 153; attributes applied to, 9, 13; congressional hearings
on, 146, 147–48, 176, 178; defined as
narcotic and gateway drug, 35, 37, 143;
demands for, 162; growing acceptance
of mundane effects, 145–46; Hearst's
campaign against, 25–26, 197–98n42;
LSD confused with, 195n58; mescaline
compared with, 52; Nixon's campaign
against, 184; penalties for possession,
145, 146; as Schedule 1 (no medical use)
drug, 176–77; theatergoers' use of, 188
Marijuana, Assassin of Youth (film), 31–32
Marijuana Girl (novel), 32
Marriott, Alice, 72–73, 86
Martin, Ralph G., 117
Marx, Harpo, 62
Mary (Marriott's friend), 72–73
Maryland: censorship board of, 20
Massachusetts: censorship board of, 20
Massachusetts Correctional Institution
(Concord), 123, 125, 126, 129, 132
Massachusetts Department of Public
Health, 125

Massachusetts Institute of Art, 127–28
mass media. *See* film; media; newspapers; popular magazines; radio; television
Mayer, Louis B., 30
Mayer, Martin, 132–33
McCall's (magazine), 155, 213n10
McCartney, Paul, 176
McClelland, David, 120–21
McClelland, George, 20
McGinniss, Joe, 173
McLuhan, Marshall, 3, 148–50
McQuail, Denis, 10
measurement issues: creativity and, 48, 67; difficulty in mystical and spiritual experiences, 47–50, 94–95, 106; "halo effect" in, 126; Leary's approach to, 122, 124–25; Marsh Chapel "Miracle" and, 125–26, 129, 132, 137–38, 139; subjects' biases and expectations, 107–8
media: entranced by psychedelic drugs, 2–3; influence of, studied, 4–10; informational role of, 50–51, 85, 109–12, 178–79; LSD introduced by, 11–14; McLuhan's views of, 148–50; Nixon's war on drug abuse in, 181–85. *See also* advertising and advertisements; agenda setting in media; diffusion theory; film; newspapers; popular magazines; radio; television
media hype: of cocaine use, 7; definition, 2–3, 131; earlier studies related to, 4–10; of magic mushrooms, 86–88
media hype of LSD: approach to studying, 1–4, 14–16; on chromosomal damage and birth defects, 13, 151, 155–59, *157, 158*; as cultural vs. political concern, 141–42; drug development and research, 42–50; historiographic context, 10–14; Huxley's drug experiences linked to, 42, 60, 62–63, 68, 72, 81, 128; "LSD as problem" fostered in, 176–80; moral panic fostered by, 151–59, *157, 158*; negative stories magnified in, 155–58, *157, 158*, 174–75; promise of depicting LSD trips, 10, 14, 178–79; sensationalization in, 3–4, 159–60, 178, 191n1; sensations of madness, 51–57, *53, 54, 58–59*, 60; shaping of story, 7–10; side-effects scare

(freak-outs and hospital admissions), 151, 154–55, 168, 169, 176, 179; summary of, 188–90. *See also* film; Los Angeles LSD experiments; moral panic; newspapers; popular magazines; psychedelic hype; radio; television
media-medicine intersection: approach to studying, 15; diffusion and acquisition of drug in, 10–11, 89–95. *See also* Los Angeles LSD experiments; physicians; psychology and psychiatry; therapeutic use of LSD
Medical Innovation (Coleman, Katz, and Menzel), 5, 89, 192–93n20
medical research. *See* therapeutic use of LSD
meditation, 13, 134, 135, 147, 166, 179–80
Mediterranean squill, 43
"medium is the message" phrase, 149–50
Méliès, George, 19
Mendez, Eva (Maria Sabina), 74, 79, 80, 81, 82, 85, 87
mental illness: biochemical theory of, 12, 47; LSD and mescaline used as insight in, 60, 90; LSD as creating sensation of madness, 51–57, *53, 54, 58–59*, 60, 105, 111; LSD research on, 44–46, 50; LSD's promise for treatment of, 104–5; LSD use linked to, 108–9, 113–14, 136, 140, 156, *158*, 170; psychosis defined, 60; schizophrenia, 45, 60, 140, 196n5; self-selected volunteers with, 107–8. *See also* brain; human consciousness; unconscious mind
Menzel, Herbert, 5, 89, 192–93n20
Merck-Sharp and Dohme (pharmaceutical company), 79
mescaline (peyote derivative): adrenaline compared with, 47; arrest for possession, 66; cost of, 108; Ellis's advocacy for, 41; experience depicted in magazines, 18, 52–53, *53*, 54; experience touted in newspaper, 98–99; Huxley's description of, 42, 60, 63–66, 68, 69, 72; Leary and, 121, 122–23; possibilities touted, 130, 137, 159; sales of, 85; scientific research on, 45, 52, 55–56, 108, 196n5. *See also* Huxley, Aldous; peyote

Metzner, Ralph, 126, 133, 140
Mexico: drugs allegedly from, 38; intoxicating plants recorded in, 69; Leary and followers ejected from, 128–29; paranormal show filmed in, 107; search for magic mushrooms in, 68, 73, 74–75, 78–81, 85, 87
Meyerhoff, Hans, 66
MGM, 188
Midnight Cowboy (film), 188
midwifery herbals, 43
migraine headaches, 32
military forces, 11, 34–35, 141
Millbrook (N.Y.): Leary's activities and estate in, 129, 146, 163, 216n86
Miller v. California (1973), 225–26n21
Miltown (tranquilizer), 51, 177, 194n47
Milwaukee Journal, 83
Missiles and Rockets (magazine), 140
Mitchum, Robert, 30, 40
Modern Romances (magazine), 156, *158*
Mod Squad (television), 183
Monk, Thelonious, 122
Monkees (group), 187
moral beliefs, 8, 151–52. *See also* social beliefs
moral panic: alleged drug involvement of school kids in, 152–53; exaggerated stories about LSD effects underlying, 13, 151–59, *157*, *158*; LSD as test case in theory of, 13, 178, 195n55; scientific research blocked due to, 162. *See also* criminal activities; fear of drugs; media hype
morning-glory seeds, 69, 129, 131
morphine, 23, 33–34, 52
Motion Picture Association of America, 187
Motion Picture Producers and Distributors of America, 21
Motion Picture Production Code (1930), 21–22, 34, 187
movies. *See* film
Movie Star, American Style (film), 186
moving-picture arcades, 19
Mue, Gon Sam, 39
murder: drug trafficking linked to, 21, *24*; as LSD-induced, 28, 148, 153, 160, 168; marijuana use linked to, 25–26, 32, 153

Murphy, Michael, 162
Murray, John Courtney, 117, 208–9n23
mushrooms. *See* magic mushrooms; psilocybin (and psilocin)
Mushrooms, Russia, and History (Wasson and Wasson), 77–78, 79, 82–83, 84
music, 176, 184, 187
Musto, David F., 4, 18, 34, 35, 177
Mycologia (journal), 80
mycology. *See* magic mushrooms
The Mystery of the Leaping Fish (film), 20–21
mystical and spiritual experiences: attempt to place LSD in context of, 160–61; cautions and skepticism about, 105–7, 108–9, 113–14; Cohen's view of, 138–39; desirability of, 13–14; expectations and valuation of, 97; experts in fields used as test subjects, 92; finding God in, 71, 117, 133–34, 137, 138, 169–70, 174; Grant on being "born again" in, 100; Huxley's description of, 42, 60, 63–66, 68; W. James's experience of, 17–18, 130; H. Luce's description of, 117; Marsh Chapel "Miracle" of, 125–26, 129, 132, 137–38, 139; nineteenth-century drug trip testimonies of, 17–18; "sacred energies" in, 147–48; science reporter on, 111–12; Wasson's description of, 81, 82. *See also* Christianity; Indian ritual drug use; LSD experiences; measurement issues; religion

Naked Lunch (Burroughs), 199n75
The Name of the Game (television), 183
narcotics: alleged sources of, 35, 38; media panics about, 6; medical uses, 2, 5; popular magazine articles on, 31, 194n47; schoolchildren's alleged addiction to, 34–35, 36–38. *See also* narcotics scare; psychedelic drugs
narcotics agents, 30, 198n63
narcotics scare (1950s): context of, 34–35; impetus for, 35–37; media coverage's effects on, 37–41
The Nation, 66, 145, 149
National Association for Mental Health, 170
National Association of Radio and Television Broadcasters code, 31

National Board of Censorship (N.Y.), 20
National Book Award winner, 33–34
National Film Board of Canada, 30
National Institute of Mental Health, 90, 113, 120, 176
National Narcotics Education Week, 25–26, 27
National Organization for the Reform of Marijuana Laws, 32
National Police Gazette, 102, 103
Native American church. See Indian ritual drug use; peyote
Navajo people, 71–72
NBC radio, 37–38
NBC television, 35, 38, 97
Neo-American Church, 169
New Age movement, 13, 84, 180
New Republic: on Cohen's The Beyond Within, 95; exaggerated stories about LSD in, 154; on Huxley's Heaven and Hell, 66; LSD prohibition opposed by, 160–61; marijuana prohibition questioned, 145; psychedelic references deplored, 176
newspapers: antidrug crusades in, 22–27; decline of interest in psychedelic experiences, 185; exaggerated stories about LSD effects in, 152–53, 156; experts on staff of, 212n92; informational reporting by, 109–12; as interpreter of cultural phenomena, 176; magazine coverage compared with, 50–51; pros/cons of LSD in, 174–75; reluctance to encourage drug taking, 129; sources and objective style of, 38–39. See also letters to the editor; and specific papers
Newsweek (magazine): on magic mushroom exhibit, 74; marijuana prohibition questioned in, 145; on mescaline research, 52–53, 53, 54; psychedelic magazine cover of, 168
—LSD COVERAGE: blindness reports, 154–55; exaggeration in, 153; experiences described, 140, 168; Leary and Alpert, 127, 131
New York (state): anti-LSD law of, 151; censorship board of, 20; Leary's activities and estate in Millbrook, 129, 146, 163, 216n86; organized crime investigations in, 36–37

New York Academy of Medicine, 29
New York City: drug effects and details in film censored in, 20; Leary's psychedelic celebrations in, 163, 164–65, 166; prosecutor's anti-LSD rhetoric in, 152–54
New Yorker, 72–73, 83
New York Herald Tribune, 76, 100–101. See also This Week
New York Journal (newspaper), 19
New York Post, 173
New York Society for the Suppression of Vice, 19–20
New York Times: agenda setting by, 7; antidrug crusade coverage in, 27; anti-drug rhetoric of, 25; as case study, 11; on China's drug exports, 35; on drugs at Harvard, 127; on drugs in movies, 187; on drug tourism in Mexico, 85; on FDA raids, 108; Huxley's books and, 64, 66; on magic mushrooms, 74, 83; on marijuana, 143; on morning-glory seeds, 131; number of narcotics-related articles in, 37–38; on peyote use, 70–71; on schoolchildren's drug addiction, 36–37; on thalidomide, 112
—LSD COVERAGE: congressional hearings, 148; criminal cases, 153; experiences described, 140, 146; Leary, 128, 129–30, 146, 148; Luces, 173–74; research, 50
New York Times Book Review, 65
New York Times Magazine, 138–39, 153–54, 167, 174
New York University, 129
Nicholson, Jack, 187
nicotinic acid, 125
Nin, Anaïs, 94
Nixon, Richard M.: on Leary, 115; mentioned, 74, 93; war on drug abuse, 181–85
Nobel Prizes, 46, 62
Normand, Mabel, 21
Novak, Steven J., 90, 208n8

obscenity: authors prosecuted for, 34; British definition of, 19; films open to charges of, 186–87; guidelines on, 225–26n21; laws on, 18, 19–22; U.S. definition, 33. See also industry codes
obstetrics, 32, 43

Odets, Clifford, 102
Ohio: censorship board of, 20
Oklahoma Territory: peyote use in, 70
One Step Beyond (television), 107
Open End (television), 140, 146
Operation Petticoat (film), 100, 101
opium: antidrug rhetoric on, 4, 24, 25, 35; criminal penalties for, 18–19, 35; film depictions of, 19–20; mescaline compared with, 63; writing on, 17, 90, 194n47
Oscar awards, 187–88
Osmond, Humphrey: Huxley's experience guided by, 62–64, 140; LSD research of, 55–56, 61–62; mescaline and adrenaline research of, 47; on new mind drugs, 168; television appearance of, 146

paganism and neopaganism, 13, 167, 180
Pageant (magazine), 168–69
Pahnke, Walter N., 125–26
Parents (magazine), 112
Parent's Magazine and Better Homemaking, 153–55
Parker, William H., 38
Parsons, Louella, 101
Pennsylvania: censorship board of, 20, 30
The People's Choice (Lazarsfeld, Berelson, and Gaudet), 4–5, 89
People Today (magazine), 66
Person to Person (television), 69, 80
peyote: debates on use, 70–72; Indian use of, 68–70; sales of and instruction for, 85. *See also* Indian ritual drug use; mescaline
phanerothyme (Huxley's term), 63
photography, 160, 168
physicians: advertising's influence on, 192–93n20; FDA's investigation of misuse of LSD by, 108; influences on prescription practices of, 5; LSD warnings from, 169; social and professional activities of, 89. *See also* Los Angeles LSD experiments; psychology and psychiatry; therapeutic use of LSD
Pickford, Jack, 21
Playboy, 133, 166–67
Poe, Edgar Allan, 17
police officers. *See* law enforcement
popular magazines: back issues and research in, 175; earlier refusal to depict drug trip experience, 39–40; exaggerated stories about LSD effects in, 151, 153–58, *157*, *158*; FBN and Anslinger's control of, 31–32; in-depth, entertaining stories in, 50–51, 56–57; on Leary and Alpert's drug experiments, 131–33, 136–37, 139; on Leary's psychedelic celebrations, 163, *164–65*, 166; on LSD and sex, 167–68; LSD articles popular in, 11, 12–13, 194n47; LSD experiences depicted in, 51–57, *53*, *54*, *58–59*, 60, 134, *135*, 136–40, 141–44, 166; LSD prohibition opposed by, 160–62; Nixon's war on drug abuse in, 182–83; on pros/cons of LSD, 167–70, *171*, *172*, 173, *174*. *See also specific magazines*
Popular Science (magazine), 166
Popular Science Monthly, 18
pornography, 32–33
Powell, Gloria, 102, *103*
Preminger, Otto, 34, 187
Price, Vincent, 60
The Primal Scream (Janow), 159
prison inmates: LSD experiments with, 50, 105, 123, 125, 126, 129, 132; recidivism statistics on, 123, 126
The Private Sea (Braden), 129
Production Code Administration, 22, 30–31, 34
Prohibition Era, 26, 170. *See also* temperance movement
prohibition of LSD: context of, 13, 15–16; effects on discourse, 185; magazines critical of, 160–62; momentum for, 176–80; state laws on, 148, 151, 162
psilocybin (and psilocin): access to, 121–22, 125; Good Friday experiment with, 125–26, 129, 132, 137–38, 139; identified in mushroom, 80, 82; Leary's experiments with, 122–23, 125, 126, 127–28, 133; possibilities touted, 130, 137. *See also* magic mushrooms
psychedelic: use of term, 63–64, 175–76
psychedelic devotees: advocacy of, 147, 148–50; Bicycle Day of, 10, 43–44; diffusion of LSD via, 10–11, 89–95. *See also* hippie counterculture; *and specific individuals*

psychedelic drugs: attempt to separate LSD from, 160–61; attitudinal change on, 143–44; decline of media interest despite insurgent popularity of, 3–4, 13–14, 15–16; defense of, 127; gratifications of, 10; historical context of, 3, 68–70; as hyena, 23–24, *24*; legal use of, 62–67; mass media entranced by, 2; media's informational reporting on, 50–51, 85, 109–12, 178–79; otherworldliness linked to, 9, 42; possibilities touted, 124, 130, 161–62; use of term, 3; warnings about, 127. *See also* LSD; magic mushrooms; marijuana; mescaline; peyote; psilocybin (and psilocin)

psychedelic experiences: alternatives to, 129, 179–80, 185; approach to studying, 15; contradictory attributes given to, 85–88; Davis's description of, 95, 106, 134; as Death, 23; desirability of effects, 13–14; in documentary on drug addicts, 29–30; films' depiction of, 185–89; Huxley's description of, 42, 60, 62–63, 68, 72, 81, 128, 185; intellectual inquiry legitimated, 66–67; Leary as icon of, 15, 142–43; Leary's celebrations of, 163, *164–65*, 166; of mescaline madness, 52–53, *53*; as "mindquake," 111–12; movies billed as, 187–88; news media's decline of interest in, 185; nineteenth-century drug trip testimonies of, 17–18. *See also* hippie counterculture; LSD experiences; mystical and spiritual experiences

psychedelic hype: call for education not punishment in, 162–63; complaints about, 159–60; exaggerated stories about LSD in, 151, 153–58, *157, 158*; Leary's sacralization of LSD as, 163, *164–65*, 166; LSD prohibition questioned in, 160–62; moral concerns set aside in, 166–67; pros/cons of LSD in, 167–70, *171, 172*, 173, 174–75; wider cultural context of, 175–76. *See also* media hype

psychology and psychiatry: breakthroughs in drugs for, 12, 46, 51; drug research on, 196n5; "existential transaction" in, 120–21, 123; experts in fields used as test subjects, 90–91; LSD's potential impact on, 111–13; LSD therapeutic applications in, 44–50, 61, 67, 97–102, 104; testing in, 55, 119, 123. *See also* measurement issues

psychosis. *See* mental illness

public: decreased knowledge about drugs, 31–32; historical cycle of drug speech in, 18; media's informational role and, 50–51, 85, 109–12, 178–79; media's introduction of LSD to, 11–14; presumed desire for surveillance, 38. *See also* psychedelic devotees

public opinion: on LSD as problem, 176–80; media and social circle influence on, 4–10, 89; most important problem identified in, 142; Nixon's antidrug campaign and, 184–85; polling techniques in, 4. *See also* fear of drugs; moral panic

Pulitzer Prizes, 38, 117

race: rhetoric on drug use and, 25, 28–29

radio: antidrug war pressures on, 184; congressional hearings on, 35–37; LSD experiences discussed on, 92, 95, 140, 146. See also *specific radio stations*

Rappe, Virginia, 21

Reader's Digest, 112, 153–54, 155, 182

Readers' Guide to Periodical Literature, 11, 112, 185, 194n47

Real for Men (magazine), 86

recreational drug use: call to ban LSD for, 108, 109; cultural moment for, 131; drug travelogues' role in, 85–86; laughing gas as, 17; LSD research vs., 91–92, 117–18; LSD used as, 93–94, 174; media coverage and rhetoric against, 4, 15, 19, 60, 66–67; motivations for, 144; Nixon's campaign against, 181; opposition to, 136–37, 176, 177–78; as still up for debate, 147; survey on, 159. *See also* diffusion theory

Reefer Madness (*The Burning Question*, film), 32

Reese, Stephen D., 3, 7, 131

Regina v. Hicklin (Britain, 1868), 19

Reid, Wally, 23

reincarnation, 99, 106

religion: attempt to place LSD in context of, 160–61; dismissed as necessary to drug experience, 85–86; Leary's sacralization of LSD as, 163, *164–65*, 166; LSD as right in, 95, 130; LSD taken as part of, 169. *See also* Christianity; Indian ritual drug use; mystical and spiritual experiences

The Reporter (biweekly), 64, 132

Richardson, Allan, 73, 79, 80, 81, 82, 83, 87

Rinkel, Max, 46–47

Ritalin, 134

Rogers, Everett M., 9, 192n11

Roosevelt, Eleanor, 35, 38

Roosevelt, Franklin D., 71

Rosenfield, Albert, 170

Ross, Jane, 85

Rosset, Barney, 122

Sabina, Maria (Eva Mendez), 74, 79, 80, 81, 82, 85, 87

Safford, William E., 78

Sahl, Mort, 147

Salem witch trials, 201n4

San Diego Evening Tribune, 98

Sandoz Pharmaceuticals: ceased production of LSD, 148; Hofmann's position at, 43; LSD distribution by, 89–91, 107, 113; LSD research and manufacturing by, 10, 44–45, 49; mentioned as source, 121; scientists skeptical about mystical experiences with LSD, 106; synthetic drug of (Gynergen), 43. *See also* Hofmann, Albert

San Francisco Call Bulletin, 110–12, 128–29

San Francisco Chronicle, 98, 109, 131

San Francisco Examiner, 22–23, *24*

San Francisco Oracle (newspaper), 162, 167

Sanger, Margaret, 19

Saskatchewan Mental Hospital, 55–56, 61

Saturday Evening Post: on chromosomal damage and birth defects due to LSD, 156, *157*; competition of, 161; Huxley's essay on drugs in, 95; on law officers' lives, 39; on Leary and Alpert's drug experiments, 133–34, *135*, 173; madness depicted in, 51; magic mushroom story rejected by, 79; on youth drug problem, 143

Saturday Review, 65, 83, 139–40

Schiller, Lawrence, 143

schizophrenia, 45, 60, 140, 196n5

Schulberg, Budd, 87–88

Science (journal), 13, 151, 155–56, 158, 185

Scientific American (magazine), 12, 29, 55

Scientific Monthly, 95

Scientology, Church of, 191n1

Senior Scholastic, 154

sexuality: LSD as aphrodisiac, 167–68; mushrooms linked to, 86–87; peyote linked to, 72; psychedelic drugs linked to, 133

sexual violence and alleged drug use, 21, 28–29. *See also* criminal activities; violence

Sgt. Pepper's Lonely Hearts Club Band (album), 176

Sheed, Wilfred, 117

Shepard, Jack, 162–63

She Shoulda Said No (a.k.a. *The Wild Weed*, film), 30

Shlain, Bruce, 48, 218n136

Shoemaker, Pamela, 6

Siberia: mushroom used in, 78

Siegel, Bugsy, 36

Sinatra, Frank, 34

Singer, Rolf, 80

Skidoo (film), 187

Slattery's Hurricane (film), 31

Smith, Huston, 150

Smith, Jackson, 136

Smithsonian Folkways (record label), 74

Smithsonian Institution, 70

Smothers Brothers, 183

Smythies, John R., 47, 55, 61–62

social beliefs: drug addiction feared as weakness, 35; drug use as analogy for rebelling against, 33–34; media influenced by, 18–19; media influence on, 9; "turn on, tune in, drop out" phrase vs. conservative, 158. *See also* fear of drugs; moral beliefs; public opinion

Solomon, Carl, 33

soma (fictional drug), 62

soma (in Rig-Veda), 84

Southern California Psychiatric Society, 109

space travel and LSD, 140

Speaker, Susan L., 22, 197n28

speech, antigovernment or political vs.
sexual, 33. *See also* drug speech; media
Sports Illustrated, 140
Stafford, Peter, 140
St. Anthony's fire, 43
State University of New York, Buffalo,
155–56
Stevens, Jay, 151
Stockings, G. Taylor, 52
Stolaroff, Myron, 108, 109, 111
Stoll, Arthur, 44
Stoll, Werner, 44
Story (magazine), 87
Strauss, Neil, 149
Stravinsky, Igor, 62
Susskind, David, 140
Swanberg, W. A., 117, 213n10
Swiss Archives of Neurology (journal), 44

Taylor, William Desmond, 21
tea: use of term, 33
telepathy (ESP or extra sensory perception), 99, 106, 107
television: congressional hearings aired
on, 35–37; drug depictions blocked
from, 12, 14, 18, 20, 21–22, 30–31, 110;
FBN and Anslinger's influence on,
31–32; LSD experiences depicted on,
51, 95–97, 110, 130, 140–41, 146–47;
magic-mushroom discovery and promotion on, 69; Nixon's war on drug
abuse in, 183–84; promotion of horror/
paranormal show on, 107; as substitute
for psychedelic experience, 16. See also
specific television programs
temperance movement, 4, 24–25, 70. *See
also* Prohibition Era
tetracycline, 5, 89, 192–93n20
thalidomide, 13, 112, 156, 195n53
The Lord of the Rings (Tolkien), 169
therapeutic use of LSD: medical findings,
12, 196n5; promise for treating alcoholism and drug addiction, 61, 104, 129, 130,
141; promise for treating mental illness,
104–5; in psychology and psychiatry,
44–50, 61, 97–102; television documentary on, 147; "therapy-in-a-bottle"
claim, 110, 111–12

This Week (magazine): cautions about LSD
in, 105; on LSD conference, 104; magic
mushroom story in, 73–74, 75, 81–82
Thomas, Olive, 21
Thomas Aquinas, 118
Thompson, Hunter S., 201n27
Thorazine (chlorpromazine), 46, 51, 126, 156
Through the Looking Glass (television), 141
Time (magazine): on audience for televised
hearings, 36; on Cohen's *The Beyond
Within*, 117–18; corporate culture of,
1–2; on drug experiments, 67; editorial
stance of, 7, 116–17; founding, 2, 116; on
Huxley's *Doors of Perception*, 64–65; on
mushroom research, 82; on Navajos and
peyote, 71–72; on schoolchildren's drug
addiction, 37; on thalidomide, 112
—LSD COVERAGE: blindness reports,
154–55; chromosomal damage and birth
defects, 156; decline of, 173; exaggeration in, 153; Hollywood, 104; Leary and
Alpert's drug experiments, 136–37;
mysticism and, 137–38, 169–70; pros/
cons of drug, 174; respectful coverage,
115, 117–18, 129, 142; sensationalization
in, 3, 191n1
Time Inc. (later Time-Life, publishing
house): corporate culture of, 1–2; *Fortune*
magazine of, 2, 32, 117; LSD documentary of, 141; mescaline use legitimated
by, 72. See also *Life*; Luce, Henry Robinson; *Time*
Times Film Corp. v. Chicago (1961), 187
The Tingler (film), 60, 186
tobacco use, 8, 65
Today's Health, 51
Toledo Blade Sunday Pictorial, 83
Tolkien, J. R. R., 169
Tonight in Saint Louis (television), 140
To the Ends of the Earth (film), 30
Travel (magazine), 71
The Trip (film), 186
Trips Festival (San Francisco), 161
True, the Man's Magazine, 83–84
True Crime (magazine), 86
truth: Cohen's view of, 90; Colbert's quip,
151; Grant on, 100; Huxley's search for,
62–66

Tucson Daily Citizen, 65
"turn on, tune in, drop out" phrase, 149–50, 158
2001: A Space Odyssey (film), 187–88

Ulysses (Joyce), 32–33
Uncensored (magazine), 86
unconscious mind: artistic representations of, 160; LSD's potential for exploring, 12, 61, 104–5, 118; mescal intoxication in understanding of, 18; perceived revisiting of childhood and repressed memory, 50, 51–52; potential of drugs to shape, 95; sanity vs. madness in, 42. *See also* brain; human consciousness; psychology and psychiatry
Understanding Media (McLuhan), 148
United Nations, 183
universities: drugs on campuses, 127, 143, 162–63; LSD research at, 105. See also *specific universities*
University of California, 105
University of Missouri, 162–63
University of Nebraska, Lincoln, 83
U.S. Bureau of American Ethnology, 70
U.S. Bureau of Indian Affairs, 70–71, 72
U.S. Camera (magazine), 160
U.S. Congress. *See* congressional hearings; laws and statutes; *and specific acts*
U.S. Constitution. *See* First Amendment
U.S. Defense Department (armed forces), 11, 141
uses and gratifications theory, 9–10
U.S. News and World Report (magazine), 112, 156, 182
U.S. Supreme Court: on censorship of film, 20; on drug-themed music lists, 184; on film censorship, 186; on free speech, 33
U.S. Treasury Department. *See* Federal Bureau of Narcotics

Valium, 194n47
The Varieties of Psychedelic Experience (Beresford and Houston), 108
The Varieties of Religious Experience (James), 17–18
Variety (magazine), 31, 34, 186
Vaughn, Roger, 166

Veterans Administration hospitals, 96, 113, 118, 138. *See also* Cohen, Sidney
violence: alleged drug use and sexual violence, 21, 28–29; allegedly due to marijuana use, 25–26, 28–29, 32, 153; magic mushrooms linked to, 86–87; peyote linked to, 72. *See also* criminal activities; murder
Virginia: censorship board of, 20
Vision (magazine), 82
visual arts, psychedelic depictions, 160, 168, 170, *171*, *172*, 173. *See also* creativity
Vogue (magazine), 79

Wainwright, Loudon, 2
Wanta, Wayne, 6, 184–85
war on drug abuse, 181–85
Washington Post: on drug use in universities, 143; on Huxley's *Doors of Perception*, 65; on possibilities of psychedelic drugs, 130; on schoolchildren's drug addiction, 37
—LSD COVERAGE: birth defects, 156; Grant's story, 102; Leary's ejection from Mexico, 128; research, 50
Wasson, Masha, 78–79
Wasson, Peter, 79
Wasson, R. Gordon: background and credentials of, 75–76; guilt for drug tourism, 85; "magic mushrooms" coined by, 68; magic mushroom story of, 69, 73, 74, 74–75, 77, 78–83, 185; media's informational reporting on, 111, 179; mushroom theories of, 81, 83–84; mycophobia concept of, 77, 86–87; narrative power of, 87–88; WORK: *Mushrooms, Russia, and History*, 77–78, 79, 82–83, 84
Wasson, Valentina Pavlovna Guercken: background, 76–77; magic mushroom story of, 73–74, 75, 81–82; mushroom search of, 78–79; WORKS: *The Chosen Baby*, 76; *Mushrooms, Russia, and History*, 77–78, 79, 82–83, 84
Watts, Alan, 11, 92, 136, 160, 179
Wavy Gravy (entertainer), 159
WBAI (radio), 140
Weil, Andrew, 124, 131–32
Weil, Simone, 169

Wenner, Lawrence A., 10
WGBH (television), 147
The White Goddess (Graves), 77
"White Rabbit" (song), 184
The Wild Weed (a.k.a. *She Shoulda Said No*, film), 30
Wiley, Harvey W., 70–71
William S. Merrell Company, 112
Wilson, Bill, 92
Wingenroth, Donna, 153, 160, 168
"With a Little Help from My Friends" (song), 184
WKCR (radio), 146
WMAL (radio), 140
WNEW (radio), 146
Woman's Christian Temperance Union, 70, 86
Woodstock (1967), 159
Wootton, Phlip H., Jr., 80

World War II: drug trafficking in aftermath, 34–35
WPIX (radio), 38
WTOP (radio), 140

Yale Daily News, 116
Yale University, 117
Yeats, W. B., 18
Yellow Submarine (film), 187
Yoder, Norman M., 154–55
Young, Jock, 8, 177, 178
youth and college students: congressional hearings on drug use by, 146, 147–48; exaggerated and sensationalized coverage of drug use, 143–44, 152–55, 162–63, 178; marijuana as drug of choice in, 145; Nixon's war on drug abuse and, 182. *See also* children and teens; universities

STEPHEN SIFF is assistant professor of journalism at Miami University, Ohio.

THE HISTORY OF COMMUNICATION

Selling Free Enterprise: The Business Assault on Labor
   and Liberalism, 1945–60   *Elizabeth A. Fones-Wolf*

Last Rights: Revisiting *Four Theories of the Press*   *Edited by John C. Nerone*

"We Called Each Other Comrade": Charles H. Kerr & Company,
   Radical Publishers   *Allen Ruff*

WCFL, Chicago's Voice of Labor, 1926–78   *Nathan Godfried*

Taking the Risk Out of Democracy: Corporate Propaganda
   versus Freedom and Liberty   *Alex Carey; edited by Andrew Lohrey*

Media, Market, and Democracy in China: Between the Party Line
   and the Bottom Line   *Yuezhi Zhao*

Print Culture in a Diverse America   *Edited by James P. Danky and Wayne A. Wiegand*

The Newspaper Indian: Native American Identity in the Press, 1820–90
   John M. Coward

E. W. Scripps and the Business of Newspapers   *Gerald J. Baldasty*

Picturing the Past: Media, History, and Photography
   Edited by Bonnie Brennen and Hanno Hardt

Rich Media, Poor Democracy: Communication Politics in Dubious Times
   Robert W. McChesney

Silencing the Opposition: Antinuclear Movements and the Media
   in the Cold War   *Andrew Rojecki*

Citizen Critics: Literary Public Spheres   *Rosa A. Eberly*

Communities of Journalism: A History of American Newspapers
   and Their Readers   *David Paul Nord*

From Yahweh to Yahoo!: The Religious Roots of the Secular Press   *Doug Underwood*

The Struggle for Control of Global Communication: The Formative Century   *Jill Hills*

Fanatics and Fire-eaters: Newspapers and the Coming of the Civil War
   Lorman A. Ratner and Dwight L. Teeter Jr.

Media Power in Central America   *Rick Rockwell and Noreene Janus*

The Consumer Trap: Big Business Marketing in American Life   *Michael Dawson*

How Free Can the Press Be?   *Randall P. Bezanson*

Cultural Politics and the Mass Media: Alaska Native Voices
   Patrick J. Daley and Beverly A. James

Journalism in the Movies   *Matthew C. Ehrlich*

Democracy, Inc.: The Press and Law in the Corporate Rationalization
   of the Public Sphere   *David S. Allen*

Investigated Reporting: Muckrakers, Regulators, and the Struggle
   over Television Documentary   *Chad Raphael*

Women Making News: Gender and the Women's Periodical Press in Britain
   Michelle Tusan

Advertising on Trial: Consumer Activism and Corporate Public Relations
   in the 1930s   *Inger L. Stole*

Speech Rights in America: The First Amendment, Democracy, and the Media   *Laura Stein*

Freedom from Advertising: E. W. Scripps's Chicago Experiment   *Duane C. S. Stoltzfus*

Waves of Opposition: The Struggle for Democratic Radio, 1933–58   *Elizabeth Fones-Wolf*

Prologue to a Farce: Democracy and Communication in America   *Mark Lloyd*

Outside the Box: Corporate Media, Globalization, and the UPS Strike   *Deepa Kumar*

The Scripps Newspapers Go to War, 1914–1918   *Dale Zacher*

Telecommunications and Empire   *Jill Hills*

Everything Was Better in America: Print Culture in the Great Depression   *David Welky*

Normative Theories of the Media   *Clifford G. Christians, Theodore L. Glasser, Denis McQuail, Kaarle Nordenstreng, and Robert A. White*

Radio's Hidden Voice: The Origins of Public Broadcasting in the United States   *Hugh Richard Slotten*

Muting Israeli Democracy: How Media and Cultural Policy Undermine Free Expression   *Amit M. Schejter*

Key Concepts in Critical Cultural Studies   *Edited by Linda Steiner and Clifford Christians*

Refiguring Mass Communication: A History   *Peter Simonson*

Radio Utopia: Postwar Audio Documentary in the Public Interest   *Matthew C. Ehrlich*

Chronicling Trauma: Journalists and Writers on Violence and Loss   *Doug Underwood*

Saving the World: A Brief History of Communication for Development and Social Change   *Emile G. McAnany*

The Rise and Fall of Early American Magazine Culture   *Jared Gardner*

Equal Time: Television and the Civil Rights Movement   *Aniko Bodroghkozy*

Advertising at War: Business, Consumers, and Government in the 1940s   *Inger L. Stole*

Media Capital: Architecture and Communications in New York City   *Aurora Wallace*

Chasing Newsroom Diversity: From Jim Crow to Affirmative Action   *Gwyneth Mellinger*

C. Francis Jenkins, Pioneer of Film and Television   *Donald G. Godfrey*

Digital Rebellion: The Birth of the Cyber Left   *Todd Wolfson*

Heroes and Scoundrels: The Image of the Journalist in Popular Culture   *Matthew C. Ehrlich and Joe Saltzman*

The Real Cyber War: The Political Economy of Internet Freedom   *Shawn M. Powers and Michael Jablonski*

The Polish Hearst: *Ameryka-Echo* and the Public Role of the Immigrant Press   *Anna D. Jaroszyńska-Kirchmann*

Acid Hype: American News Media and the Psychedelic Experience   *Stephen Siff*

The University of Illinois Press
is a founding member of the
Association of American University Presses.

_____

Composed in 10.5/13 Marat Pro
by Lisa Connery
at the University of Illinois Press
Manufactured by Cushing-Malloy, Inc.

University of Illinois Press
1325 South Oak Street
Champaign, IL 61820-6903
www.press.uillinois.edu